The European Public Prosecutor's Office

L.H. Erkelens · A.W.H. Meij
M. Pawlik
Editors

The European Public Prosecutor's Office

An Extended Arm or a Two-Headed Dragon?

ASSER PRESS

Springer

Editors
L.H. Erkelens
A.W.H. Meij
M. Pawlik
EU Law
T.M.C. Asser Instituut
The Hague
The Netherlands

ISBN 978-94-6265-034-3 ISBN 978-94-6265-035-0 (eBook)
DOI 10.1007/978-94-6265-035-0

Library of Congress Control Number: 2014948751

Published by T.M.C. ASSER PRESS, The Hague, The Netherlands www.asserpress.nl
Produced and distributed for T.M.C. ASSER PRESS by Springer-Verlag Berlin Heidelberg

Printed on acid-free paper

Springer is part of Springer Science+Business Media (www.springer.com)

Foreword

The conference on the plans to create a European Public Prosecutor's Office (EPPO) held by the T.M.C. Asser Institute in The Hague early September 2013 took place at a highly opportune moment. July 2013 had seen the publication of the European Commission Proposal for a Council Regulation on the establishment of the EPPO.[1] The conference was thus the first opportunity to discuss, from a scholarly perspective, both the proposal itself and the problems identified in a number of political commentaries. One of the questions it addressed was whether the EPPO should be seen as 'an extended arm or a two-headed dragon': should it operate as the long arm of the law, reaching down from European level to tackle at national level crimes that harm the EU's financial interests, or is it likely to become an ungovernable monster, with its European and national 'heads' squabbling about who is in control?

This book is the outcome of discussions at the conference. Debate on the proposal is now in full swing. From the outset, the Commission had a less than easy ride: parliaments in 11 Member States, including the Dutch assembly, gave it a yellow card because they believed the proposal did not comply with the subsidiarity principle. This compelled the Commission to take another look at the matter to see if modification or even withdrawal was the next logical step. However, the Commission saw no reason to do either, and decided to maintain the original proposal.

On 12 March 2014, the European Parliament adopted a resolution on the proposal on the EPPO. The resolution entailed a rather long range of 'political guidelines' addressed to the Council. At the same time, it suggested some amendments. These recommendations included strict observance of the right to a fair trial, precise determination of the scope of the EPPO's competence, and the availability of uniform investigative tools and investigation measures compatible with the legal systems of the Member States. The optimistic response of the Commission's Vice-President Viviane Reding, the EU's Justice Commissioner, and Algirdas Semeta, the EU Anti-Fraud Commissioner, to the European Parliament's

---

[1] COM (2013) 534 final of 17 July 2013.

backing was: 'Today's vote by the European Parliament is good news for Europe's taxpayers and bad news for criminals. The EPPO will make sure that every case of suspected fraud against the EU budget is followed up so that criminals are brought to justice'.

I use the word 'optimistic' in light of the next step along the road to establishing the EPPO: the proposal will now be submitted to the Council of the European Union. To pass this hurdle, the proposal must be adopted unanimously, in accordance with Article 86, paragraph 1, second sentence of the Treaty on the Functioning of the European Union. As yet, unanimity is far from guaranteed. Even before the yellow cards were issued, it was clear that the chance that the Member States would unanimously accept the proposal was small. The objections of the 11 parliaments made that even clearer. The Commission and the Parliament are therefore assuming that the EPPO will come into being via the 'enhanced cooperation' procedure also laid down in Article 86, paragraph 1. This entails a compromise in which at least nine Member States will jointly set up an EPPO which can only operate in the participating states. In this case too unanimity is an issue, since a proposal for enhanced cooperation requires consensus in the European Council. Part V of this book deals with questions regarding the feasibility—and consequently the effective functioning—of the EPPO if it is established under the enhanced cooperation procedure.

But this is just one of the issues covered in this book. At the root of the problems identified above and the criticism of the proposal lies a political question: what kind of Europe do the Member States want? For some the proposal does not go far enough; they believe the Commission has missed the opportunity to create European rules of criminal procedure alongside the EPPO. Others are convinced the decentralised model chosen by the Commission, in which prosecution is based on the criminal procedure of the Member State in question, is in itself too great an interference with the sovereignty of the Member States in criminal matters, since the initiative to prosecute will come from Europe. In this book, these opposing political views are being discussed from a scholarly viewpoint.

This book offers a useful basis for further debate on whether an EPPO is desirable and feasible, and if so, how it should work.

The Hague, May 2014

J.W. Fokkens
Procurator General at the
Supreme Court of the Netherlands

Contents

Abbreviations

Acquis	*acquis communautaire*: the accumulation of EU Treaties, EU legislation and EU Court decisions
AFSJ	Area of Freedom, Security and Justice
AG	Advocate General (at the European Court of Justice)
AIDP	l'Association Internationale de Droit Pénal
Cepol	European Police College
CFR	Charter of Fundamental Rights
CISA	Convention Implementing the Schengen Agreement
CMS	Case Management System
COM	European Commission
EAW	European Arrest Warrant
EC	European Community
ECHA	European Chemicals Agency
ECHR	European Convention of Human Rights
ECJ	European Court of Justice
ECLAN	European Criminal Law Academic Network
ECtHR	European Court of Human Rights
EDP	European Delegated Prosecutors
EDPS	European Data Protection Supervisor
ENCS	Eurojust National Coordination System
EPP	European Public Prosecutor
EPPO	European Public Prosecutor's Office
EU	European Union
EUCrim	European Criminal Law Association's Forum
Eurojust	European Union Agency for Criminal Justice Cooperation
Europol	European Union's Law Enforcement Agency
IGC	Intergovernmental Conference
JIT	Joint Investigation Team
MLA	Mutual Legal Assistance
OHIM	Office for Harmonization in the Internal Market

OJ	Official Journal of the EU
OLAF	Office de Lutte Anti-Fraude (European Anti-Fraud Office)
PIF	Protection des Intérêts Financiers (Protection of EU Financial Interests)
PPS	Public Prosecution System
REACH	Regulation on Registration, Evaluation, Authorisation and Restriction of Chemicals
RIDP	Revue Internationale de Droit Pénal
SWD	Staff Working Document (European Commission)
TEU	Treaty on European Union
TFEU	Treaty on the Functioning of the European Union
TWF	Temporary Work File
UK	United Kingdom
USA	United States of America
ZIS	Zeitschrift für Internationale Strafrechtsdogmatik

Chapter 1
Introduction

Criminal Law Protection of the European Union's Financial Interests: A Shared Constitutional Responsibility of the EU and Its Member States?

Leendert Erkelens

Abstract A brief historic account is given of the institutional endeavours and extensive legal research projects preceding the proposal on the establishment of a European Public Prosecutor's Office finally delivered by the Commission in July 2013. Marked by this history, the proposed Council regulation walks a fine line between trying to respect legal identities and essential state functions of Member States and to allow as much as possible for efficiency requirements which though will lead to a centralised system, legally as well as organisationally. The different authors in this book do investigate this dilemma as well as a few other issues. Their contributions are briefly presented.

Keywords Financial interests of the Union · Corpus juris · Treaty changes · Lisbon Treaty · Identity clause · Article 86 TFEU · European public prosecutor's office

Contents

Rather obviously, everybody wants to have their money protected against stealing, abuse or misuse by others. In the same vein, States, natural and legal persons, including international organisations, do have an equal need to protect their assets

---

Leendert H. Erkelens is a Visiting Research Fellow at the T.M.C. Asser Instituut in The Hague, The Netherlands.

L. Erkelens (✉)
T.M.C. Asser Instituut, The Hague, The Netherlands
e-mail: l.erkelens@asser.nl

L.H. Erkelens et al. (eds.), *The European Public Prosecutor's Office*,
DOI 10.1007/978-94-6265-035-0_1

and financial means. Alas! Fraud against public means is not uncommon. Precautionary measures to help ensure the necessary protection are required. However both, States, natural and legal persons, are dependent on financial institutions entrusted with dealing with their money on one hand and from law enforcement authorities responsible for enforcing the law on the other. The same holds true for the European Union (EU),[1] which for a long time has been trying to enhance the level of security of its own budget. From 1958 to 1970 the EEC (and Euratom) budget was financed by a system of Member States' contributions[2] effectively until 1971,[3] when a system of own resources for the general budget was introduced intended to progressively replace the financial contributions from Member States. According to the European Commission, this allocation of own resources to the Community triggered the idea of specifically furthering criminal law protection of the Community's financial interests.[4] To that end in 1976, the Commission proposed a draft amendment to the Treaties to permit the adoption of common rules on the protection of the financial interests of the Communities[5] and the prosecution of infringements of the Treaty provisions.[6] In this instance, the proposed common rules on the protection of its financial interests made explicit provision that the criminal provisions of each Member State relating to infringements causing damage to the Member State's financial interests applied in an equivalent manner to acts or omissions causing such a damage to the financial resources and budget of the Communities.[7] The Commission's proposal implied that the protection of the financial interests of the Communities should be placed in the hands of the Member States. In accordance with their criminal policies on investigating and prosecuting crimes affecting the State's financial interests, their criminal law authorities should actively investigate and prosecute offences against EU fraud. This original proposal applying the principle of equivalence did not make it, but nevertheless it created the baseline.

Since then, the EU has come a long way till the most recent Commission proposal of July 2013 to establish a Public Prosecutor's Office.[8] In the intervening

[1] The EU also in its capacity as successor of the European Community (EC).

[2] European Commission 2008, p. 18 and further.

[3] Council Decision of 21 April 1970 on the replacement of financial contributions from Member States by the Communities' own resources (70/243 ECSC, EEC, EURATOM). *OJ* L 094, 28/04/1970, pp. 19–22.

[4] European Commission 2001, p. 5.

[5] This refers to all three European Communities functioning at that time: the EEC, the European Coal and Steel Community (ECSC) and the European Atomic Energy Community (Euratom).

[6] Draft for a Treaty amending the Treaties establishing the European Communities so as to permit the adoption of common rules on the protection under criminal law of the financial interests of the Communities and the prosecution of infringements of the provisions of those Treaties, *OJ* C 222/2, 22.9.1976.

[7] See Articles 14 and 15 of the Protocol attached to the Draft for a Treaty amending the Treaties, supra n. 6.

[8] Proposal for a Council Regulation on the establishment of the European Public Prosecutor's Office; Brussels, 17 July 2013, (COM 2013 534 final).

period new developments took place. The Convention on the protection of the financial interests of the EC (1995) was signed[9] and a new provision of the Amsterdam Treaty led to the establishment of a new agency entrusted with administrative powers to combat fraud against the Communities' budget, known by its French acronym OLAF.[10] OLAF is a part of the Commission and has the task of conducting 'external administrative investigations for the purpose of strengthening the fight against fraud, corruption and any other illegal activity adversely affecting the Community's financial interests'. In other words, OLAF's competences are limited and of administrative nature only; no judicial powers to investigate and prosecute the aforementioned illegal activities have been conferred on OLAF.

While emphasising the scale and impact of fraud cases against the Community's financial interests, the Commission continued its quest for providing criminal law measures especially by means of a European Prosecutor to help protect these interests. To that end, preceded by almost 10 years of preparatory work, in 2001 a Green Paper on this matter was issued by the Commission.[11] The most important part of that work consisted of the rather famous Corpus Juris, originally brought about under the direction of Professor Delmas-Marty, it entailed a set of rules for the criminal law protection of the Community's financial interests.[12] The Corpus Juris was not just an intellectual exercise but an outcome of an academic undertaking solidly based on a comparative study of national criminal law systems of those days' Member States. According to the Corpus Juris' rules of criminal procedure, the territory of the Member States of the Community would constitute one single area within which a European Public Prosecutor would become the authority responsible for investigating, prosecuting, and the committal for trial and the execution of sentences imposed for offences against the financial interests of the Community.[13] Definitions of these offences were provided in a separate, substantive part of the Corpus Juris. This approach abandoned the principle of equivalence and introduced a radical reversal of the criminal law perspective and the relationship between Community and Member States in comparison with the base line proposed by the Commission in 1976. It abandoned the idea of common rules attributing jurisdictional competence to the criminal law systems of the Member States to investigate and prosecute these offences. On the contrary, powers in this area were to be invested in the Community itself. In fact, the Corpus Juris drew a new line in the sand providing a fresh starting point for future developments in this area.

The academic efforts on this issue provided also a substantive impetus for intergovernmental negotiations on the idea of a European Public Prosecutor. During

---

[9] *OJ* C 316, 27.11.1995, 49. This Convention entered into force on 17 October 2002.

[10] Office de Lutte Anti-Fraude (OLAF), based upon Article 280 TEC and established by a Commission Decision of 28 April 1999. *OJ* L 136, 31 May 1999, 20.

[11] European Commission, Green Paper 2001.

[12] Delmas-Marty 1997.

[13] See Article 18 of the revised version of the Corpus Juris known as the 'Florence version' of May 1999, available at http://ec.europa.eu/anti_fraud/documents/fwk-green-paper-corpus/corpus_juris_en.pdf (Accessed May 2014).

the Intergovernmental Conference (IGC) in Nice (2000), the Commission vainly proposed the introduction of a new provision regarding the appointment of a European Public Prosecutor and the conditions for the exercise of its functions.[14] The idea of creating an EPPO was taken up again by the 2004 IGC and inserted in the Constitutional Treaty. With some amendments it finally landed in the Lisbon Treaty (Article 86 TFEU).

The entering into force of the Lisbon Treaty in December 2009, while entailing in Article 86 TFEU a legal base for the establishment of the EPPO, did effectively accelerate and deepen the debate[15] and intellectual efforts regarding the European Public Prosecutor and related issues such as his investigative and prosecutorial powers and competences, the functioning of his Office, the relationship with national criminal law, rights of the defence and legal remedies. In this regard, a most outstanding academic undertaking was the research project 'European Model Rules for the European Public Prosecutor's Office', carried out at the University of Luxembourg and directed by Professor Katalin Ligeti.[16] A monumental project, among others providing a comparative overview of 20 criminal law jurisdictions of 19 Member States based on a full description of the pre-trial phase of criminal procedure of the respective 20 systems and the investigative measures and prosecutorial tools available to the authorities as well as procedural safeguards. All this was followed by 'model rules'. These Model Rules were '(…) delineating the investigative and prosecutorial powers of a European Public Prosecutor's Office (EPPO), the applicable procedural safeguards and the evidential standards'.[17] while building upon the rules of the Corpus Juris. The two legal projects together

[14] Additional Commission contribution to the Intergovernmental Conference on institutional reforms—The criminal protection of the Community's financial interests: A European Prosecutor 29.9.2000.

[15] Since the entering into force of the Lisbon Treaty many conferences and meetings were devoted to the EPPO, wholly or in part. Most recently (as of 2012) held were among others the following: Eurojust held a conference in The Hague ('10 Years Of Eurojust') on 12 and 13 November 2012 spending half a day EPPO. Almost at the same time, 7–9 November 2012, OLAF held a conference in Berlin entitled: 'Cooperation of a future European Public Prosecutor's Office with National Prosecution Services'. ERA held a conference in Trier on 17 and 18 January 2013 entitled: Towards the European Public Prosecutor's Office (EPPO)'. The 7th European Jurists' Forum organised a conference in Barcelona from 18 to 20 April 2013 during which half a day was spent to EPPO. The 6th Meeting of the Network of Public Prosecutors or equivalent institutions at the Supreme Judicial Courts of the Member States of the European Union, Cracow, 15–17 May 2013. In Rome a 2 day international conference was held with the support of OLAF—Hercule II from 12 to 14th June 2013 on 'Protecting fundamental and procedural rights from the investigations of OLAF to the future EPPO'. The European Academic Criminal Law Network in Brussels held a Conference on 2 July 2013, entitled: 'Les Apéros du Droit Européen—"The European Public Prosecutor: sooner or later?"'

[16] Ligeti 2013, 2014.

[17] Katalin Ligeti, Introduction to the model rules. Available at: http://eppo-project.eu/design/eppodesign/pdf/converted/index.html?url=c982b9eef093cee8cebfbfcb2b0556d1.pdf&search (Accessed May 2014).

provided fundamental groundwork for the legislative proposal on the EPPO of the Commission of July 2013.

The present publication provides a selection of legal issues and questions related to the Commission's legislative proposal itself. All contributions have been written by experts in the area of Justice and Home Affairs or related areas of EU law. In September 2013, the T.M.C. Asser Instituut organised a first conference entitled 'Criminal law protection of the European Union's financial interests: a shared constitutional responsibility of the EU and its Member States?', which was solely focused on the Commission's proposal on the establishment of an EPPO.[18] Speakers at the conference were so kind to contribute to this book elaborating and recasting the original texts of their conference speeches. In addition, Mr Martin Wasmeier of OLAF was kind enough to contribute his ideas on the choice of forum by the EPPO in a separate chapter.

The underlying theme of the Asser conference as well as of this publication pertains to constitutional issues of balancing powers, competences and interests of the Member States and the Union. Will the Commission's legislative proposal (finally) deliver a well-structured body, able to apply in a satisfactorily balanced manner European and national rules of procedure, evidence and review? Vera Alexandrova presents a general overview of the Commission proposal. The Treaty on the Functioning of the EU stipulates rather enigmatically that the Office of the European Public Prosecutor shall be established 'from Eurojust'.[19] The draft regulation offers now some insight into its features and implications regarding the relationship between an intergovernmental agency like Eurojust and the new Office modelled as a Union body. In this perspective, Michèle Coninsx provides an overview of the main characteristics of the proposal especially in the light of the constitutional obligation that EPPO has to be established 'from Eurojust'.

The title of this publication attempts to grasp the balancing act between the positions of the Union and its Member States: '*The European Public Prosecutor's Office: an extended arm or a two headed dragon?*' It conveys two ways the EPPO could be viewed. One image is of the EPPO as an organisation assisting Member States in their endeavours to crack down on EU fraud. The other image is referring to Hydra, the multi-headed and almost invincible monster from Greek mythology. For each head cut off it grew two more. Substituting head for 'competence creep' endows this image its European connotation and symbolises the concerns of some Member States. These rather contrasting options are elaborated in a much more subtle way by Katalin Ligeti and Anne Weyembergh in their contribution on certain constitutional issues emanating from the Commission proposal. Bernardus Smulders explores the constitutional balance between Eurojust and its tasks and competences as a horizontally oriented agency and those attributed to the new, vertically organised body. He maintains that, while taking into account an urgent financial

---

[18] Background information available at: http://intranet.asser.nl/events.aspx?archive=1&id=368&site_id=34 (Accessed May 2014).

[19] Ligeti and Simonato 2013 on the relationship between EPPO and Eurojust.

problem resulting from a suboptimal enforcement of EU rules at national level, the Commission proposal strikes the right balance.

The advent of a European Public Prosecutor in the Area of Freedom, Security and Justice having exclusive power in all Member States to investigate and prosecute criminal offences against the Union's financial interests is without precedent and could involve far reaching consequences. One could assert that it impinges on the distribution of powers and therefore immediately raises questions with regard to constitutional principles of subsidiarity, proportionality and conferral of competences. It could also be claimed that the Office with its new powers will affect the (exclusive) power of a State to assert its jurisdiction on its own territory, even though this Office would only be concerned with fraud against the EU funds, thus offences not directly within the sphere of national sovereignty. However, national competences to determine the criminal justice priorities and the subsequent capacities of law enforcement, justice and the penitentiary system to implement those priorities will be affected by the new Office. Culturally, national values and norms of what is considered 'good' and 'bad' seem to lack a common focal point.[20] In other words, the question may and has to be brought up as to the extent this legislative proposal sufficiently satisfies the constitutional requirement that the Union shall respect the national identities of the Member States and their essential state functions in the sense of Article 4, para 2 TEU.[21] According to Guastaferro, the so-called 'identity clause' could become, to a certain extent, a constraint on the EU legislator.[22] The clause could be interpreted as a general constraint on the EU legislator, requiring it to favour the measure which less pre-empts the Member State's scope of action.[23] From that point of view the new Office needs sound and balanced operational foundations.

In this volume Kai Lohse, in his capacity as a practising public prosecution officer, comes forward with practical solutions to establish such a foundation by practical proposals to ease off the tension between the proposed vertical powers of EPPO and the necessity to acknowledge the jurisdictional responsibilities and competences of Member States with regard to crimes violating their own legal order. Marta Pawlik and André Klip provide a critical assessment of the proposed legal arrangement of the material powers of the new Office, the lack of

[20] Many of these questions respectively critical remarks were brought forward by national Parliaments in their reasoned opinions issued in accordance with Protocol No 2 to the Treaties on the application of the principles of subsidiarity and proportionality. See: European Commission 2013.

[21] Article 4, para 2 TEU: 'The Union shall respect the equality of Member States before the Treaties as well as their national identities, inherent in their fundamental structures, political and constitutional, inclusive of regional and local self-government. It shall respect their essential State functions, including ensuring the territorial integrity of the State, maintaining law and order and safeguarding national security. In particular, national security remains the sole responsibility of each Member State'.

[22] Guastaferro 2012, p. 46.

[23] Ibid, p. 51.

accountability and provisions regarding the cooperation between EPPO and EU Member States. Catherine Deboyser scrutinises in great detail the consequences of the proposed tasks and competences of EPPO for Eurojust and ways of cooperation and interaction between both bodies.

Another area being explored in this publication pertains to the administrative structure, the legal bases and procedures for EPPO operations and judicial review, as well as the division of rules of substance and procedure governing EPPO's operations between the Union and the national level. Further, some constitutional issues related to Eurojust and the EPPO will be scrutinised. Martin Wasmeier focuses in particular on questions related to the choice of *forum* by a supranational authority working within a pluralistic legal framework. Jan Inghelram scrutinises the competence to review search and seizure measures. Contrary to the Commission's proposal, Inghelram argues that EPPO investigation measures will not be governed only by the law of the Member States nor will in every respect their courts be competent to review the validity of those measures. Inghelram sets out that in relation to crucial aspects the reviewing of the validity of EPPO investigation measures will be a matter for the EU courts. Arjen Meij explores issues regarding the legality and legitimation of a multilevel administration consisting of composite levels of integrated administration in a particularly sensitive area. He questions whether the hierarchical structure of the proposed model, including national operational resources, is the least intrusive model as regards national institutional autonomy. Also, serious doubts are raised in respect of the legal fiction provided for, turning the EPPO into a national authority for the purposes of judicial review of its procedural measures.

The present book closes with tackling the rather challenging topic of 'enhanced cooperation'. With a view to enable Member States that are determined to make progress and integrate their polities in a certain area the Treaties provide for a special cooperation framework, the so-called 'enhanced cooperation' framework. Under certain conditions Member States that wish to cooperate on a certain issue can make use of this specific legal figure. Alongside the horizontal clauses on enhanced cooperation, the Treaty provides for a special legal regime on the establishment of EPPO as entailed in Article 86. The procedures under this regime differ significantly—though not completely—from those of the general system on enhanced cooperation. The topic has become rather acute since the UK, Denmark and Ireland already declared that they will not participate in EPPO.[24] A wealth of legal and constitutional questions is emerging from this specific framework and the way it could be or will be applied. Julian Schutte especially investigates the implications of enhanced cooperation for the decision making procedures. Szymon Pawelec focuses on the implications of enhanced cooperation for the EPPO model and the interactions and ways of cooperation with non-participating Member States.

---

[24] See: Point 6 of the Legal Service Contribution to Working Party on Cooperation in Criminal Matters (COPEN) of 7 February 2014, Council of the European Doc 6267/1, available at: http://register.consilium.europa.eu/doc/srv?l=EN&f=ST%206267%202014%20INIT (Accessed May 2014).

In the form of an Appendix to this book has been attached the corpus of the proposed Council regulation on the EPPO. The Explanatory Memorandum together with the 75 articles of the proposal have been included though without the Annex to the proposed regulation, the Legislative Financial Statement and the Estimated Financial Impact of the Proposal/Initiative.

References

Delmas-Marty M (1997) Corpus Juris, introducing penal provisions for the purpose of the financial interests of the European Union, Paris

European Commission (2001) GREEN PAPER on criminal-law protection of the financial interests of the Community and the establishment of a European Prosecutor, 11 Dec-2001, COM (2001) 715 final. http://eur-lex.europa.eu/LexUriServ/LexUriServ.do?uri=COM:2001:0715:FIN:EN:PDF. Accessed May 2014

European Commission (2008) European Union public finance, 4th edn, pp 135–136. http://ec.europa.eu/budget/library/biblio/publications/public_fin/EU_pub_fin_en.pdf. Accessed May 2014

European Commission (2013) COMMUNICATION from the Commission to the European Parliament, the Council and the national parliaments on the review of the proposal for a Council Regulation on the establishment of the European Public Prosecutor's Office with regard to the principle of subsidiarity, in accordance with Protocol No 2. COM (2013) 851 final, of 27 November 2013

Guastaferro B (2012) Beyond the exceptionalism of constitutional conflicts: the ordinary functions of the identity clause. New York University School of Law, New York. http://centers.law.nyu.edu/jeanmonnet/papers/12/documents/JMWP01Guastaferro.pdf. Accessed May 2014

Ligeti K (ed) (2013) Toward a prosecutor for the European Union. A comparative analysis, vol 1. Hart Publishing, Oxford

Ligeti, K (ed) (2014) Toward a prosecutor for the European Union. Draft rules of procedure, vol 2. Hart Publishing, Oxford (forthcoming)

Ligeti K, Simonato M (2013) The European Public Prosecutor's Office: towards a truly European Prosecution Service? New J Eur Crim Law 4(1):7–21

Part I
Presentation of the Main Features of the Proposed EPPO

Chapter 2
Presentation of the Commission's Proposal on the Establishment of the European Public Prosecutor's Office

Vera Alexandrova

Abstract This article provides an introduction to the proposal for a Council Regulation on the establishment of the European Public Prosecutor's Office, adopted by the European Commission on 17 July 2013. The author outlines the governing structure of this office, its competences and the investigative measures available, as well as forms of judicial remedies. The proposal foresees the creation of an independent, decentralised and integrated prosecution office to effectively combat crimes affecting the financial interests of the Union. This novel approach, which is based on the Treaty of Lisbon, would constitute a significant development in the field of EU criminal law policy and bring about the desired added value and coherence in the protection of the financial interests of the Union.

Keywords Article 86 TFEU · Crimes against the financial interests of the Union · Eurojust · European Public Prosecutor's Office · Lisbon Treaty

Contents

The author is Policy Officer at the European Commission, DG Justice, Unit B2 (Criminal Law).

V. Alexandrova (✉)
European Commission, Brussels, Belgium
e-mail: vera.alexandrova@ec.europa.eu

L.H. Erkelens et al. (eds.), *The European Public Prosecutor's Office*,
DOI 10.1007/978-94-6265-035-0_2

2.1 Introduction

Many different opinions have been expressed on what the European Public Prosecutor's Office (EPPO) should look like. The debate has been going on for many years.[1] Practitioners, politicians and academia have expressed enthusiasm, commitment, but also doubts and disapproval. The topic remained challenging. At the present stage, however, the nature of the discussion has changed fundamentally compared to previous years following the adoption of the Proposal for a Council Regulation on the Establishment of EPPO on 17 July 2013.[2] Some blame the Commission for being too ambitious in its proposal; others recognise its modesty. The fact is that the Lisbon Treaty entails a legal basis providing for a much larger ground than the present proposal actually does. It is always a matter of proper tailoring in order to cover the ground at once or making progress step by step.

The Treaty on the Functioning of the European Union (TFEU) explicitly foresees the possibility to establish the EPPO[3] giving some clear indications on the area of competence and the powers, as well as on the structure and other important aspects of the future Office. In its proposal the Commission builds on the following objectives: to provide an efficient structure, to be able to protect better the financial interests of the Union and to ensure operability, which will enable the Office to work within the legal systems of the Member States while building a genuine European prosecution policy.[4]

These objectives are broad and ambitious and deserve long-lasting attention. However, in view of the overall theme of this book the following issues have been selected to be dealt with in this chapter: the governance structure (Sect. 2.1); the competence (Sect. 2.2); some procedural aspects, in particular the investigative measures (Sect. 2.3) and judicial review (Sect. 2.4).

2.2 Governance Structure of EPPO

Many options have been subject to the Commission's analysis.[5] Bearing in mind the objectives mentioned above, the Commission has opted for an integrated, but decentralised model of governance.

First, the integrated model implies an independent European body with separate legal personality which will be able to provide efficient response to the existing gap

---

[1] See Chap. 1 of this volume: 'Introduction'.

[2] COM 2013 534. See the Appendix to this Volume. Hereafter 'EPPO proposal'.

[3] Article 86 TFEU.

[4] See the Impact Assessment accompanying the Commission's proposal, SWD (2013) 274 of 17.7.2013.

[5] For more details, see the Impact Assessment supra n. 4.

in the protection of the Union's financial interests. Such a model will also be able to ensure equivalent protection throughout the Union.

Second, the decentralised model proposes a structure which builds on the national law enforcement and prosecution services. Article 86 TFEU already gives some indication in that respect. It foresees that the concerned criminal cases must be prosecuted before the national courts. The advantage of this choice is that in such way EPPO will benefit from the proximity of the place of crime. Moreover, this is already a hint for the division of labour between the European and the national judicial authorities. This issue will be dealt with in more detail in Sect. 2.5, dealing with judicial review aspects.

The Commission considers that this decentralised model offers the best balance between European and national decision making, but furthermore also the best chances that EPPO will be genuinely effective and accepted at Member State level.

The structure of EPPO, as foreseen in the Commission's proposal, comprises two layers. The first consists of the European Public Prosecutor (EPP) and his/her four Deputies.[6] They shall be appointed by the Council with the consent of the European Parliament in an open competition applying a transparent procedure.[7] The fact that the two arms of the EU budgetary authority will be the appointing authorities of the head of the EU office responsible for the protection of the Union's financial interests is of a significant importance which adds to its legitimacy. This appointment procedure gives the necessary guarantees for the independence of the EPP and its Deputies which is of fundamental importance for its efficiency and its added value. The EPP and his/her Deputies will be located in the headquarters.

The second layer of the EPPO structure consists of the European Delegated Prosecutors (EDPs), who will be appointed by the EPP, on the basis of a list of at least three candidates submitted by the Member State concerned.[8] This procedure of appointment reflects the EDPs' double-hatted status (see below) and seeks to ensure the best balance between the integrity and acceptance from both sides. The EDPs will each stay in their own Member State.

The role of the EPP will be to exercise the central coordination and steering in order to ensure consistency and equivalent protection of the Union's financial interests.[9] This is the core function of the office, and its central position will allow to develop a genuine EU wide prosecution policy.

In order to be able to pursue this main function, the EPP shall monitor during the investigation phase the investigations and ensure their coordination. According to the proposal he/she will instruct the EDPs where necessary[10] or also may reallocate the case to another EDP or even take up the investigations himself/ herself if certain

---

[6] Article 6.1 of the EPPO proposal.

[7] Articles 8(1) and 9(1) of the EPPO proposal.

[8] Article 10(1) of the EPPO proposal.

[9] Recital 12 of the EPPO proposal.

[10] Article 18(4) of the EPPO proposal.

conditions are fulfilled.[11] During the prosecution phase the EPP receives for review the summary of the case with the draft indictment and the list of evidence.[12] In the event the EDP considers the investigation completed, the EPP may instruct to dismiss the case, to bring it before the national court, to refer it back for further investigations, or to bring himself/herself the case before the national court.[13] The choice of jurisdiction is with the EPP in close cooperation with the EDPs, based on objective criteria set up in the draft regulation.[14] This is the only decision which shall be centralised. The initiation of the investigation on the other hand can be done at local level by the EDPs.

The *European Delegated Prosecutors* maximise the efficiency and minimise the costs.[15] They are the emanation of the principle of decentralisation which has an impact on their specific status. The EDPs originate from national prosecution bodies and maintain their powers as national prosecutors (their national hat). And yet acting on behalf of and under the authority of the EPP, they are integral part of EPPO (their European hat).

This 'double-hatted' status has, both, institutional and operational implications. In institutional terms, before being appointed, the EDPs must be already national prosecutors with relevant experience and qualification. Moreover, they shall keep their status as national prosecutors during the whole mandate as EDPs.[16] This requirement has essential operational and practical reasons. It aims at ensuring smooth operational cooperation between the EDPs and the national law enforcement authorities. Furthermore, it allows the EDPs, to the extent compatible with their EPPO status and powers, to use their national prosecutorial powers and apply the relevant national legal framework, e.g., regarding the modalities for carrying out investigative measures or procedural rules applicable in the trial phase.[17]

Also, the EDPs cannot be dismissed as national prosecutors by the competent national authorities without the consent of the EPP during the exercise of their functions on behalf of EPPO.[18] This provision should not be considered as an unjustified interference with the national decision making on the career development of the prosecutors but as a guarantee for the EDPs' independence.

Moreover, the EDPs cannot receive nor seek instructions from their national superiors as regards EU fraud cases. According to the Commission's proposal EPPO will have exclusive competence to deal with EU fraud cases and therefore, the national authorities will not be competent to give instructions on these cases.[19]

---

[11] Article 18(5) and (6) of the EPPO proposal.

[12] Article 27(2) of the EPPO proposal.

[13] Criteria laid down in Article 28 of the EPPO proposal.

[14] Article 27(4) of the EPPO proposal.

[15] Recital 13 of the EPPO proposal.

[16] Article 10(2) of the EPPO proposal.

[17] Article 26(2) of the EPPO proposal.

[18] Article 10(3) of the EPPO proposal.

[19] See Article 6(5) second sentence of the EPPO proposal.

Consequently, conflicting instructions on EU fraud cases shall not occur. The national law enforcement authorities will work on EU fraud cases but only on the basis of EDPs' instructions.

At the same time the EDPs shall be an integral part of EPPO. They shall be appointed by the EPP and act under his/her exclusive authority.[20] As a consequence, their acts shall be attributed to EPPO.[21] These are logical consequences of the establishment of a genuine European prosecutorial authority.

The EDPs may exercise their functions as national prosecutors as well if there is no EU fraud case assigned to them. To ensure efficiency and resolve potential conflicting assignments, the EDPs shall notify the EPP if the exercise of EDPs' function as national prosecutors is in conflict with their function as European prosecutors. Following consultation with the national prosecution authorities, the EPP may instruct EDPs to give priority to the European fraud case and inform the national authorities thereof.[22] Acceptance of this EU priority by national authorities stems from the obligations imposed on the Member States to combat criminality affecting the financial interests of the Union[23] and the principle of sincere cooperation envisaged in Article 4 TEU, which requires the Member States to facilitate the achievement of the Union's tasks and refrain from measures that could jeopardise their attainment. A similar obligation is stated by the proposed EPPO regulation.[24]

Another important aspect which deserves special attention is whether the Treaty reference to the establishment of EPPO 'from Eurojust' means that EPPO shall have a Eurojust-like collegial structure. The Commission considers that creating EPPO with an intergovernmental collegial structure would seriously hamper the independence of EPPO to take decisions on prosecutions. It would also slow down the decision making and therefore be inefficient.[25]

Firstly, there is a need to ensure that EPPO will be able to take decisions independently. A collegial structure as foreseen for Eurojust allows pursuing national interests in the field of judicial cooperation and in this form contravenes the notion to create an independent prosecutorial office. Such model echoes the intergovernmental approach of the pre-Lisbon cooperation in criminal matters which is neither compatible with the current legal framework nor in line with the objective to develop a genuine EU wide prosecution policy. In addition, a collegial structure following the model of Eurojust could mean that any action to be taken by EPPO would require an agreement of the Member State concerned with regard to the investigation and/or prosecution, creating the possibility for national interests to outweigh Union ones.

---

[20] Article 6(5) of the EPPO proposal.

[21] Article 6(7) of the EPPO proposal.

[22] Article 6(6) of the EPPO proposal.

[23] An obligation as provided for in Article 325(1) TFEU.

[24] Article 11(7) of the EPPO proposal.

[25] See Impact Assessment supra n. 4.

Secondly, a collegial structure like Eurojust's, would be cumbersome, and could mean serious delays in the operational decision making during the investigation (e.g. searching premises or arresting suspects in several Member States), in the prosecution phase (e.g. choice of jurisdiction, indictments), and in particular in cases of conflicts of jurisdiction.

Thirdly, a collegial structure for taking decisions on prosecutions is found nowhere in the Member States' systems—even in cases where the general prosecution policy is determined by the highest judicial authorities, the individual decisions, whether or not to prosecute, are always taken by the individual prosecutor in order to avoid political interference with the administration of justice.

Last but not least, in the case of Eurojust the Member States, whose national members are sitting in the college, have retained their competence to investigate and prosecute crimes. This situation differs fundamentally from the set-up of EPPO, which according to the Treaty will have its own European competence to investigate, prosecute and bring cases before the court.

The Commission has analysed carefully the arguments raised by those who defended the collegial structure of EPPO, and the need for a close cooperation between the headquarters and the EDPs has been recognised. The Commission's proposal foresees a forum of 10 members (the EPP, his four Deputies and five European Delegated Prosecutors) with the competence to decide on the internal rules of procedure of EPPO. These rules are of major operational importance since they will cover, *inter alia* the organisation of the work of the Office, as well as the general rules on the allocation of cases. This approach does not compromise the independence of the Office, neither its efficient decision-making process.

2.3 EPPO Competence

2.3.1 Exclusive Competence

The exclusive competence of EPPO[26] has a crucial operational function: to avoid parallel investigations at EU and national level. It shows clearly who does what and who takes the responsibility for conducting investigations and prosecutions.

However, this does not mean that the national authorities are excluded from the process or that their obligation to protect the financial interests of the Union diminishes. The decentralised structure of EPPO allows for the involvement of national law enforcement authorities into the process. The purpose is not to exclude national authorities but to work better together.

[26] Article 11(4) of the EPPO proposal.

2.3.2 Mandatory Prosecution Versus Discretion to Prosecute

The Commission has opted for mandatory prosecution based on the following reasoning; EPPO's discretion to decide whether or not to prosecute a criminal case falling within its remit would mean that the Office could decide not to handle a case despite clear indications that a crime affecting the financial interests of the Union has been committed. Such possibility would be incompatible with the strong commitment of the Union towards legality and legal certainty and the policy of zero tolerance for these offences. This means in practice that whenever EPPO has reasonable grounds to believe that a criminal offence within its competence was committed, it has an obligation to initiate a criminal investigation.

Moreover, the principle of mandatory prosecution is a logical consequence of the exclusive competence of EPPO to deal with crimes against the financial interests of the Union. Since EPPO will be the only Office to deal with these offences, there should be no discretion whether or not to prosecute in case of sufficient evidence. This does not mean that minor offences will be always prosecuted in court; EPPO may dismiss cases where the offence is minor and refer them to OLAF or to national authorities for administrative follow-up.

2.3.3 Material Competence—Offences Against the Financial Interests of the Union

The Treaty[27] foresees the possibility to establish EPPO to combat crimes affecting the financial interests of the Union. The European Council may by a unanimous decision and after obtaining the consent of the European Parliament and consulting the Commission, extend the powers of EPPO by including serious crimes having a cross-border dimension. Such a decision would require a detailed analysis of the operational activities of EPPO first as well as the political will to introduce such a major change. Article 74 of the proposal foresees that such analysis be conducted 5 years after the regulation's application.

2.3.4 Ancillary Competence

Ancillary competence is a well-known concept in law. It aims at an efficient use of resources and better administration of justice, given that EU fraud is generally not committed alone but in conjunction with other crimes. The proposed provision on ancillary competence[28] says that only according to strictly determined criteria and

---

[27] Article 86 TFEU.

[28] Article 13 of the EPPO proposal.

on a case-by-case basis EPPO might be competent to investigate and prosecute offences other than EU fraud, if these other offences are inextricably linked with EU fraud, both offences are based on the same facts, and the EU fraud is preponderant. On the same basis, national prosecution services might be competent to investigate and prosecute EU fraud following the same criteria, if EU fraud is not preponderant EPPO. The national prosecution authorities shall consult each other on this matter.

The ancillary competence of the EPPO should not be understood as an extension of the EPPO competences as provided for by Article 86(4) TFEU. This Treaty provision indeed refers to serious and cross-border crime (e.g. trafficking in human beings, terrorism). It is not likely that those crimes can be committed together with EU fraud and on the basis of the same facts, as required by the Commission's proposal. In that sense the Commission's proposal on the ancillary competence of EPPO does not circumvent Article 86(4) TFEU. Essentially, the Commission proposal aims at avoiding unnecessary duplication of investigations and prosecution rather than artificially separating cases.

2.4 Procedural Aspects: Investigative Measures

According to the Commission's proposal, EPPO will rely on, both, EU and national rules of investigation and prosecution.

EPPO will have the power either to request authorisation from a national court, or, depending on the circumstances, to order itself, the investigative measures listed by the proposed EPPO regulation.[29] The proposal foresees a catalogue of investigative measures which will be at the disposal of the EPP / EDPs throughout the territory of the Member States. Among others, the investigative measures at the disposal of EPPO include the search of premises, property and computer systems, the interception of telephone conversations and the questioning of the suspected person(s) and witnesses.

The proposal refers to the national rules as regards the conditions for applying the investigative measures, as well as for the procedural rules for the trial phase.

This common toolbox will ensure consistency and uniformity of the protection of the Union's financial interests as the investigative measures will not depend on the choice of jurisdiction. Some of these measures are more intrusive than others. For the most intrusive measures the proposal requires prior judicial authorisation by national courts.[30]

The second key procedural element of the proposed regulation is the rule on the admissibility of evidence.[31] The proposal foresees a provision which ensures that evidence lawfully gathered in one Member State shall be admissible in the courts of

[29] Article 26 of the EPPO proposal.

[30] Article 26(4) of the EPPO proposal.

[31] Article 30 of the EPPO proposal.

all (participating) Member States, if—according to the trial court—the admission would not adversely affect the fairness of proceedings or the rights of the defendant as enshrined in the Charter of Fundamental Rights. This does not deprive the trial court from its right to assess the evidentiary value of the evidence in question. This provision is of fundamental importance for the efficient follow-up of criminal cases as confirmed by Commission Communications[32] and recent OLAF reports.[33]

2.5 Judicial Review

The provision on judicial remedies is one of the shortest provisions in the proposed regulation. And yet it brings one of the most important changes to the well-known system of judicial remedies of the EU.[34] The well-established case law[35] of the ECJ says that the national courts cannot assess the validity of the acts of European institutions. And yet, in line with Article 86(3) TFEU, Article 36 of the proposal creates a legal fiction. It provides that for the purpose of judicial review EPPO shall be considered as a national authority when adopting procedural measures in the performance of its function. As a result, national courts will be entrusted with the judicial review of all EPPO's challengeable acts of investigation and prosecution, both during the pre-trial and trial stages.

The Commission's view is that it would not be feasible to foresee the ECJ's competence for this purpose given the potential volume of cases to be handled (an estimate of 2,500 cases per year) and the absence of a specialised EU court.[36]

There are many reasons for this innovative approach. EPPO's acts of investigation are closely related to an eventual prosecution and will mainly deploy their effects in the legal orders of the Member States. In most cases, they will also be carried out by national law enforcement authorities acting under EPPO's

---

[32] Communication from the Commission to the European Parliament, the Council, the European Economic and Social Committee and the Committee of the Regions on the protection of the financial interests of the European Union by criminal law and by administrative investigations, COM (2011) 293, see p. 6 and following.

[33] See in particular OLAF Report 2011, p. 35 and following, mentioning among others that: '[…] practitioners have pointed out that mutual legal assistance has its limits, that the use of evidence in cross-border cases is sometimes problematic and that there is a tendency to limit prosecutions to domestic cases and disregard the European dimension'. http://ec.europa.eu/anti_fraud/documents/reports-olaf/2011/olaf_report_2011_en.pdf (Accessed June 2014).

[34] Article 36 of the EPPO proposal:
Judicial review:
1. When adopting procedural measures in the performance of its functions, the EPPO shall be considered as a national authority for the purpose of judicial review.
2. Where provisions of national law are rendered applicable by this Regulation, such provisions shall not be considered as provisions of Union law for the purpose of Article 267 of the Treaty.

[35] Judgment of 22 October 1987, Foto-Frost/Hauptzollamt Lübeck-Ost, Case 314/85.

[36] See the Impact Assessment supra n. 4.

instructions, sometimes after having obtained the authorisation by a national court. EPPO is therefore a Union body whose actions will mainly be relevant in the national legal orders. It is therefore appropriate and coherent to consider EPPO as a national authority for the purpose of the judicial review of its acts of investigation and prosecution. This solution provides a significant benefit to the extent that suspects and their defence lawyers will work within the national legal systems which they know well.

This innovative approach is without prejudice to the competence of the Court of Justice of the European Union to give preliminary rulings.[37] The Court's powers in this respect will not become affected by the proposed regulation. In accordance with Article 267 TFEU, national courts are able or, in certain circumstances, bound to refer to the Court of Justice questions on the interpretation or the validity of provisions of Union law which are relevant for EPPO's acts of investigation and prosecution. The preliminary rulings procedure will thus ensure that this regulation is applied uniformly throughout the Union.

[37] Article 267 TFEU.

Chapter 3
The European Commission's Legislative Proposal: An Overview of Its Main Characteristics

Michèle Coninsx

Abstract This chapter puts the European Commission's proposal on the establishment of a European Public Prosecutor's Office in a wider perspective, taking as a starting point the current framework for the protection of the EU's financial interests at European judicial level. Implications from institutional, procedural and substantive law points of view, which need to be kept in mind when implementing Article 86 of the Treaty on the Functioning of the European Union in the existing landscape of judicial cooperation in criminal matters, are analysed. Against this background, the main characteristics of the European Commission's proposal are explored and features essential for a future European Public Prosecutor's Office to be able to function in practice are highlighted. The argument is made that the European Public Prosecutor must act as part of a coherent system to bring added value to the fight against crimes adversely affecting the EU's financial interests. To be workable, the proposal needs to ensure solid synergies between all national and European actors involved, especially Eurojust, as stipulated in the Lisbon Treaty.

Keywords Crimes against the financial interests of the European Union · European Public Prosecutor's Office · Eurojust · Lisbon Treaty · Article 325 Treaty on the functioning of the European Union · Judicial cooperation in criminal matters · Mutual recognition principle

Contents

The author is President of Eurojust and National Member for Belgium.

M. Coninsx (✉)
Eurojust, The Hague, The Netherlands
e-mail: mconinsx@eurojust.europa.eu

L.H. Erkelens et al. (eds.), *The European Public Prosecutor's Office*,
DOI 10.1007/978-94-6265-035-0_3

The development of legislation in the area of Freedom, Security and Justice is impressive, but it has shortcomings in terms of overlapping and a certain lack of coherence.[1]

3.1 Introduction

With the entry into force of the Lisbon Treaty, the European Area of Freedom, Security and Justice (AFSJ) is moving towards a new phase in combating crimes adversely affecting the EU's financial interests in a more effective manner. The Lisbon Treaty leaves room for manoeuvre when it comes to the options for an enhanced role for Eurojust, the European Union's judicial cooperation unit, on the basis of Article 85 of the Treaty on the Functioning of the European Union (TFEU), as well as for the establishment of a European Public Prosecutor's Office (EPPO) *from* Eurojust, on the basis of Article 86 TFEU.[2]

The European Commission seized the opportunity provided by the Lisbon Treaty to propose a package reform based on a multi-faceted integrated approach to tackling EU fraud.[3] In June 2012, the European Commission proposed a directive on the fight against fraud to the EU's financial interests by means of criminal law to create greater harmonisation of the existing criminal provisions in this area.[4] Thereafter, in July 2013, two parallel proposals were issued on the basis of Articles 85 and 86 TFEU.

[1] European Council, Stockholm Programme: an open and secure Europe serving and protecting citizens (2010/C 115/01), p. 5.

[2] Article 86(1) TFEU.

[3] Viviane Reding, Strengthening the basis for EU criminal law and judicial cooperation, speech to the CRIM Special Committee, European Parliament, Brussels, 19 March 2013, p. 2, http://ec.europa.eu/.

[4] Proposal for a Directive on the fight against fraud to the Union's financial interests by means of criminal law, COM 2012 363 final of 11 July 2012.

Firstly, the European Commission issued a proposal for a new Eurojust regulation to improve its governance and democratic accountability framework and, ultimately, to strengthen the operational work of Eurojust in the fight against cross-border crime.[5]

Secondly, the European Commission issued a proposal for a Council regulation on the establishment of an EPPO, a novel European actor that would specifically centralise investigations and prosecutions regarding offences against the financial interests of the European Union and bring criminals to justice.[6] The proposals for regulations on 'Lisbonising' Eurojust on the one hand and on the establishment of the EPPO on the other hand are—and must be—very much interlinked. Accordingly, the two drafts must—ideally in parallel—be read and developed in the negotiating process at Council and Parliament level to ensure complementarity of competences and enable operational interaction in a common approach to more effectively protect the financial interests of the European Union.

This package reform brought by the European Commission is intended to overcome the current fragmentation of national law enforcement efforts to investigate and prosecute offences adversely affecting the EU's financial interests and bring them to judgement. The European Commission argues that the current stand-alone competence of Member States to prosecute offences against the EU budget results in unequal protection of the EU's financial interests and an insufficient level of deterrence achieved by current anti-fraud measures. According to the European Commission, the EPPO—centralising investigations and prosecutions regarding such offences—would better equip the European Union in the fight against fraud that damages its budget.[7] Despite its noble ambitions, the establishment of the EPPO raises some issues and concerns, not only at political level, but also from legal, institutional and procedural points of view.

Against this background, two pertinent questions emerge:

- Does the proposal adequately correspond to the existing national criminal justice systems and the EU criminal justice framework?
- Will the proposal prove to be workable in practice?

An assessment of the concrete, published proposal should be carried out, taking into account the range of instruments that already exist at EU level. Such assessment should also attempt to determine the potential obstacles to the proper functioning of the European judicial area as a whole and the added value of the EPPO within it.

---

[5] Proposal for a Regulation of the European Parliament and of the Council on the European Union Agency for Criminal Justice Cooperation (Eurojust), COM 2013 535 final. As from now referred to as: draft Eurojust regulation.

[6] Proposal for a Council Regulation on the Establishment of the European Public Prosecutor's Office, COM 2013 534 final. See the Appendix to this Volume. As from now referred to as: EPPO proposal.

[7] Explanatory Memorandum of the proposal for a Council Regulation on the establishment of the European Public Prosecutor's Office, COM 2013 534 final.

3.2 The Current Framework

3.2.1 A Shared Constitutional Responsibility

As the wording of Article 325 TFEU suggests, the Lisbon Treaty advocates that the European Union and Member States share responsibility equally in countering fraud and any other illegal activity affecting the EU's financial interests.[8] Accordingly, any EU action in this field as far as based on this provision should comply with the principles of subsidiarity and proportionality.

The unique feature characterising offences adversely affecting the EU's financial interests, the so-called *Protection des Intérêts Financiers* (PIF) offences, is that they are not only committed *in* Europe but are also directed *against* the European Union. This characterisation led the European Commission to consider these crimes as European by nature and to determine the European level as the appropriate level to tackle them. The logical consequence of this reasoning for the European Commission has been the necessity to put in place an autonomous EU actor to ensure equal protection of the EU's financial interests. Viviane Reding, Vice-President of the European Commission and EU Commissioner for Justice, Fundamental Rights and Citizenship, explained the logic behind the establishment of the EPPO in these terms: 'If you have a "federal budget"—with money coming from 27 Member States to promote common European interests—then you also need federal instruments to protect this budget.'[9] The European Commission drew attention to the federal system developed in the USA, where the first criminal case that the police could prosecute across the state borders was the evasion of federal taxes.[10] Given the shared constitutional responsibility of the judicial protection of the EU's financial interests, Member States will first of all assess whether the European Commission's proposal strikes a reasonable balance between national and EU competences, reflecting the principles of subsidiarity and proportionality.

In any event, a European logic of action must be ensured in complex cross-border cases, including fraud and any other illegal activity affecting the EU's financial interests.[11] The need for coordination and cooperation between the competent national authorities of the Member States in this field is also strongly

[8] Article 325(1) TFEU: 'The Union and the Member States shall counter fraud and any other illegal activities affecting the financial interests of the Union through measures to be taken in accordance with this Article, which shall act as a deterrent and be such as to afford effective protection in the Member States, and in all the Union's institutions, bodies, offices and agencies.'

[9] Interview with Commissioner V. Reding in *Eurojust News*, Issue No. 8 (May 2013), p. 5, available on Eurojust website: http://www.eurojust.europa.eu/doclibrary/corporate/Pages/newsletter.aspx.

[10] *Id.*

[11] Interview with Prof. Dr. J. Monar, College of Europe, *Eurojust News*, Issue No. 8 (May 2013), p. 13, available on Eurojust website: http://www.eurojust.europa.eu/doclibrary/corporate/Pages/newsletter.aspx.

emphasised by Article 325 TFEU. The principle of mutual recognition forms the core of a European logic of action in a framework of horizontal judicial cooperation between Member States.

3.2.2 *The Principle of Mutual Recognition*

The Corpus Juris refers to the European Union as a 'single legal area',[12] yet the European Union comprises interactions among 30 different legal systems. Such differences between national legal systems must be taken into account, when considering further steps in the fight against PIF crimes at the EU level. As the Lisbon Treaty asserts, EU judicial criminal cooperation, including cooperation in the fight against PIF crimes, is based on the key principle of mutual recognition. This principle is based upon respecting the differences between legal systems, and attempts to neutralise the negative impact these differences may have on judicial cooperation. Accordingly, as this principle allows for coordination without harmonisation, it was initially presented as an alternative to the approximation of national legislation. Nonetheless, to the extent necessary to facilitate mutual recognition the approximation of substantive and procedural national criminal law, as well as the adoption of measures to prevent and settle conflicts of jurisdiction between Member States, is foreseen in the Lisbon Treaty.[13]

With regard to PIF crimes, a first important step in the direction of the approximation of legislation was already taken by the European Commission when it adopted on the basis of Article 325 TFEU a proposal for a directive on the fight against fraud to the EU's financial interests by means of criminal law.[14] Indeed, mutual recognition of judicial decisions among Member States can only function if mutual trust prevails. As the European Council suggested: 'Mutual trust between authorities and services in the different Member States and decision-makers is the basis for efficient cooperation in this area. Ensuring trust and finding new ways to increase reliance on, and mutual understanding between, the different legal systems in the Member States will thus be one of the main challenges for the future'.[15]

Eurojust was created in this spirit, to help address the challenge through the building up of mutual trust. By providing a common roof for all 28 EU national prosecution authorities, enabling them to have daily contact, and by supporting and strengthening coordination and cooperation between national investigation and prosecution authorities of Member States, Eurojust fosters mutual trust. Indeed, as

---

[12] Article 18 *Corpus Juris*.

[13] Articles 82 and 83 TFEU.

[14] Proposal for a Directive of the European Parliament and of the Council on the fight against fraud to the Union's financial interests by means of criminal law, COM 2012 363, 11 July 2012.

[15] European Council, Stockholm Programme: an open and secure Europe serving and protecting citizens (2010/C 115/01), p. 5.

Eurojust's experience shows, mutual trust requires direct contact through personal presence.

The European Commission's next step in the fight against PIF crimes was the adoption of a proposal establishing the EPPO. Although this European body would specifically centralise investigations and prosecutions regarding offences against the financial interests of the European Union, it would act within different national legal systems. If established, the EPPO's success will therefore heavily rely on the principle of mutual trust and on its capacity to operate as part of a coherent system.

3.3 Fighting Against Crimes Affecting the EU's Financial Interests Today

Currently, protection of the financial interests of the European Union is mainly regulated through the European Anti-Fraud Office (OLAF) Regulation, the Council Decision on Eurojust[16] and national legislation. In short, OLAF carries out administrative investigations regarding fraud, corruption and any other illegal activities adversely affecting the Community's financial interests, and submits the results to national authorities. The judicial follow-up of these cases is entrusted to national authorities, which may request the assistance of Eurojust.

Against this background, Eurojust can be considered a key player in the fight against PIF crimes, as it is the only judicial body in the European Union ensuring coordination and cooperation between the competent authorities of the Member States in cases that fall within its competence. Eurojust plays a vital role in enabling judicial authorities to overcome the main difficulties encountered by national competent authorities in this field. Such difficulties mainly touch upon the complexity of the cases, the amount of information, the speed of exchange of information, or the lack of exchange of information, and the execution of mutual legal assistance requests.

Indeed, Eurojust has developed efficient tools to facilitate information exchange between national competent authorities, and to bring together law enforcement and judicial authorities, allowing for strategic and targeted operations, the resolution of practical difficulties and the resolution of potential conflicts of jurisdiction. Notably, the Eurojust National Coordination System (ENCS) ensures coordination of the work of national authorities by Eurojust.[17] Furthermore, over the past 11 years,

[16] Council Decision 2009/426/JHA of 16 December 2008 on the strengthening of Eurojust, amending Council Decision 2002/187/JHA setting up Eurojust with a view to reinforcing the fight against serious crime.

[17] Eurojust paper on ENCS structure and tasks and the ideal profile of national correspondents for Eurojust, available on: http://www.eurojust.europa.eu/Practitioners/objectives-tools/Pages/eurojust-national-coordination-system.aspx.

Eurojust has been active in facilitating the rapid execution of mutual legal assistance requests, European Arrest Warrants, and confiscation and asset recovery.[18]

For the system employed in the fight against PIF crimes to work effectively, all concerned European actors must join forces. Therefore, on the basis of the 2008 Practical Agreement,[19] collaboration between Eurojust and OLAF has been enhanced, with an increased exchange of case referrals, case summaries, and case-related information, as well as a regular follow-up of ongoing cases. However, to provide judicial follow-up in cross-border investigations related to PIF crimes, closer cooperation with OLAF and the involvement of Eurojust in the early stages of relevant cases are necessary. The new OLAF Regulation is expected to greatly contribute to future operational cooperation between Eurojust and OLAF, as it specifically refers to the transmission of relevant information to Eurojust.

Viewing the creation of the EPPO as progress *per se*, isolating it from the current police and judicial cooperation system, would be a mistake. This new actor will be successful in fulfilling its mission only if integrated in the current landscape made up of national and EU authorities. Therefore, in order to bring real added value it will be crucial to reach for the broadest possible understanding and consent among EU Member States and their competent national authorities on the organisational structure and competences of this new actor.

3.4 Points of Attention When Thinking of EPPO

Institutional, procedural and substantive law aspects must be kept in mind. The following points take stock of the current framework in the fight against PIF crimes, reflect on the provisions of the Lisbon Treaty, and are inspired by the opinions expressed by practitioners from Member States on future prospects.

3.4.1 Enhanced Cooperation

As Article 86 TFEU specifies, the EPPO can only be established in accordance with a special legislative procedure. The regulation establishing the EPPO needs to receive unanimous approval of the Council after obtaining the consent of the European Parliament. Given this veto power granted to each Member State, Article 86 TFEU further grants the possibility to establish the EPPO through the mechanism of enhanced cooperation.

[18] Eurojust Annual Report 2012. http://eurojust.europa.eu/doclibrary/corporate/eurojust%20Annual%20Reports/Annual%20Report%202012/Annual-Report-2012-EN.pdf (Accessed June 2014).

[19] Practical Agreement on arrangements of cooperation between Eurojust and OLAF, 24 September 2008.

In addition, given the 'opt-out' right of the UK, Ireland and Denmark in the AFSJ, inevitably not all Member States will participate in the establishment of the EPPO.[20]

Obviously, the creation by some Member States of an actor responsible for protecting the interests of the European Union as a whole raises difficult conceptual questions regarding the choice of EPPO's model, as well as practical questions regarding its operation.

In particular, the need emerges to coordinate its actions with the national authorities of Member States not involved in the EPPO. As the Consultative Forum of Prosecutors General and Directors of Public Prosecutions of the Member States suggested, the legislator should consider the role that Eurojust could play in this context.[21] Eurojust's expertise in preventing and solving possible conflicts of jurisdiction could also bring added value in the coordination between future EPPO and non-EPPO Member States.

3.4.2 A Model Integrated in the National Systems

The centralisation of the investigation and prosecution of PIF crimes conveyed by the wording of Article 86 TFEU suggests that the EPPO would have a vertical structure. Article 86 TFEU provides flexibility as regards the concrete design of this organisational set-up.

Nonetheless, such design needs to ensure that both European and domestic interests would be adequately reflected in decisions taken by the EPPO, concerning investigations and prosecutions conducted in Member States. Furthermore, the vertical set-up of the EPPO should complement and build on the collegial and horizontal manner in which Eurojust works with the national authorities in Member States. To be feasible, the establishment of the EPPO should build upon existing structures, as stated in the European Commission's Impact Assessment.[22]

Accordingly, once the EPPO has been established, a close link with Eurojust's structure and with each of the Member States needs to be ensured. In this context, the ENCS could be of great use. ENCSs are set up at national level to facilitate cooperation and coordination and a structured information exchange between the Member States and Eurojust. National correspondents for Eurojust are appointed in each Member State, responsible for the functioning of the ENCS. This network

[20] Protocol (no. 21) on the position of the United Kingdom and Ireland in respect of the AFSJ; Protocol (no. 22) on the position of Denmark (TEU—TFEU).

[21] Council document 11628/13 of 27 June 2013, Meeting of the Consultative Forum of Prosecutors General and Directors of Public Prosecutions of the Member States of the European Union, The Hague—26 April 2013.

[22] European Commission Impact Assessment accompanying the proposal for a Council Regulation on the establishment of the European Public Prosecutor's Office, SWD (2013) 274 final, p. 55.

connectivity with each of the Member States enables Eurojust to maintain the necessary ties with national systems and authorities. In addition, the unique position of the Eurojust National Members as national prosecutors has enabled Eurojust to establish efficient bridges between national authorities of the Member States. This working method could also be of great use to future EPPO.

3.4.3 Clearly Defined Set of Competences

Article 86(1) TFEU indicates that the EPPO's main competence relates to 'crimes affecting the financial interests of the Union'. However, the wording of the Lisbon Treaty is less clear regarding whether this competence should be exclusive or shared. In this respect, the possibility of having a threshold for the EPPO to investigate and prosecute PIF crimes, so that minor cases and non-complex cases would still be investigated and prosecuted by Member States, deserves to be considered.

In addition, a reasonable balance needs to be found with respect to the extent of prosecutorial powers to be granted to the EPPO. Indeed, the supremacy or priority in exercising jurisdiction by the EPPO can be defined in different ways. One option would be to give the EPPO the possibility to decide first if it wants to exercise its jurisdiction; in this case, national authorities would exercise their jurisdiction by delegation. Another option would be for the EPPO to have a right of evocation. In this option, even if both the EPPO and a Member State would have jurisdiction over a PIF crime, whenever the EPPO would decide to exercise its jurisdiction, it would exclude the Member State's authorities from exercising their own jurisdiction. To provide legal certainty, a choice must be made between these two options. Indeed, while the first solution could leave the authorities of Member States in limbo until an EPPO has taken a decision on its intention to act, the second solution would ensure that Member States' authorities may take investigative measures prior to any decision of an EPPO to assume responsibility for the case. In addition, the evocation option would allow for appropriate solutions and a reasonably simple procedure in the event the EPPO would not consider a case to be of sufficient importance to be investigated at EU level.

Furthermore, the creation of the EPPO inevitably raises questions about how to deal with cases in which suspects of crimes affecting the EU's financial interests are involved in other serious transnational crimes falling outside the competence of an EPPO. The necessity arises to consider how to deal with these so-called 'connected crimes'. Eurojust's experience demonstrates that distinguishing fraud against the financial interests of the European Union from other serious cross-border crimes is a rather artificial operation, as criminal networks do not limit themselves to a single criminal area. To avoid gaps or overlaps in dealing with such cases, the jurisdictional competences of and coordination mechanisms among the national prosecutorial authorities of the Member States, the EPPO and Eurojust must be explored and defined precisely. In addition, in cases where connected crimes should be investigated and prosecuted separately, coordination will need to be ensured between the efforts of the EPPO and those of the competent national authorities. In any event, Eurojust's assistance and coordination tools could be particularly valuable given the experience it has developed in this field; they are at the disposal of the competent national authorities.

3.4.4 Adequate Procedural Safeguards and Judicial Review Mechanisms

The impact assessment accompanying the European Commission's proposal for establishing the EPPO states: 'Since Article 86 TFEU provides for the establishment of an EPPO, this provision must be read, interpreted and implemented in full compliance with the Charter of Fundamental Rights of the EU ("the Charter")'.[23]

In line with the rights prescribed in the Charter, procedural safeguards should be put in place in the draft proposal on the establishment of the EPPO to ensure effective judicial control of the criminal investigations undertaken by the EPPO.

The lack of approximation of procedural legislation applicable to the EPPO's activities could be considered bearing the risk of a drawback. The diversity of procedural rules among Member States can be a source of disagreement, especially with regard to admissibility of evidence or investigative and coercive measures undertaken. Serious consideration thus needs to be given to this aspect, also with a view to rights of the suspect.

In addition, establishing the EPPO that specifically centralises investigations and prosecutions in an area still characterised by a variety of criminal and procedural rules may result in a higher risk of forum shopping. To avoid such risk, clear criteria should be defined to determine the competent forum. Given the experience and expertise Eurojust has acquired over the past 11 years in the field of prevention and of resolution of conflicts of jurisdiction,[24] it should be explored which role it could play in this regard. In accordance with Article 86 TFEU, the EPPO proposal also determines the rules applicable to the judicial review of procedural measures taken by the EPPO while performing its functions. These draft rules do give rise to the question which authority should be competent for such a review. This is a controversial issue on which practitioners not yet have reached consensus.[25]

---

[23] European Commission Impact Assessment accompanying the proposal for a Council regulation on the establishment of the European Public Prosecutor's Office, SWD (2013) 274 final, p. 27.

[24] See also Eurojust Annual Report 2003 http://eurojust.europa.eu/doclibrary/corporate/eurojust%20Annual%20Reports/Annual%20Report%202003/Annual-Report-2003-EN.pdf (Accessed June 2014).

[25] See A. Meij, Chap. 7 in this book.

The discussions of the Consultative Forum[26] highlighted the choice of either giving such competence of judicial review of procedural measures taken by the EPPO to the national courts or to the European Court of Justice. Most practitioners, however, pointed out that judicial review of EPPO's activities should be neither exclusive national, nor exclusive European competence, and that the competent authority should be determined on a case-by-case basis.[27]

3.4.5 From Eurojust

The wording of Article 86 TFEU, spelling out that the EPPO should be established 'from Eurojust',[28] implies that the relationship between the EPPO and Eurojust should be of an essential nature. Eurojust is certainly called upon to play a special role, and an integrated concept, forming a strong link between Eurojust and the EPPO, must be ensured. EPPO and Eurojust should act in synergy, the two future regulations should use the same terminology, and their provisions should mirror each other to avoid discrepancies and achieve a coherent and effective system of investigation and prosecution of PIF crimes.

Further, Eurojust's competence should be adapted in such a way that both actors can complement each other without diminishing the core mission of Eurojust: supporting and strengthening cooperation and coordination upon request and when needed. As the Impact Assessment of the European Commission specifies, 'Whichever option is chosen, Eurojust's role as the Union's coordination agency for cross-border judicial cooperation in criminal matters will remain unaffected'.[29]

On the contrary, given that the EPPO would need to act within a limited scope in substance and will most likely be subject to territorial constraints, Eurojust will be called upon to perform a new task: avoiding gaps in the police and judicial cooperation system that may arise with a future new EU actor on board. The EPPO can certainly take advantage of Eurojust's expertise and operational experience in international judicial cooperation and the tools developed therefor, such as information gathered by Eurojust, the Eurojust coordination meetings and operational coordination centres, and its work in Joint Investigation Teams (JITs). All these tools will certainly contribute to the future success of the EPPO. In addition, participation of the EPPO in the meetings of the College of Eurojust on operational

---

[26] Council document 11628/13 of 27 June 2013, Meeting of the Consultative Forum of Prosecutors General and Directors of Public Prosecutions of the Member States of the European Union, The Hague—26 April 2013.

[27] *Id.*

[28] Article 86(1) TFEU.

[29] European Commission's Impact Assessment accompanying the proposal for a Council Regulation on the establishment of the European Public Prosecutor's Office, SWD (2013) 274 final, p. 31.

PIF-related matters and the daily contact at the operational level between the Eurojust's National Desks and the EPPO would be mutually beneficial.

The efficiency expected from the centralisation of investigations and prosecutions of PIF crimes performed by the EPPO would certainly be undermined by a lack of synergies between all involved actors. Both effectiveness and cost efficiency would be ensured by the setting up of an infrastructure ensuring close ties with Eurojust. However, while the establishment of the EPPO is intended to fight an important criminal domain more effectively, this domain remains limited when compared to the wide spectrum of competences of Eurojust. As Hans G. Nilsson pointed out, 'You cannot have a weaker Eurojust in relation to very serious crimes when, at the same time, you have a stronger European Public Prosecutor's Office in relation to fraud against the financial interests of the EU'.[30] Thus, the establishment of the EPPO should not result in a transfer of resources to the detriment of Eurojust.

3.5 Overview of the European Commission's Proposal

3.5.1 An Office at EU Level Directing Double-Hatted European Delegated Prosecutors

The European Commission's proposal sets out an indivisible and hierarchical structure for the EPPO. In this design, the EPPO is headed by a European Public Prosecutor, who is assisted by four deputies. This specialised core group at EU level would direct and supervise the activities carried out by the European Delegated Prosecutors in each Member State. The European Commission conceived these European Delegated Prosecutors as national prosecutors who, when dealing with PIF crimes, are fully independent of national prosecuting bodies and act under the exclusive authority of the European Public Prosecutor.[31] The structure created by the proposal relies mainly on these European Delegated Prosecutors, who can, under the authority of the European Public Prosecutor, undertake investigative measures on their own or instruct the competent national law enforcement authorities to do so.[32]

Nonetheless, the proposal does not clarify concretely how relations amongst European Delegated Prosecutors would take place and whether the European Public Prosecutor and the European Delegated Prosecutors would meet in a common structure to take decisions. Despite the vertical set-up provided for the EPPO, this

[30] Interview: Mr Hans G. Nilsson, Head of Unit, Fundamental Rights and Criminal Justice, General Secretariat of the Council of the EU, *Eurojust News*, Issue No. 8 (May 2013), p. 12, available on Eurojust website: http://www.eurojust.europa.eu/doclibrary/corporate/Pages/newsletter.aspx.

[31] Article 6 of the EPPO proposal.

[32] Article 18 of the EPPO proposal.

European body will face the same operational boundaries that horizontal cooperation faces today. Each European Delegated Prosecutor will act within his/her own Member State and will need to have effective means to communicate across Europe. As Eurojust's experience demonstrates, this matter is not purely administrative; it has an important operational dimension as well. In this context, the use of the ENCS for the European Delegated Prosecutors seems to be a logical conclusion.

A key feature of the EPPO, as envisaged by the European Commission, consists of the two 'hats' of the European Delegated Prosecutors. They are integrated into the EPPO while remaining national prosecutors. As Eurojust's experience shows, two hats can be very useful, notably with regard to access to national databases and the establishment of efficient bridges between national and European interests. However, such a design may raise important issues both at national level and at the level of the EPPO.

On national level, the proposal gives the European Delegated Prosecutors the power to instruct competent law enforcement authorities in the Member State where they are located. While such power may not raise particular concerns in Member States in which prosecutorial powers on PIF offences are centralised, concerns might be raised in more decentralised Member States.

On EPPO level, in the event of a conflict of priorities, the proposal gives the power to the European Public Prosecutor to instruct the European Delegated Prosecutors to give priority to their functions deriving from the EPPO Regulation, following a consultation with the competent national authorities. This design, in which a specialised core group at EU level has the power to instruct these double-hatted prosecutors, constitutes a remarkable new concept in decision making and resource allocation in the area of EU criminal matters. The question legislators must pose is whether this shift is both acceptable and feasible.

3.5.2 Maximal Competences Within a Limited Scope

According to the proposal, the EPPO shall have exclusive competence to investigate and prosecute crimes adversely affecting the financial interests of the European Union.[33] Furthermore, no threshold is mentioned in the proposal under which the competence to investigate and prosecute PIF crimes could be left to the Member States. The lack of a threshold reflects the principle of mandatory prosecution underlying the EPPO's investigation and prosecution activities, so as to ensure 'zero tolerance' towards offences adversely affecting the EU's financial interests, as advocated by the European Commission.[34]

---

[33] Article 11(4) of the EPPO proposal.

[34] Recital 20 of the EPPO proposal.

Nonetheless, the proposal acknowledges that the EPPO should have the possibility to dismiss a case in which the offence is minor.[35] Consequently, it sets a case-by-case threshold unilaterally defined by the EPPO.

The proposal appears to advocate the delegation option concerning the extent of the powers to be granted to the EPPO within its competences, since the proposal prescribes that, in principle, authorities of Member States should only act at the request of the EPPO.[36] Even if an exception is foreseen for urgent measures, the option chosen by the European Commission might raise concerns about the possibility for Member States' authorities to take investigative measures prior to any decision of the EPPO to take over the case.

Turning to the question of connected crimes, the proposal specifies that the EPPO would have an ancillary competence to investigate and prosecute offences that are inextricably linked with PIF crimes in cases in which PIF offences are preponderant. Determining the competent authority when linked offences are present will therefore become a preliminary step. In this context, one must keep in mind that Article 86 TFEU specifies that an extension of powers of the EPPO necessitates a special legislative procedure. The EPPO's ancillary competence can therefore not result in an indirect extension of its competences in breach of the Treaties. Eurojust's role in facilitating the agreement on the determination of the ancillary competence between the EPPO and the national prosecution authorities is clearly recognised in the draft EPPO regulation[37] and should be mirrored in the Eurojust regulation. Less clear, however, is how the determination of such competence will be accomplished in practice, since the proposal only specifies that Eurojust 'may be associated' where appropriate.

Eurojust's added value is also acknowledged with regard to specific acts of investigation regarding connected crimes and crimes falling outside the territorial competence of the EPPO. The draft EPPO regulation provides for the possibility for the EPPO to include Eurojust in cross-border or complex cases by requesting Eurojust to participate in the coordination—or to make use of its powers, attributed by Union or national law, thereto—of specific aspects of investigations that may fall outside the material or territorial competence of EPPO.[38] Further clarification and enhancement of Eurojust's role in coordinating and enhancing cooperation between an EPPO and national authorities can maximise the added benefit that Eurojust can bring.

Overall, even though the scope of competence of the EPPO is limited to PIF crimes, the proposal provides for a maximum of competences within this limited scope. Indeed, the EPPO would have an exclusive competence not subject to any threshold; national authorities would only exercise their jurisdiction by delegation from the EPPO, and the EPPO might even be competent for connected crimes

[35] Recital 31 of the EPPO proposal.

[36] Recital 23 and Article 17 of the EPPO proposal.

[37] Articles 13 and 57(c) of the EPPO proposal.

[38] Article 57(2)(b) and (2)(d) of the EPPO proposal.

inextricably linked to PIF crimes if certain conditions are fulfilled. Whether such maximising of the competences of the EPPO for PIF crimes is sufficiently justified by the 'zero tolerance' approach remains to be seen in the legislative process.

3.5.3 Exchange of Information in the EU Context

Once established, the EPPO will obviously need to have access to all relevant information concerning offences that fall within its competence. Several information databases relating to these offences already exist within the European Union. Finding a method of granting the EPPO access to all the information needed to effectively carry out its investigations and prosecutions is important. One must bear in mind that creating a new database is costly in terms of time and resources. Besides, national authorities may consider transmitting data to an additional entity burdensome.

The European Commission's proposal provides for three main sources of information for the EPPO. First of all, the EPPO would have access to the national criminal investigation databases of participating Member States through the European Delegated Prosecutors.[39] In addition, the EPPO shall have access to all relevant information concerning an offence within its competence from EU institutions, bodies, offices and agencies.[40]

Finally, the proposal provides for the establishment of an autonomous Case Management System with a mechanism for automatic cross-checking of data with Eurojust's Case Management System.[41] Eurojust's experience can be of great value in assessing the required functionalities and resources involved in creating a Case Management System for the EPPO. Eurojust currently uses its own, sophisticated Case Management System.[42] It took several years to put it in place and refine and configure it for operational purposes. Tools for a structured and secure transmission of information from national authorities to Eurojust have been developed following the last revision of Eurojust's framework in 2008, where the emphasis was placed, *inter alia*, on strengthening the information flow towards Eurojust,[43] taking into account a highly developed data protection regime.

---

[39] Article 20 of the EPPO proposal.

[40] Article 21 of the EPPO proposal.

[41] Article 22 of the EPPO proposal.

[42] Articles 16–16b Council Decision on Eurojust.

[43] Article 13 Council Decision on Eurojust.

3.5.4 Choice of Forum—A Hybrid System

The European Commission's proposal gives the power to each European Delegated Prosecutor to carry out investigations in his/her Member State and relies solely on the principle of mutual recognition when dealing with the question of admissibility of evidence, without tackling the question of an approximation of legislation.[44] Will the *status quo* be sufficient to avoid the risk of inadmissibility of evidence regarding investigations carried out by the EPPO?

The proposal leaves the choice of the forum to the EPPO in consultation with the European Delegated Prosecutor submitting the case.[45] A few criteria have to be taken into account by the EPPO when taking such decision, but no order of priority is given nor has a role for Eurojust been provided for in this context. Is the discretion of the EPPO with respect to the choice of forum compatible with fundamental rights?[46]

The Explanatory Memorandum rightly points out that the operation of the EPPO should be governed by the principle of procedural neutrality, and should be subject to judicial review. However, when determining which court should be competent for such a review, the proposal specifies that the EPPO 'shall be considered as a national authority for the purpose of judicial review'.[47] Should the judicial review of procedural measures taken by an—at its core—EU entity be an exclusively national matter?

Even if the EPPO would carry out the same activities as national prosecutors—investigating a case and bringing it to judgment, it would remain a European entity and the rules governing these activities would be both national and European. The burden put on national courts by this creative construction might be heavy. National courts will not easily carry out such a judicial review and will certainly need to refer to the European Court of Justice for preliminary rulings.

3.5.5 Special Relationship with Eurojust

Both the proposed Eurojust regulation[48] and the proposal for establishing the EPPO[49] refer to the 'special relationship' between Eurojust and the EPPO, which is 'based on close cooperation and the development of operational, administrative and management links'. Despite the wording 'from Eurojust' of Article 86 TFEU, Eurojust is not mentioned in the provision of the EPPO proposal stipulating the

[44] Article 30 of the EPPO proposal.
[45] Article 27(4) of the EPPO proposal.
[46] See M. Wasmeier, Chap. 9 in this book.
[47] Article 36 of the EPPO proposal.
[48] Article 41 of the draft Eurojust regulation.
[49] Article 57(1) of the EPPO proposal.

structure and organisation of the EPPO.[50] The proposal seems to create a new body rather than a new actor closely linked to Eurojust, hence moving away from the formulation of the Treaty.

In addition, some discrepancies exist in the European Commission's proposals concerning the articulation of competences for PIF crimes between Eurojust and the proposed EPPO. Indeed, the current formulation of the proposed Eurojust regulation excludes in principle Eurojust's competence *ratione materiae* for the crimes for which the EPPO is competent,[51] yet the list in Annex 1 newly includes the category of 'crime against the financial interests of the Union'. The same need for clarification of the 'combined reading' of the two proposed regulations rises with regard to provisions on operational support. How this 'close cooperation' will be worked out in operational terms is less clear from other provisions. For example, in relation to third States and international organisations, both proposals provide for the possibility to conclude working arrangements and designate contact points to third States.[52] Nonetheless, duplication of contacts and working arrangements with third States and international organisations by Eurojust and the EPPO could be avoided. Consequently, due consideration should be given to one of the options put forward in the European Commission's Impact Assessment, whereby the EPPO would profit directly from Eurojust's existing cooperation agreements.[53] Regarding cooperation with other important partners such as Europol and OLAF, the EPPO Regulation does not provide much detail. EPPO could certainly benefit from the working relationships as established between Eurojust and respectively Union bodies and third States.

Some issues arise as well regarding the administrative support that Eurojust is asked to bring to the EPPO. According to the draft Eurojust regulation, Eurojust is expected to assist the EPPO through support provided by its staff in almost all fields related to the functioning of the body; the list is non-exhaustive and includes technical support in programming, security, IT, financial management, HR and 'any other services of common interest'. The details need to be laid down in an agreement between Eurojust and the EPPO.[54] However, according to the estimated financial impact of the European Commission proposal, the support provided by Eurojust to the EPPO is expected to be given on a 'zero-cost basis'.[55] This important involvement and responsibility of Eurojust in the functioning of the EPPO might raise the question of the availability of resources granted to Eurojust to

[50] Article 6 of the EPPO proposal.

[51] Article 3(1) of the draft Eurojust regulation.

[52] Article 59 of the EPPO proposal and Articles 42 and 43 of the draft Eurojust regulation.

[53] European Commission Impact Assessment accompanying the Proposal for a Council Regulation on the establishment of the European Public Prosecutor's Office, SWD (2013) 274 final, p. 39.

[54] Article 41(7) of the draft Eurojust regulation.

[55] Explanatory Memorandum, draft Eurojust regulation.

carry out its mission. If one wants to have a strong EPPO established from Eurojust, one needs strong support from Eurojust and, thus, strong Eurojust.

Finally, on the question of the seat of the EPPO, the preamble refers only to the decision already made at the highest level. Is it, however, realistic to envisage that Eurojust would be able to strongly support the functioning of the EPPO—as recommended by the European Commission—and that the two bodies enjoy a 'special relationship', if they do not work together under the same roof?

3.6 Conclusion

The legislative proposal on the establishment of the EPPO is intended to tackle the current fragmentation of the system used in the investigation and prosecution of crimes adversely affecting the EU's financial interests. The proposal has great potential. To ensure solid synergies amongst all of the actors involved in the fight against PIF crimes at national and EU levels is a complex challenge; the design chosen needs, above all, to avoid further fragmentation of the EU framework. Thus, future EPPO should not be conceived as an isolated actor, but rather seen in the context of part of a multilevel interaction. To bring added value, the EPPO needs to be fit for purpose in practice. In this time of economic crisis, thought needs to be given to the responsible use of resources.

The negotiation process which is currently taking place in the Council of the European Union and in the European Parliament is the momentum to shape the future landscape of the European Union. Indeed, one must take a step back and adopt a global approach to the framework of police and judicial cooperation and coordination in criminal matters to ensure that this proposed novel actor fills in the gaps, avoids duplication of efforts and ensures legal certainty. From a practitioner's point of view, the guiding questions should be: What is needed? How could it work in practice?

Part II
From Eurojust to the European Public Prosecutor's Office: A Reversal of Constitutional Perspective?

Chapter 4
Is the Commission Proposal for a European Public Prosecutor's Office Based on a Harmonious Interpretation of Articles 85 and 86 TFEU?

Ben Smulders

Abstract One may wonder whether it is not because the Lisbon Treaty, through its abolition of the EU's pillar structure, has solved the institutional problems resulting therefrom that it may have created a new one. More particularly, has the new treaty, by abolishing in particular the Justice, Liberty and Security (JLS) pillar, which was so respectful of Member States' sovereignty in the area of criminal law, whilst at the same time introducing Articles 85 and 86 TFEU with their far reaching scope, not triggered the question whether we will be facing a reversal of the constitutional perspective if the European Commission's proposal for an EPPO were to be adopted? The answer should be negative. Where that may be true as a result of the creation of its legal basis, i.e. Article 86 TFEU, it would be exaggerated to claim that the limited use the Commission has made thereof in connection with the EPPO proposal amounts to a reversal of the constitutional paradigm prevailing today in some of the EU Member States as regards criminal justice. Against a background of increasing and widespread Euro scepticism and mindful of the limits of the EU Treaty, the Commission proposal should rather be considered as an attempt to find an effective and proportionate European solution to an urgent financial problem of a certain magnitude resulting from a suboptimal enforcement of EU rules at national level. Following an extensive impact assessment of its proposal, the Commission reached the conclusion that simply strengthening Eurojust's role is not an option in this respect given the limits of its Treaty mandate.

Keywords European Public Prosecutor's Office · EPPO · Articles 85 and 86 TFEU · *Corpus Juris* · Horizontal cooperation v communitarisation · *Sui generis* nature EU financial interests

---

Ben Smulders is Director and Principal Legal Advisor in the Legal Service of the European Commission and Professor of International and European Competition Law at the Free University of Brussels. The views expressed in this article are exclusively those of the author.

B. Smulders (✉)
Legal Service of the European Commission, Brussels, Belgium
e-mail: Bernardus.Smulders@ec.europa.eu

L.H. Erkelens et al. (eds.), *The European Public Prosecutor's Office*,
DOI 10.1007/978-94-6265-035-0_4

Contents

4.1 Introduction

It is approximately 10 years ago that the Asser Institute organised a conference dedicated to a problem which today is no problem anymore: the relationship between the three pillars of the European Union and the institutional issues resulting therefrom?[1] One may wonder whether it is precisely because these issues have been solved in the meantime, that a new one is created. The EU's third pillar, which was so respectful of Member States' sovereignty in the area of criminal law, is now abolished. At the same time, the new treaty introduces Articles 85 and 86 TFEU, allowing the EU to interfere considerably with the Member States' administration of justice. Hence, the question whether we, as a result of the Lisbon Treaty, will be facing a reversal of the constitutional perspective if the European Commission's Proposal for an European Public Prosecutor's Office (EPPO),[2] based on the new Article 86 TFEU, were to be adopted? The answer should be answered in the negative. Where that may be true as a result of the 'creation' of its legal basis in the new treaty, it would be exaggerated to claim that the proposed modest and nuanced 'use' of that legal basis in view of the 'creation' of EPPO amounts to a reversal of the constitutional paradigm prevailing today in some of the EU Member States as regards criminal justice. It is also submitted that in doing so, the Commission took due account of the role and purpose of Eurojust, as defined in Article 85 TFEU.

Already at the end of the nineties an effort was made to organize an EPPO in order to protect the financial interests of the EU in the context of the *Corpus Juris* project.[3] It was launched by a group of academics with the financial and substantive

[1] Smulders 2002, p. 9.

[2] European Commission 2013. See also the Appendix to this Volume.

[3] Delmas-Marty M / J.A.E. Vervaele 2000.

support of the Commission services and members of the European Parliament. Inspired by the Rome Statute of the International Criminal Court,[4] the objective at the time was the establishment of a single legal area for the purposes of not only investigation and prosecution, but also trial and execution of sentences for the offences described in the project. Its geographical scope comprised the territory of 'all' the Member States of the EU. In its Opinion of 26 January 2000 to the Intergovernmental Conference (IGC), which eventually led to the Nice Treaty, the Commission recommended to supplement the current provisions relating to the Community's financial interests by a legal basis in view of setting up a system of rules relating to criminal proceedings in cross-border fraud, notably by the establishment of a European Public Prosecutor (EPP). However, the proposal was not considered by the IGC which instead referred it back to the Commission with the request to examine its practical implications in more depth.[5] One had to wait for the Lisbon Treaty 10 years later to have it accepted in the form of the current Article 86 TFEU. In the meantime, the issue had been discussed extensively in Working Group X 'Freedom, Security and Justice' of the European Convention. It transpires from its final report of 2 December 2002,[6] that the members of the Group were much divided about the issue. Some favoured the creation of a EPP responsible for detecting, prosecuting and bringing to judgment in the national courts the perpetrators of crimes prejudicial to the Union's financial interests and they pleaded therefore for the introduction of a legal basis in the treaty to the effect. Others considered that a convincing case had not been made for the creation of such a body and that there were strong objections on both practical and accountability grounds. A third category of members took the view that there was a need for a proper EPPO with a scope of action going 'beyond' the protections of the financial interests of the Union and that Eurojust could evolve towards that Office.

4.2 Criticism About the Possible Creation and Functioning of EPPO at the Beginning of the Century

Still today it is worthwhile considering the criticism made by leading academics about the very idea of creating a body like EPPO, as developed in the 2001 Commission Green Paper.[7] Indeed, their views continue to be useful as a

[4] See 1998 Rome Statute of the International Criminal Court, 2187 UNTS.90.

[5] See for an account of the 1999 IGC discussions on this issue Killmann and Hofmann 2011, p. 759 and Ladenburger 2008, p. 27.

[6] European Convention 2002, Final Report of Working Group X 'Freedom, Security and Justice', p. 20.

[7] European Commission 2001 Green Paper on criminal law protection of the financial interests of the Community and the establishment of a Public Prosecutor, Document COM (2001) 715 final of 11 December 2001, available at: http://ec.europa.eu/anti_fraud/documents/fwk_green_paper_document/green_paper_en_pdf.

benchmark in order to judge the Commission proposal for the creation of EPPO, in particular against the background of Article 85 TFEU which defines Eurojust's competences and tasks. The criticism voiced at the time was in essence based on the following allegations.[8]

- Little is known about the precise scale of EU fraud. The basic processes of this type of crime take place locally, so that efforts to combat it properly are primarily dependent on competent and decisive local (i.e. national) structures.
- Where penal interventions are the appropriate course of action, the more benefit should be expected from investments in intergovernmental cooperation in the judicial network and in Eurojust than from the creation of an EPPO.
- EPPO gives rise to enormous problems in relation to national penal authorities. Not only there are shortcomings with regard to political responsibility for the actions of an EPPO, the construct of an EPP with Deputy Prosecutors in the Member States makes moreover the latter somewhat *Fremdkörper* within their own national Public Prosecution Systems (PPS). In addition, the latter's task are made impossible because of their lack of control over the deployment of human and material resources in the investigations to be conducted.
- The right to bring proceedings should not be governed by the principle of 'mandatory' criminal prosecution but of 'discretionary' proceedings. It is submitted that uniformity of proceedings and independence of the EPPO are not necessarily better enhanced through this obligation. Arguably, also the discretionary prosecution principle can be applied uniformly within the Member States. Furthermore, one could not justify within a national system that financial damage 'to the EU' always leads to criminal proceedings, but that similar harm 'to the national State' will not. It is also questionable whether there should be this drastic obligation in the event of financial loss for a 'legal' entity within a national regime that may be less oriented towards protection in cases of serious loss resulting from injury to 'natural' persons? Furthermore, in a transnational context it requires little imagination to think of terrorism, trafficking in women and in human beings in general, or organised crime involving drugs. In such cases, it would be arbitrary to rule out, on the basis of the principle of mandatory prosecution, any power of balancing of interests only where (also) EU fraud is concerned. Finally, in Member States which for whatever reasons are less 'enthusiastic' to prosecute crimes affecting the EU's financial interests, this obligation could lead, with a certain predictability to a kind of 'displacement' effect, i.e. a different approach to investigations leading to a situation where fewer cases would be 'solved' so that there would be nothing more to decide with regard to possible criminal proceedings. This could only be remedied, arguably, if the EPP had a direct say as to the scale and specific deployment of investigative resources within the Member State.

[8] See e.g. Fijnaut and Groenhuijsen 2001, pp. 325–333.

4.3 Why Does the Lisbon Treaty Allow for the Creation of EPPO Despite This Criticism and in Particular the Existence of Eurojust?

Looking at the way the views of the Commission about EPPO have been evolving since the beginning of this century and evaluating how they have concretely culminated in its latest proposal, one should start by making some considerations of a general and historical nature.[9] The 2007 Lisbon Treaty brought a significant gain in resources for European security as it provided for the radical change of Treaty foundations of the two EU bodies active in the field of police and judicial co-operation, Europol and Eurojust, supplemented with the possibility to create a EPPO from Eurojust. The relevant articles concerning these bodies, seen in the context of the 'communitarisation' of the third pillar, are marked by a new philosophy and allow for a substantial overhaul of both bodies. The novelty is that these provisions give some leeway to the EU legislator to confer new tasks and powers, including those of an 'operational nature', on both bodies and also to settle corollary institutional issues, such as their internal functioning, the modalities of parliamentary oversight by the European Parliament together with national parliaments, and modalities of judicial control by the European Court of Justice. This power given to the legislator is in contrast to the previous Treaty, which defined directly the tasks of both bodies in more detail and in a more limitative way. However, under the Lisbon Treaty there are still important limits to the operational tasks that can be conferred to Eurojust and Europol, as follows from Articles 85(2) and 88(2) TFEU. The same limits do not apply to the EPPO (cf. Article 86 TFEU). The latter article provides for a legal base to create a EPPO, 'from Eurojust'. The new Treaty thus does not establish the Office directly, but only provides the legislator (i.e. the Council) with the possibility to do so. The new Article 86 had to arbitrate between two schools of thought.[10] One, earlier developed by the Commission and the European Anti-Fraud Office OLAF, favoured a Prosecutor specifically for the protection of the Union's financial interests, and a second which saw a more urgent need for such a body in areas of organised crime coming under Europol's remit. The final article combines both options and leaves the choice to the European Council. The wording 'from Eurojust' also leaves various options open on the relations between such a possible future body and Eurojust. One may ask where precisely the border lies between further developments of Eurojust, by qualified majority and co-decision, and the creation of a European Prosecutor's Office. This line appears to be drawn in Article 85(2) TFEU: Eurojust cannot take formal acts of judicial procedure, i.e., act directly before a national criminal judge, whereas the whole point of creating a prosecutor's office is for it to take precisely

---

[9] See for an account of the 2007 IGC discussions on Europol, Eurojust and EPPO: Killmann and Hofmann 2011, pp. 760–761 and Ladenburger 2008, pp. 35–40.

[10] See Ladenburger 2008, pp. 35–36.

such formal acts itself. A last intriguing question that will have to be resolved by the legislator on the basis of the Commission's proposal is about judicial control of the Prosecutor's Office. As a new Union body, acts of that Office having legal effects would be submitted in principle to Article 263 TFEU. On the other hand, as will be explained in more detail below, the point of the Office is to act before national judges under national criminal law, be it simply 'in the shoes' of national prosecution authorities or pursuant to special procedural rules to be defined in accordance with Article 86(3) TFEU. The legislator thus needs to devise a delicate formula of burden sharing between the Union's and the national judicial resources.

4.4 Which Use Has the Commission Actually Made of the Lisbon Treaty?

Turning more specifically to the Commission's proposal and thereby using as a benchmark the points of criticism referred to above, how should it be evaluated in terms of substance and procedure? The following elements of the proposal show that a genuine attempt has been made to find a middle way, bearing in mind the possibilities offered and constraints imposed by the treaty legal base.

First, EPPO's remit *ratione materiae*, as proposed, is limited to 'criminal offences affecting the financial interests of the EU'.[11] Admittedly, it may cover other offences but only if these are inextricably linked with the first category of offences and their investigation and prosecution are 'in the interest of a good administration of justice'.[12]

Second, the proposal covers only the stages of investigation and prosecution, excluding in principle the stages of trial and execution of sentences[13] as was envisaged e.g. in the *Corpus Juris* project referred to earlier and in the Rome Statute of the International Criminal Court.

Third, as regards the question whether Delegated Prosecutors will become *Fremdkörper* in their own national PPS, it seems to be more of a psychological than a legal or managerial nature. Indeed, what matters from the latter point of view is that there are clear (and from the national PPS distinct) lines of command between the EPP and these Delegated Prosecutors and these lines are provided for.[14]

Fourth, equally important is that Article 6(2) of the proposal stipulates that the EPP 'direct its activities and organises its work'. In other words: the EPP 'does' control the deployment of resources in order to conduct his investigation and prosecution.

---

[11] See Article 12 of the EPPO proposal.

[12] See Article 13(1) of the EPPO proposal.

[13] The only exception can be found in Article 31 of the proposal providing for disposition of assets following a final court ruling on their confiscation.

[14] See Articles 6(5) and 6(6) of the EPPO proposal.

Fifth, as regards admissibility of evidence, an attempt has been made to address some concerns about forum shopping, also expressed by academics[15] at the beginning of the century and which can be summarised as follows: whilst there is some merit in the argument that in order to avoid 'forum shopping' the EPP must be prevented from conducting prosecutions in the Member State that has the most flexible rules concerning the admissibility of evidence and that therefore a certain form of recognition of acts of investigation undertaken abroad is justified, a premium should not be placed on concentrating investigation activities in countries with overdue or incomplete legislation. The proposal's response to that concern is therefore the following: starting point is some form of mutual recognition of evidence but subject to a review by the trial court, which is limited nevertheless to Articles 47 and 48 of the EU Charter (fairness of the procedure and rights of defence). Moreover, from a purely practical point of view, it is difficult to see how the EPPO in its investigation could be led by anything else than efficiency considerations where, on the basis of objective factors, there are different jurisdictions involved.

4.5 Why Does the Commission Adhere to the Principle of Mandatory Prosecution?

The Commission proposal provides that the EPP 'shall' initiate an investigation where there are reasonable grounds to believe than an offence within the competence of the EPPO is being or has been committed.[16] It is therefore obvious that the Commission has made a clear choice in favour of the principle of mandatory prosecution whilst being aware that this is a subject in terms of procedure which inevitably triggers controversy since only few Member States adhere to that principle at national level. However, the differences between the principle of mandatory prosecution and the principle of discretionary prosecution should not be overestimated, since to both apply exceptions and limitations leading to some degree of convergence in practice. This is e.g. the case where overburdening of courts needs to be avoided and where the potential impact of proceedings on the outcome of the case or the effectiveness of recovery of sums corresponding to the financial interests that are violated are to be considered. In the specific context of the proposal, particular attention should be paid to Articles 28 and 29 of the proposal, which allow for the dismissal of cases (e.g. in case of certain minor offences or lack of relevant evidence) and transactions (if they serve the purpose of proper administration of justice and after the damage caused by the offence has been compensated). More generally, however, in a period of increasing and widespread euro scepticism, one should not be surprised that the Commission advocates that

---

[15] See e.g. Fijnaut and Groenhuijsen 2002, p. 330.

[16] See Article 16(1) of the EPPO proposal.

minimum discretion is best as regards offences related to tax payers' money spent on European Union. In that respect, the situation has changed dramatically as compared to 10 years ago. Uniformity of action is all the more necessary given that today Member States, to varying degrees, are paying lip services to the fight against EU fraud instead of using resources, both material and procedural in nature, which are no less decisive if not more than the measures taken to avert comparable infringements of national law.

4.6 Are There Any Better Alternatives to the Commission's Proposal, e.g. Strengthening Eurojust's Role?

In order to better understand which policy considerations prompted the Commission not only to make a proposal but specifically the one which it has tabled and not a proposal for a different set up of EPPO, it is worthwhile reading the voluminous report on the impact assessment which preceded the adoption of the proposal.[17] Not only does the report address the classic questions of the problem definition, the choice of the legal base and the need for compliance with the principle of subsidiarity but it examines in extenso five different policy options, using as a base-line scenario—no policy change at all. Two of the policy options considered relate to Eurojust, ranging from strengthening the powers of Eurojust to the creation of an EPPO within Eurojust. Others include the creation of a College-type EPPO, a centralised integrated EPPO and a decentralised integrated EPPO, the option eventually retained by the Commission.[18]

Taking into account the weaknesses in the available data, for the purposes of this Impact Assessment it has been assumed that about €3 billion per year could be at risk from EU fraud. Of course, one should immediately concede that, given the weaknesses in the available data and the difficulties inherent in measuring the scale of the criminal activities that are undetected, the true figure cannot be calculated precisely. But every year at least several hundred million euros appear to be fraudulently diverted from their intended purpose. Only a small fraction of these losses are ever recovered from the criminals. In fact, the Commission's annual statistics demonstrate that while fraud against the Union's financial interests is pervasive and causes substantial damage every year to the tax payer, national criminal enforcement efforts lag behind and vary much from Member State to Member State. In particular, OLAF's cases which are transferred to national investigation and judicial authorities are not always equally effectively followed-up. The rate of successful prosecutions concerning offences against the EU budget varies indeed considerably across the EU (from approximately 20 % to over 90 %),

---

[17] European Commission 2013 Staff Working Document—Impact assessment accompanying the Proposal for a Council Regulation on the establishment of the EPP, Document SWD (2013) 274 final, available at: http://ec.europa.eu/justice/newsroom/criminal/news/130717_en.htm

[18] European Commission Staff Working Document—Impact Assessment 2013, §§ 3–7.

partly owing to the complexity of the cases, the lack of sufficient national resources and the frequent need to gather evidence outside the national territory.

Against that background, why not simply strengthening Eurojust's role, thus minimising the risk of upsetting the national administration of criminal justice? The answer given in the impact assessment report[19] is (relatively) short and simple: because Eurojust's treaty mandate only allows it to coordinate and encourage investigations and prosecutions, and to assist with information exchange. This means that Eurojust in general only becomes active where Member States themselves take the initiative on a certain case. However, in the context of the impact assessment the Commission has been looking particularly at the problem that such action is often not taken. And if a Member State prosecution service is reluctant to investigate or prosecute a case, Eurojust cannot compel it to do so. The national members of Eurojust frequently lack the powers to ensure effective follow-up in the Member States, or if they do, they usually refrain from using the powers which they derive from national laws—most decisions on these issues are arrived at through consensus. Moreover, even the most far-reaching reform of Eurojust is limited by the TFEU. As a consequence, Eurojust activities can only build on Member States' action and in doing so, at the most, coordinate and facilitate that action. Article 85 TFEU does not provide the possibility to entrust Eurojust with conducting investigations: at the maximum, Eurojust could be given the power to initiate investigations, but not conduct them. This means that the current disparities and fragmentation of national prosecution efforts would not be solved. Instead, following the impact assessment, the Commission has decided to go for an option that would have a limited impact on Eurojust. Eurojust would remain a separate body as regards crime areas other than offences affecting the EU's financial interests. It would carry on with its core activity of coordinating and stimulating judicial cooperation within the EU with regard to other serious cross-border crimes and remain a coordination body at the service of Member States. However, in the interest of synergies and cost-savings, according to Article 57 of the proposal, Eurojust would provide administrative support to the EPPO, including functional support (finance, human resources) and technical services (security, Information Technology). EPPO may also associate Eurojust in operational matters. In practical terms, Eurojust's administrative structure would cover the needs of both Eurojust and the EPPO. This administrative structure would ensure coordinated budgetary planning and execution, various aspects of staff management and the provision of all other support services.

This is, in a nutshell, the way the Commission has interpreted the notion of establishing an EPPO 'from Eurojust' in the sense of Article 86(1) TFEU. Compared to the other options assessed as being able to deliver no more than incremental improvements to the current situation, the creation of the EPPO would represent a significant change in the approach to defending the EU's financial

[19] European Commission 2011 Staff Working Document—Impact Assessment 2013, § 6—policy options. On the policy options as regards the relationship between EPPO and Eurojust (in particular the notion '*from Eurojust*') following the entry into force of the Lisbon Treaty, *see* also Peers, p. 860; Killmann and Hofmann 2011, p. 761; Zieder 2010, p. 220; Vervaele 2008, p. 182.

interests, in particular due to the independence of the EPPO guaranteed through this option. The new powers conferred to the EPPO, as well as the improved access of information for concerned authorities, would deliver the needed improvements to the investigative and prosecutorial tools available. As compared to a collegial body or a unit within Eurojust, the hierarchical structure of the EPPO would also imply important advantages in terms of efficiency: a faster decision-making process, and clear lines of responsibility. It can be expected that a much greater number of cases —as much as twice as many as under the current arrangements—will be brought before courts and may result in convictions, so that a substantially higher amount of illegally received Union money will be recovered and a much larger number of crimes would be deterred.[20]

4.7 Final Considerations: Avoiding the Trap of Comparing Apples with Pears

A reflection of a more general nature may help to come to a synthesis. Given the *sui generis* nature of EU fraud, as acknowledged by e.g. Van Gerven already back in 2000,[21] one may wonder what the right benchmark should be when judging the merits (and the lack thereof) of the Commission's proposal in terms of proportionate EU interference with the Member States' choices as regards their own administration of justice. Should one compare what is proposed in relation to investigation and prosecution of fraud against *EU* financial interests with what exists in Member States in relation to investigation and prosecution of fraud against 'national' financial interests? Or should the benchmark be to compare investigation and prosecution of fraud against EU financial interests 'in one Member State' with investigation and prosecution of the same type of fraud 'in another Member State'? It is submitted that the latter should be the case as that comparison makes plain disparities that are socially unacceptable and legitimises EU action. Hence, it is questionable whether in this context one should engage in highly sophisticated constitutional considerations about the divide between Articles 85 and 86 TFEU. Instead, it may be more useful to adopt a more down-to-earth approach and to search for the most effective and proportionate solution available under the current treaty in order to address an urgent financial problem of a certain magnitude resulting from suboptimal enforcement.[22] In doing so, for the reasons explained in

[20] European Commission Staff Working Document—Impact Assessment 2013, *ibidem*.

[21] Van Gerven 2000, p. 318 accepting that the proposals contained in the *Corpus Juris* with regard to the investigation, prosecution and trial of the serious trans-border crimes referred to in the former Article 29 TEU, for which efficient criminal proceedings as well as adequate legal protection is to be ensured.

[22] See for a similar approach the methodology followed in the Deloitte Enterprises Risk Services 2011 report, commissioned by the Budget Control Committee of the European Parliament.

the previous paragraphs, action is taken at EU level that is in full harmony with the rationale of Articles 85 and 86 TFEU respectively.

References

Delmas-Marty M, Vervaele JAE (2000) The implementation of the *Corpus Juris* in the member states: penal provisions for the protection of European finances, vol 1–4. Intersentia, Paris

Deloitte Enterprises Risk Services (2011) Improving coordination between the EU bodies competent in the area of police and judicial cooperation: moving towards a European Prosecutor, study commissioned by the European Parliament's Budgetary Control Committee. http://www.europarl.europa.eu/studies

European Commission (2001) Green paper on criminal law protection of the financial interests of the community and the establishment of a Public Prosecutor. Document COM (2001) 715 final of 11 December 2001, available at: http://ec.europa.eu/anti_fraud/documents/fwk_green_paper_document/green_paper_en_pdf

European Commission (2013), Proposal for a Council Regulation on the establishment of the European Public Prosecutor, Document COM (2013) 534 final of 17 July 2013. http://ec.europa.eu/justice/newsroom/criminal/news/130717_en.htm

European Commission (2013) Staff working document—Impact assessment accompanying the proposal for a Council regulation on the establishment of the European Public Prosecutor. Document SWD 274 final. http://ec.europa.eu/justice/newsroom/criminal/news/130717_en.htm

European Convention (2002) Final report of working group X 'Freedom, Security and Justice', European Document CONV 426/02 of 2 December 2002. http://european-convention.eu.int/

Fijnaut C, Groenhuijsen MS (2002) A European public prosecutor service: comments on the green paper. Eur J Crime Crim Law Crim Justice 10(4):321–336

Killmann B-R, Hofmann M (2011) Perspektiven für eine Europäische Staatsanwaltschaft. In: Sieber (ed) Europäisches Strafrecht. Nomos, Baden Baden, pp 757–766

Ladenburger C (2008) Police and criminal law in the Treaty of Lisbon—A new dimension for the Community method. Eur Const Law Rev 4:20–40

Peers S (2011) European Public Prosecutor. In: EU Justice and Home Affairs Law, 3rd edn. Oxford University Press, pp 858–860

Smulders B (2002) Enkele bespiegelingen omtrent de verhouding tussen de drie pijlers van de Europese Unie. In: 'Veiligheid' en het recht van de Europese Unie. Asser Instituut Colloquium Europees Recht. Tweeëndertigste zitting, T.M.C. Asser Press, The Hague, pp 9–18

Van Gerven W (2000) Constitutional conditions for a public prosecutor's office at the European level. Eur J Crime Crim Law Crim Justice 8(5):296–316

Vervaele JAE (2008) The shaping and reshaping of Eurojust and OLAF—investigative judicial powers in the European judicial areas. Eucrim Max Planck Inst Foreign Int Crim Law 3 (4):180–192

Zieder F (2010) Europstrafrecht aktuell—Ausbau der Einrichtungen zur Zusammenarbeit—Teil 2: Kommt eine Europäische Staatsanwaltschaft? J Für Strafrecht 6:217–221

Chapter 5
The European Public Prosecutor's Office: Certain Constitutional Issues

Katalin Ligeti and Anne Weyembergh

Abstract The EPPO proposal proclaims a new generation of EU judicial body with, on the one hand, vertical/supranational integration aspects and, on the other hand, horizontal/intergovernmental elements. This chapter analyses the balance achieved between both types of features in the Commission's proposal for a Regulation.

Keywords Applicable law · Cooperation · Eurojust · European area · European Public Prosecutor's Office · European territory · Evidence · Fair trial · Forum shopping · Judicial control · Integration · Legal certainty · Legality principle · Procedural guarantees · Verticalisation

Contents

K. Ligeti is Professor of Criminal Law at the University of Luxembourg and coordinator of the European Criminal Law Academic Network (ECLAN).A. Weyembergh is Professor of criminal law at the *Université Libre de Bruxelles* (ULB) and coordinator of the European Criminal Law Academic Network (ECLAN).

K. Ligeti (✉)
University of Luxembourg, Luxembourg, Luxembourg
e-mail: katalin.ligeti@uni.lu

A. Weyembergh
Université Libre de Bruxelles, Brussels, Belgium
e-mail: aweyembe@ulb.ac.be

L.H. Erkelens et al. (eds.), *The European Public Prosecutor's Office*,
DOI 10.1007/978-94-6265-035-0_5

5.1 Introduction

The European Commission published its EPPO proposal in July 2013. The proposal is a part of a legislative package consisting of a proposal for a Regulation on the establishment of the European Agency for Criminal Justice Cooperation (hereafter Eurojust proposal)[1] and a Communication on the European anti-Fraud Office's (OLAF) governance and the enhancement of procedural guarantees in investigations, in view of establishing the European Public Prosecutor's Office [hereafter the EPPO proposal].[2] The legislative package is accompanied by a communication explaining the package.[3]

The EPPO proposal represents a symbolic move towards a single European criminal jurisdiction and strives to pave the way for a new era of criminal justice cooperation in the EU. This move is, however, not without drawbacks and it sensitively challenges national criminal justice sovereignty as shown by the position of certain governments and national parliaments.[4] In order to understand the Proposal, this chapter shall first briefly highlight the legislative and political struggles leading to its adoption (Sect. 5.2). This will then be followed by a recast

---

[1] Proposal for a Regulation on the European Union Agency for Criminal Justice Cooperation (Eurojust), 17 July 2013, COM (2013) 535 final (hereafter: ‘Eurojust proposal’).

[2] Proposal for a Regulation on the establishment of the European Public Prosecutor's Office, 17 July 2013, COM (2013) 534 final (hereafter: ‘EPPO proposal’). See also the Appendix to this Volume.

[3] Better protection of the Union's financial interests: Setting up the European Public Prosecutor's Office and reforming Eurojust', 17 July 2013, COM 2013a 532 final.

[4] Ever since the idea of an EPPO was launched by the *Corpus Juris*, it has always met resistance by the Member States that denied the need and added value of a new supranational institution (see the Follow-up report on the Green Paper on criminal-law protection of the financial interests of the Community and the establishment of a European Prosecutor, 19 March 2003, COM 2003 128). Similar resistance was encountered by the proposal of a Regulation on the EPPO: fourteen national Parliaments sent reasoned opinions to the Commission (the so-called ‘yellow card’) triggering the Subsidiarity control mechanism provided for in Article 7 of Protocol no. 2 to the Treaties on the application of the principle of subsidiarity and proportionality. The Commission had therefore to review the proposal to decide whether to maintain, amend or withdraw it. On 27 November 2013 the Commission confirmed that it maintains its original proposal, stressing that the protection of the EU budget against fraud can be better achieved at EU level (COM (2013) 851 final).

of the main features of the Proposal, first assessing the new elements of vertical integration (Sect. 5.3) and subsequently turning towards the features of more traditional horizontal cooperation (Sect. 5.4). This analysis does not aim to be exhaustive, but represents an evaluation of the Proposal in the light of the constitutional objectives of the Treaty and against the present background of judicial cooperation in criminal matters in the EU. As certain aspects of the Proposal, in particular the issue of judicial control of the acts of the EPPO, are treated by other authors in this book, this chapter remains brief on this matter. The concluding remarks of the authors take into account the current outcome of the negotiations and aim to assess whether the Proposal can achieve its main objective, namely an efficient and equivalent protection of the financial interests of the EU.

5.2 The EPPO Proposal: The Road to a Compromise

It was not until the Lisbon Treaty that the Member States reached the political agreement to abolish the pillar structure of the Treaty and to bring criminal law under the community method.[5] Thereby, the entry into force of the Lisbon Treaty opened up the possibility to move on with criminal justice integration in the EU. Hence, Articles 84–86 TFEU now provide for reinforcing the powers of existing European criminal law enforcement bodies and for developing new ones. Certainly, one of the most innovative provisions relating to the Area of Freedom, Security and Justice is Article 86 TFEU, which provides for setting up the EPPO. By prospecting the creation of a new European judicial body, the Treaty allows to overcome the present fragmentation of the Area of Freedom, Security and Justice. Whereas the current Area of Freedom, Security and Justice is based on mutual recognition that requires enforcing national decisions beyond national borders, the distinctive feature of setting up the EPPO would be that European decisions should be enforced directly throughout the whole EU. In concrete terms, instead of mutually recognising national prosecutorial decisions, European decisions of a European prosecution service including the opening of an investigation, the launching of a prosecution and bringing charges should be directly enforced in the Member States.[6] This represents a conceptual challenge and a qualitative change in criminal justice integration.

Although Article 86 TFEU does not *ipso jure* establish the EPPO, but rather provides for a legal basis for its subsequent establishment, the EU institutions, the Member States and the already existing EU criminal justice bodies and agencies felt the need to take a position on the implementation of Article 86 TFEU. This resulted in a rich debate with two focal points. One central theme of the debate addressed the

---

[5] Title V of the TFEU.

[6] However, Article 86 TFEU allows the EU legislator to create this single legal area only for the pre-trial procedure. As regards the trial phase, the multitude of 28 systems shall remain.

institutional design of the EPPO. Article 86 TFEU says little on the institutional aspects of the future office apart from the statement that the EPPO shall be established 'from Eurojust'. The Treaty is silent on the aspects of, for instance, structure, appointment, accountability and immunity. The institutional design of the EPPO determines the status and powers of this new office as well as its relationship with national authorities and EU bodies and agencies. It makes the transfer of sovereignty visible for the Member States and is, therefore, very sensitive. Ever since the EPPO was proposed by the Corpus Juris, there has been general consensus that the new prosecutorial body should be independent both from national governments and from EU institutions.[7] Subordinating the EPPO to either EU institutions or to national governments has always been considered a threat to its legitimacy.[8] There is equally general understanding that in order to counterbalance the independence of the EPPO it will be necessary to provide for an effective mechanism of accountability allowing 'to some extent for the requisite democratic control of an institution that would have a direct influence on the rights and freedoms of citizens'.[9] Beyond the general agreement as to independence and accountability, there have been, however, three approaches voiced in the debate as possible EPPO models: a central structure, a decentralised structure and a combination of these two, i.e. the integrated structure.[10] The idea of an entirely supranational prosecution service composed of a chief prosecutor and several specialised deputy prosecutors at the central level acting throughout the territories of the Member States did not receive any support in the debate. The arguments aimed more at defining the right level of decentralisation. Should the EPPO embark on the collegial structure of Eurojust and become itself a collegial body composed of prosecutors appointed by the Member States participating in the EPPO,[11] or should it combine central coordination and hierarchy in the investigative phase with local enforcement?[12]

The second focal point of the discussions preceding the Commission's proposal was the procedural framework of the EPPO. Article 86(3) TFEU states that

> 'The regulation [...] shall determine the general rules applicable to the EPPO, the conditions governing the performance of its functions, the rules of procedure applicable to its activities, as well as those governing the admissibility of evidence, and the rules applicable to the judicial review of procedural measures taken by it in the performance of its functions'.

Accordingly, the EPPO regulation should determine the rules applicable to the procedure of the EPPO. These rules shall not only prescribe the powers of the

---

[7] The independence was foreseen both in the *Corpus Juris* (Article 18) and in the Green Paper on criminal-law protection of the financial interests of the Community and the establishment of a European Prosecutor, COM (2001) 715 (para 4.1.1). See Delmas-Marty and Vervaele 2000, p. 314 et seq.

[8] See Van den Wyngaert 2004.

[9] Zwiers 2011, p. 373.

[10] See Ligeti and Simonato 2013, p. 7 et seq.

[11] See Vermeulen et al. 2012, p. 475 et seq.

[12] See Vervaele 2010, p. 189 et seq.; Ligeti and Simonato 2013, p. 15 et seq.

EPPO but will also govern the admissibility of evidence and judicial control[13] of the measures undertaken. The Treaty gave several options to the Commission for developing the procedural framework of the EPPO. It could propose to establish an EPPO working either with a certain combination of European procedural rules and national criminal procedural laws of the Member States[14] or, rather, a full set of European rules of criminal procedure describing the investigative and prosecutorial powers of the EPPO.[15] Here once again, the debate exposed the level of acceptable Europeanisation of criminal procedure.

The debate that evolved around the structure and the procedural framework of the EPPO was further stimulated by two additional elements. First, the Commission presented, in July 2012, a Proposal for a Directive on the fight against fraud to the Union's financial interests by means of criminal law (hereafter PIF Directive).[16] The proposed PIF Directive—under discussion in the European Parliament at the time of writing[17]—allowed to speculate to what extent this proposal covers all forms of misconduct in the sense of Article 86(1) TFEU and thereby defines the material scope of action of the EPPO.[18] A second element that substantially influenced the design of the EPPO proposal was the reflection on the upgrading of Eurojust based on Article 85 TFEU. According to Article 85 TFEU, Eurojust may receive powers to issue binding decisions on solving conflicts of jurisdiction and to

---

[13] See Durdevic 2013, p. 986 et seq.

[14] The procedural framework of the EPPO cannot be based entirely on national criminal procedural laws. The very fact that the EPPO is a European body presupposes a minimum of European rules for decisions to be taken by the EPPO such as, for instance, the decision to open an investigation, to start prosecution or to choose the forum for bringing charges. Conversely, evidence can be gathered either by using the national criminal procedural laws of the Member States or by a set of harmonised European rules.

[15] The Model Rules are reprinted in several languages in Ligeti 2014b. Also available at www.eppo-project.eu.

[16] See Proposal for a Directive of the European Parliament and of the Council on the fight against fraud to the Union's financial interests by means of criminal law, COM 2012 363 final, Brussels, 11 July 2012. The proposal not only 'Lisbonises' the existing *acquis*, but also includes two additional offences not covered by previous third pillar instruments, namely fraud in public procurement or grant procedures and misappropriation. The Commission has reflected on including the other offences mentioned in the Corpus Juris, namely a specific offence of abuse of office and the breach of professional secrecy. However, the Commission decided not to include a special offence on abuse of office as 'it has been considered a superfluous addition to the offence of misappropriation. Similarly, an offence of breach of professional secrecy has not been included in the proposal as the conduct is already covered under the disciplinary-law measures of the EU Staff Regulations.' See Kuhl 2012.

[17] The main discussion point was less the content of the proposal as such, but the legal basis proposed by the Commission. The Commission intends to use Article 325(4) TFEU that allows for all necessary measures with a view to affording effective and equivalent protection to the EU budget. Conversely, Member States argue that the proposal should be based on Article 83(2) TFEU which is the general legal basis for the approximation of substantive criminal law. The advantage of using Article 325(4) TFEU is that the directive would be binding for all Member States, including Denmark, Ireland and the UK.

[18] See in detail Ligeti 2013, p. 73 et seq.

initiate criminal investigations. In particular the phrase according to which the tasks of Eurojust may include 'the initiation of criminal investigations [...] conducted by competent national authorities' triggered discussions. What should be the future role of Eurojust, once an EPPO is created?

The EPPO proposal drafted against the background of this debate is certainly marked by the views expressed by Member States and national practitioners as to the idea of a supranational 'parquet' instructing national law enforcement authorities. At the same time it displays the cautious approach of the European Commission itself, that tried to avoid projecting the image of an omnipotent 'European prosecution service' which could fuel resistance and controversy among Member States.

The EPPO proposal provides for setting up the EPPO for investigating and prosecuting offences against the financial interests of the EU as defined in the respective PIF Directive.[19] The EPPO should be a hierarchically organised EU body with a decentralised structure composed of a European Public Prosecutor and European Delegated Prosecutors in the Member States.[20] The European Delegated Prosecutors should work directly under the European Public Prosecutor who may give them instructions to them in relation to offences falling in the remit of the EPPO.[21] At the same time the European Delegated Prosecutors shall remain integrated in the judicial systems of their respective Member States ('double hat').[22] Although the delegates shall work exclusively for the EPPO on PIF cases, they may, however, perform national investigations in relation to other offences.[23] According to the European Commission, the double hat model is the best guarantee of integration of the delegates into the national systems of criminal justice. The EPPO should operate on the territory of the Union's Member States as within a single legal area.[24] The EPPO should have the powers as enlisted in the proposal and its actions should be safeguarded by a set of procedural safeguards.[25]

---

19 Articles 4 and 12 of the EPPO proposal.

20 Articles 3(1) and 6(1) of the EPPO proposal.

21 Article 6(4), (5), (6) of the EPPO proposal.

22 The 'double hat' approach has been advocated ever since the *Corpus Juris* (see Delmas-Marty and Vervaele 2000b, p. 79 et seq.). It entails that delegated prosecutors will maintain their status within their national justice systems and will simultaneously form part of the EPPO, in order to ensure a certain proximity to the field work of investigations. However, this approach could raise concerns as to the independence of the EPPO, since delegated prosecutors would be confronted with the dilemma of serving two masters at the same time.

23 Article 6(6) of the EPPO proposal.

24 Article 25(1).

25 Articles 4, 5 and 8 of the EPPO proposal. See also recital 10 of the preamble of the proposal.

5.3 Innovative and Ambitious Features of the Proposal

The EPPO Proposal certainly contains innovative features that one may interpret as signs of a new era of criminal justice integration in the EU.

5.3.1 Binding Powers of the EPPO

The first innovating feature of the EPPO is the fact that the proposal is of a different nature and is more ambitious than the mutual recognition. The principle of mutual recognition relies on the concept of horizontal cooperation between the national criminal justice systems. In the system of mutual recognition, the judicial authorities of one Member State recognise and execute the decisions of (judicial) authorities of other Member States, with the minimum of formality and on the basis of mutual trust. In other words, the decision of the issuing state takes effect 'extraterritorially', i.e. within the legal system of the executing state. Although it is not automatic and the executing authorities still have a possibility (sometimes a duty) to refuse the cooperation, the principle of mutual recognition constitutes a developed form of horizontal cooperation mechanisms as it principally provides for the execution of foreign decisions. As such, it is a representative of the notion of an EU area of criminal justice.

By attributing binding powers to the EPPO, the proposed regulation clearly goes beyond mutual recognition as it forms a passage from horizontal cooperation to vertical integration. The EPPO shall have autonomous powers, albeit limited ones; it shall decide on opening an investigation,[26] launching a prosecution and bringing the defendant to justice.[27] These three powers are central decisions of the EPPO that will bind also the national authorities. The EPPO is expected to exercise these powers in the European interest, serving the EU area of criminal justice. It is one of the main drawbacks of the current setting that OLAF's administrative investigations are not followed up in the Member States[28] due to non-recognition or low prioritisation of these European interests. The purpose of the EPPO proposal is to overcome such situation.

---

[26] Article 16 of the EPPO proposal.

[27] Article 27 of the EPPO proposal.

[28] See the Commission Staff Working Paper of 26 May 2011, SEC (2011) 621 final, Table 2.2, p. 7. See also the *Eleventh operational report of the European Anti-fraud Office(OLAF)*, 1 January to 31 December 2010, available at http://ec.europa.eu/anti_fraud/about-us/reports/olaf-report/index_en.htm (Accessed 21 March 2014) http://bookshop.europa.eu/en/eleventh-operational-report-of-the-european-anti-fraud-office-pbOBAC11001/.

The proposal is also more ambitious than the previous generation EU actor competent in the field of criminal justice, i.e. Eurojust. It is well known that presently Eurojust is still just a mediator, a facilitator, without any decision-making competences or binding powers with regard to national authorities.[29] The outcome of its interventions is dependent on the power of persuasion that it exercises over the authorities concerned. If the national authorities fail to comply with its request or recommendations, Eurojust may record these situations in its reports[30] but it does not have any means, any sanctioning power, for obliging them to comply. The allocation of binding powers to the EPPO is thus quite an important difference compared to Eurojust in its current form. This difference will be maintained even in the light of the Eurojust proposal, which was published on the same day as the EPPO proposal.[31] Indeed, the political choice made by the Commission was not to implement Article 85(1) third sentence of the TFEU, which allows to confer limited binding powers to Eurojust,[32] but to further approximate the powers of the national members of Eurojust. These powers remain limited to the currently existing three categories: ordinary powers, powers exercised in agreement with a competent national authority and powers exercised in urgent cases.[33] According to the Eurojust proposal, national members shall have the power to issue and execute requests themselves[34] (under the current Eurojust Decision that can be exercised only in agreement with the competent national authority[35]) and, as a new power in urgent cases, they shall have the power to order investigative measures.[36] Besides the abolition of the national safeguard clause, currently provided for by Article 9e of the Eurojust Decision,[37] these novelties should allow more consistency in the powers conferred to national members and should also, generally speaking, lead to strengthening of the national members' powers. However, in comparison to the EPPO proposal, such strengthening remains quite limited. For instance, the above-mentioned new powers in urgent cases are exceptional and quite restricted, making it clear that the main function of Eurojust is still the coordination of transnational investigations in serious crimes.[38]

---

[29] Flore 2009, p. 589 et seq.

[30] Regarding this aspect, see, especially, Bures 2010.

[31] Eurojust proposal, *op. cit.*

[32] Weyembergh 2013b.

[33] Article 8 of the Eurojust proposal.

[34] See Article 8(1)(a) *in fine* of the Eurojust proposal.

[35] See Article 9c(1)(a) and (b) of the Eurojust Decision as revised in 2008.

[36] See Article 8(3) and (2)(a) combined of the Eurojust proposal.

[37] This is a wide scale and vague exemption allowing for not granting the powers exercised in agreement with a 'competent national authority' or the powers exercised in urgent cases, when granting any such powers to the national member is contrary to constitutional rules or fundamental aspects of the criminal justice system.

[38] See Weyembergh 2013a.

5.3.2 *Exclusive Competence of the EPPO*

The second important feature of the EPPO proposal marking vertical integration is the principle of exclusive competence as stated by its Article 11(4).[39] This is certainly one of the most far reaching features of the EPPO's competence and this provision goes beyond what has been suggested in the Corpus Juris or in the Model Rules. The exclusive competence of the EPPO means that in cases falling into the substantive scope of competence of the EPPO, or in other words the 'PIF crimes' as defined in the current Proposal for a PIF Directive, only the EPPO can investigate and prosecute. As a consequence, national authorities lose their competence in relation to PIF offences. Such choice made by the Commission is of course quite sensitive and could be considered by the Member States as affecting their national sovereignty.

5.3.3 *The EPPO Is a Single European Office*

Third feature that is conceived in the Commission's proposal, is that the EPPO shall be a single European office—not a college or a team. It is organised in a decentralised fashion: the idea of the proposal is indeed to combine the existence of a central European body with local enforcement. The European Delegated Prosecutors located in the Member States form part of this European Office.[40] They shall act under the exclusive authority of the European Public Prosecutor and follow his instructions, guidelines and decisions only when they carry out investigations and prosecutions assigned to them.[41] The EPPO is a hierarchically organised European prosecution service. This is once again an important difference to Eurojust. Eurojust is composed of 28 national members forming a college, which has, however, no power to pass binding decisions on the national members. Eurojust remains a coordination body, and it is not envisaged or organised as a single hierarchical prosecution service.

According to the EPPO proposal, when the European Delegated Prosecutors act within their 'regulation mandate', they shall be fully independent from the national prosecution bodies and have no obligations towards them.[42] They may also exercise their function as national prosecutors, however, in the event of conflicting assignments, the European Delegated Prosecutors shall notify the European Public Prosecutor, who may, after consultation with the competent national prosecution authorities, instruct them in the interest of the investigations and prosecutions of the EPPO to give priority to their functions deriving from the Regulation. In such cases,

[39] See also Article 14 and recitals 5 and 26 of the preamble of the EPPO proposal.
[40] Article 6(1) of the EPPO proposal.
[41] Article 6(5) of the EPPO proposal.
[42] Article 6(5) of the EPPO proposal.

the European Public Prosecutor shall immediately inform the competent national prosecution authorities thereof.[43] The idea is thus to combine, on the one hand, the 'two hats' model, which is the best guarantee of integrating the delegates into the national systems of criminal justice and, on the other hand, the prevalence/pre-eminence of the European identity on their national quality.

Here again, the difference is to be noticed comparing to Eurojust. Even though Eurojust is marked by its hybridity,[44] its national members acting as national judicial authorities and members of the College of Eurojust ('two hats' system), but without prevalence of the EU interest being 'organised'. However, it is worth pointing out, that the Eurojust proposal also tends to strengthen the European nature of Eurojust. Such trend is particularly represented by the fact that, according to the proposal, national members should always be acting as 'Eurojust' when exercising their operational functions and not as national authorities anymore. The Eurojust proposal thus introduces the abolition of the distinction between the national members' powers exercised as competent national authorities and as Eurojust national members. This is of course an important novelty if it favours the emergence of the European interest and if it allows the national members to better serve the EU criminal justice area.[45]

5.3.4 Free Movement of Evidence

The submission of evidence to the relevant court will be a major challenge for the European Public Prosecutor. Its effectiveness will especially be measured on the basis of its ability of using at trial the evidence it has gathered.[46] On the ground of Article 86(3) TFEU, the EPPO proposal establishes the rules governing the admissibility of evidence: according to Article 30(1) of the proposal, the evidence gathered by the EPPO shall be admitted in the trial where the court considers that its admission would not adversely affect the fairness of the procedure or the rights of defence. Under this last condition, it results in the free movement of evidence within the EU. It means that, even if the national law of the Member State where the court is located provides for different rules on the collection or presentation of evidence, the evidence collected and presented by the EPPO should be admitted. Such choice for mutual admissibility is somehow similar to the approach of the

---

[43] Article 6(6) of the EPPO proposal.

[44] Concerning this Eurojust's hybrid nature, see especially Flore and De Biolley 2003, p. 623; Flore 2009, p. 567; Vlastnik 2008, p. 37.

[45] However, such change does not result in the end of the well-known Eurojusts' hybridity. The national members still keep 'two hats': they would act only as members of the college of Eurojust in their *operational* functions but as national representatives in their *management* functions.

[46] See the Commission's Green Paper on the criminal-law protection of the financial interests of the Community and the establishment of a European Prosecutor, COM (2001) 715 final, 11 Dec. 2001, point 6.3.4, and Hamran and Szabova 2013.

Commission's Green Paper on the criminal-law protection of the financial interests of the Community and the establishment of a European Prosecutor.[47]

This is of course quite ambitious, especially when a comparison is made with what has happened in the field of horizontal cooperation. For a long time, many efforts have been made to develop and smoothen horizontal cooperation in the field of cross-border gathering evidence. Such efforts have recently taken the form of mutual recognition.[48] However, in spite of the Conclusions of Tampere[49] and the wording of Article 82(2) TFEU,[50] no concrete proposal has been put forward to implement a system of mutual admissibility of evidence across the EU. The issue of admissibility of evidence has thus so far been neglected. Among the reasons for this situation are the important differences that exist between the national rules governing the collection of evidence and the fact that the Member States still want to keep a margin of discretion to exclude evidence gathered abroad, especially when it has been collected in a way that violates the fundamental principles of their national laws.

5.4 Elements of Horizontal Cooperation in the Proposal

Besides the innovative features, the EPPO proposal is also marked by the reservations of the Member States and the restraints of the European Commission. The tension between the original ambitions of the European Commission and the reality of political negotiations leading to the adoption of the proposal resulted in a discrepancy between the preamble and the actual text. The ambitions invoked in the preamble of the EPPO proposal are not always matched by the actual text. In the following four points of the EPPO proposal that are still confined to the old logic of horizontal cooperation need to be particularly highlighted: (i) the lack of reference to the European territoriality principle, (ii) the lack of common rules both substantive and procedural, (iii) the lack of clarity concerning the identification of the

---

[47] COM (2001) 715 final, 11 Dec. 2001, point 6.3.4, p. 58: 'Neither unification in the form of a complete code on the admissibility of evidence, nor a simple reference to national law but mutual admissibility of evidence is the most realistic and satisfactory solution here'.

[48] See Framework Decision 2003/577/ JHA of 22 July 2003 on the execution in the European Union of orders freezing property or evidence, Framework Decision 2008/978/JHA of 18 December 2008 on the European evidence warrant for the purpose of obtaining objects, documents and data for use in proceedings in criminal matters and the future Directive of the European Parliament and of the Council regarding the European Investigation Order in criminal matters (the EIO Directive).

[49] Para 36: '(…) evidence lawfully gathered by one Member State's authorities should be admissible before the courts of other Member States, taking into account the standards that apply there'.

[50] It states that 'the European Parliament and the Council may, by means of directives adopted in accordance with the ordinary legislative procedure, establish minimum rules. They shall concern: (a) mutual admissibility of evidence between Member States…'.

applicable national legal system and choice of forum and (iv) the vagueness and restraints of the proposal concerning judicial control.

5.4.1 Area or European Territory?

Among the formal and symbolic expressions of such restraint, the fact that the proposal does not explicitly word the European territoriality principle is to be mentioned. It is true that, according to Article 25(1) of the proposal, '(...) the territory of the Union's Member States shall be considered a single legal area (...)'. But the explicit words 'EU or European territory or territoriality' are not to be found. This is a difference compared to the *Corpus Juris*[51] or the Model Rules.[52,53] Such absence is most probably deliberate: it can be considered an important signal sent to the Member States as to the proclaimed level of integration. It shows the Commission's restraint or moderation in terms of ambitions. On the other hand, such 'silence' could also be understood as based on a EU constitutional argument since Title V of Part III of the TFEU only speaks about a EU area and not about a EU territory.[54]

5.4.2 European Prosecution Service Based on National Laws?

As it has been mentioned earlier, the legal framework of the functioning of the EPPO, both the substantive and procedural, was subject to controversial debates prior to the adoption of the EPPO proposal.

The discussions on substantive law are a result of the wording of Article 86 TFEU that offers two possibilities in respect of the material scope of competence of the EPPO. According to para 1 the EPPO shall be established '[i]n order to combat crimes affecting the financial interests of the Union'. However, according to para 4, the competence of the EPPO can be extended—by unanimous decision of the Council—'to include serious crimes having a cross-border dimension'. The discussions in relation to paras 1 and 4 of Article 86 TFEU raised mainly two questions. The first one is related to the narrower versus broader vision of the material scope of competence of the EPPO, i.e. whether the EPPO should be in charge of

---

[51] See Delmas-Marty and Vervaele 2000a, especially pp. 37 and 190.

[52] Rule 2 of the Model rules is entitled 'European territoriality'.

[53] The 2001 Commission's Green Book did not establish the EU territoriality principle as such but mentioned several times the 'Community territory' (see for instance p. 23).

[54] The notion of 'Union territory' is however not completely absent in the Treaty (see Article 153, (1)(g) of Title X on social policy).

investigating and prosecuting only offences affecting the financial interests or whether other serious cross border crimes should be also included. The second question was more of a technical nature and related to the interpretation of Article 86(1) TFEU. The latter namely requires that the regulation establishing the EPPO 'determines' the offences for which the EPPO should exercise its powers. Would it be sufficient, if the future regulation makes reference to the new PIF Directive and the national implementing provisions? Or does Article 86(1) TFEU require that the regulation itself defines the offences falling into the remit of the EPPO, thus constituting a legal basis for the harmonisation of substantive criminal law in the EU?

The EPPO proposal made a clear choice in favour of a reference to the proposed PIF Directive. Article 12 of the European Public Prosecutor's Office proposal states that 'The EPPO shall have competence in respect of the criminal offences affecting the financial interests of the Union, as provided for by directive 2013/xx/EU and implemented by national law'. Thereby the European Public Prosecutor's Office proposal refrains from providing for definitions of criminal offences in respect of which the European Public Prosecutor's Office should exercise its functions. By making reference to the PIF Directive, the EPPO proposal accepts that the offence definition will be given by national (implementing) law.

The EPPO proposal does not only lack common offence definitions, but it also refrains from defining the investigative powers of the EPPO. Although the recitals of the Preamble refer to uniform investigation powers throughout the Union[55] and Article 25(1) states that 'For the purpose of investigations and prosecutions conducted by the EPPO, the territory of the Union's Member States shall be considered a single legal area in which the EPPO may exercise its competence' it becomes clear from the reading of Articles 11 and 18 that these powers are fully dependent upon national laws and territories. The EPPO proposal sets up a mixed model consisting of a minimum of European rules to be extended by national criminal procedural laws.[56] Article 26 lists the investigative measures that the EPPO shall have, but, at the same time, Article 11(3) stipulates, that 'National law shall apply to the extent that a matter is not regulated by this Regulation.' Furthermore, Article 18 (6) states that: 'Where the investigation is undertaken by the European Public Prosecutor directly, he/she shall inform the European Delegated Prosecutor in the Member State where the investigation measures need to be carried out. Any investigation measure conducted by the European Public Prosecutor shall be carried

[55] The preamble of the proposal proclaims in recital 7 that the EPPO 'requires *autonomous powers of investigation and prosecution*, including the ability to carry out investigations in cross-border or complex cases' (emphasis added). The notion of autonomous powers points into the direction of a set of uniform powers for investigation and prosecution, independent from those of the national authorities of the Member States.

[56] As explained in recital 19 of the preamble: 'As it would be disproportionate to provide detailed provisions on the conduct of its investigations and prosecutions, this Regulation should only list the measures of investigation that the European Public Prosecutor's Office may need to use and leave the other matters, in particular rules related to their execution, to national law.'

out in liaison with the authorities of the Member State whose territory is concerned. Coercive measures shall be carried out by the competent national authorities'.

The combination of Articles 26, 11 and 18 lead to a situation where the investigative powers of the EPPO are defined by the national criminal procedural law of each Member State. Since the EPPO proposal only enlists the powers, but, apart from the need for judicial authorisation, does not set any further requirements as to those powers, Member States are free to stipulate the conditions for the individual investigative measures of the EPPO. Accordingly, the EPPO shall have as many sets of powers as Member State participate in the EPPO. Moreover, it follows from Article 18 that the sets of powers are confined to the territory of the Member State in which the EPPO investigates. The EPPO proposal does not even require the national authorities to mutually recognise the authorisation given for coercive measures. Accordingly, if a coercive investigative measure needs to be undertaken in various Member States (e.g. telephone tapping), the EPPO needs to request authorisation for the same measure in each Member State where the measure is to be carried out.

In summary, the legal framework—both substantive and procedural—of the EPPO laid down in the EPPO proposal is based on national law. Although the EPPO proposal contains a minimum of European rules both in respect of the offence definitions and the investigative measures, the details are always defined by national (implementing) legislation. This leads to a situation where it depends on national law and national territory whether the EPPO can investigate and prosecute a certain offence and which powers it may exercise.

The dominant role given to national law in the legal framework of the EPPO is explicable in the light of the requirement of respect for national diversity, which is enshrined in Article 4(2) TEU and Article 67(1) TFEU. Thus the Treaty itself provides for a strong EU constitutional argument in favour of references to national law. This is, however, counterbalanced by the Treaty objectives such as establishing an Area of Freedom, Security and Justice (Article 3 TEU), endeavouring a high level of security (Article 67(3) TFEU) and ensuring an effective PIF protection (Article 325 TFEU).

In light of the requirements and objectives pronounced in the Treaty, the legal framework of the EPPO raises three types of concerns.

First, it is doubtful whether the proposed system referring so much to national law will allow to implement the above-mentioned constitutional objectives. The practical concern that led to devising a European prosecutor is the quest to establish a coherent European system for investigating offences which prejudice the European budget.[57] The new system should be more effective and efficient than the current system based on national investigations and prosecutions and mutual assistance between national authorities. The aim is to overcome the current

[57] According to recital 12 '[t]o ensure consistency in its action and thus an equivalent protection of the Union's financial interests, the organisational structure of the European Public Prosecutor's Office should enable central coordination and steering of all investigations and prosecutions within its competence. The European Public Prosecutor's Office should therefore have a central structure where decisions are taken by the European Public Prosecutor.'

fragmentation of national prosecutions. The question, however, remains whether this mixed system of European minimum rules and national substantive and criminal procedural law is a solution to existing problems, and, more generally, whether it is a workable model.

Second, the lack of common substantive and procedural rules also raises concerns as to the compatibility of the proposed system with the basic EU principles. The lack of common rules is problematic from the point of view of the legality principle, the principle of legal certainty and the requisite of a fair trial as provided for in the EU Charter on Fundamental Rights.

The lack of offence definitions in the EPPO proposal ultimately means that the EPPO will have as many definitions of its competence as the number of Member States participating in its establishment. Equally, the lack of definition of investigative measures in the proposal means that the EPPO will have no uniform powers, but as many sets of powers as the number of the Member States participating in it. Both the material scope of competence and the powers of the EPPO, therefore, may vary from Member State to Member State. This may cause substantial problems in investigating and prosecuting transnational cases.

Furthermore, it must be borne in mind that the notion 'crimes affecting the financial interests of the Union' is an autonomous notion of EU law that has to be interpreted independently and uniformly throughout the EU. EU citizens and economic operators must be able to rely on a uniform application accordingly. Especially, if investigations and prosecutions of the EPPO also involve a standard of procedural safeguards and judicial review which is different from national criminal procedure, EU citizens and economic operators will have a fundamental right following from the right to a fair trial to know which prosecuting authority (national or European) is in charge of the case. The right to a fair trial requires that in all the stages of the criminal procedure, including pre-trial proceedings, the applicable law is foreseeable.

Third, and beyond any constitutional consideration, it is also unclear how these completely decentralised and nationalised systems can assure the admissibility of evidence in the forum state. As seen previously, Article 30 of the EPPO proposal provides for the mutual admissibility of evidence, which represents an interesting and important step forward. Nevertheless, it is highly improbable that such principle will work and be accepted without being 'accompanied' by some common rules in the field of investigation and collection of evidence. In this regard, it should be reminded that from the follow-up report on the 2001 Green Paper it resulted that many respondents considered such a system of mutual admissibility of evidence to raise serious problems both for defence rights, as well as for the legal certainty principle. Numerous answers underlined the need to adopt common minimum rules as a necessary prerequisite for the acceptance of such principle.[58]

---

[58] Follow-up report on the Green Paper on the criminal-law protection of the financial interests of the Community and the establishment of a European Prosecutor, Brussels, 19 March 2003, COM 2003, 128 final, p. 18.

5.4.3 What Is the Applicable Law?

According to Article 11(3), the national law applicable to investigations and prosecutions, will be the law of the Member State 'where the investigation or prosecution is conducted'. This wording, however, is unclear in respect of the applicable law. Especially in case of transborder measures, such as e.g. interception of telecommunication, it is unclear whether the law of the Member State where the measure was ordered, or the law of the Member State where the measure is executed should be the applicable one. This may also mean, that for the ordering and the execution of the very same measure, different national laws would apply. The phrase 'is conducted' is not specific enough to give guidance for such situations.

In view of the lack of common rules and the diversity between applicable national laws, especially in cases where several Member States are concerned, there is a real risk of forum shopping, both with regard to the investigations, on the one hand, and prosecution and bringing the case to judgement, on the other hand. European Delegated Prosecutors could be tempted to investigate or execute some investigative measures where the rules are the most flexible for the investigator, or to prosecute where the definition of the offences is the broadest. The risk of forum shopping should not be overestimated since the favourable nature of the rules is not the only criterion or element that the EPPO will take into consideration. Other important criteria such as the location of the suspect, of the evidence, etc. will play a major role.[59] But, even if it is limited, the risk of forum shopping clearly exists and is, as such, problematic. The lack of clarity concerning the identification of the applicable national legal system and choice of forum is also problematic from the point of view of defendants' rights. As it has been stated above, the right to a fair trial requires that in all stages of the criminal procedure, including pre-trial proceedings, the applicable law is foreseeable. The suspected person must have clarity as to the Member State and the national law he/she will be accountable to, because this is the only way to ensure effective defence in pre-trial investigations. However, the EPPO proposal is far from ensuring such 'predictability'.

5.4.4 No Judicial Control by a European Court?

The fourth drawback of the proposal is its vagueness and timidity as to judicial control in general and especially concerning the judicial control by the ECJ. This aspect will not be thoroughly analysed in this chapter because it is the precise topic of other chapters in this book.[60] Nevertheless, some remarks are to be made.

---

[59] One should also be aware of the fact that it is not easy in practice to transfer the file several times. Getting acquainted with a file—especially when it is a complex file—takes time. Therefore transferring/'delocalising' implies also a loss of time and energy.

[60] See infra n. 63.

First, some provisions of the EPPO proposal are unclear, as for instance Article 13(4) about ancillary competence which states that 'The determination of competence pursuant to this Article shall not be subject to review'. Does it mean 'not be subject *to any review*'[61] or only 'not be subject to review *at the EU level*'? Besides, and more fundamentally, Article 36, which is the main provision of the proposal on judicial review, as it is worded, gives the impression of being essentially aimed at reducing as much as possible the control by the ECJ.[62] It means for example that there will be no 'direct' judicial control at the European level of the EPPO's decision on the choice of forum because such decision is considered to be a national one. Therefore, it should be submitted to judicial review at the national level. But in this respect, no specific duty is provided for by the proposal. Although individuals will not have the possibility to directly challenge the EPPO's decision and although the national competent authorities will not be allowed to introduce a preliminary ruling to the ECJ concerning the validity of the EPPO's decision, the national authorities will be allowed to introduce such preliminary ruling concerning the interpretation or validity of the provisions of the regulation (for example concerning the interpretation of the criteria listed in Article 27(4) of the proposal).

What is striking, is the contradiction between, on the one hand, the insistence on the status of the EPPO being a European body and, on the other hand, the fact of considering its acts as acts of a national authority, in order to exclude a possible direct control by the ECJ. This is at least difficult to reconcile with EU primary law, in particular with Article 267 TFEU, which, since the Lisbon Treaty, explicitly covers the preliminary rulings concerning interpretation and validity of acts of the EU bodies, offices and agencies of the Union. It can be considered as bypassing EU primary law and, as such, it is of course a dangerous precedent.[63]

5.5 EPPO 'From' or 'Next To' Eurojust?

The EPPO should become a new judicial body with operative jurisdiction in the EU. This ultimately means that its relations to existing EU bodies and agencies of criminal law enforcement have to be defined.

---

[61] This would mean in some cases exclusion of an existing national judicial review (as in Belgium where the decision of the *chambre des mises en accusation* can in principle be submitted to a *pourvoi en cassation*).

[62] Along the same lines see also recital 38 of the preamble ('In accordance with Article 267 of the Treaty, national courts are able or, in certain circumstances, bound to refer to the Court of Justice questions for preliminary rulings on the interpretation or the validity of provisions of Union law, including this Regulation, which are relevant for the judicial review of the acts of investigation and prosecution of the European Public Prosecutor's Office. National courts should not be able to refer questions on the validity of the acts of the European Public Prosecutor's Office to the Court of Justice, since those acts should not be considered acts of a body of the Union for the purpose of judicial review').

[63] See in this regard, Arjen Meij in Chap. 7 and Jan Inghelram in Chap. 8 in this book.

In this respect, the EPPO proposal deals rather extensively with the relationships with Eurojust and announces that 'special rules apply to the relationship of the EPPO with Eurojust given the special links that tie them together in the area of operational activities, administration and management'[64] and Article 57 develops these 'special links'.[65]

Conversely, in respect of OLAF, Article 58 of the proposal only states that 'The European Public Prosecutor's Office shall cooperate with the Commission, including OLAF, for the purpose of implementing the obligations under Article 325 (3) of the Treaty. To this end, they shall conclude an agreement setting out the modalities of their cooperation'.[66] The EPPO proposal is also similarly brief in relation to Europol when it states that the EPPO 'shall develop a special relationship with Europol'.

Although the EPPO proposal clearly allocates more attention to the relationship between the EPPO and Eurojust than between the EPPO and OLAF or Europol, the respective provisions of the legislative package are far from clear. The proclaimed 'special relationship' between Eurojust and the EPPO is (at least) twofold: structural/institutional on the one hand and functional/operational on the other hand.

As regards the structural relationship, Article 86 TFEU stipulates that the EPPO shall be established from Eurojust. This phrasing of the Treaty led already in the forerun of the proposal to consider various possible scenarios. The first saw the EPPO as a completely separate and autonomous entity; an EPPO alongside Eurojust, but outside its structure.[67] According to the second option the EPPO could be designed as a specialised unit within Eurojust. In this second option the EPPO would organisationally be a part of Eurojust, the horizontal and vertical functions

64 Explanatory memorandum of the Proposal on the EPPO Regulation, p. 8. According to recital 40 of the Proposal, 'they should organically, operationally and administratively co-exist, co-operate and complement each other'; furthermore, Article 3(3) of the Proposal states that '[t]he European Public Prosecutor's Office shall cooperate with Eurojust and rely on its administrative support in accordance with Article 57.'

65 Article 57 of the EPPO proposal corresponds to Article 41 of the Eurojust proposal. Some discrepancies between their provisions can be however noticed as to terminology: it is unclear the reason of such inconsistency that could complicate the readability of the proposals.

66 In particular the relationship between the EPPO and Olaf gave room for a lot of speculation prior of tabling the EPPO proposal. A European prosecution service with powers to investigate and prosecute PIF offences in the Member States would automatically render the administrative investigations of OLAF superfluous. The integrationist view supported by OLAF itself suggested, therefore, that OLAF should become the '*police judicière*' of the EPPO acting at the central level. It is, however, doubtful whether Article 86 TFEU provides legal basis for such a scenario. See Inghelram 2011, p. 270 et seq.

67 Many argued that this is the most straightforward solution in terms of accountability and internal organisation. It would have the further advantage that since the two entities (EPPO and Eurojust) would be kept completely separate it would be clear that there is one unit for judicial cooperation in general whereas the other one is for investigating and prosecuting EU fraud.

would, however, not merge.[68] Finally, a third option was raised in which the EPPO could merge with Eurojust so as to form one (new) body.

The EPPO proposal and the one on Eurojust make an implicit, but clear choice: the EPPO will be a separate entity next to Eurojust. It seems that the invoked special link is in fact rather loose. Articles 12 and 16 of the Eurojust proposal provide for some forms of cooperation, in particular a possibility for the EPPO to participate at the Eurojust College meeting—albeit without the right to vote—in case of the issues relevant for it; the same regards the meetings of the Executive Board of Eurojust, in this case with a possibility to address written opinions to which the Executive Board shall respond in writing without undue delay. Especially the Eurojust proposal gives the impression that the EPPO is a sort of 29th member of Eurojust, albeit with very limited powers. This impression is further confirmed by Article 41 of the Eurojust proposal according to which requests for support by the EPPO should be treated by Eurojust as if they had been received from a national authority.

As regards the functional/operational relationship between the EPPO and Eurojust, the two main aspects influencing this relationship are linked to the material scope of competence in those cases in which PIF crimes are 'inextricably linked' with non-PIF crimes[69] on the one hand, and to the territorial scope of the EPPO (enhanced cooperation), on the other hand.

In respect of the material scope of competence on 'hybrid cases', Articles 13(2) and 57 of EPPO proposal favours the 'unification of competence': after consultation involving also the Eurojust College, only one authority (the EPPO or the national authority of the respective Member State) should be in charge of the investigations. This means that the EPPO does not only have exclusive competence for investigating and prosecuting PIF offences, but it should also have primary authority for coordinating PIF investigations and prosecutions of non-PIF crimes when 'joint investigation and prosecution are in the interest of a good administration of justice', provided that PIF offences 'are preponderant and the other criminal offences are based on identical facts'. Consequently, PIF offences are excluded from the scope of competence of Eurojust.[70]

[68] In this case the EPPO would be located on Eurojust's premises in order to be able to use Eurojust's facilities, but it would function independently from Eurojust.

[69] Article 13(1) of the EPPO proposal.

[70] This is confirmed by Article 3 para 1 of the proposal on Eurojust which explicitly excludes Eurojust's competence in the field of PIF. Simultaneously, however, Annex 1 of the same proposal mentions PIF among the fields of competence of Eurojust. This contradiction can be alleviated by interpreting Article 3 of the Eurojust proposal in a way that it excludes the competence of Eurojust only in those cases in which EPPO actually exercises its competence. It makes sense because (i) there might be non-EPPO states, (ii) the EPPO may decide to refer the case to national authority and (iii) if the competence in case of connected crimes is allocated to Member States, then Eurojust should be competent to exercise its functions. However, even in cases where the EPPO actually exercises its competence, the EPPO may need support functions of coordination from Eurojust e.g. in relation to non-EPPO countries. Here, Article 3 of the Eurojust proposal is problematic as it excludes verbatim any competence for Eurojust. It has been suggested by Catherine Deboyser in Chap. 6 in this book, to read it in a way that Eurojust may act in PIF cases only on request of the EPPO.

A further aspect of the functional relationship between the EPPO and Eurojust may arise, if the EPPO is established via enhanced cooperation. In this case the EPPO may encounter transnational PIF offences that took place both in EPPO-participating Member States, as well as in non-participating ones. None of the proposals provide for a possibility of consultation in order to confer the competence to the EPPO in such cases. Consequently, the EPPO has to work alongside and with Eurojust, provided that Eurojust has been involved by the competent national authorities of the non-participating Member States concerned.

Finally, the EPPO proposal foresees that the EPPO may request the support of Eurojust in the transmission of its decisions or requests for mutual legal assistance in cases involving Member States which are not Member States of the EPPO or third countries. That provision must be read in combination with Article 41(3) of the Eurojust proposal providing that Eurojust shall make use of its agreements with third countries and its liaison magistrates in order to support the cooperation of the EPPO with third countries. However, it should be noted that, like Eurojust, also the EPPO may establish working arrangements (including the secondment of liaison officers to the EPPO) with third countries and international organisations and may designate contact points in third countries.[71] This raises the risk of duplication of efforts and questions whether this cooperation can effectively work in practice: does Eurojust have an added value for the EPPO in cases where a request for assistance is needed regarding non-participating states?

However, it must be borne in mind that the operational support and expertise of Eurojust will be crucial for the effectiveness of EPPO's action. This is reflected by the provisions of the two proposals on exchange of information. Of course, the EPPO will need to have access to all relevant information concerning offences that fall within its competence. Consequently, both proposals insist on the importance of exchange of information, including personal data between Eurojust and the EPPO under certain conditions.[72] We can find an obligation for Eurojust to report to the EPPO,[73] the obligation to transmit information when requested[74] and other provisions on the sharing of relevant information between the two bodies.

In particular, the effectiveness of the exchange of information will depend on the concrete mechanisms in place to guarantee an effective exchange. In this regard, we know that Eurojust has developed its CMS (case management system). Article 24 of the Eurojust proposal foresees that the CMS and its temporary work files shall be made available for use by the EPPO. At the same time, Article 22 of the EPPO proposal provides for the establishment of the EPPO's own 'Case Management System, index and temporary files'. It is, however, unclear how the two systems

[71] Article 59 of the EPPO proposal.

[72] Article 41(4) Eurojust proposal and Article 57(4) of the EPPO proposal.

[73] Article 15 of the EPPO proposal.

[74] Article 21 of the EPPO proposal.

should interact. Will it be guaranteed by the envisaged automatic cross-checking of data by Eurojust as provided for in Articles 41(5) and 41(6) of the Eurojust proposal and Article 57(3) of the EPPO proposal?[75]

Considering the EPPO and Eurojust as two separate entities reveals a remarkably cautious understanding of the term 'from Eurojust' as used in Article 86 TFEU. This approach is reflected in the administrative support to be given by Eurojust to the EPPO.[76]

5.6 Conclusions

The Commission's task of drafting the proposal for a regulation on the EPPO was formulated against the requirement that Article 86 TFEU only allows for *partial* verticalisation of criminal justice integration in the EU. The Treaty itself requires that the adjudication remains in the competence of national courts. Verticalisation of the PIF enforcement system shall, therefore, be limited to the pre-trial phase and must be in line with the legal systems of the Member States.

Hence, the EPPO proposal proclaims a new generation of EU judicial body with, on the one hand, vertical/supranational integration aspects and, on the other hand, horizontal/intergovernmental elements. This combination is of course not per se disputable. But it obliges the EU legislator to find a sound balance between both types of elements.

The EU legislator in its effort to strike a sound balance could profit from previous reflections, such as the *Corpus Juris*, the consultations performed in the context of the 2001 Commission's Green Paper, and the more recent academic studies conducted for the purposes of the preparation of the EPPO proposal. Initially, OLAF—which due to historical and legal reasons assumed an active role in promoting the setting up of the EPPO[77]—commissioned a series of comparative and empirical studies,[78] namely the 'Rethinking Criminal Justice' study,[79] the

[75] It is interesting to note that this mechanism of automatic cross checking goes further than the system imagined by Eurojust and the European Parliament and successfully submitted to the Commission as a proposal to be inserted in both draft regulations on Eurojust and on Europol. That system put in place with Europol is not automatic. It respects the restrictions indicated by the owner of the information and provides for similar conditions for access to information for both organisations.

[76] See Article 41(7) of the Eurojust proposal. The list contained in this provision is non-exhaustive and includes technical support in programming, security, IT, financial management, HR, and 'any other services of common interest': the details will be specified in an agreement between Eurojust and the EPPO.

[77] See in detail, Ligeti 2014a, b.

[78] All of these studies embarked on the *Corpus Juris* study Delmas-Marty and Vervaele 2000b.

[79] Sieber and Wade 2010, Volumes 1–5, Manuscript.

'Euro Needs' study[80] and the 'Model Rules' study.[81] These studies highlighted the legal and practical impediments of an efficient protection of the financial interests of the EU by national law and national authorities. In particular, the Model Rules Study argued in favour of elaborating a set of common European provisions for defining the investigative and prosecutorial powers of the EPPO.[82] After having analysed the relevant aspects of national pre-trial proceedings in the Member States, the Model Rules Study concluded that, though inspired by the European Convention on Human Rights and the respective case law of the Strasbourg Court, there is not sufficient common ground between the various national criminal procedural laws of the Member States. On the contrary, the comparison of the national systems revealed an extreme diversity regulating the pre-trial phase of the criminal procedure in the Member States in general and in relation to special investigation techniques in particular.[83] Due to these substantial differences the Model Rules study concluded that the EPPO cannot, for its supranational investigations, rely on the investigative measures of the territorial state. Rather, it will need a distinct set of harmonised supranational investigative powers for gathering evidence.

Such degree of harmonisation, however, proved out of reach in the context of the negotiations conducted by the Commission prior to publishing the EPPO proposal. The two Directorate Generals of the Commission (OLAF and DG Justice) have been engaged in intense consultations with the Member States and with associations of practitioners prior to adopting the proposal in order to prepare the terrain for the EPPO. During these negotiations, the Commission's ambitions met the resistance of the Member States and of the national practitioners. Most notably, Germany and France sent a joint letter to the EU Commission in order to demonstrate their joint position.[84] It was clear that the content of the joint French-German letter was supported by several Member States. The letter made two substantial points: the structure of the EPPO should resemble the more intergovernmental structure of Eurojust and the powers of the EPPO should be governed by national criminal procedural law only. Against this background, the European Commission had to strike its balance with respect to the reality of negotiations.

The French-German letter came at a decisive period of the pre-consultations and had a large impact on the text of the proposal. The Commission put on hold the provisions that related to the harmonisation of investigative measures, but

80 Study on evaluating the need for and the needs of a European Criminal Justice System, available at http://www.mpicc.de/shared/data/pdf/euroneeds_report_jan_2011.pdf (Accessed 21 February 2014).

81 Study on European Model Rules for the Procedure of the future European Public Prosecutor's Office, published in Ligeti 2014a, b.

82 The Model Rules are reprinted in several languages in Ligeti 2014b.

83 For a description of special investigative techniques see Vervaele 2009.

84 Joint letter of S. Leutheusser Schnarrenberger and C. Taubira addressed to the Vice-President of the EU Commission, Vivianne Reding and to the Commissioner responsible for Taxation, Customs, Statistics, Audit and Anti-Fraud, Algridas Semeta, 20 March 2013 (available at www.eppo-project.eu).

maintained, to a large extent, its original position in relation to the institutional design of the EPPO. The so adopted proposal once again reveals the tension between different avenues of criminal justice integration in the EU. Much of the originally envisaged unification has been abandoned in order to give more room to national diversity.

However, so conceived system of a minimum European procedural rules combined with national procedural laws does not ultimately lead to reducing the current complexity. On the contrary, giving as much room as possible to national procedural law it conserves, to a large extent, the present scenario where the different national criminal justice systems need to interact in the investigation and prosecution of transnational offences on the basis of mutual recognition. Basing the functioning of the EPPO on national rules of investigation requires, that the investigative measures (and the information obtained by using them) of the delegated prosecutors of the EPPO are mutually recognised.

Taking into consideration the resistance of Member States towards the vertical integration/supranational aspects—and especially the views of some of the Member States it wanted to count on—led the Commission to a considerable decrease of its own ambitions. Such situation unfortunately gives good argument to sceptics, arguing that time was not ripe to introduce such a proposal and that the 'good governance time line' has been circumvented.[85] Such argument seems to be also supported by the fact that 14 Chambers of national parliaments sent reasoned opinions to the Commission, thus triggering the subsidiarity control mechanism provided for in Article 7(2)2 of the protocol No 2 to the Treaties (i.e. the yellow card procedure).[86] As it is well known, the Commission did not withdraw its proposal nor did it amend it. It declared, however, that it will take good account of the reasoned opinions of the national parliaments during the legislative process.[87]

Finally, and in order to conclude on a positive note, regardless of the deficiencies that the proposal for a regulation on the EPPO might have, the very fact that Member States are negotiating at the Council level about setting up the EPPO is already a major achievement. The proposal is an essential first step and will most probably have an important driving force. If the regulation is eventually adopted, time will probably prove that, to work efficiently, the EPPO needs common rules, both substantive and procedural. Let us hope that the negotiations within the

[85] It indeed seems to support the reasoning according to which the Commission should have waited more, namely for the complete assessment of the 2008 decision on Eurojust, for the strengthening of Eurojust's powers through the adoption of a Regulation adopted on the basis of Article 85 TFEU, for a full evaluation of such Regulation and, then finally, if this was still not sufficient, pass to the establishment of an EPPO.

[86] V. Franssen, National Parliaments Issue Yellow Card against the European Public Prosecutor's Office, European Law Blog, 4 November 2013, available at http://europeanlawblog.eu/?p=2025 (last visited on 21 March 2014).

[87] See COM 2013b 853 final, 27 Nov 2013.

Council and the taking into consideration of the European Parliament's views[88] will allow the EU legislator correcting the most important imbalances affecting the proposal and building a more balanced system, which will not be detrimental to the rights of the concerned '*justiciables*', to the efficiency of the mechanism, and overall to the implementation of the EU constitutional objectives.

References

Bures O (2010) Eurojust's fledging counterterrorism role. Journal of contemporary European Research, 6(2):236 et seq

COM (2003) Follow-up report on the green paper on the criminal-law protection of the financial interests of the Community and the establishment of a European Prosecutor, Brussels, 19 March 2003, p 128 final

COM (2013a) Better protection of the Union's financial interests: setting up the European public prosecutor's office and reforming Eurojust', 17 July 2013, 532 final

COM (2013b) 853, final, 27 Nov 2013

Commission Staff (2011) Working paper of 26 May 2011, SEC 621 final

Delmas-Marty M, Vervaele JAE (eds) (2000a), Corpus juris 2000 Florence version. Antwerp, Intersentia

Delmas-Marty M, Vervaele JAE (eds) (2000b) The implementation of the corpus juris in the member states, vol 1. Intersentia, Antwerp

Delmas-Marty M, Vervaele JAE (eds) (2000c) The implementation of the corpus juris in the member states, vols 1–4. Intersentia, Antwerp

Durdevic Z (2013) Judicial control in pre-trial criminal procedure conducted by the European public prosecutor's office. In: Ligeti K (ed) Toward a prosecutor for the European Union, vol 1. A comparative analysis. Hart Publishing, Oxford, p 986 et seq

Eleventh operational report of the European Anti-fraud Office (OLAF), 1 January to 31 December 2010. http://ec.europa.eu/anti_fraud/about-us/reports/olaf-report/index_en.htm (last visited on 21 March 2014) http://bookshop.europa.eu/en/eleventh-operational-report-of-the-european-anti-fraud-office-pbOBAC11001/

European Parliament resolution of 12 March 2014 on the proposal for a Council regulation on the establishment of the European public prosecutor's office (COM(2013)0534—2013/0255 (APP))

Flore D (2009) Droit pénal européen. Les enjeux d'une justice pénale européenne, Brussels, Larcier

Flore D, De Biolley S (2003) Jurisdictional bodies in criminal matters for the EU, in Cahiers de droit Européen, 2003, p 623 et seq

Franssen V (2013) National parliaments issue yellow card against the European public prosecutor's office. European Law Blog, 4 Nov 2013. available at http://europeanlawblog.eu/?p=2025 (last visited on 21 March 2014)

Green paper on the criminal-law protection of the financial interests of the Community and the establishment of a European prosecutor, COM (2001) 715 final, 11 Dec. 2001

Hamran L, Szabova E (2013) European public prosecutor's office—cui bono? New J Eur Crim Law 4(1–2):54 et seq

[88] See especially European Parliament resolution of 12 March 2014 on the proposal for a Council regulation on the establishment of the European Public Prosecutor's Office COM (2013) 0534—2013/0255(APP).

Inghelram JFH (2011) Legal and institutional aspects of the European Anti-Fraud Office (OLAF). Europa Law Publishing
Kuhl L (2012) The initiative for a directive on the protection of the EU financial interests by substantive criminal law, in Eucrim 2:65 et seq
Leutheusser Schnarrenberger S, Taubira C (2013) Addressed to the vice-president of the EU Commission, Vivianne Reding and to the commissioner responsible for taxation, customs, statistics, audit and anti-fraud, Algridas Semeta, 20 march 2013. www.eppo-project.eu
Ligeti K (2013) Approximation of substantive criminal law and the establishment of the European public prosecutor's office. In: Galli F, Weyembergh A (eds.) Approximation of substantive criminal law in the EU, IEE, p 73 et seq
Ligeti K (ed) (2014a) Toward a prosecutor for the European Union. vol. I: Draft rules of procedure, Hart Publishing, Oxford (forthcoming)
Ligeti K (ed) (2014b) Toward a prosecutor for the European Union. vol. II: Draft rules of procedure, Hart, (forthcoming)
Ligeti K, Simonato M (2013) The European public prosecutor's office: towards a truly European prosecution service? New J Eur Crim Law 4(01–02)
Proposal for a directive of the European Parliament and of the Council on the fight against fraud to the Union's financial interests by means of criminal law, COM (2012) 363 final, Brussels, 11 July 2012
Proposal for a regulation on the establishment of the European public prosecutor's office, 17 July 2013, COM (2013) 534 final
Proposal for a regulation on the European Union Agency for Criminal Justice Cooperation (Eurojust), 17 July 2013, COM (2013),p. 535 final
Sieber U, Wade M (eds) (2010) Structures and perspectives of European criminal justice, vol 1–5. Manuscript
Study on evaluating the need for and the needs of a European criminal justice system. http://www.mpicc.de/shared/data/pdf/euroneeds_report_jan_2011.pdf (last visited on 21 February 2014)
Van den Wyngaert C (2004) Eurojust and the European public prosecutor in the corpus juris model: water and fire? In: Walker N (ed) Europe's area of freedom, security and justice. Oxford University Press, Oxford, p 231 et seq
Vermeulen B, De Bondt W, Ryckman C (2012) Rethinking international cooperation in criminal matters in the EU. Maklu, Antwerp
Vervaele JAE (2009) Special procedural measures and the protection of human rights. General report for Section III of the AIDP, RIDP 2009, vol (1–2), pp 75–123
Vervaele JAE (2010) Quel statut pour le ministère public? in Quelles perspectives pour un ministère public européen? Protéger les Intérets Financiers et Fondamentaux de l'Union, Dalloz
Vlastnik J (2008) Eurojust—a cornerstone of the federal criminal justice system in the EU? In: Guild E, Geyer F (eds) Security versus justice? Police and judicial cooperation in the EU. Ashgate Publishing, Hampshire
Weyembergh A (2013a) An overall analysis of the proposal for a regulation on Eurojust. EUCrim 2013(4):127–131
Weyembergh A (2013b) Coordination and initiation of investigations and prosecutions through Eurojust, in ERA Forum, 14(2):177 et seq
Zwiers M (2011) The European public prosecutor's office. Intersentia, Antwerp

Chapter 6
European Public Prosecutor's Office and Eurojust: 'Love Match or Arranged Marriage'?

Catherine Deboyser

Abstract The draft regulations on Eurojust and the European Public Prosecutor's Office (EPPO) complement each other. To get a full comprehension of the relations between both proposals, they must be read and analysed simultaneously. According to those draft regulations the scope of material competence of the EPPO would in principle be seamlessly delimited, as Eurojust would not be competent for the crimes for which the EPPO is competent and vice-versa. However, provisions in both draft regulations regulate operational cooperation between the two bodies, which consists mainly of sharing information and the possibility for the EPPO to address specific requests to Eurojust. Moreover, in line with the requirement of Article 86 TFEU and for reasons of cost efficiency, the development of the EPPO as envisaged by the Commission will heavily rely on the support to be provided by Eurojust.

Keywords European Public Prosecutor's Office · Eurojust · Fraud against financial interests of the EU · PIF · Article 85 TFEU · Article 86 TFEU

Contents

The author is Head of the Legal Service of Eurojust. The opinions expressed in this article are those of the author and may not be attributed to Eurojust. The author would like to thank Laura Surano, Legal Officer at Eurojust, for the fruitful exchange of views, and Jacalyn Birk, for her precious assistance.

C. Deboyser (✉)
Eurojust, The Hague, The Netherlands
e-mail: cdeboyser@eurojust.europa.eu

L.H. Erkelens et al. (eds.), *The European Public Prosecutor's Office*,
DOI 10.1007/978-94-6265-035-0_6

6.1 Introduction

The imperative included in Article 86 of the Treaty on the Functioning of the European Union (TFEU) to establish the European Public Prosecutor's Office (EPPO) 'from Eurojust' has apparently been taken literally by the European Commission. Pending the final outcome of the 6th round of mutual evaluations devoted to the implementation of the Eurojust Decision, the draft regulations on Eurojust[1] and the EPPO[2] were presented—on the same day—as a reform intending to create the EPPO and to strengthen Eurojust. The provision on the establishment of the EPPO[3] stipulates that the Office shall cooperate with Eurojust and rely on its administrative support. Additionally, both legislative proposals refer to 'the special relationship' between Eurojust and the EPPO, which is to be based on 'close cooperation and the development of operational, administrative and management links'.[4] According to recital (41) of the EPPO proposal, Eurojust and the EPPO should 'organically, operationally and administratively co-exist, co-operate and complement each other'. What is exactly the meaning of this recital?

The wish for an extensive functional and administrative support that Eurojust is called upon to provide to the EPPO through its services and staff is made clear, although some of the provisions implementing such desire leave room for interpretation. The two drafts envisage a close organic coexistence consolidated by regular meetings of the European Public Prosecutor and Eurojust's President.[5] The European Public Prosecutor is granted the right to participate in all College and Executive Board meetings[6] and to address written opinions to the Executive Board

[1] Proposal for a Regulation of the European Parliament and of the Council on the European Union Agency for Criminal Justice Cooperation (Eurojust) (COM(2013) 535 final), 17.7.2013, referred to in this article as the 'Eurojust proposal'.

[2] Proposal for a Council Regulation on the establishment of the European Public Prosecutor's Office (COM(2013) 534 final, 17.7.2013, referred to in this article as the 'EPPO proposal'. See also the Appendix to this book.

[3] Article 3 of the EPPO proposal.

[4] Article 41 of the Eurojust proposal and Article 57 EPPO of the proposal.

[5] Article 41(1) of the Eurojust proposal.

[6] Articles 12(3) and 16(7) of the Eurojust proposal.

and to the College, which shall be responded to in writing without undue delay. The EPPO will draw on the resources of the administration of Eurojust for all its essential needs and its functioning as an organisation.[7]

Both proposals state that the details of the services to be provided by Eurojust to the EPPO must be laid down in an agreement. The intention here is clearly to create synergies, avoid duplication of resources and achieve cost efficiency. Undoubtedly, in that respect the proposals, if adopted, will most probably reach their goals. Although no mention is made as to whether this future agreement could provide reimbursement of the costs of these services and despite the Legislative Financial Statements in both proposals claiming that support should be provided by Eurojust on a zero-cost basis, invoicing and reimbursement or another form of financing can indeed be anticipated.

The present chapter focuses on operational aspects of this 'special relationship', ensuing in the following question: has the Commission taken the full measure of the potential interaction and the possible structural links that could be developed between the two bodies, or has it mainly had in mind the economy of scale and the practical advantages that a coexistence of the two bodies could bring?

This question will be examined through an analysis of those provisions of both proposals which are dealing with the scope of competence of the two bodies, the regime proposed in both proposals regarding the exchange of information, and the legal requirements with regard to the requests that the EPPO, on the basis of the proposals, could address to and expect from Eurojust.

6.2 Scope of Competence of the EPPO and Eurojust

According to the EPPO proposal, the Office will have exclusive competence to tackle crimes against EU funds until the trial phase.[8] In other words, in cases where a criminal offence affects the EU's financial interests, the EPPO will be competent to investigate, prosecute and bring it to judgment, regardless of whether national interests are also involved. The intention of the proposal is to avoid parallel jurisdictions with regard to PIF offences. However, the division of tasks will be based on a weighing exercise,[9] with the EPPO being exclusively competent if the crime affecting EU's financial interests is the most significant factor of the offence. The EPPO's competence may be extended to other, though inextricably linked offences, but the decisions thereto will have to be made in consultation with the national authorities.[10]

[7] Article 57(6) of the EPPO proposal.

[8] Article 11(4) of the EPPO proposal.

[9] Article 13(1) of the EPPO proposal.

[10] Article 13(2) of the EPPO proposal.

In this respect two questions require further analysis with regard to the position of Eurojust: the impact of the EPPO's competence on Eurojust's role, and the role of Eurojust in the determination of the ancillary competence of the EPPO.

6.2.1 The Impact of the EPPO's Competence on Eurojust's Role

According to Annex 1 to the Eurojust proposal, crime against the financial interests of the Union is listed amongst the crimes for which Eurojust is competent for. At the same time, however, Article 3(1) of the same document excludes in principle Eurojust's competence *ratione materiae* in those crimes for which the EPPO is competent.[11] Considering that the EPPO shall be exclusively competent for crimes against EU's financial interests, this listing might seem like an error on drafters' part. But it only seems so at first sight.

As a preliminary remark, it must be stated that the roles and powers of Eurojust and of the EPPO cannot be compared. The EPPO will be competent to investigate, prosecute and bring a case to judgment before the national courts; it will thus exercise the competences normally exercised by the national competent authorities of the Member States. In contrast, Eurojust's role in supporting national authorities is more that of a mediator, called to support and strengthen coordination and cooperation between national investigating and prosecuting authorities.

Consequently the creation of the EPPO and the affirmation of its exclusive competence should mainly affect the competence *ratione materiae* of the national prosecuting authorities and not Eurojust's. In principle the impact on Eurojust's competence will only be indirect, which is the meaning of the statement contained in Article 3(1) of the Eurojust proposal. If Member States are not competent, then Eurojust, the statutory mission of which is to assist the Member States, would logically not be competent either.

However, this statement—according to which Eurojust's competence would be 'slavishly' attached to that of Member States and restricted in the same way by the creation of the EPPO—does not take into account the proposed new distribution of roles. In addition to the task given to Eurojust in supporting Member States, the two proposals on Eurojust and EPPO provide Eurojust with a new mandate, which is to support the activities of the EPPO, comprehensively from a functional and a structural point of view and, though to a lesser extent, also from an operational point of view.[12]

---

[11] Article 3(1) of the Eurojust proposal: 'Eurojust's competence shall cover the forms of crime listed in Annex 1. However, its competence shall not include the crimes for which the European Public Prosecutor's Office is competent'.

[12] Support provided by Eurojust to the EPPO consists among others in the determination of ancillary competence of the EPPO and responding to requests from the EPPO on specific acts, especially in the field of external relations; and a consultative role in issues of indictment and prosecution.

Overlooking the different roles and competences of parties involved in EU criminal law enforcement in general and PIF offences in particular, a new configuration, resembling a triangle formed by the Member States, the EPPO and Eurojust, emerges. Ideally, in this triangle, the new role given to Eurojust should be better reflected in the provisions of the Eurojust proposal devoted to the regulating of tasks, competences and operational functions and the way all three attributes are to be exercised.[13] However, such legal provisions clarifying these issues are lacking though would have provided an opportunity for spelling out how the new mandate given to Eurojust in providing operational support to the EPPO should be exercised.[14]

Given also the far-reaching role played by national competent authorities through the involvement of European Delegated Prosecutors, the combination of the various actors called to play a prosecutorial role in the future PIF landscape could be described by a division into three categories, helping to put the concept of exclusive competence of the EPPO in respect of investigation and prosecution of PIF crimes in a proper perspective:

1. In Member States not taking part in Eurojust nor in the EPPO, national authorities will continue to exercise their exclusive competence.
2. In Member States taking part in Eurojust and not taking part in the EPPO, national authorities will exercise their exclusive competence with the support of Eurojust.
3. In Member States participating both in Eurojust and the EPPO, the EPPO will exercise its competence with the support of the competent authorities of those Member States and with the support of Eurojust (except in those criminal cases where the national authorities will remain competent in accordance with the EPPO proposal).

Thus, contrary to what one might think at first reading, the issue of division of competences understood in terms of three (and not two) parties involved, comes as the primary remark. These parties, each of them endowed with their own competences, do constitute a triangle.

Secondly, it should be remarked that regarding the nature and extent of the intended exclusion of competence, EPPO's exclusive competence to investigate and prosecute as affirmed by Article 11(4) of the EPPO proposal is not absolute. The two proposals do not exclude the competence of Eurojust for the 'types' of crimes for which the EPPO will be competent, i.e. PIF crimes as provided for by the proposed PIF Directive[15] once they are implemented by national law. Article 3(1)

---

[13] Articles 2–5 of the Eurojust proposal.

[14] See infra, Sect. 6.3.2.2.

[15] Proposal for a Directive of the European Parliament and of the Council on the fight against fraud to the Union's financial interest by means of criminal law (COM (2012) 363 final) (2012/0193 (COD)), 11.7.2012.

of the Eurojust proposal[16] must be read in conjunction with other provisions[17] of both texts, from which the conclusion can be drawn that Eurojust will maintain competence in dealing with PIF crimes. The reasons for this conclusion are threefold.

The first reason is that EPPO shall be able to dismiss a case if the offence is minor according to national law implementing the PIF Directive.[18] The EPPO may refer such a case to OLAF or to competent national administrative or judicial authorities for recovery or administrative follow-up or monitoring.[19] The EPPO proposal does not indicate a possibility for the judicial authorities to 'inherit' such a case to ensure proper judicial follow-up. It is difficult to understand why the proposal does not clearly entrust national authorities with the possibility to investigate, prosecute and bring to judgment a case dismissed by the EPPO, should they consider taking such action with a view to avoid impunity. What type of actions regarding these cases could be authorised by national authorities, in particular judicial authorities, remain unclear. In any event, following such a referral to national authorities, Eurojust could be called to play its legally prescribed role in supporting and coordinating national authorities (although, the offence being by definition 'minor', it is rather unlikely that Eurojust would be called to assist).[20]

Secondly, Eurojust would maintain its competence in PIF cases through the provisions related to the EPPO's ancillary competence. If the conditions extending EPPO's competence to inextricably linked offences are not met, the Member State that is competent to prosecute those crimes shall also be competent for the PIF crimes in that particular case[21] (through an agreement between EPPO and the national prosecution authorities or, in case of disagreement, by a decision of the national judicial authority competent to decide). In such a situation Eurojust might be requested by the concerned Member States' authorities to assist in the case, and thus remain competent in the area of PIF crimes.

Thirdly, the non-participating Member States will maintain their competence in prosecuting PIF crimes and analogically their right to may request Eurojust to cooperate within that area.

In the light of the abovementioned arguments, it must be concluded that Annex I of the Eurojust proposal, which lists the crimes for which Eurojust will be competent, thus logically and correctly includes '[the crime] against the financial interests of the Union'. Article 3(1) of the Eurojust proposal must therefore be

---

16 See supra, n. 11.

17 These provisions will be dealt with in the paragraphs hereafter.

18 Article 28(2) of the EPPO proposal.

19 Article 28(3) of the EPPO proposal.

20 See recital 5 of the Eurojust proposal: 'Whilst the European Public Prosecutor's Office should have exclusive competence to investigate and prosecute crimes affecting the Union's financial interests, Eurojust should be able to support national authorities when they are investigating and prosecuting these forms of crime in accordance with the Regulation establishing the European Public Prosecutor's Office'.

21 Article 13(2) of the EPPO proposal.

interpreted as indicating that, with respect to the crimes (or part(s) of the crimes) for which the EPPO will not exercise its competence, Eurojust will exercise its own competence on request of a Member State or on its own initiative.

In conclusion, the Eurojust proposal could perhaps be improved by adding a reference to its new and important role of supporting the EPPO in addition to its primary role of assisting the Member States.[22] Similarly, the Eurojust's material scope of competence in relation to PIF crimes could be defined better by stating that, in cases in which the EPPO does not exercise its competence, Member States may request the assistance of Eurojust. It is thus suggested to amend the Eurojust proposal with a view to clarify the operational functions and powers of Eurojust in assisting the EPPO, so as to mirror the provisions of the EPPO proposal.

6.2.2 The Role of Eurojust in Determining EPPO's Ancillary Competence

The EPPO proposal provides, under certain conditions, for an extension of the competence of the Office to non-PIF crimes. Those crimes have, however, to be inextricably linked with the PIF offences and 'their joint investigation and prosecution [must be] in the interest of a good administration of justice'.[23] According to the Commission, the extension of the EPPO's competence to ancillary offences should not be seen as an attempt to circumvent the Treaty provision on the possible extension of EPPO competences to serious and cross-border crimes.[24] This contribution will, however, not discuss the compatibility with constitutional orthodoxy of that extension, but only the role of Eurojust in determining which authority should be competent to deal with cases in which PIF offences are connected to other offences.

Two conditions are foreseen for extending the competence of the EPPO to the other offence(s): the PIF offence must be preponderant, and additionally it must be based on identical facts as the 'other' criminal offence(s). If these conditions are not met, the Member State competent for the other offences shall also be competent for the PIF offences.[25] The procedure foreseen in the subsequent paragraphs[26] establishes a consultation requirement between the EPPO and the national prosecution authorities in order to determine which authority has competence. In case of

[22] Such change could be made in Articles 2–5 of the Eurojust proposal, which determine Eurojust's tasks, competence, operational functions and the way they are exercised,

[23] Article 13(1) of the EPPO proposal.

[24] Conclusions of the conference organised by the Lithuanian Presidency in cooperation with the European Commission and the Academy of European Law 'European Public Prosecutor's Office: A Constructive Approach towards the Legal Framework' (Vilnius, 16–17 September 2013), Doc. Council 13863/1, 13–14 October 2013, p. 9.

[25] Article 13(1) of the EPPO proposal.

[26] Articles 13(2) and 13(3) of the EPPO proposal.

disagreement, the decision shall be taken by the national judicial authority competent to decide on the attribution of competences concerning prosecution at national level. In any case, the 'determination' of competence shall not be subject to review. According to Article 13(2) of the EPPO proposal, Eurojust may be associated to the consultation procedure 'where appropriate'. In this respect two questions arise.

First: can the national competent authorities also request the assistance of Eurojust in this procedure? Article 13(2) of the Eurojust proposal specifies that Eurojust may be associated 'in accordance with Article 57'. Article 57(2)(c) of the EPPO proposal in that respect states that [the EPPO] may associate Eurojust by 'facilitating the agreement between the EPPO and the Member States concerned [...]'. Unlike other tasks foreseen in this paragraph the word 'request' is not used suggesting that the concerned Member State(s) could not ask for Eurojust to facilitate an agreement between them and EPPO. Clarification in that respect would be useful and, in doing so, indicating that Member States may also request the assistance of Eurojust.

Second: should Eurojust's opinion, prompted by a request for assistance in determining the ancillary competence addressed by the EPPO, be given by the concerned National Member(s) of Eurojust or by its College? According to Article 5(2)(a)(ii),[27] Eurojust shall act as a College 'when the case involves investigations or prosecutions which have repercussions at Union level or which might affect Member States other than those directly concerned'. On the one hand, it could be argued that determining the ancillary competence of a Union body already entrusted with far reaching powers is a sensitive and complicated matter. It may not just lead up to extending its powers in a specific case, but could affect other Member States. Additionally, it could create a precedent thereby (implicitly) extending its powers over time. Such a task should be dealt with by the College ensuring that all National Members are involved in the consultations. This might lead to the conclusion that such opinion should be an action taken by the College. On the other hand, the College will also comprise National Members from non-participating Member States. Their participation in the adoption of EPPO-related opinion, given their lack of involvement in the Office, could raise serious questions.

6.3 Operational Cooperation

Having considered the scope of competence of the two agencies and concluded that in some instances they will interfere, it is now necessary to analyse the mode of this interference, namely the operational cooperation. The fields of cooperation between the two bodies as envisaged by the draft regulations concern the exchange of information, including personal data, the possibility for the EPPO to request the

[27] Article 5(2) of the Eurojust proposal.

assistance of Eurojust regarding acts falling outside the material or geographical scope of its own competence, as well as the facilitation of mutual legal assistance (MLA) with Member States non-participating in the EPPO. The key provisions are Article 41 of the Eurojust proposal and Article 57 of the EPPO proposal. To a large extent both articles complement and mirror each other, although not completely.

6.3.1 Exchange of Information

In addition to the provisions on the exchange of information between the EPPO and other EU bodies, as well as international organisations and the competent authorities of third States,[28] the EPPO proposal entails specific provisions concerning its relationship with Eurojust: like any other national or EU body, Eurojust has the obligation to inform the EPPO immediately of any possible offences falling within the scope of its competence.[29] Furthermore, for the purpose of its investigations, the EPPO can request and obtain from Eurojust (as well as from Europol) any relevant information concerning an offence within its competence.[30] Both draft regulations insist on the exchange of information, including personal data, between the EPPO and Eurojust, under certain conditions.[31] The EPPO may share information on decisions relating to the bringing to judgment or dismissal of a case and transaction, before submission to the EPP, 'where Eurojust's competences may be affected and this is appropriate in the light of Eurojust's previous involvement in the case'.[32] The sharing of information between both bodies would be facilitated, from an operational point of view, by the alignment of the data protection regime and supervision scheme of the EPPO to that of Eurojust and by granting the EPPO access to a mechanism for automatic cross-checking of data inserted in Eurojust's Case Management System (CMS). These two aspects merit further exploration from the point of view of data protection, as well as the sensitivity of data exchanged through the CMS.

6.3.1.1 Data Protection

The right to protection of personal data is explicitly recognised by the European Union's Charter of Fundamental Rights.[33] Additionally, the TFEU provides rules on data protection for all activities within the scope of EU law. Article 16 TFEU

---

28 Article 56 of the EPPO proposal.

29 Article 15(1) of the EPPO proposal.

30 Article 21(1) of the EPPO proposal.

31 Article 41(4) of the Eurojust proposal and Article 57(4) EPPO proposal.

32 Article 57(2)(e) of the EPPO proposal.

33 Article 8 of the European Union's Charter of Fundamental Rights.

affirms the right of each person to the protection of his personal data and stipulates that European institutions and bodies shall protect personal data. Naturally the EPPO constitutes no exception to that rule.

Both legislative proposals[34] provide for the application of Regulation 45/2001[35] to the two bodies. This instrument regulates the processing of personal data carried out by—Community—institutions and bodies in the exercise of their activities within the scope of Community law (*ex* 'first pillar') and was therefore not made applicable yet to Eurojust. The data protection regime of Eurojust is currently governed by a set of data protection provisions that have been complemented by the Rules of Procedure on the Processing and Protection of Personal Data at Eurojust, implementing and further specifying the principles of the Council of Europe Convention.[36]

Regulation 45/2001 established also the European Data Protection Supervisor (EDPS) as an independent supervisory authority with the responsibility to monitor the processing of personal data by the (former) Community institutions and bodies. Since this Regulation was not applicable to Eurojust, created as a 'third pillar' body, neither was EDPS competent for it; and it still is not at present. Nevertheless, the EDPS should become competent for both Eurojust and the EPPO, if the Proposals are adopted.

The Eurojust and EPPO proposals repeat the Eurojust rules on data protection, but provide also that they should only particularise the processing of data—in principle governed by Regulation 45/2001—as far as operational personal data are concerned.

Such a combination of rules is likely to create important difficulties in practice. The application of Regulation 45/2001 could seriously impede the speed and efficiency of the operational support that Eurojust offers to national judicial authorities. For example, requirements like the consent of the 'data subject' as a legal ground for processing personal data, or the right of the 'data subject' to object such processing are hardly imaginable in the context of police and justice operations. Therefore, consideration should be given to restricting the application of Regulation 45/2001 to administrative processing operations, and regulating the issue of case-related data processing operations entirely in the new Eurojust regulation. Such an amendment could be made in conformity with the Commission proposal for a regulation on Europol.[37] The Europol proposal restricts the application of Regulation 45/2001 to the personal data of Europol 'staff members' and 'administrative

[34] Article 37(5) of the EPPO proposal; Article 27(5) of the Eurojust proposal.

[35] Regulation (EC) 45/2001 of 18 December 2000 on the protection of individuals with regard to the processing of personal data by the Community institutions and bodies and on the free movement of such data, *OJ* L 8, 12.01.2001, p. 1.

[36] Council of Europe Convention of 28.1.1981 for the Protection of Individuals with regard to Automatic Processing of Personal Data.

[37] Article 28 of the Proposal for a Regulation of the European Parliament and of the Council on the European Union Agency for Law Enforcement Cooperation and Training (Europol) and repealing Decisions 2009/371/JHA and 2005/681/JHA (COM (2013) 173 final), 27.3.2013, hereinafter the 'Europol proposal'.

personal data', which means[38] that all personal data are processed separately from those that are processed to meet its operational objectives. According to our understanding, there is no need to take an approach different to the one as adopted by the Commission in its proposal on Eurojust.

The same reasoning applies even more, in the opinion of this author, to the EPPO and the operational, investigative, as well as prosecutorial tasks it will be called to exercise. Unless it is revised, with a view to provide exceptions to certain provisions on the law enforcement sector, or unless clear derogations are introduced in the EPPO proposal, Regulation 45/2001 does not seem to provide a suitable set of rules applicable to the processing of case-related data by the EPPO.[39]

6.3.1.2 Case Management System

The Case Management System (CMS) of Eurojust and its temporary work files (TWF) shall be made available to the EPPO.[40] According to the Commission Communication on the Protection of the Union's financial interests and the Reform of Eurojust,[41] the permission to be given to the EPPO to use Eurojust's IT infrastructure, including its CMS and TWF, is justified by potential cost savings. Recital 14 of the EPPO proposal ambiguously states that 'the data processing system of the EPPO should build on the CMS of Eurojust, but its temporary work files should be considered case-files from the time an investigation is initiated'. Furthermore, Article 22(1) of the EPPO proposal states that 'the EPPO shall establish a CMS composed of temporary work files and of an index which contain personal data as referred to in the Annex and non-personal data'. According to Article 24 of the proposal, the European delegated prosecutors and their staff shall have access to the CMS and the TWF.

Whether the two entities will actually use the same CMS is difficult to ascertain from these provisions. If so, special features would need to be put in place to guarantee proper protection of the data entered. As an alternative, only the software developed by Eurojust over the years will be used for creating and developing a new CMS for the EPPO. Both options could be envisaged from a technical point of

38 In accordance with Article 2(o) of the Europol proposal.

39 It should be mentioned that the Framework Decision 2008/977/JHA of 27 November 2008 on the protection of personal data processed in the framework of police and judicial cooperation in criminal matters (*OJ* L 350/60, 30.12.2008) regulates the protection of personal data in the field of police and judicial cooperation in criminal matters and is for the time being only applicable to the transfer of data between competent authorities in the Member States.

40 Article 24(8) of the Eurojust proposal provides that 'The provisions on access to the Case Management System and the temporary work files shall apply mutatis mutandis to the European Public Prosecutor's Office. However, the information entered into the Case Management System, temporary work files and the index by the European Public Prosecutor's Office shall not be available for access at the national level'.

41 'Better protection of the Union's financial interests: Setting up the European Public Prosecutor's Office and reforming Eurojust' (COM (2013) 532 final, 17.7.2013).

view and both could achieve the same results, i.e. provide secure databases that would in principle be technically impenetrable and accessible only for the post-holders of the other entity, based on a proper legal basis, and formed in accordance with principles of confidentiality and data protection. Strategically, the second option, consisting of a separate system using the same technology, would probably be preferable, as it would appear to offer more guarantees to information providers.

Furthermore, the two draft regulations provide that Eurojust shall put in place a mechanism for automatic cross-checking of data entered in the CMS to find matches between data entered by the EPPO and data entered by Eurojust.[42] This provision raises concerns as to the negative impact such automatic cross-checking of Eurojust data could have on the exchange of sensitive information between Eurojust and the competent national or EU authorities. Those authorities might show reluctance towards the exchange of sensitive information with Eurojust since this could automatically provide EPPO with access to it. This risk would most probably occur in cases where it is compulsory for judicial authorities to exchange certain types of information with Eurojust.[43]

This mechanism of automatic cross-checking goes well beyond the system introduced by the Commission in both draft regulations on Eurojust and Europol, which does not provide for an automatic cross-checking of data, but for an indirect access on the basis of a hit/no hit of wanted data. This indirect access respects the restrictions indicated by the owner of the information and especially those as provided for by other suppliers of these data to Eurojust.[44] Therefore, a system of indirect access would preferable also be set up between the EPPO and Eurojust as it would give the information supplier more solid guarantees on the possible use of the information provided to another organisation. Receiving the information from its partners would consequently be less likely to negatively impact the trust put in that organisation.

6.3.2 EPPO's Requests to Eurojust in Relation to Specific Acts Outside Its Competence and Mutual Legal Assistance with Non-EPPO States

Besides the exchanging of information between Eurojust and the EPPO, other forms of operational support may also be provided by Eurojust to the EPPO. However, such support is of a limited nature and could only be triggered by a request of the

42 Article 41(5) of the Eurojust proposal mirroring Article 57(3) of the EPPO proposal.

43 Such obligations are provided for e.g. in Article 13 of the Eurojust decision, a provision that is further reinforced by Article 21 of the Eurojust proposal. That provision enumerates situations in which national authorities are obliged to inform Eurojust, even if they do not require assistance from Eurojust, such as the emergence of serious cases in which at least three Member States are involved or the setting up of joint investigation teams or organising controlled deliveries affecting three countries (comprising at least two Member States).

44 See Article 40 of the Eurojust proposal and Article 27 of the Europol proposal.

EPPO. According to both legislative proposals the requesting of assistance by the EPPO (beyond the exchange of information) is exclusively foreseen in three instances (a) in cases in which the EPPO, due to the limitations of its geographical and material competence, cannot act,[45] (b) in cases where a benefit can be derived from agreements with third States already concluded by Eurojust[46] and finally with regard to the transmission of EPPO decisions to specific third parties.[47]

The transmission of EPPO decisions must also be read in combination with Article 41(3) of the Eurojust proposal, stipulating that—with a view to the special relationship between Eurojust and the EPPO—Eurojust shall make use of its agreements with third States and its liaison magistrates in order to support cooperation of the EPPO with third States.

Regrettably, the proposals do not exploit more ambitiously the potential benefit that the EPPO could gain from the expertise, experience and tools developed by Eurojust over the last decade in the field of judicial coordination and cooperation in criminal matters. The EPPO may request 'Eurojust or its competent national member(s)' to participate in the coordination or to use its powers, but it is only for 'specific' acts regarding 'specific' aspects which are falling outside its material or territorial competence.

Nevertheless, the aforementioned provisions do raise a few questions. Namely what real added value could Eurojust bring to the EPPO in the field of external relations? Which actual situations referred to in the proposals can prompt a request from EPPO to Eurojust? What will be the exact status of such an EPPO's request? Who shall issue the request and to whom? And finally, who should be responsible for responding the request? The following paragraphs will attempt to answer those questions.

6.3.2.1 External Relations

The importance of EPPO's relations with third States must not be underestimated in quantitative terms, given the significant amount of financial resources spent by the

[45] Article 57(2)(b) of the EPPO proposal: 'requesting Eurojust or its competent national member (s) to participate in the coordination of specific acts of investigation regarding specific aspects which may fall outside the material or territorial competence of the European Public Prosecutor's Office;'

[46] Article 57(2)(d) of the EPPO proposal: 'requesting Eurojust or its competent national member (s) to use the powers attributed to them by Union legislation or national law regarding specific acts of investigation which may fall outside the material or territorial competence of the European Public Prosecutor's Office'.

[47] Article 57(2)(f) of the EPPO proposal: 'requesting Eurojust or its competent national member (s) to provide support in the transmission of its decisions or requests for mutual legal assistance to, and execution in, States members of Eurojust but not taking part in the establishment of the European Public Prosecutor's Office or third countries'. Actually, while referring to 'States members of Eurojust but not taking part in the establishment of the EPPO', this appears to be the single one provision in the EPPO proposal implying that the EPPO might be established on the basis of an 'enhanced cooperation' framework.

European Union outside its borders 'to make Europe count in the world'.[48] The Multi-annual EU budget for 2014–2020 in the area of external action provides for a global amount of EUR 92.980 billion, to cover a full range of external support under the EU budget in the field of development and cooperation.[49] This creates multiple possibilities for crimes against EU's financial interests being committed also outside its borders.

When EU subsidies are fraudulently diverted by non-EU nationals to a third State, the investigation and prosecution can in principle only be conducted by the third State's authorities. But even if EU nationals are involved, assistance of the third State's authorities will be needed. Efficient cooperation with third States is therefore a key factor in ensuring the overall effectiveness of the EPPO's actions.

Under the Lisbon Treaty, the procedures for concluding agreements with third parties have been put on a new footing. Whilst Eurojust, like any other EU Justice and Home Affairs body, can—under its current legal framework—negotiate and conclude agreements with third States and international organisations with the goal of, *inter alia*, exchanging information, Article 218 TFEU prescribes that any cooperation agreement between the European Union and a third State or international organisation shall be concluded by the Council following the procedure defined in that article.

This new principle has been transposed into both proposals, providing very similar rules on external relations. The proposals provide that the transfer of information, including personal data, to an authority of a third State or an international organisation can only take place on the basis of a decision of the European Commission stating that that third party ensures an adequate level of data protection ('adequacy decision') or on the basis of an agreement between the European Union and that third State or international organisation, 'adducing adequate safeguards with respect to the protection of privacy and fundamental rights and freedoms of individuals'.[50]

However, under certain conditions may be derogated form these main new rules on concluding international agreements. First, by way of a transitional arrangement, Eurojust may uphold its international agreements already concluded prior to the entry into force of the new Eurojust regulation. These agreements remain legally valid.[51] Secondly, and only on a case by case basis, under certain pressing conditions derogatory rules are foreseen regarding the transfer of personal data to third

---

[48] Remarks by President Barroso on the Commission's proposals for the 2014–2020 Multi-Annual Financial Framework on 29 June 2011. SPEECH/11/487 http://europa.eu/rapid/press-release_SPEECH-11-487_en.htm.

[49] See the Multiannual Financial Framework adopted on 2 December 2013: the Heading 'Global Europe' covers all external action ('foreign policy') by the EU such as development assistance or humanitarian aid. The total amount indicated is at 2011 prices and, in addition to the EUR 58.704 billion designated for Global Europe in the Multiannual Financial Framework, includes the EUR 34.276 billion for the European Development Fund, outside the EU budget.

[50] Article 61 of the EPPO proposal and Article 45 of the Eurojust proposal.

[51] Articles 66(5) (on transitional arrangements) of the Eurojust proposal.

countries or international organisations.[52] Thirdly, the possibility remains for the EPPO and Eurojust to conclude working arrangements to implement the international agreements concluded by the European Union.[53] Finally, the Eurojust proposal maintains the possibility for Eurojust to designate contact points in third States for the purpose of facilitating cooperation; such possibility will also be offered to the EPPO.[54]

At the same time, some divergences between the two proposals must be noted. The Eurojust proposal no longer includes an explicit reference (provided for in the current Eurojust decision) to the possibility for third States to second liaison magistrates to Eurojust, while the posting of liaison officers by third States and international organisations to the EPPO is foreseen.[55] Conversely, the EPPO is not granted the possibility to post liaison magistrates to third States by the EPPO proposal, whilst such possibility, introduced in the Eurojust decision by the 2009 reform but not yet implemented by Eurojust, remains in the Eurojust proposal. Moreover, the EPPO proposal opens two major and daring avenues with regard to the external relations of the EPPO which, if adopted and implemented, will endow the EPPO with powerful tools in the exercise of its mandate regarding fraud committed outside the borders of the European Union. First, on the basis of Article 218 TFEU, specific agreements may be concluded between third States and the EPPO regarding cooperation in mutual legal assistance and extradition in cases falling under the competence of the EPPO.[56] Secondly, the EPPO proposal obliges Member States to recognise either the EPPO—within the remit of its material competence—as a competent authority for the purpose of the implementation of their international MLA and extradition agreements or, 'where necessary', to alter those agreements to ensure that the EPPO can exercise its functions on the basis of those agreements.[57]

In summary, the EPPO draft regulation as it stands now, provides the Office with a possibility to establish its own network of contact points in third States, facilitating cooperation with liaison officers and, at the same time, providing them with a privileged status. All on the basis of international agreements to be concluded by the European Union with the concerned third States. Therefore, it seems that Eurojust can provide very little added value in terms of cooperation with third States. With one exception, however. The cooperation agreements already concluded by Eurojust, as well as the Eurojust liaison magistrates, are not at the EPPO's disposal in the field of external relations. These tools could possibly enable Eurojust to assist the EPPO in its relations with third States. In addition, and certainly in the initial

[52] Articles 42(2) and 42(3) of the Eurojust proposal; Articles 61(2) and 61(3) of the EPPO proposal.

[53] Article 45(1) *in fine* of the Eurojust proposal; Article 61(1) *in fine* of the EPPO proposal.

[54] Article 43(2) of the Eurojust proposal; Article 59(2) of the EPPO proposal.

[55] Article 59(1) of the EPPO proposal.

[56] Article 59(3) of the EPPO proposal.

[57] Article 59(4) of the EPPO proposal.

phase of its existence, the EPPO should also benefit from the experience and expertise built up by Eurojust over the years in dealing with third States and from the trust it has acquired in its relations with third parties.

6.3.2.2 Status of the EPPO's Requests

The Eurojust proposal stipulates that Eurojust shall treat any request from the EPPO without undue delay and as if it had been received from a competent national authority.[58] Participants to the Eurojust seminar on the new Eurojust proposal have taken the view that a request from the EPPO to Eurojust must not be understood as an order, and that Eurojust must have the possibility to refuse to comply with the EPPO's request, if it has good reasons to do so, in the same way that Eurojust can refuse to execute a request addressed by a competent authority of a Member State. Two arguments were expressed to ground such opinion. The first one is that a request is by nature not binding. Secondly, Articles 85 and 86 TFEU represent two complementary models. The model set up by Article 85 for Eurojust is a horizontal cooperation model in which the EPPO's role would be more akin to that of a national competent authority than to that of a hierarchically superior entity.[59]

A subsequent issue pertains to the question through which mechanism such requests has to be dealt with by Eurojust. Article 4 of the Eurojust proposal defines the operational functions of Eurojust. Subsequently, Article 5 defines whether these functions will be. exercised by Eurojust acting through one or more National Members, or as a College. To which category would a request for assistance issued by the EPPO belong? According to Article 5, Eurojust shall act through one or more of the National Members concerned when taking action referred to in Article 4(1) or (2). It shall act as a College when taking action referred to in Article 4(1) or (2) if so requested by one or more National Members concerned, or when the case involves investigations or prosecutions that have repercussions at EU level, or that might affect Member States other than those directly concerned.

Since the support offered by Eurojust to the EPPO has not been envisaged as a new major task for Eurojust, Article 5 is silent as to which category requests from the EPPO would belong. Article 57(2)(c) of the EPPO proposal stipulates that the EPPO requests shall be addressed to 'Eurojust or its competent national members (s)'. This wording is not entirely in line with the Eurojust proposal, which abolishes the notion of 'powers exercised by National Members as national authorities' and exclusively envisages tasks exercised by Eurojust (acting either through its National Members or as a College).[60] Any request addressed by the EPPO should therefore

---

[58] Article 41(2) of the Eurojust proposal.

[59] See Conclusions of Workshop IV of the seminar, 'The new Eurojust Proposal: an Improvement in the fight against cross-border crime?' (The Hague, 14–15 October 2013), Doc. Council 17188/1/13 REV 1, 4 December 2013, p. 39.

[60] Articles 5(1) and 5(2) of the Eurojust proposal.

be addressed to Eurojust and Eurojust should have the discretion to evaluate, on a case-by-case basis, whether it will respond to it acting through its National Member (s) concerned or as a College.[61]

6.3.3 Sharing of the EPPO's Prosecution Decisions: Information or Consultation?

According to the EPPO proposal the European Public Prosecutor shall be conferred three different options to decide on a completed criminal investigation. He or she shall decide either to bring the case to judgment, to dismiss it, or to propose a transaction.[62] If the European Public Prosecutor opts for an indictment, he or she shall, in close cooperation with the European Delegated Prosecutor(s), choose the jurisdiction of the trial and determine the competent national court, taking into account the criteria set out in Article 27(4). The EPPO shall, 'where necessary for the purposes of recovery, administrative follow-up or monitoring', notify the competent national authorities and EU bodies, including Eurojust, about the indictment.[63]

At the same time the EPPO proposal contains an interesting provision, according to which information regarding prosecution decisions (indictment, dismissal or transaction) may be shared with Eurojust previously to their submittal to the European Public Prosecutor 'where Eurojust competences may be affected and this is appropriate in the light of Eurojust's previous involvement in the case'.[64] The information should be shared with 'Eurojust or its competent national members...'. However, as has been mentioned before,[65] the role of national members acting as national authorities has been abolished in the Eurojust proposal and thus, it is such information should be addressed to Eurojust rather than to the National Member(s) concerned only.

On the other hand the wording, full of precautionary language ('may share', 'may affect', 'where appropriate'), and the timing of the sharing of information suggests that, despite a mere reference to information, the intention of the drafters was in fact to provide an opportunity to consult Eurojust before the decision is formalised and submitted to the European Public Prosecutor. This and the fact that, according to Article 57(2)(e) this shall take place where 'Eurojust competences may be affected [...] in the light of Eurojust's previous involvement' could lead to a conclusion that the purpose is not only to consult Eurojust, but also to enable it to propose alternative solutions.

---

[61] This question is already raised in Sect. 6.2.

[62] Articles 27–29 of the EPPO proposal.

[63] Article 27(5) of the EPPO proposal.

[64] Article 57(2)(e) of the EPPO proposal.

[65] See Sect. 6.3.2.2.

6.3.4 Example

In practical terms, the operational cooperation envisaged between the EPPO and Eurojust could be illustrated by the following hypothetical scenario.

An investigation related to a large fraud case involving Belgium and France (assuming their participation in EPPO) reveals suspicions of facts that consist of both PIF offences as well as other types of offences not falling within the scope of competence of the EPPO. The EPPO, considering that the offences are inextricably linked, consults the French and Belgian national authorities in order to determine whether the PIF offences are predominant. The EPPO may involve Eurojust in order to facilitate an agreement. The concerned authorities agree that the PIF offences are preponderant and that, consequently, the EPPO is competent to investigate and prosecute the case. Subsequently, in the course of their investigations, French and Belgian Delegated Prosecutors discover connections with the UK (assuming its non-participation in EPPO, but participation in Eurojust), Israel and the USA. EPPO could exchange information with Eurojust on these links. Additionally, the EPPO will probably have a contact point or an agreement with the UK authorities to which it will ask for information and assistance. In addition, and where appropriate, it could also ask Eurojust to facilitate and coordinate the exchange of information with the UK authorities, as well as to use its powers to execute investigative acts addressed to the UK authorities (house searches, arrests, hearings, execution of EAWs). The EPPO could also request Eurojust to use its contact point in Israel to obtain information on mutual legal assistance; or it could use Eurojust's privileged contacts with the USA: the Eurojust-US agreement and the US liaison prosecutor seconded to Eurojust.[66]

6.4 Conclusions

The legislative proposals on the EPPO and on Eurojust undeniably reflect the wish of the European legislator to link the creation of the EPPO with the further development of Eurojust. The Commission's vision seems, however, not to be that Eurojust should develop into the EPPO—as one could have expected and hoped—but rather that the two bodies should coexist, side by side, and so to say 'get married'—for better or for worse.

This approach is particularly clear regarding the functional support expected from Eurojust, since the objective here is unmistakably to ensure economies of scale, avoid duplication and achieve cost efficiency. Although the EPPO is envisaged as a separate legal entity—*indépendance oblige*—in the Commission's view it

---

[66] Subject to implementation of Article 59 of the EPPO proposal, i.e. the recognition of the EPPO as competent authority under an international agreement or alteration of such agreement.

should nevertheless hugely rely on the support and resources of Eurojust's administration for its vital needs.

The operational cooperation between the two bodies on the other hand has been envisaged by the Commission in a minimalist fashion, i.e. only with a view to compensate the limitations of EPPO's competence, that will be much narrower than Eurojust's, both *ratione materiae* and, most probably, *ratione loci*. However, since a large range of facilities, powers and connections available to EPPO through its entrenchment in the national systems will make it highly 'self-sufficient', only some investigations and prosecutions will require acts exceeding its material and geographical scope of competence.

The Commission has regrettably not envisaged a closer cooperation, where the EPPO could benefit from Eurojust's operational role, as well as its well established facilities in the field of judicial cooperation.

The Commission's interpretation of TFEU's Article 86 predicate resembles a marriage of convenience (defined by the Oxford Dictionary as 'a marriage that is arranged for practical, financial, or political reasons'). Undoubtedly such arrangement could be a good basis for long and peaceful life together. Over the course of time, it might even turn out to be a love marriage.

Part III
Administrative Structure, Judicial Review and Jurisdiction

Chapter 7
Some Explorations into the EPPO's Administrative Structure and Judicial Review

Arjen Meij

Abstract The Commission proposal for an EPPO purports to establish an intricate structure of multilevel administration of justice in that it seeks to centralise and at the same time decentralise the novel prosecutorial function for the EU. Fragmentation of the substantive and procedural provisions in various legal instruments among divergent national systems is bound to give rise to shortcomings in the appropriate protection of citizen's rights. Legitimation derived from the role of national courts is profoundly ambiguous, to the extent that the obvious risks of forum competition and output incoherencies are generally recognised. The EU courts provide the effective remedy required by the principle of the rule of law, an individual is entitled to as against acts of EU bodies. The mere reference in Article 86 TFEU to the possibility to adopt rules applicable to judicial review, does not imply a power to set aside the entire Treaty system of judicial protection. The effort to restrict the preliminary jurisdiction of the ECJ introduces an arbitrariness which does not correspond to prevailing perceptions of the EU legal order as based on the rule of law. The unprecedented system of judicial protection in national courts as against acts of a single, integrated EU body raises questions of consistency in the light of the general pattern of coherent judicial protection in the refined multilevel court system of the EU.

Keywords Access to court · Attributed powers · Coherent judicial protection · Criminal justice · Democratic or institutional legitimation · Double-hatted delegated prosecutor · European Public Prosecutor's Office · Institutional autonomy · Judicial review · Legality requirements · Integrated administration · Shared administration · 255 panel

---

Arjen W.H. Meij, former Judge at the General Court of the EU, is at the time of writing Visiting Research Fellow at the T.M.C. Asser Instituut, Guest Professor at the University of Luxembourg and Honorary Professor at Utrecht University.

A. Meij (✉)
T.M.C. Asser Instituut, The Hague, The Netherlands
e-mail: a.meij@asser.nl

L.H. Erkelens et al. (eds.), *The European Public Prosecutor's Office*,
DOI 10.1007/978-94-6265-035-0_7

Contents

7.1 Introduction

The Commission's proposal for a European Public Prosecutor's Office enters relatively new substance territory in view of the creation of a fresh EU body with limited, albeit within their scope far reaching powers in the area of criminal justice. It may not come as a surprise, therefore, that the proposal does not shy away from charting new avenues to connect EU and national levels of administration and jurisdiction. Even so, from an EU law generalist's perspective, it looks like a wonderland of institutional imagination and, at the same time, a roller coaster occasionally coming close to a constitutional shipwreck.

Article 86 of the TFEU itself turns common images of multilevel administration in the EU and entailing judicial functions upside down where it provides for a European Public Prosecutor (EPP) exercising its prosecutorial functions in the competent courts of the Member States. Indeed, ways and means of implementing and administering EU policies as shared between the Union and its Member States may be multiple and diverse. However, a constant common feature seems to be that judicial review of EU decisions directly (and individually) affecting individuals lies with the EU courts. A legal action affecting an individual more directly than prosecution is hardly conceivable. Admittedly, prosecution in a criminal court is not the same as an application for judicial review in an administrative court. Still, even if the legal substance, the procedural concept, the initiative as well as the judicial function in both types of proceedings referred to may be different, from an EU constitutional point of view it remains hard to imagine that an EU body needs to bring its (EU) cases in various national courts under diverse rules of criminal procedure. Setting up a Union body for the prosecution at Union level in cases of Union interest in the variable environment of national courts appears to be a *contradictio in terminis*. It may well be that the creation of a complete criminal court system at EU level, did not look particularly appealing to the authors of Article 86 for various reasons. Also, clearly, as in other areas, in this particular subject-matter the Union cannot do without relying in several respects on the services of the Member States. This does not mean, however, that the solution presently laid down in Article 86 as regards the competent trial courts is the most appropriate. However this may be, even if the conception of Article 86 sheds some light—or shadow, depending on the perspective—on the choices made in the proposal implementing this provision, the purpose of this chapter is not to discuss this Treaty provision.

The proposal, then, is equally innovative to the extent that it seeks to centralise and, at the same time, decentralise the novel prosecutorial function for the EU and in doing so couples EU and national authorities in an unprecedented manner. It is not unusual for Member States' administrations to participate in the implementation and application of the Union's policies or to facilitate the achievement of the Union's tasks, as follows from the principle of sincere cooperation enshrined in Article 4(3) TEU. The duty of sincere cooperation, however, addresses the Member States, usually leaving it to their own constitutional systems to determine the internal distribution of powers and obligations to that effect.[1] This approach has become known as the principle of national institutional autonomy. In the present proposal each participating Member State shall have at least one of its national prosecutors appointed as European Delegated Prosecutor (EDP). This national official is not only appointed as EDP by the EPP, but also acts under the EPP's exclusive authority.[2] The proposal purports to establish an intricate structure of multilevel administration of justice in that it provides for an independent office on the Union level which in itself consists of a multilevel structure. Indeed, each Member State may submit a shortlist of three candidates for appointment as an EDP, but according to the proposed provisions the Member State must make sure that the appointee is at the same time a national prosecutor. The provisions of Article 6 of the EPPO proposal in particular raise issues of legal qualification which may impact the transparency, the accountability and the justiciability of the EPPO's operations.

A key element in respect of transparent division of competences and responsibilities becomes manifest in the light of recent developments as regards fundamental rights protection. Since the entry into force of the EU Charter of Fundamental Rights any EU action of legal consequence is subject to an autonomous regime of fundamental rights, alongside the ECHR and the constitutional traditions of the Member States, as Article 6 TEU has it. As a consequence any form of an EPPO—to whichever extent it may be (de)centralised or conceived in a cooperative model with Member States' prosecution services—acts under the full range of fundamental rights provided for by virtue of Article 6 of the TEU. The EPPO proposal expressly refers to the Charter in several instances: in Article 11(1),

[1] Cf. e.g. Case C-8/88, Germany v Commission.

[2] Articles 6, para 5 and 10, paras 1–2 of the EPPO proposal.

as a basic principle to be ensured in its activities, and again in its fourth chapter on procedural safeguards, where various procedural rights also provided for in the Charter are spelled out for the purposes of investigation and prosecution, by reference to the relevant EU directives and more generally to the applicable national laws.

Article 51 of the Charter specifies that it addresses not only the institutions but also the bodies, offices and agencies of the Union, thus anyhow including the EPPO. As regards the Member States the wording of Article 51 to the effect that the Charter applies 'only when they are implementing Union law', has been reset in the Åkerberg case to refer to 'all situations governed by EU law', thus 'binding the Member States when they act in the scope of Union law', as the judgment has it with reference to the explanations relating to Article 51 of the Charter.[3] Even if the Åkerberg case law is assumed to be broad enough to cover any EPPO-related action, the question creeps up for instance of whether or not a police action following the applicable national rules of criminal procedure and carried out upon instruction of a national prosecutor who is on the verge of initiating in the same case an investigation in the capacity of EDP, must be deemed to be governed by EU law in the sense of Åkerberg.

It is somehow reassuring that the vehicle of an EPPO, including its (EDP) trailers of various national origins, will not travel anywhere without the Charter of Fundamental Rights coming along, eventually even with the ECtHR in the backseat. However, piling up layers of fundamental rights instruments, on the one hand, and executive 'hats' of different levels, on the other, may not necessarily be helpful from a point of view of delimitation of powers and responsibilities within an EPPO framework, neither apt to avoid subsequent ambiguity in terms of legal protection. Key issues of fundamental rights' protection are therefore in the transparency of an EPPO's organisation and procedures, as well as in the conception of the ensuing judicial review of its activity.

Given the complex and innovative structure of the proposed EPPO, it would appear appropriate first to explore tentatively how the proposal relates to fundamental principles governing the exercise of administrative authority. The meaning of such principles, e.g. of legality and of conferral of powers, for the proposal as well as elementary notions of sharing jurisdiction through mechanisms of delegation and mandate will be analysed against the backdrop of existing conceptions of administrative structures characterising the implementation of EU law and policies so far (Sect. 7.2).

In this connection, subsequently, the issue arises of how the fundamental principle of a fair trial, including transparent access to court, is guaranteed in such a complex multilevel structure, essentially concerned with far reaching powers in

[3] Judgment of 26 February 2013 in Case C-617/10, Åkerberg Fransson, pts. 19–20. The question whether the right to good administration, provided for in Article 41 of the Charter specifically in respect of the institutions, bodies, offices and agencies of the Union, also applies to the Member States implementing EU law, is pending in Case C-372/12, referred by the Council of State of the Netherlands.

respect of individuals. The artificial transformation, in Article 36 of the proposal, of the EPPO in a national authority for the purposes of judicial review raises questions in this regard and more generally on how the proposal fits into the current EU system of coherent judicial protection as conceived since the Lisbon Treaty and shared between the EU courts and the Member States' courts (Sect. 7.3).

7.2 An Unprecedented Structure

7.2.1 Legality Requirements

In spite of the important movements over the past decades of broadening and deepening of the integration process—including the administration of criminal justice—the EU has remained an international organisation as between states and as such is firmly based on the principle of conferral of competences, reaffirmed in Article 5, paras 1 and 2, and further specified in Article 13, para 2, TEU for the exercise by the institutions of the powers conferred on them. It would appear essential, therefore, that a legislative act providing such far reaching powers of investigation and prosecution as the present proposal, defines these powers with utmost clarity. In so far, the principle of conferral may be seen as an expression of the legality principle underlying any exercise of public authority in a rule of law-based system of government.

The late Advocate General Geelhoed distinguished two aspects of a legislative act as an expression of the legislature's will in a community of law, such as the European Union. On the one hand, a legislative act is an instrument to pursue justified objectives of public interest and, on the other, it constitutes a guarantee of citizens' rights in their dealing with public authority. In his view, its wording and structure must strike an acceptable balance between the powers granted to the implementing authorities and the guarantees granted to citizens.[4] For the purposes of the present proposal, the question then is how such a balance is ensured in a multilevel construction as proposed. The legality principle, in this context, is generally assumed to embrace, on top of the attributive function contained in the above-mentioned principle of conferral, a role of legitimating as well as one of regulating the conferred powers.[5] The nature of the proposal as an instrument of criminal prosecution imposes an additional requirement of foreseeability.[6]

[4] Opinion of April 5, 2005 in Joined Cases C-154 and 155/04, Alliance for Natural Health, pt. 88.

[5] Cf. Verhoeven and Widdershoven 2011, at p. 58. See also Besselink et al. 2011 at p. 6 *et seq*.

[6] Cf. for punitive sanctions in the area of competition law ECJ Case C-266/06P, Evonik Degussa, of 22 May 2008, pts. 38 *et seq*. See also Case C-308/06, Intertanko, of 3 June 2008, pts. 69–71.

7.2.2 [In]Direct, Shared or Integrated Administration

The model adopted for the EPPO in the present proposal seems to go largely beyond any existing notion of EU administration so far. It need not be recalled that in the early days direct exercise of administrative authority by the EC institutions was an exception, virtually limited to the Commission's role in the enforcement of competition law. The EC institutions essentially acted as an *administration de conception* providing legislative and often also secondary provisions, as well as budget for the implementation e.g. of the common agricultural policy and the structural funds, by the administrative authorities of the Member States. This practice has come to be designated as indirect or shared administration.[7] To the extent EU legislation left implementing provisions, individual application and enforcement to the Member States, the latter preserved variable forms of institutional autonomy to organise these implementing administrative tasks, on the basis of the principle of sincere cooperation, in accordance with the principles of equivalence and effectiveness as developed in abundant case law.

In recent doctrine a gradual shift of the organisation of administrative implementation of EU law and policies is unveiled. Ongoing processes of overall administrative cooperation have developed in various areas, defined as 'integrated administration', in which reportedly the traditional distinction between direct and indirect administration tends to become blurred. In case studies in such different policy areas as competition, telecom, food safety, and environment, it has been found that national agencies act in a double-hatted manner, constituting part of national administrations while, at the same time, becoming part of a multilevel Union administration. Not all of these forms of integrated administration are necessarily fitted with full swing executive and legal equipment. However, tension and conflict between the various levels are by no means uncommon.[8] In governance terms bodies such as the European Medicines Agency and the European Food Safety Agency in which representatives of the Member States play an important role, represent perhaps integrated co-administrations. From a strictly legal point of view they are, however, as EU agencies considered a manifestation of direct administration.[9]

Similarly, the Office for Harmonisation in the Internal Market, charged with the administration of the Community Trade Mark, as well as the Community Plant Variety Office and the European Chemicals Agency (ECHA) constitute direct administrations at Union level, complete with their own Boards of administrative appeal and direct judicial review in the EU courts.

---

[7] Cf. E. Chiti 2009 at pp. 9–33 and P. Craig 2009 at pp. 34–62. See also Harlow 2011, pp. 439–464. On the early forms of shared administration and judicial protection Meij 1993, pp. 75–87.

[8] Cf. Curtin 2009, p. 167 *et seq.*

[9] Cf. Dubos 2013 at p. 301.

A comparison with the network structure for the implementation of competition policy is not necessarily appropriate as in that area the European system really is the precursor and the Commission is quite naturally in a position to take the lead. Moreover, recently undertaken research does not show ground for the affirmation that various forms of administrative cooperation within the competition network and judicial review of its operations work smoothly,[10] to such extent that it provides an appropriate model for an even more critical sector such as the administration of criminal justice.

7.2.3 *How 'Integrated' is EPPO?*

Undoubtedly, recent experiences with various types of agencies have inspired the present proposal. It is not self-evident, however, that in the amalgam of variable forms of attribution and/or delegation of powers to implementing bodies, whether on EU or national level or both, a coherent continuum may be discerned on which to position the EPPO proposal. The particular nature of the proposed structure is also apparent from the fact that the Common Approach on Decentralised Agencies, recently adopted by the institutions,[11] has merely inspired the chapter on general provisions of the proposal.[12]

The present proposal providing for a central EPP with deputies and double-hatted delegated prosecutors on the national level in a single structure is perhaps not the very first integrated multilevel EU office of a pre-eminently legal 'justice' administration.[13] As compared to Eurojust, the principal structural characteristic of the proposal resides in its combination of centralised coordination and steering and decentralised operational activities. According to Article 6 of the proposal, the EPP, assisted by four Deputies, shall direct the activities and organise the work of the office. However, as a rule, the investigations and prosecutions of the office shall be carried out by at least one EDP in each Member State, under the direction and supervision of the EPP. The provisions of Article 6 specify expressly that the EDP's are an integral part of the EPPO, act under the exclusive authority of the EPP and follow only the EPP's instructions, guidelines and decisions while carrying out the investigations and prosecutions assigned to them. The same article continues to add that when acting within their mandate, the EDP's shall be fully independent from the national prosecution bodies they are part of and have no obligations with regard

[10] Cf. Böse 2012, pp. 840–870.

[11] Cf. Joint Statement of the European Parliament, the Council and the Commission on decentralised agencies, of 19 July 2012; comment by Scholten 2012. For an extensive analysis of the process leading up to the Common Approach, Zwiers 2011, pp. 191 and 201 *et seq.*

[12] Explanatory Memorandum pt. 3.3.9.

[13] With regard to Eurojust see the contributions of M. Coninsx in Chap. 3, B.P.M. Smulders in Chap. 4, and C. Deboyser in Chap. 6 of this book.

to them. Also, in case of conflicting national and EPPO assignments the EPP may instruct the EDP to give priority to the EPPO functions.[14]

This idiosyncratic structure has been defined as integrated administration in two opposite directions. In a single, integrated structure, on the one hand, the EDP stemming from the national level forms an integral part of the EPPO and, on the other, the EDP is part of the national administration of justice as an extended arm of the EPPO. The EDP's act with a double-hat to the extent that they maintain their position within their national administration of justice and simultaneously form part of EPPO.[15] Apparently, the idea is that, even if the two hats must be strictly distinguished, the EDP acting in EPP's capacity disposes fully of the equipment of its national position, including workforce services, as well as legal and procedural tools.

From a governance point of view the expression 'integrated administration' possibly has some attractiveness. For the purpose of legal analysis, however, it may not be particularly helpful. Rather than integrating hats, lawyers tend to distinguish functions, competences, and responsibilities. A striking feature, from such angle, is the strict hierarchy between the central EPP and the decentralised EDP's, making up for a network structure which appears completely different from other 'integrated' agencies. Indeed, the national prosecutors investigating and prosecuting in their capacity as EDP's do not operate under a form of delegation of powers or co-governance, but straightforward on the basis of an organic mandate upon instructions of the EPP. In spite of their definition as 'delegated' European prosecutor, EDP's are apparently not acting as national officials implementing certain powers derived from the EPP, but acting as part of the EPPO. As a consequence, any action of the EDP conducted on behalf of the EPP or rather in the EDP's capacity as EPP must be attributed to the EPPO.[16] In addition, provisions on the conduct of investigations reconfirm that the EDP designated for a given case leads the investigation on behalf of and under the instructions of the EPP. In this connection the proposal breaks further into the national organisational structure where it provides that the EDP may instruct the competent law enforcement authorities of his or her Member State to take the necessary investigation measures and that these authorities are obliged to comply with such instructions.[17]

Taking into account that terminology tends to remain a tricky issue in the European context, the provisional upshot may be that, in an unprecedented move, the proposal purports that the new EU body for the purposes of its mandate under the regulation 'integrates' a national official appointed as EDP, including the enforcement services under his/her instruction, without leaving this EDP room for autonomous manoeuvre. Even stronger, any potential conflict in the bosom of the

[14] Article 6, paras 5–6, of the proposal.

[15] Ligeti and Simonato 2013, p. 7 et seq., at p. 15 predicting with foresight that the integrated model would be the most likely approach of the Commission, with further references.

[16] Article 6, para 7, of the proposal.

[17] Article 18, para 1, of the proposal.

double-hatted official is solved by priority instructions in favour of the EDP hat. It would appear therefore that, at least according to the proposed rules, the hat forwarded by the extended arm of the EPP is somewhat bigger and more solid than the national hat of the EDP. From this point of view the attributive structure of the proposal appears fairly clear. Not only the EPP and the deputies, also the EDP derives its powers from the EU regulation, even if the latter requires for the EDP a concomitant foundation in the national prosecution services.

7.2.4 Conditions Governing the Exercise of the Attributed Powers

For the definition of the substance matter of the EPPO's competences, the proposal refers to the equally proposed directive on the offences affecting the financial interests of the Union. As a consequence, the scope of the EPP's operations is to be determined by reference to the directive and its implementation in the Member States. According to standing case law directives cannot by themselves impose obligations on individuals.[18] Therefore, in the context of this proposal the ultimate reference for the purpose of foreseeability is in the provisions of each Member State implementing the directive. Conspicuously, the definition of the offences for the investigation and prosecution of which typically an EU office was considered necessary, results from national law. As regards the requirements of the legality principle, EU directives, particularly in the area of criminal law, are somewhat uneasy company because the legitimising process is complete neither at the conception of the directive at EU level, nor at the stage of its implementation at national level.[19] In principle, Member States' discretion in the implementation of directives only concerns form and method, not content. The question whether the definitions of the offences within the EPPO's powers show discrepancies from one implementing Member State to another, depends therefore largely on the precision and detailed nature of the definitions given by the directive. At this point it may be noted that Article 325(4) TFEU, providing a specific legal basis for measures necessary to combat fraud affecting the financial interests of the Union, purports to afford 'effective and equivalent protection in the Member States and the Union institutions', leaving open the choice of the most appropriate legal instrument.[20]

Furthermore, the proposal provides for a wide range of provisions governing the operations of the Office. Although the proposal contains a list of investigative measures it may request or order in the exercise of its powers,[21] in many respects

[18] Case 80/86, Kolpinghuis, 1987 ECR 3969.

[19] Cf. in particular Verhoeven and Widdershoven 2011, at p. 59 *et seq.*

[20] See further K. Ligeti and A. Weyembergh, Chap. 5 in this book, at Sect. 5.1.

[21] Article 26.

these operations will have to rely on further detailed national rules and practices.[22] Equally in this respect, the proposal typically is part of an area of shared competence between the Union and the Member States,[23] for which Article 2(2) TFEU stipulates an 'as long as' arrangement to the effect that the Member States exercise their competence to the extent that the Union has not exercised its competence and again to the extent that the Union has decided to cease exercising its competence. As a result, in such areas of shared competences and shared legislative techniques, legality also must be conceived as a shared concept. In view of the variable sources of applicable regimes as well as the divergences between Member States' provisions, it is questionable whether the definition and the regulation of the powers attributed to the EPPO are sufficiently clear and transparent.[24] It remains to be seen whether the 'as long as' status quo as it stands in the proposal conceals a serious drawback for the EPPO's coherent operability or a powerful harmonising development potential. Or both at the same time.

7.2.5 A Duly Legitimised EPPO?

From the viewpoint of democratic or institutional legitimation a series of sources may be taken into account. In the first place, the EPPO as proposed may be distinguished from the great majority of other EU agencies by the fact that it finds its legal basis in the Treaty itself. However, the Treaty provides an optional legal basis, not an obligation. Against this background, one may wonder whether the yellow card drawn by no less than 14 national parliamentary chambers does outweigh the favourable position initially taken by the European Parliament. In its response, the Commission has maintained its entire proposal, underlining in particular, on the one hand, that the principles of efficiency, independence, and accountability lie at the heart of the proposal which, on the other, is based on respect of the national legal traditions and judicial systems of the Member States.[25]

Secondly, while, as it appeared above under Sect. 7.2.4, legitimation derived from the applicability of national rules is not per se convincing, broad application of national provisions may also hamper at least efficiency, if not as well overall independence and accountability. In addition, legitimation derived from the role of national courts is profoundly ambiguous, to the extent that the obvious risks of forum competition and output incoherencies are generally acknowledged.[26]

Thirdly, looking at the institution of an EPPO itself, it is to be noted that the double-hatted EDP, unlike the EPP and the Deputies, relies on a double mandate

---

[22] See Ligeti and Weyembergh, supra n. 20, Sects. 5.3.2 and 5.3.3.

[23] Article 4, para 2, under (j) TFEU.

[24] See Ligeti and Weyembergh, supra n. 20, Sects. 5.3.2 and 5.3.3, and Perillo 2012, at p. 47.

[25] COM(2013)851.

[26] See Ligeti and Weyembergh, supra n. 20, Sect. 5.4.3.

based on two separate appointments, on the national and on the EU level. A comparison springs to mind with national judges, in particular those specialised in EU relevant areas, and judges in the EU courts. The national judges referred to fulfil, on top of their mandate derived from national law, also a European mandate, every time they are called upon to apply rules of EU law. Although they operate on the basis of a single national appointment, their autonomous role for the purposes of the application of EU law, for which they may rely on the authority of the ECJ, is by and large uncontroversial. From the viewpoint of professional deontology, integrity and personal independence, the statutory position of prosecutors is essentially similar to that of judges. An essential distinctive feature, however, resides in the variable degrees of hierarchical dependence of prosecutors on political superiors in various Member States. Obviously, against this background the risk of loyalty conflicts within the double-hatted EDP serving two different hierarchies is substantially larger than for independent judges exercising a double mandate. For the purposes of legitimation and acceptation of the exercise of attributed powers by the appointed officials it is very appropriate therefore that the appointment provisions provide for consultation of a professional advisory panel after the example of the so called 255 panel for the appointment of judges in the ECJ and the General Court.[27] In view of the very important role the 255 panel has come to play for the EU courts, it is an omission that the same is not provided for the appointment of the Deputy European Public Prosecutors and in particular also for the EDP. Surprisingly, there is no provision either for an oath of office.[28]

7.2.6 An Acceptable Balance of Powers and Guarantees?

According to the Explanatory Memorandum of the proposal, the analysis of the Impact Assessment has shown that the model of a decentralised integrated office, which relies on national judicial systems, offers the most benefits and generates the lowest costs. During the preparation of the proposal the Commission has gone at great length to assemble materials through research projects and extensive consultations in order to draft the optimal instrument justified by the objective of the protection of the financial interests of the Union. Admittedly, the objections put forward by a number of national parliaments were largely inspired by resistance against the creation of yet another EU body competing, albeit in a very limited area, with cherished national institutions and traditions, rather than by the substance of the matter.

27 Article 8, para 3 of the proposal; and see Article 255 TFEU and also the panel referred to in Article 3 of Annex I to the Statute of the Court of Justice of the EU concerning the Civil Service Tribunal of the EU.

28 Remarkable also in comparison to the EU courts, is it that the EPP adopts its own internal rules and administrative rules, cf. Articles 7 and 69 of the proposal.

More problematic is the balance at the level of the guarantees for citizens. Fragmentation of the substantive and procedural provisions in various EU legal instruments and among potentially divergent national systems, without provision for a coherent system ensuring overall judicial protection, is bound to give rise to shortcomings in the appropriate protection of citizen's rights. Indeed, one may wonder whether the administration of criminal justice, where *ipso facto* rights and interests of citizens are at stake, constitutes appropriate experimental playground for a double-hatted structure, in which controversy over reciprocal delimitation of competences and applicable law, as well as internal tensions as a consequence of clash of cultures are undoubtedly inherent.

7.3 An Unprecedented System of Judicial Review

7.3.1 Common Images Turned Upside Down

If, as signalled above, Article 86 TFEU turns common images of multilevel administration and judicial review in the EU upside down by providing the exercise of EPPO's prosecutorial functions in national courts, this appears all the more so for the transformation of EPPO in a national authority for the purpose of judicial review.[29] The chapter of the proposal concerning judicial review, in the context of criminal justice perhaps not the least important, is certainly the briefest of all chapters. It contains nevertheless some curious elements concerning the division of tasks between the EU courts and national courts. Apart from the legal implications of this proposal, one is tempted to wonder whether it makes sense to organise a strictly hierarchical new office on EU level, integrating even national officials, but certainly not acting in a national capacity, in order to then suddenly turn it around for the purpose of judicial review. Although it certainly is an imaginative solution, a hint of inconsistency is in the air.

The Explanatory Memorandum is a little more elaborate on this chapter. It explains that Article 86(3) TFEU allows the Union legislator to determine the rules applicable to judicial review of the EPPO's procedural measures in view of the specific nature of the EPPO requiring special rules regarding judicial review. It goes on to explain that acts of pre-trial investigation are closely related to eventual prosecution, that they deploy their effects in the national legal order and are carried out by national law enforcement authorities, sometimes after having obtained the authorisation of a national court. In short, the EPPO's action will mainly be relevant in the national legal orders and therefore the judicial review of all challengeable acts of investigation and prosecution of the EPPO should be with national courts. As EPPO's acts of investigation and prosecution shall be considered as acts of a national authority for the purpose of judicial review, in the Commission's view, the

[29] Article 36, para 1, of the proposal.

EU courts will have no jurisdiction for actions for annulment, actions for failure to act or actions for damages regarding those acts or the absence thereof. In addition, recital 38 to the proposal, picking up on the Explanatory Memorandum, considers that national courts should not be able to refer preliminary questions on the validity of acts of the EPPO to the Court of Justice since by virtue of the legal fiction[30] of article 36(1), those acts cannot be considered acts of a body of the Union for the purpose of judicial review.

Curiously, the final part of the Explanatory Memorandum on this chapter concedes that national courts, if not on validity, remain able to refer preliminary questions on interpretation to the Court regarding EPPO's acts. The idea probably is that questions cannot be referred on the interpretation of the EPPO acts themselves, as the Court would not have jurisdiction to interpret acts of a national authority; however, any question on the interpretation of the proposed regulation or of any other rule or principle of EU law that may be relevant to the appreciation of the act of EPPO at issue before the national court, may or must be referred under Article 267 TFEU. Also the above-mentioned reference to the unavailability of the action for damages under Article 268 TFEU as regards acts of the EPPO appears inconsistent with Article 69 of the proposal which precisely provides for jurisdiction of the Court for damage caused by the EPPO in the performance of its duties in so far as it may be imputed to it, without distinguishing different causes. The idea behind this apparent inconsistency may be that the hypothesis of the proposed Article 36, on the basis of the empowerment of the legislator by Article 86 (3), to determine the rules for judicial review, is that the general system of the Treaty does not apply at all; as a consequence the proposed regulation reconfirms the applicability of the EU action for damages. It keeps turning around.

7.3.2 A Coherent System of Judicial Protection

In order to put this part of the proposal in perspective, it is perhaps appropriate to recall the broad outline of the EU system of judicial protection. A first observation, then, is that the EU Courts exercise specifically conferred jurisdiction in accordance with the principle of conferral of powers. The national courts of the Member States act as courts of general jurisdiction in EU matters where no specific jurisdiction of the EU Courts is available. The jurisdiction of the EU courts is called exceptional as it is the exception to the general jurisdiction of national courts. However, where it is provided this exceptional jurisdiction also is exclusive.

A second observation concerns the pattern of conferral as it is organised by the Treaties. The general mission entrusted to the three branches of the institution Court of Justice is according to Article 19(1) TEU to ensure that the law is observed in the interpretation and the application of the Treaties. Since the Treaty of Lisbon, the

[30] Cf. J. Inghelram, Chap. 8 in this book, Sect. 8.3.4.2.

second sentence of the same paragraph requires that the Member States shall provide remedies sufficient to ensure effective legal protection in the fields covered by Union law. The third paragraph of Article 19 TEU sets out three ways to implement the general mission, i.e. (a) direct actions by Member States, institutions and private individuals, (b) preliminary rulings requested by national courts and (c) other cases. These three categories of proceedings are spelled out further in the form of various actions provided for in Articles 258 *et seq.* TFEU. Moreover several provisions complement this set-up, e.g. confirming that national courts remain competent with the exception of jurisdiction conferred on the Court (Article 274) and Member States may not settle disputes in a way different from the Treaty provisions (Article 344).[31]

According to the general pattern of this division of powers an action for annulment under Article 263 TFEU in the EU Courts is available against acts of EU institutions, bodies, offices, and agencies, intended to produce legal effects, whereas jurisdiction lies with the courts of the Member States in cases where EU acts are implemented on the national level. The key to coherence of this multilevel system of judicial protection is the preliminary reference procedure of Article 267 TFEU providing for an interface for intensive cooperation between the Court and national courts in charge of the application of EU law in cases before them. An essential element of this interface is that it is for the Court to determine the proper interpretation of EU acts and rules, as well as the validity of EU acts and for the national courts to determine the validity and interpretation of national law, eventually in the light of the interpretations of EU law given by the Court. Thus, on the basis of specific and exclusive jurisdiction conferred on the EU courts and general jurisdiction remaining in the competent national courts, an overall system of judicial protection has developed, ensuing the—either European or national—level of administrative intervention towards individuals, with the EU Court's jurisdiction on preliminary references as key to the coherence between national courts and the EU courts. Access to either system of courts, on national or EU level, follows the origin of the act undertaken, jurisdiction of either court level is qualified by the EU or national nature of the body producing the act. Interestingly, standing case law recognises the criterion of attribution of causation as a public law collision rule to distinguish liability of EU bodies from liability of national bodies in the exercise of powers derived from EU law.[32] It follows that the EU courts are the courts providing the effective remedy, required by the principle of the rule of law or the *gesetzliche Richter* enshrined in Article 47 of the Charter and Article 6 of the ECHR, an individual is entitled to as against acts of EU bodies and national courts vice versa.

[31] See also Inghelram, supra n. 30, Sect. 8.3.4.3 on Article 276.

[32] Cf. joined cases 97, 99, 193 and 215/86, Asteris, 1988 ECR 2208. See Meij 1993 p. 85.

7.3.3 An Appropriate Interpretation of Article 86?

It is suggested that the interpretation of Article 86(3) TFEU put forward in the EPPO proposal is inconsistent with common approaches to EU judicial protection usually based on coherence, uniform application and consistent review. Firstly, the mere reference in Article 86(3) to the possibility to adopt rules applicable to judicial review, does not imply a power to set aside the complete Treaty system of judicial protection. Even if, as a consequence of the provision of Article 86(2), the EPPO must bring the cases it pursues in the competent national court, the effect of this provision making an extraordinary exception to the general system of the Treaty cannot be but narrowly interpreted. Indeed, it is concerned with trial jurisdiction in criminal cases hitherto not provided in the general EU court system. This reasoning for para 2, however, does not mean that para 3 may be taken as broad as to deny the EU Courts' specifically conferred jurisdiction, e.g. to review the EPPO's forum choice or any other decision taken in the pre-trial stage intended to produce legal effect.

Secondly, the phrase 'rules applicable to judicial review' may perhaps constitute a basis for procedural rules for the proper operation of the EPPO, rules in the nature of particular provisions as also given in the founding statutory rules for certain agencies, such as the Community Trademark Office (OHIM)or the ECHA agency and for the appropriate application of the Aarhus convention, but not as a basis for rules on jurisdiction. Without any reference to the general system provided for in the above-mentioned Treaty provisions, such implementing rules may not be considered as equalling power to modify the general Treaty provisions on judicial review or to provide a complete derogation thereof. It is hard indeed to see in the wording of Article 86(3), a foundation proper to set aside the Treaty system for judicial review.

In addition, thirdly, the concept of rules applicable to judicial review in Article 86 perfectly corresponds to the notion of specific conditions and arrangements concerning actions brought by natural or legal persons against acts of bodies, offices and agencies of the Union, which by virtue of Article 263 may be provided in acts setting up such bodies. Obviously, the idea of this new provision of Article 263, introduced with the Treaty of Lisbon at the same time as Article 86, is not to set aside the provisions of this article altogether.

Fourth, the proposal faces a constitutional dilemma. To the extent that Article 36 finds no appropriate legal basis in Article 86 TFEU, this legal fiction of the proposed Article 36(1), providing that for the purpose of judicial review of its procedural measures the EPPO shall be considered as a national authority, amounts to depriving applicants of the legal remedy they are entitled to under Article 47 of the Charter. This is equally true for the second branch of Article 36, providing that provisions of national law rendered applicable by the EPPO regulation, shall not be considered as provisions of Union law for the purpose of Article 267 TFEU. Such an effort to restrict the preliminary jurisdiction of the Court, doing away with classic approaches to coherence of EU law and practical possibilities to achieve consistency of EPPO action, introduces in the legislative process a certain arbitrariness which does not correspond to prevailing perceptions of the EU legal order as based on the rule of law.[33]

On a more general score, one wonders whether the consequences of the choices laid down in Article 86 of the Treaty and in Articles 27 and 36 of the proposal may not be less desirable than purported, all the more so where these choices are not substantially compensated by a full-fledged preliminary reference system. In particular in the absence of more rigorous unification of procedural rules as developed in the Model Rules,[34] the pressure on the overall coherence of the actions of the EPPO in national courts in trial and pre-trial stages may become disproportionate. Admittedly, in various instances the Commission appears in national courts, e.g. where it brings cases for breach of contract or for damages[35] in the competent national courts or where it acts as *amicus curiae* in competition cases and state aid cases. However, as the latter role properly fits into the Commission's monitoring functions in these areas and the former follows from regular rules of jurisdiction, such experience may not be very indicative for the position of an EPPO in national courts.

All this is not to say that pre-trial review in the EU courts and trial in national courts should be an ideal solution. Within the framework of a fairly complete set of rules of criminal procedure, the Model Rules provide for jurisdiction of the EU courts, so far only for *ex post* judicial review.[36] Not only regulations setting up EU bodies, offices and agencies as referred to in Article 263(5) TFEU, such as concerning the Community Trade Mark or concerning the marketing of chemical substances (REACH), also instruments such as the Aarhus Regulation (environment) and the Regulation on Access to Documents provide for specific regimes of access to the EU Courts. Further research may establish whether, in a similar vein, Article 86(3), TFEU may be construed as an 'other case[s] provided for in the Treaties' in the sense of Article 19(3) TEU, to the effect that the EU Courts may exercise jurisdiction to rule on requests for prior authorisation of coercive measures as against natural or legal persons by an EPPO. Clearly, such jurisdiction as well as jurisdiction in cases brought against an EPPO's pre-trial decisions without prior authorisation would require accompanying legislation on procedural safeguards and appropriate arrangements for the organisation of the EU Courts, provided that where required coercion would be exercised by national enforcement officials under instruction of the EPPO. Even so, it may well be that an intermediate approach of sharing jurisdiction and regulation between both levels in appropriately fitting roles will turn out to be the most preferable solution. In Case C-94/00, *Roquette Frères*,

---

[33] See in more detail Inghelram, supra n. 30, Sect. 8.3.4 and Zwiers 2011, p. 407, who tends to consider Article 86 a *lex specialis*.

[34] Model Rules for the EPPO, available at http://www.eppo-project.eu/index.php/EU-model-rules (Accessed July 2014), and in Ligeti 2014.

[35] Cf. recently Case C-199/11, Otis a.o.

[36] Rules 7 and 31 of the Model Rules, referred to in n. 34 supra. See also Perillo 2012, p. 28.

the ECJ drew a subtle line distinguishing the exclusive competence of the EU Courts to review the legality of the Commission's investigative action in the area of competition law enforcement from the national courts' power to verify whether the coercive measures requested by the Commission of the national authorities are proportionate. It is doubtful whether measures taken by national prosecutors, even with police assistance acting as extended *bras de fer* of an EDP may still be reviewed by national courts rather than solely by the EU Courts. Even if the present proposal recognises that coercive measures remain the province of the Member States, this presumably does not take away the actor's EPPO quality. To the extent that the national prosecutor in question acts upon the EPPO's instruction without exercising any discretion, there is no need for a *dédoublement* of review.[37]

From an integrationist perspective a less constitutionally cumbersome, truly innovative approach could be to designate in each Member State a specialised trial court in which EPPO cases would be brought before one or more chambers of 3 and 5 judges, among whom respectively one and two judges would be recruited on a case by case basis from a pool of judges from other Member States than the trial court. Appeal on points of law could then lie with a special chamber of the ECJ or the General Court. For judicial review or authorisation of measures in the pre-trial stage, a distinction could be made between the stage of proceedings as from the choice of the trial jurisdiction following the criteria of Article 27 of the proposal and the preceding stage during which, in the absence of a choice of a trial court cases could be attributed to a specialised central jurisdiction, to begin with the existing Civil Service Tribunal.

7.4 Final Observations

The present proposal for an EPPO sets out imaginative new approaches to multi-level administration and entailing court provisions in the EU in a particularly sensitive area. Unsurprisingly, a unique structure of central steering and coordination of decentralised operational activities in a single body calls for complex searches of elements of legality and legitimation shared by the composite levels of integrated administration. The strictly hierarchical structure of the proposed model, including national operational resources, raises the question whether indeed it is the least intrusive model on national institutional autonomy as claimed. It remains to be seen whether the status quo of reliance on national procedural provisions will turn out to be a drawback for the EPPO's coherent operability or rather a powerful incentive for further harmonisation. As regards democratic legitimation, the yellow card drawn by no less than 14 national parliamentary chambers raises questions as to the feasibility of the proposal for the Union as a whole, which however appeared

[37] See, however, Inghelram, supra n. 30, Sect. 8.3.4.3.

limited from the outset. If anything, most probably a more or less extensive enhanced cooperation is the only option.

The unprecedented system of judicial protection in national courts as against acts of a single, integrated EU body raises questions of consistency and arbitrariness in the light of the general pattern of coherent judicial protection in the refined multilevel court system of the EU. Further research, on top of many years of arduous research that have enabled the staging of the present proposal, may demonstrate which intermediate approach of sharing jurisdiction and regulation is most appropriate. The shift in the Council debate to a mitigated college model seems to reflect a stagnating discussion on a common approach for an agency's framework and a fixed position of some important Member States falling short of the Commission's ambitions.[38]

References

Besselink LFM et al (2011) Introduction: legality in multiple legal orders. In: Besselink LFM, Pennings FJL, Prechal A (eds) The eclipse of the legality principle in the European Union, Kluwer Law International, Alphen a/d Rijn, pp 3–10, at 6 et seq

Böse M (2012) The system of vertical and horizontal cooperation in administrative investigations in EU competition cases. In: Ligeti K (ed) Toward a prosecutor for the European Union, a comparative analysis, vol 1. Hart Publishing, Oxford, pp 840–870

Chiti E (2009) The administrative implementation of European Union law: a taxonomy and its implications. In: Hofmann HCH, Türk AH (eds) Legal challenges in EU administrative law, Edward Elgar Publishing, UK, pp 9–33

Craig P (2009) Shared administration and the regulatory state. In: Hofmann HCH, Türk AH (eds.) Legal challenges in EU administrative law. Edward Elgar Publishing, UK, pp 34–62

Curtin D (2009) Executive power of the European Union. Oxford University Press, Oxford

Dubos O (2013) Objectif d'efficacité de l'exécution du droit de L'Union européenne: la tectonique des compétences In: Neframi E (ed) Objectifs et compétences dans l'Union européenne. Bruylant, Brussels, pp 293–314

Harlow C (2011) Three phases in the evolution of EU administrative law. In: Craig PP, de Búrca G (eds) The evolution of EU law, Oxford University Press, Oxford, pp 439–464

Ligeti K (ed) (2014) Toward a prosecutor for the European Union. Draft rules of procedure, vol 2. Hart Publishing, Oxford (forthcoming)

Ligeti K, Simonato M (2013) The European public prosecutor's office: towards a truly European prosecution service? New J Eur Crim Law 4:7 et seq.

Meij AWH (1993) Rechtsbescherming bij gedeeld bestuur in de EG, Nederlands Tijdschrift voor Bestuursrecht 93(1):75–87

Perillo E (2012) Le droit pénal substantiel et l'espace de liberté, de sécurité et de justice, deux ans après Lisbonne: une analyse *de jure condito* et quelques perspectives *de jure condendo*, Institutional Report to the Fide conference, Tallinn, p 47

---

[38] See Council of the EU 7095/14 Press 106 PR CO 11 of 4 March 2014 and Presidency Note 9834/1/14 rev 1 of 21 May 2014 in Interinstitutional File: 2013/0255(APP) in the light of the Common Position of the Ministers of Justice of France and Germany on the European Public Prosecutor's Office submitted to the competent Commissioners in March 2013, at the time accessible on www.justice.gouv.fr. Cf. Ligeti and Weyembergh, supra n. 20, Sect. 5.6.

Scholten M (2012) The newly released 'common approach' on EU agencies: going forward or standing still? Columbia J Eur Law Online 19(2)
Verhoeven M, Widdershoven R (2011) National legality and European obligations. In: Besselink LFM, Pennings F, Prechal S (eds) The eclipse of the legality principle in the European Union, Kluwer Law International, Alphen a/d Rijn, pp 5–72
Zwiers M (2011) The European public prosecutor's office. Intersentia

Chapter 8
Search and Seizure Measures and Their Review

Jan Inghelram

Abstract The Commission's proposal on the European Public Prosecutor's Office defines the investigative competences which the EPPO will have by virtue of Article 86(2) TFEU. According to the Commission's proposal, EPPO investigation measures will predominantly be governed by the law of the Member States and their courts will be competent to review the validity of those measures. It is however argued that, in relation to crucial aspects, those measures will in any event be governed by EU law and, in particular, by the Charter of Fundamental Rights of the EU and that reviewing the validity of EPPO investigation measures under EU law will be a matter for the EU courts.

Keywords European Public Prosecutor's Office · Investigative competences · Applicable law · Coercive measures · Judicial review · Prior authorisation proceedings · Review of validity under EU law

Contents

The author is Référendaire at the Court of Justice of the EU. The views expressed in this article are strictly personal.

J. Inghelram (✉)
Court of Justice of the EU, Luxemburg, Luxemburg
e-mail: jan.inghelram@curia.europa.eu

L.H. Erkelens et al. (eds.), *The European Public Prosecutor's Office*,
DOI 10.1007/978-94-6265-035-0_8

8.1 Introduction

According to Article 86(2) TFEU, the European Public Prosecutor's Office (hereinafter the 'EPPO')[1] will not only have prosecutorial but also investigative competences. In particular, it will be 'responsible for investigating [...] the perpetrators of, and accomplices in, offences' falling within the scope of that provision.[2] In the Commission's Proposal for a Council Regulation on the establishment of the European Public Prosecutor's Office[3] (hereinafter the 'Commission's proposal'), this investigative competence is qualified as a competence to 'direct and supervise investigations'[4] or, more generally, to 'investigate'[5] or to 'conduct investigations'.[6]

This chapter focuses on this investigative competence of the EPPO and, in particular, on search and seizure measures. Starting from the Commission's proposal, it intends to analyse the EPPO's investigative competence in a broader institutional context, thereby taking into consideration the (administrative) investigation competences which already exist at the EU level, for instance in the competition law area and in the field of the protection of the financial interests of the EU. Particular attention will be given to the issue of judicial review.

8.2 The Commission's Proposal

8.2.1 Overview

Search and seizure measures are dealt with in Article 26 of the Commission's proposal. This provision contains a detailed list of 21 investigation measures which

[1] For recent studies on the EPPO, see, e.g., Zwiers 2011 and Ligeti 2013.

[2] The French text of the TFEU uses the word 'rechercher' instead of 'enquêter'. However, it does not seem possible to deduce from that wording that an EPPO would not have an investigative competence in the common sense of the word, see also Flore 2008, p. 232. In Dutch, the word 'opsporen' is used.

[3] Proposal for a Council Regulation on the establishment of the European Public Prosecutor's Office, COM(2013) 534 final (hereinafter, the 'Commission's proposal'). See also the Appendix to this book.

[4] Article 4(2) of the Commission's proposal.

[5] See, e.g., Article 11(4) of the Commission's proposal.

[6] See, e.g., Article 11(5) of the Commission's proposal.

the EPPO can use in the investigations and prosecutions conducted by it. Apart from these measures, the EPPO can also order or request other investigation measures, but only if they are available under the law of the Member State where the measure is to be carried out.[7]

The 21 investigation measures listed in Article 26(1) are divided into two categories. The first 10 measures are subject to authorisation by the competent judicial authority of the Member States where they are to be carried out.[8] Searches of premises, land, means of transport, private home, clothes and any other personal property or computer system[9] as well as freezing of assets and of financial transactions[10] belong to this first category of investigation measures.

The last 11 measures listed in Article 26(1) of the Commission's proposal are only subject to judicial authorisation if so required by the national law of the Member State where the investigation measure is to be carried out.[11] Seizure of objects which are needed as evidence[12] belongs to this second category.

Whatever may be the category to which the investigation measure belongs, the final outcome of the Commission's proposal will always be that, if a prior judicial authorisation mechanism exists in a Member State for a given investigation measure listed in Article 26(1), the EPPO will have to comply with that procedure if it wants to order or request an investigation measure in that Member State. This seems to express, in relation to the sensitive issue of the varying extent of judicial control of investigation measures in the Member States,[13] the Commission's willingness to ensure that the impact of the proposed regulation on the legal orders and the institutional structures of the Member States is the least intrusive possible.[14]

With its list of 21 investigation measures, the Commission's proposal is more detailed than previous proposals have ever been before. Nevertheless, the Commission's proposal clearly builds upon these previous proposals, among which the *Corpus Juris*[15] and the Model Rules for the Procedure of the EPPO[16] (hereinafter the 'Model Rules'). In these previous proposals, search measures also formed part of the investigation measures which a European Public Prosecutor could carry out and it was always envisaged that they would be subject to prior judicial

[7] Article 26(2) of the Commission's proposal.

[8] Article 26(4) of the Commission's proposal.

[9] Article 26(1)(a) of the Commission's proposal.

[10] Article 26(1)(d) and (h) of the Commission's proposal.

[11] Article 26(5) of the Commission's proposal.

[12] Article 26(1)(m) of the Commission's proposal.

[13] See also Đurđević 2013, p. 992.

[14] See recital 6 in the preamble of the Commission's proposal.

[15] http://ec.europa.eu/anti_fraud/documents/fwk-green-paper-corpus/corpus_juris_en.pdf. Accessed 31 March 2014.

[16] Model Rules for the Procedure of the EPPO, available at: http://www.eppo-project.eu/index.php/EU-model-rules/english. Accessed 9 October 2013.

authorisation.[17] The same is true for seizure measures, except for some nuances with regard to prior judicial authorisation.[18]

8.2.2 No Specific Rules on Investigation Measures in the EU Institutions

The Commission's proposal does not contain any specific rules on EPPO investigation measures in the EU institutions. This is a major difference compared to OLAF, whose competences are based on the fundamental distinction between internal investigations (in the EU institutions and bodies) and external investigations (in the Member States and third countries), with different rules governing both categories of investigations.[19] It appears, therefore, to be the Commission's intention to submit EPPO investigation measures in the EU institutions and bodies to the same rules as such measures in the Member States.

From a pure criminal law point of view, the Commission's proposal represents a continuation of the current situation. Indeed, criminal law investigations in relation to offences committed in the EU institutions or by EU officials are currently a matter for the Member State authorities.[20] Insofar as the EPPO will, in fact, step in for those authorities within the limits of its competences, it seems normal that it will have to comply with the same rules as those authorities when criminal investigations in relation to such offences are concerned.

However, the Commission's proposal has important practical consequences. Indeed, although being an EU body, the EPPO would have to obtain prior judicial authorisation from a Belgian *juge d'instruction* in order to carry out a search in the offices of an EU institution located in Brussels, if one applies Article 26 of the Commission's proposal. This raises the question as to whether a national judge is the best placed authority to exercise such a competence, at the investigation stage, in a pure EU environment.

Furthermore, the procedure to be followed by the EPPO is far more burdensome than the one currently applying to OLAF, which is competent to carry out searches in the offices of the EU institutions with almost no formalities at all.[21] The

---

[17] See, respectively, Article 20(3)(d) of the *Corpus Juris* and Rule 48 of the Model Rules.

[18] In Article 20(3)(d) of the *Corpus Juris*, seizure measures are subject to judicial authorisation, in Rule 39 of the Model Rules, seizure of evidence is not, and in the Commission's proposal, seizure of objects which are needed as evidence is, as indicated above, subject to judicial authorisation if so required by the national law of the Member State where the seizure measure is to be carried out.

[19] Reg. (EU, Euratom) No 883/2013 of the European Parliament and of the Council of 11 September 2013 concerning investigations conducted by the European Anti-Fraud Office (OLAF) and repealing Regulation (EC) No 1073/1999 of the European Parliament and of the Council and Council Regulation (Euratom) No 1074/1999, *OJ* 2013, L 248/1, Articles 3–4.

[20] Ibid., Article 11(5).

[21] Ibid., Article 4(2)(a).

temptation could, therefore, exist for the EPPO to use information obtained through searches in the EU institutions carried out by OLAF, supposing the latter continues to exist as it is now, rather than organising its own searches. This would, however, raise questions as to whether the applicable rules and procedural guarantees have been complied with by the EPPO.

The Commission appears to be aware of this problem. On the same day when it launched its EPPO proposal, it announced that it would submit proposals to improve OLAF's governance and reinforce procedural safeguards in investigations in view of the establishment of an EPPO.[22] In practice, OLAF's search and seizure measures in the EU institutions and bodies would become subject to the prior opinion of the Controller of procedural safeguards (for EU staff) or to a prior quasi-judicial authorisation (for members of EU institutions).

Such proceedings in the context of OLAF investigations would reduce the procedural differences between EPPO and OLAF search measures and could thus render the use by the EPPO of information obtained through OLAF searches less problematic.[23] The question remains, however, whether a mere opinion (by the Controller of procedural safeguards) suffices, in this respect, as a procedural guarantee in comparison with a quasi-judicial or judicial prior authorisation procedure. Moreover, as the European Court of Human Rights' ruling in the *Tillack* Case shows, it will in any event remain delicate for one authority to investigate on behalf of another.[24]

8.2.3 Admissibility of Evidence Obtained Through EPPO Investigation Measures

It follows from Article 30(1) of the Commission's proposal that evidence obtained through EPPO investigation measures, for instance a house search, carried out in one Member State is admissible in the trial in another Member State even if the national law of the Member State where the court is located provides for different rules on the collection of such evidence. Mutual recognition is, however, not absolute since admissibility is explicitly made subject to the condition that the court considers that admitting the evidence would not adversely affect the fairness of the

22 COM(2013) 533 final. See further on OLAF's future when the EPPO will be established, e.g., Covolo 2012, pp. 86–87.

23 Even without the establishment of an EPPO, one may argue that such proceedings in the context of OLAF investigations are necessary, see Inghelram 2012b, pp. 68–70.

24 *Tillack* v. *Belgium*, judgment of 27 November 2007, no. 20477/05, para 64. In that case, a house search and seizures carried out by Belgian judicial authorities on behalf of OLAF were found to have violated Article 10 of the Convention for the Protection of Human Rights and Fundamental Freedoms (freedom of expression).

procedure or the rights of defence as enshrined in Articles 47 and 48 of the Charter of Fundamental Rights of the EU (hereinafter the 'Charter').[25]

The question arises in this respect why Article 30(1) of the Commission's proposal only refers to Articles 47 and 48 of the Charter.[26] In relation to search measures, the right to privacy as enshrined in Article 7 of the Charter is particularly relevant[27] and it appears difficult to see why only a violation of Articles 47 or 48 and not of Article 7 of the Charter could be an obstacle to the admissibility of evidence obtained through a house search. However, the practical implications of the wording of Article 30(1) are most likely limited. Indeed, evidence obtained through a house search which violates the fundamental right to privacy may well be considered to adversely affect the fairness of the procedure and thus fail the admissibility test on those grounds.

8.3 Institutionally Relevant Issues in Relation to Search and Seizure Measures

The topic of search and seizure measures and of investigation measures in general is interesting because it lies at the crossroads of several institutionally or even constitutionally relevant issues for both Member States and the EU. Four issues will be dealt with below, namely (1) the nature of the body responsible for investigations, (2) competence *versus* responsibility in relation to coercive measures, (3) the rules applicable to investigation measures and (4) judicial review of those measures.

8.3.1 The Nature of the Body Responsible for Investigations

When the EPPO will be established, the EU, for the first time in its history, will be competent to conduct criminal investigations through one of its bodies.[28] This is the

[25] See for a broader analysis of judicial control in the context of mutual recognition, Weyembergh 2013.

[26] Contrary even to recital 11 in the preamble of the Commission's proposal, which, in the same context, refers to the Charter in general.

[27] See, to that effect, Joined Cases 46/87 and 227/88, *Hoechst* v. *Commission* [1989] ECR 2859, para 19.

[28] Until now, the EU only has administrative investigation competences, although, in relation to OLAF, opinions may differ as to the exact qualification of these competences. See, e.g., Braum 2009, p. 302.

major difference between Eurojust[29] and the EPPO. Whereas, briefly stated, Eurojust coordinates criminal investigations conducted by 'national authorities',[30] the EPPO will be an 'EU body' conducting criminal investigations. This clear-cut difference between both scenarios[31] follows from a mere reading of the relevant Treaty Articles—Article 85 TFEU for Eurojust and Article 86 TFEU for the EPPO. Articles 15–19 of the Commission's proposal, which deal with the conduct of investigations, confirm that it is the EPPO which has the authority to investigate. The consequence is that the responsibility for conducting investigations shifts from the Member State level (in the Eurojust scenario) to the EU level (in the EPPO scenario). This, in turn, has consequences for the issue of judicial review. Indeed, whereas, in the Eurojust scenario, there is no doubt about the fact that the Member State level is the only appropriate level for exercising judicial control over investigation measures, the EPPO scenario raises the question as to whether such control should take place at the Member State or the EU level. This question will be further dealt with below.

8.3.2 Competence versus Responsibility in Relation to Coercive Measures

The fact that an EU body will conduct investigations does not mean that this body will carry out all investigative acts itself. In particular, Article 18(6) of the Commission's proposal explicitly states that '[c]oercive measures shall be carried out by the competent national authorities'. There will, therefore, be no FBI-style EU police force carrying out house searches or other investigation measures for the EPPO.

In this respect, the Commission's proposal does not change anything about what appears to be a basic characteristic of the EU, namely that it does not have powers of coercion of its own—those powers which are typical for a sovereign state. Expressions of this basic characteristic can be found in Article 88(3) TFEU, which explicitly states in relation to Europol that '[t]he application of coercive measures shall be the exclusive responsibility of the competent national authorities', as well

---

[29] Council Decision 2002/187/JHA of 28 February 2002 setting up Eurojust with a view to reinforcing the fight against serious crime, *OJ* 2002, L 63/1, as last modified by Council Decision 2009/426/JHA of 16 December 2008 on the strengthening of Eurojust and amending Decision 2002/187/JHA setting up Eurojust with a view to reinforcing the fight against serious crime, *OJ* 2009, L 138/14.

[30] See further on Eurojust, e.g., Nilsson 2000 and Vervaele 2008. The Commission's Proposal for a Regulation of the European Parliament and of the Council on the European Union Agency for Criminal Justice Cooperation (Eurojust), COM(2013) 535 final, launched together with its EPPO proposal, does not change this characteristic of Eurojust's competences, see Article 2(1) of the Eurojust proposal.

[31] See also Ligeti and Simonato 2013, p. 11. See, however, for a proposal which combines both scenarios, White 2013, pp. 38–39.

as in the case-law of the Court of Justice of the EU (hereinafter the 'ECJ') on the Commission's investigative competences in the competition law area.[32]

However, the fact that coercive measures are executed by national authorities does not discharge the EPPO from its responsibility in relation to those measures. Indeed, Article 18(1) of the Commission's proposal confirms that, when executing the investigation measures assigned to them, the competent law enforcement authorities in the Member State act under the instructions of the European Delegated Prosecutor who, in turn, acts under the instructions of the European Public Prosecutor. Individuals affected by EPPO investigation measures executed by national authorities are, therefore, entitled to consider that they are affected by measures of the EPPO itself and thus of an EU body. This again is important for the question as to the level at which judicial control in relation to such measures should be exercised.

8.3.3 The Rules Applicable to EPPO Investigation Measures

Article 26(2) of the Commission's proposal mentions that the 21 investigation measures listed in para 1 of that Article 'shall be subject to the conditions provided for in this Article and those set out in national law'. However, since that Article contains very few conditions,[33] it may be assumed that it is the Commission's intention that those measures will essentially be governed by conditions set out in national law.

The question of whether investigation measures of the EPPO should be governed by national law or by EU law is often presented as a policy choice. The Common Position of the Ministers of Justice of France and Germany on the EPPO, sent to the European Commission on 20 March 2013, confirms this view by claiming that EPPO investigations should be pursued in accordance with the national law of the Member States in which the inquiries are being made.[34]

This choice is, however, to a large extent a virtual choice. It is clear that the EPPO as an EU body will have to comply with the provisions of the Charter of

[32] See, e.g., Joined Cases 46/87 and 227/88, *Hoechst* v. *Commission* [1989] ECR 2859, para 31. See, for another expression of this basic characteristic, Articles 280 TFEU and 299 TFEU, according to which enforcement of judgments of the ECJ and decisions of the Council or the Commission which impose a pecuniary obligation on persons other than States, is governed by the rules of civil procedure in force in the State in the territory of which enforcement is carried out.

[33] The only exceptions appear to be the rules on prior judicial authorisation (Article 26(4)–(6) of the Commission's proposal) and the condition that the individual investigation measure shall not be ordered without reasonable grounds and if less intrusive means can achieve the same objective (Article 26(3) of the Commission's proposal).

[34] http://www.eppo-project.eu/index.php/Home/News/Position-of-Germany-and-France-on-EPPO. Accessed 9 October 2013. See para 30.

Fundamental Rights of the European Union.[35] This compliance, especially with Articles 47 and 48 of the Charter, is even particularly important since the admissibility of evidence presented by the EPPO in front of the trial court is subject to it.[36]

Moreover, in the context of investigation measures, several fundamental rights provided by the Charter are relevant, such as the fundamental right to privacy, as defined by Article 7 of the Charter, which applies to search measures,[37] and the fundamental right to property, as defined by Article 17 of the Charter, which applies, for instance, to the freezing of assets and financial transactions.[38] Furthermore, the fundamental right to property includes a right to be heard in case of considerable interference with that right.[39]

It appears therefore an illusion to think that investigation measures of the EPPO can be solely governed by the law of the Member States. In relation to crucial aspects, those measures are, in any event, governed by EU law, which would prevail in case of a conflict with national law of the Member States.[40] Moreover, the second *Kadi*-Case illustrates the extent to which fundamental rights can give rise to the existence of very concrete rules in practice.[41]

If the absence of specific EU legislation in relation to investigation measures ordered or requested by the EPPO does not prevent EU law from being applicable to those measures, such absence is, however, not without effect on the way in which EU law, and in particular the Charter, applies to those measures.

Indeed, limitations on the exercise of fundamental rights are subject to certain conditions set out in Article 52(1) of the Charter—also called the horizontal exception clause.[42] One of the conditions is that limitations must be 'provided for by law'.[43]

However, if there are no EU common rules in relation to investigation measures, it remains unclear to which extent the exercise of fundamental rights applicable to those measures can be adequately limited, how important such limitations may be for the EPPO to be able to effectively exercise its mission.

---

[35] See also Article 11(1) of the Commission's proposal.

[36] Article 30(1) of the Commission's proposal.

[37] See, to that effect, Joined Cases 46/87 and 227/88, *Hoechst* v. *Commission* [1989] ECR 2859, para 19.

[38] Joined Cases C-402/05 P and C-415/05 P, *Kadi and Al Barakaat International Foundation* v. *Council and Commission* [2008] ECR I-6351, para 358.

[39] Ibid., paras 368–370.

[40] Case C-617/10, *Åkerberg Fransson* [2013] not yet reported, para 29.

[41] Joined Cases C-584/10 P, C-593/10 P and C-595/10 P, *Commission and Others* v. *Kadi* [2013] not yet reported, paras 111–134.

[42] See ibid., para 101, and Case C–300/11, *ZZ* [2013] not yet reported, para 51.

[43] See, on the relevance of this condition, Case C-407/08 P, *Knauf Gips* v. *Commission* [2010] ECR I–6375, para 91, and Joined Cases C-92/09 and C-93/09, *Volker und Markus Schecke and Eifert* [2010] ECR I-11063, para 66.

Rule 48(5) of the Model Rules provides an illustration in this respect. According to this Rule, '[h]omes and other private premises may not be searched between 10.00 p.m. and 6.00 a.m. *This restriction does not apply if the evidence sought would be lost unless the search was conducted immediately*'.[44] The last sentence clearly contains what could be qualified, under the horizontal exception clause, as a limitation on the exercise of the fundamental right to privacy. However, without a similar provision in the Commission's proposal, it is less certain that the exercise of the right to privacy under Article 7 of the Charter can be limited in the same way. This would require that there exist a similar restriction in the national law applicable to an EPPO search measure and, most importantly, that this national law can qualify as a limitation, under the horizontal exception clause, of an EU fundamental right.

Therefore, the fact that the EU legislator does not adopt common rules on investigation measures may well lead to the paradoxical situation that the EPPO is faced with more stringent rules on those measures, derived from fundamental rights, than if the EU legislator had adopted such rules.[45]

8.3.4 Review of Search and Seizure Measures

Review of EPPO acts, and judicial review in particular, has always been an issue of reflection and debate.[46] Whereas the *Corpus Juris*[47] and the Commission's Green Paper[48] expressed a preference that the review function during the investigation stage be exercised by national courts, the Model Rules propose to give certain competences to the European Court.[49] Since the EPPO 'shall exercise the functions of prosecutor in the competent courts of the Member States',[50] the role of these courts in reviewing EPPO acts is clearly intended by the authors of the TFEU to be important. However, the question remains whether this important role justifies those courts to be exclusively competent to exercise such a review.

---

[44] Emphasis added.

[45] See further Inghelram 2012b, p. 81.

[46] See on this issue, e.g., Covolo 2011, pp. 148–153 and, for a detailed study, Böse 2012.

[47] Article 25bis(1) of the *Corpus Juris*.

[48] Green Paper on criminal-law protection of the financial interests of the Community and the establishment of a European Prosecutor, COM(2001) 715 final, pp. 62–63, Sect. 6.4.3, and pp 73–74, Sect. 8.2.2. A Follow-Up Report was adopted on 19 March 2003, COM(2003) 128 final.

[49] Rule 7(1) of the Model Rules.

[50] Article 86(2) TFEU.

8.3.4.1 Prior Authorisation Proceedings

The Commission's proposal does not break new ground where it gives the judicial authorities of the Member States the competence to authorise certain investigation measures of the EPPO,[51] including search measures. In the area of competition law, national judicial authorities also authorise the implementation of certain investigation measures ordered by the Commission in the Member States.[52]

Moreover, the current system of EU judicial protection, as organised by the TFEU, is based on a limited set of actions and proceedings,[53] which does not include prior authorisation proceedings.[54] The circumstance that specialised courts may be attached to the EU General Court under Article 257 TFEU[55] is not in itself an argument in favour of the possibility of creating, under the existing Treaty provisions, a specialised (chamber of an) EU court competent to issue prior authorisations in relation to investigation measures taken by an EPPO. Article 257 TFEU allows for the establishment of specialised courts competent 'to hear and determine at first instance certain classes of action or proceedings brought in specific areas', which implies that these courts hear and determine classes of action or proceedings which the EU General Court would normally hear and determine. Introducing a completely new class of actions or proceedings would go beyond the scope of that provision. In the same way, creating a prior authorisation procedure under Article 261 TFEU, which provides for the possibility to give the EU courts unlimited jurisdiction with regard to penalties, would imply an extensive reading of the scope of that provision.[56]

A major obstacle to granting a prior authorisation competence to EU courts is, however, the fact that EPPO investigations measures will also—and even predominantly—be governed by national law.[57] Examining compliance with national law is not the EU courts' task.[58] Therefore, granting a prior authorisation competence to EU courts in relation to EPPO investigation measures would either imply a questionable extension of their competences insofar as those measures are governed

[51] Article 26(4)–(5) of the Commission's proposal.

[52] See, e.g., Case C-94/00, *Roquette Frères* [2002] ECR I-9011.

[53] The most important actions are the action for infringement of the Treaty (Article 258 TFEU), the action for annulment (Article 263 TFEU), the action for failure to act (Article 265 TFEU), the preliminary ruling procedure (Article 267 TFEU) and the action for compensation for damage (Article 268 TFEU).

[54] Article 81 of the Euratom Treaty provides for a similar kind of procedure, which, however, does not seem to exceed the context of that provision.

[55] The only such specialised court currently is the Civil Service Tribunal.

[56] Even if one admits unlimited jurisdiction to be an 'autonomous' procedure, its objective always seems to be to amend or cancel sanctions which have been imposed, see further Lenaerts et al. 2006, para 15–003. See however Böse 2012, pp. 184–188, who considers that Article 261 TFEU can be used as a legal basis for a prior authorisation procedure at the EU level.

[57] Article 26(2) of the Commission's proposal.

[58] Article 19(1) TEU.

by national law or require a duplication of prior authorisation proceedings with one procedure at the national level to examine compliance with national law and another one at the EU level to examine compliance with EU law. Even if theoretically possible, the latter solution seems all but efficient.

Therefore, it would not be obvious to create a special EU court, or a special chamber within the EU General Court, exercising a prior authorisation competence in relation to EPPO investigation measures.

8.3.4.2 Judicial Review of the Validity of an EPPO Investigation Measure Under EU Law

The Commission's proposal is innovative insofar as judicial review of the validity of investigation measures of the EPPO is concerned. Article 36(1) of the Commission's proposal contains a legal fiction in this respect: when adopting procedural and investigation measures in the performance of its functions, the EPPO shall be considered as a national authority for the purposes of judicial review.[59] The result of this legal fiction is that national courts, and not EU courts, will be competent to review the validity of investigation measures of the EPPO.[60]

This is a major change compared to the current situation of judicial review under the EU Treaties, insofar as those measures are governed by EU law. Indeed, in spite of the aforementioned legal fiction, the EPPO undoubtedly is an EU body[61] and it is, until now, settled case-law that the EU courts alone have jurisdiction to determine whether the act of an EU institution or body is invalid (under EU law).[62] The Commission's proposal amounts to creating an exception to this basic rule of judicial review, to which there has not yet been any exception until now and which is, according to the ECJ's settled case-law, firmly established in primary EU law.[63] Moreover, since 'the tasks attributed to the national courts and to the [ECJ]

[59] Article 36(1) of the Commission's proposal only mentions 'procedural measures', but it follows from recital 37 in the preamble that this provision is intended to also apply to investigation measures.

[60] This is also the intention of this legal fiction, as recitals 37 and 38 in the preamble demonstrate.

[61] Article 3(1) of the Commission's proposal.

[62] See, to that effect, Case C-461/03, *Gaston Schul Douane-expediteur* [2005] ECR I-10513, para 22 and case-law cited. See also Joined Cases C-188/10 and C-189/10, *Melki and Abdeli* [2010] ECR I–5667, para 54. This case-law does not only apply to EU legislative acts, but also to individual acts adopted by EU institutions, see Case C-119/05, *Lucchini* [2007] ECR I-6199, para 53, where this case–law was applied to a Commission decision in the area of state aid. For an analysis of this case-law in the area of criminal law, see Schonard 2012, pp. 63–64.

[63] 'The possibility of a national court ruling on the invalidity of [an EU] act is [...] incompatible with the necessary coherence of the system of judicial protection instituted by the [TFEU]. [...] By Articles [263 TFEU] and [277 TFEU], on the one hand, and Article [267 TFEU], on the other, the Treaty established a complete system of legal remedies and procedures designed to ensure review of the legality of acts of the institutions and has entrusted such review to the [EU] Courts', Case C-461/03, *Gaston Schul Douane-expediteur*, cited supra n. 62, para 22.

respectively are indispensable to the preservation of the very nature of the law established by the Treaties',[64] the question remains whether this exception is possible at all.

The practical implications are important. Since national courts will be called upon to review the legality of EPPO investigations measures under, for instance, the Charter, such review can give rise to opposing results in two different Member States in relation to one and the same investigation measure. Indeed, theoretically, a court can authorise a house search in one Member State,[65] considering that this house search does not violate Article 7 of the Charter, whereas a court in another Member State can refuse to admit evidence obtained through this house search at the trial,[66] because it is of the opinion that that provision has nevertheless been violated. This may lay a burden on the system of mutual recognition, since it will ultimately be the court on which the duty to recognise rests, which will be called upon to interpret the limit to that duty by ruling whether the investigation measure is valid or not under the Charter.

Moreover, it is far from certain that the objective of the Commission's proposal to let national courts review the validity of EPPO acts will be achieved in practice. Indeed, although recital 38 in the preamble states that '[n]ational courts should not be able to refer questions on the validity of the acts of the [EPPO] to the [ECJ]', such questions can nonetheless be submitted to the ECJ through a request for a preliminary ruling, not on the validity of the investigation measure, but on the interpretation of EU law. Indeed, a question on the validity under the EPPO regulation or the Charter of an investigation measure can easily be formulated—at the initiative of the national court or the ECJ itself—as a question of interpretation of that regulation or the Charter. This is current practice when national courts submit questions for a preliminary ruling to the ECJ on the validity of national law. Since it is not competent to rule on the validity of national law, the ECJ usually qualifies the question as a question of interpretation of EU law in order to give a useful answer to the national court submitting the question.[67]

Therefore, even if, under the Commission's proposal, national courts will *not* be *bound* to submit a question for a preliminary ruling to the ECJ on the validity of an investigation measure of the EPPO, they will *still* be *able* to do so. Faced with an entirely new and complex area of EU law and perhaps eager to avoid *Köbler*-inspired claims for damages,[68] national courts may well submit such questions more often than expected.

Furthermore, the EU courts may possibly participate in the review of the legality of acts of the EPPO through the action for damages. Under Article 69(5) of the

---

[64] Opinion 1/09 [2011] ECR I-1137, para 85.

[65] Article 26(4) of the Commission's proposal.

[66] Article 30(1) of the Commission's proposal.

[67] See, e.g., Case C-53/04, *Marrosu and Sardino* [2006], ECR I-7213, paras 31–32 and case-law cited.

[68] Case C-224/01, *Köbler* [2003] ECR I-10239, para 50.

Commission's proposal, the EU courts have jurisdiction in disputes over compensation for damage caused. It is precisely this kind of action which has allowed the development of judicial review of investigation measures carried out by OLAF.[69]

8.3.4.3 An Alternative Solution?

Considering the above, the question arises whether an alternative solution exists which takes due account of, on the one hand, the basic rule that EU courts are exclusively competent to review the validity under EU law of the acts of an EU body and, on the other hand, the important role given by Article 86 TFEU to the courts of the Member States.

In this respect, it appears interesting to refer to the division of competences between national courts and the EU courts in relation to judicial review of investigation orders of the Commission in the area of competition law.[70] In Case C-94/00, *Roquette Frères*,[71] the ECJ underlined the exclusive competence of the EU courts to review the lawfulness of the assessment by the Commission of the need for investigations in the area of competition law.[72] Nevertheless, in accordance with the general principle of EU law affording protection against arbitrary or disproportionate intervention by public authorities in the sphere of the private activities of any person, a national court having a prior authorisation competence in relation to search and seizure measures is required to verify that such measures sought in pursuance of a request by the Commission for assistance are not arbitrary or disproportionate to the subject matter of the investigation ordered.[73]

The ECJ's reasoning in Case C-94/00, *Roquette Frères*, is based on fundamental rules which are applicable in the EU context under all circumstances. These are essentially the following: the need for protection of fundamental rights; the exclusive competence, in principle, of the EU courts to review the validity of EU acts; and the principle of cooperation between the EU institutions and the Member States. In this respect, the ruling could serve as a guideline for defining the extent to which national courts and EU courts share the competence of reviewing investigation measures of an EPPO, insofar as those are governed by EU law.[74]

Applying the *Roquette Frères*-solution to judicial review of the validity under EU law of EPPO acts does not seem contrary to Article 86 TFEU which, in any

[69] See further Inghelram 2012a.

[70] For a general study on the relevance for the EPPO of the cooperation mechanisms in EU competition law, see Böse 2013.

[71] See supra n. 52.

[72] Idem, para 39.

[73] Idem, para 99, first indent.

[74] For an application of this solution to two hypothetical examples (house search and committal for trial), see Inghelram 2011, pp. 268–270.

event, does not make mention of an exclusive competence of the Member States' courts under all circumstances. Furthermore, even if it is true that, under such a solution, review exercised by the national court would be limited—only insofar as the application of EU law is concerned[75]—to examining whether the EPPO investigation measure sought is not arbitrary or disproportionate to the subject matter of the investigation, this is not necessarily problematic from a perspective of the fundamental right to an effective remedy, as enshrined in Article 47 of the Charter. The review procedure as a whole should indeed be taken into consideration, which would also include the EU courts' participation through, for instance, a request for a preliminary ruling submitted to it by the national court concerned if the latter has real doubts on the validity under EU law of the EPPO investigation measure applied for.

Furthermore, Article 276 TFEU is not necessarily an obstacle to such a solution either.[76] It indeed seems possible to argue that this provision specifically applies to the particular circumstances mentioned at the end of that provision, i.e. the 'maintenance of law and order' and the 'safeguarding of internal security', and, hence, not to operations carried out by the police or other law enforcement services of a Member State on behalf of the EU itself.

Finally, several instruments exist for a rapid intervention by the EU courts, if necessary, such as the urgent preliminary ruling procedure[77] which can be applied in the Area of Freedom, Security and Justice and hence to requests for a preliminary ruling in relation to EPPO acts. Furthermore, it is theoretically possible to transfer jurisdiction to hear and determine such requests to the EU General Court.[78]

8.4 Final Remarks

The Commission's proposal raises interesting legal questions as to the division of competences between the Member States and the EU, well-illustrated by the investigative competences which a future EPPO will have by virtue of Article 86(2) TFEU. An important challenge in this respect is that of defining a system of judicial review which takes due account of, on the one hand, the basic rule that EU courts are exclusively competent to review the validity under EU law of the acts of an EU body, which the EPPO will in any event be, and, on the other hand, the important

---

[75] The national court would remain fully competent to examine compliance of the investigation measure with the applicable national law.

[76] According to this provision, '[i]n exercising its powers regarding the provisions [...] relating to the area of freedom, security and justice, the [ECJ] shall have no jurisdiction to review the validity or proportionality of operations carried out by the police or other law enforcement services of a Member State or the exercise of the responsibilities incumbent upon Member States with regard to the maintenance of law and order and the safeguarding of internal security.'

[77] Articles 107–114 of the Rules of Procedure of the ECJ.

[78] Article 256(3) TFEU.

role given by Article 86 TFEU to the courts of the Member States. The Commission's proposal gives priority to the latter consideration by conferring exclusive competence on those courts to review the validity of EPPO investigation measures. Apart from any questions as to the legality of such a solution, such a review will nonetheless most likely end up being, in practice, a shared responsibility between the national and the EU courts. This shared responsibility is the quintessence of EU judicial review[79] and any proposal on judicial review of EPPO investigation measures seems bound to face this reality.

References

Böse M (2012) Ein europäischer Ermittlungsrichter—Perspektiven des präventiven Rechtsschutzes bei Errichtung einer Europäischen Staatsanwaltschaft. Rechtswissenschaft 3:172–196

Böse M (2013) The system of vertical and horizontal cooperation in administrative investigations in EU competition cases. In: Ligeti K (ed) Toward a prosecutor for the European Union, vol 1, a comparative analysis. Hart Publishing, Oxford, pp 838–869

Braum S (2009) Justizförmigkeit und europäische Betrugsermittlung—Bemerkungen zum Fall Eurostat (EuG T-48/05, Urteil vom 8. 7. 2008). JuristenZeitung 64:298–304

Covolo V (2011) Et la judiciarisation de l'espace pénal de l'Union fût … mais où se cache le juge pénal européen? Cahiers de droit européen 47:103–154

Covolo V (2012) From Europol to Eurojust—towards a European public prosecutor. Where does OLAF fit in? Eucrim 2012:83–88

Đurđević Z (2013) Judicial control in pre-trial criminal procedure conducted by the European public prosecutor's office. In: Ligeti K (ed) Toward a prosecutor for the European Union, vol 1, a comparative analysis. Hart Publishing, Oxford, pp 986–1010

Flore D (2008) La perspective d'un procureur européen. ERA Forum 9:229–243

Inghelram J (2011) Legal and Institutional aspects of the European Anti-Fraud Office (OLAF)—an analysis with a look forward to a European public prosecutor's office. Europa Law Publishing, Groningen

Inghelram J (2012a) Judicial review of investigative acts of the European Anti-Fraud Office (OLAF): a search for a balance. Common Market Law Rev 49:601–628

Inghelram J (2012b) Fundamental rights, the European Anti-Fraud Office (OLAF) and a European Public Prosecutor's Office (EPPO): some selected issues. Kritische Vierteljahresschrift für Gesetzgebung und Rechtswissenschaft 95:67–81

Lenaerts K et al (2006) Procedural law of the European Union, 2nd edn. Sweet & Maxwell, London

Ligeti K (ed) (2013) Toward a prosecutor for the European Union, a comparative analysis, vol 1. Hart Publishing, Oxford

Ligeti K, Simonato M (2013) The European public prosecutor's office: towards a truly European prosecution service. New J Eur Crim Law 4:7–21

Nilsson H (2000) Eurojust: the beginning or the end of the European public prosecutor? Europarättslig tidskrift 3:601–621

Schonard P (2012) Judicial review of EU acts affecting criminal proceedings. Eur Crim Law Rev 2:61–76

Vervaele J (2008) The shaping and reshaping of Eurojust and OLAF—investigative judicial powers in the European judicial area. Eucrim 2008(3–4):180–186

[79] See, e.g., Opinion 1/09 [2011] ECR I-1137, para 69.

Weyembergh A (2013) Traverse report on judicial control in cooperation in criminal matters: the evolution from traditional judicial cooperation to mutual recognition. In: Ligeti K (ed) Toward a prosecutor for the European Union, vol 1, a comparative analysis. Hart Publishing, Oxford, pp 945–985

White S (2013) Towards a decentralized European public prosecutor's office? New J Eur Crim Law 4:22–39

Zwiers M (2011) The European public prosecutor's office. Intersentia, Antwerp

Chapter 9
The Choice of Forum by the European Public Prosecutor

Martin Wasmeier

Abstract The European Public Prosecutor's Office will be a supranational authority working within a pluralistic legal framework and, thus, often be able to choose from several jurisdictions. Since this choice determines the law applicable to its investigations and prosecutions, it will have a high impact on the legal position of the persons involved and on the outcome of proceedings. Unlike in the current scheme of 'horizontal' cooperation, within the substantial and geographical spheres of EPPO's competence, there will be no more parallel proceedings in various participating Member States. As an agent on Union level, EPPO will select the forum in a multilateral instead of a national perspective. With regard to its unique position and powers, the necessary flexibility needs to be balanced with legal certainty, i.e. its discretion should not be unlimited but framed by appropriate rules on Union level. This article examines the Commission's proposal from this point of view and highlights certain points where it could be fine-tuned and/or complemented in order to exclude any doubts on the transparency, legitimacy and reasonableness of the forum choice.

Keywords European Public Prosecutor's Office · Conflicts of jurisdiction · Choice of forum · Applicable law · Judicial review · Procedural rights · Indictment · Dismissal · Transaction · Legality principle · Fair trial

The author was Head of Unit Legal Advice at the European Anti-Fraud Office (OLAF). Momentarily he is staff member of the Legal Service of the European Commission. The views expressed are exclusively those of the author and may not in any circumstance be regarded as expressing an official position of the European Commission.

M. Wasmeier (✉)
European Commission, Brussels, Belgium
e-mail: martin.wasmeier@ec.europa.eu

L.H. Erkelens et al. (eds.), *The European Public Prosecutor's Office*,
DOI 10.1007/978-94-6265-035-0_9

Contents

9.1 Introduction

According to Article 86(2) TFEU, the European Public Prosecutor's Office (EPPO) shall exercise the functions of prosecutor in the competent courts of the Member States. Since it is part of the Area of Freedom, Security and Justice (AFSJ), the Union legislator has an enhanced obligation to respect the different legal systems and traditions of the Member States, as expressed in Article 67(1) TFEU which goes beyond the general principle in Article 4(2) TEU. Therefore, whatever the institutional design of the Office may be,[1] it will operate in a pluralistic legal environment. Consequently, the Commission's proposal for a regulation on the establishment of EPPO[2] (EPPO proposal) frequently refers to national law. It builds upon a combination of mutual recognition and a moderate approximation of national criminal laws.[3]

Where more than one Member State has jurisdiction,[4] EPPO will have to make a choice on where to bring charges. The present article focuses on the conclusive stage, especially the indictment, but it will also examine decisions at earlier stages which may initially set the course. EPPO should have sufficient flexibility and discretion to determine in each case the most appropriate Member State to

[1] For an overview of the main models, see Ligeti and Simonato 2013, p. 12 et seq.

[2] COM(2013)534 final.

[3] See Articles 11(3), 18(2), 26(2), 27, 30, 32(3), 32(5), 33 et seq., 36 of EPPO proposal (Appendix to this book). On the relevant criminal offences, Article 12 refers to the proposed Directive on the fight against fraud to the Union's financial interests by means of criminal law, COM(2012) 363 final.

[4] Unless indicated otherwise, 'jurisdiction' is used here in a wide sense, comprising the jurisdiction to prescribe, to adjudicate and to enforce. In criminal law the latter two depend usually on the first, see Luchtman 2013, p. 29. For an overview of jurisdictional rules in the Member States, see Sinn 2012, pp. 532–534.

prosecute. However, this flexibility needs to be balanced with legal certainty, since this choice has an enormous impact on the position and interests of all parties involved—not only factually (e.g. with regard to languages, travelling, financial and psychological burdens), but also on their rights and obligations. The choice of forum is intrinsically linked to the applicable law, not only in procedural but also in substantive terms, because the Member States' 'international criminal law'[5] is dominated by the *lex fori* principle, i.e. their courts apply the law of their own state.[6] While foreign substantive criminal law can come into play where a state requires dual criminality and/or restricts its penalty range in view of a foreign *lex mitior*,[7] such complementary references do not change the principle that Member States apply their own criminal law.

Thus, the choice of forum is of crucial importance for the process and outcome of the prosecution. It determines the scope and conditions of criminal liability, the sentencing, range and type of penalties, time limits and other grounds for barring prosecution, the latter's limits of discretion, the competent court, the nature of the procedure (e.g. adversarial or inquisitorial)[8] and any procedural issues from the position and rights of the defendants or victims to the scope of judicial review and possibilities to appeal.

9.2 The Larger Picture: Conflicts of Jurisdiction in AFSJ

9.2.1 Background (Need for a Legal Framework on Jurisdiction)

Before analysing the specific situation regarding EPPO, it is worth taking a step back and looking at the general framework of judicial cooperation in criminal matters laid down in Title V, Chap. 4 TFEU. Principally, this chapter deals with 'horizontal' cooperation, i.e. cooperation among the Member States' competent authorities. Its *Leitmotiv* is the principle of mutual recognition, complemented and supported by a limited approximation of laws, as set out in Articles 82 and 83 TFEU. The dominance of mutual recognition in EU criminal law has been

---

5 In the present article, this term refers to 'national law' on the scope of a State's criminal law and its *ius puniendi* (comparable to the term 'international private law'). It is used differently in the context of supranational or transnational criminal law, see Kreß 2009.

6 Green Paper COM(2001)715 final, p. 55; Green Paper, Annex SEC(2005)1767, pt. 1; Sinn 2012, p. 537; Vervaele 2013a, p. 171. Cf. the contributions on national systems in: Sinn (ed.) 2012, p. 181 et seq. and the 'synoptic comparison' at: http://www.zeis.eak-ok.de/inJurisdex.php. Accessed 7 November 2013.

7 Böse 2013, pp. 86–87, proposes that foreign law should generally be applied in case of extraterritorial jurisdiction (conceding, however, that this may be controversial). A different issue is the implicit relevance of foreign civil law ('*Vorfrage*', see Schmidt-Kessel 2012, pp. 68–71).

8 For a general comparison, see Spencer 2002, p. 25 et seq. Cf. Spronken 2013, p. 96 et seq.

criticised, particularly regarding the admission of evidence. In any case, it is nowadays widely recognised that it needs to be complemented by a stronger emphasis on individual rights (through approximation and/or grounds for refusal) and by rules on jurisdiction.[9] With regard to Eurojust, Article 85 TFEU adds an institutional component, featuring some cautious supranational elements. But in its operational dimension Eurojust remains in the context of coordination and essentially 'horizontal' cooperation.[10] In contrast, Article 86 TFEU foresees a 'vertical', i.e. supranational or hierarchical structure. This disparity is clearly expressed in both Treaty articles.[11] Nonetheless, EPPO is embedded in the same framework of primary law, shares its overall objectives and will have to build on the Union *acquis* in the AFSJ.

The topic at stake is addressed twice in the TFEU: Article 82(1)(b) calls on the Union to adopt measures to prevent and settle conflicts of jurisdiction ('shall');[12] according to Article 85(1)(c), Eurojust can be entrusted with the resolution of such conflicts. This double reference and call for action underlines that the authors of the Treaties considered such measures as an integral part of an AFSJ—even more so as both articles allow for regulations.[13] It is clear that the word 'conflict' refers both to 'positive' (i.e. several prosecutions) and 'negative' conflicts (i.e. absence of prosecution). As to the distinction between 'concrete' conflicts (i.e. dissent on who should prosecute a concrete case) and 'abstract' conflicts (i.e. where the law of several States confers jurisdiction, comparable to the term 'conflicts of law'),[14] there are reasons to believe that the two abovementioned provisions do not only refer to concrete, but also to abstract conflicts. Although this matter does not have to

---

[9] On this debate see Klip 2012, p. 198 et seq., 472 et seq.; Mitsilegas 2013, p. 5; Asp et al. 2013; Gless 2013a, p. 95 et seq.; Gless 2013b, pp. 4–7, and the author's contribution in: *Handbuch Europäisches Strafrecht*, 2nd edn., Nomos, Baden-Baden (forthcoming), § 32 paras 57–67. The Stockholm programme (OJ C 115, 04/05/2010, pp. 1–38, see Sects. 2.4., 3., 3.1.1.) recognises the need to support and complement mutual recognition with regard to procedural rights and jurisdiction; see also Council Resolution of 30.11.2009 ('Roadmap for procedural rights'), OJ 2009 L 295/1; Green Paper COM(2005)696 final.

[10] See European Parliament 2012. In view of the present author, the adjunct 'horizontal' is more appropriate than 'intergovernmental', also for the cooperation under ex-Article 29 et seq. TEU, as the law of the former "third pillar" had already transcended classical inter-state cooperation, cf. ECJ 16 June 2005 Case C-105/03, *Pupino* [2005] ECR I-5285.

[11] See on the one hand Article 85(2) TFEU, on the other hand Article 86(2) and (3) TFEU. Cf. Weyembergh 2011, pp. 83, 98; Ligeti and Simonato 2013, pp. 10–12.

[12] The noteworthy difference in language as compared to Article 81(2)(c) TFEU (the latter just refers to the 'compatibility' of national rules) indicates that this matter is less acute in private law, where the Union framework on jurisdiction is developed much further (cf. Regulation 1215/2012, O.J. 2012 L 351/1).

[13] Article 82(2) and 83 TFEU are limited to Directives setting 'minimum rules'. In contrast, 'measures' in Article 82(1)(c) include regulations; Article 85(1)(c) provides for regulations only; see also Article 83(3) ('emergency brake').

[14] Cf. Van der Beken et al. 2002, p. 18.

be decided here, in the following the term conflict of jurisdiction will be used in this wider sense.[15]

In a single market without internal borders and free movement of persons, services, goods and capital, such situations are likely to occur frequently. This would even be the case if Member States were to restrict their jurisdiction to the territoriality principle (as is the case in the UK with its three different jurisdictions),[16] since today this concept is usually construed as comprising the State where a damage or effect of crime occurs. The single element the principle requires is a nexus with the territory of the regulating state, as determined by national law.[17] In cases of transnational crime, it is very common that the *locus delicti* spreads over the territory of several Member States, especially where the perpetrators act via the internet,[18] which is of course happening more frequently in a rapidly growing digital market. And particularly, the effect and/or benefit of financial crimes are often not limited to the same State wherein the behaviour is incriminated. Moreover, both the EU and the international community promote extraterritorial jurisdiction and often make it obligatory, in order to avoid 'negative' conflicts and possible impunity.[19] The downside of this is an enhanced chance of 'positive' conflicts.

Today, there is a wide consensus that a legal framework for the prevention and settlement of conflicts of jurisdiction is essential for the functioning of a justice area built on mutual recognition.[20] In criminal matters, mutual recognition began without such a framework—unlike in civil matters, where it went hand in hand with jurisdictional rules from the outset.[21] While caution is required in any comparison between civil and criminal matters, it appears appropriate to say that in both areas there is an intrinsic link between jurisdiction and mutual recognition. In fact, in criminal law this link is even tighter because of the dominance of the *lex fori* rule, whereas civil law courts often apply foreign law (for instance, as *lex causae*), based on multilateral rules on conflicts of law, which as such do not exist in criminal law.[22]

---

[15] Also, at the indictment and/or the trial phase, the terms jurisdiction and forum will be used interchangeably.

[16] See Spencer 2013, pp. 64, 71 ('territoriality and nothing more'). Some authors propose to restrict the jurisdiction to prescribe to the territoriality principle, see e.g. Böse 2013, p. 86; Klip 2012, p. 474.

[17] Klip 2012, p. 191.

[18] Cf. Article 10(2) Framework Decision 2005/222 on Attacks against Information Systems, *OJ* 2005 L 69/67. See also Böse 2013, p. 80.

[19] For examples see Klip 2012, p. 194 et seq.; Green paper, Annex SEC(2005)1767 pt. 4.

[20] See COM(2000)495 final, pt. 13.2; Green paper COM(2005) 696 final and Annex SEC(2005) 1767. Haag Programme, O.J. 2005 C 53/1, pt 3.3.1; see also the references supra n. 9.

[21] See Regulation 44/2001, O.J. 2001 L 12/1, based on the 'Brussels I' Convention of 1968; cf. Regulation 2201/2003, O.J. 2003 L 338/1. For a parallel example in public law (driving licences) see Klip, p. 474.

[22] See Regulation 593/2008, O.J. L 177/6, based on the 'Rome I' Convention of 1980; Regulation 864/2007 (Rome II), *OJ* L 119/40. For a related comparison of criminal and civil law, see Schmidt-Kessel 2012, p. 74 et seq.

In sum, there are four main arguments for the creation of an EU framework on conflicts of criminal law jurisdiction. Firstly, in its absence, there will be parallel and/or overlapping procedures in different Member States on the same acts ('positive' conflicts), which entail increased burdens for the persons involved and a reduced efficiency and/or effectiveness of prosecution. Besides, in a real area of justice, parallel proceedings may be considered as antagonistic to this end. Secondly, without clarity there may be a lack of ownership and responsibility which leads to 'negative' conflicts, i.e. a total or partial absence of prosecution. Thirdly, it is increasingly argued that an arbitrary choice of jurisdiction ('forum shopping') should be excluded, i.e. executive discretion must have a limit, especially with a view to the principle of legality and the right to a fair trial (Articles 6, 7 ECHR, Articles 47–49 CFR).[23] The case law of the ECtHR provides for a test of a reasonable, non-arbitrary and (to a certain extent) foreseeable choice of jurisdiction, free from extraneous influence.[24] The *ratio* of this case law also applies to an AFSJ, based on the rule of law, common fundamental rights and principles and a Union citizenship.

Fourthly, in the absence of common denominators on the choice of jurisdiction and where the relevant criteria and procedure remain unclear, it will be difficult to achieve and maintain a high degree of mutual trust between the national authorities.[25] Unless there is a guarantee that the legitimate interests of all Member States involved will be taken into account, their authorities will not be able to transcend their traditional, i.e. national perspective. Instead of identifying the most suitable forum from a European perspective, they will continue to focus on the protection of their own particular interests and, therefore, insist upon numerous, extensive exceptions from mutual recognition, so they can keep relevant cases as far as possible in their 'own house'.[26] This can partly explain the rather limited progress achieved so far in putting mutual recognition in criminal law into reality.[27] Mutual trust requires that Member States can be sure that their interests are taken into account and given appropriate weight in the choice of jurisdiction.[28]

[23] See Van der Beken et al. 2002, pp. 30, 35; Luchtman 2013, pp. 22, 25, 29 et seq., 49 et seq. and several other contributions in: Luchtman (ed.) 2013; Asp et al. 2013, pp. 432, 440–442. Cf. ECtHR 17 September 2009 *Scoppola* v. *Italy* (No. 2), application no. 10249/03, para 92.

[24] ECtHR 22 June 2000, application nos. 32492/96 et al. *Coeme and others* v. *Belgium*, paras 148, 149; 12 July 2007, *Jorgic* v. *Germany*, application no. 74613/01, para 64; 22 January 2013 *Camilleri* v. *Malta*, application no. 42931/10, para 34 et seq. and dissenting opinion by judge Kalaydjieva.

[25] Cf. supra n. 20.

[26] For instance, the *Bundesverfassungsgericht* requires German nationals to be prosecuted in their own country if there is a significant link thereto (*maßgeblicher Inlandsbezug*), see judgment of 18 July 2005 on the European Arrest Warrant 2 BvR 2236/04, para 84 et seq. This approach promotes positive conflicts of jurisdiction. Therefore, from an EU perspective, it should be decisive whether there is a predominant, rather than just a significant link, cf. Wasmeier 2006, p. 33 et seq.

[27] Cf. Spencer 2013, pp. 69–70, with further references.

[28] Green Paper, Annex SEC(2005)1767, pt. 2.

9.2.2 Achievements So Far

So where do we stand today? Two instruments apply to ongoing procedures: Eurojust can mediate, coordinate and/or request a national authority to take on a case or to accept that another authority is better placed.[29] A framework decision of 2009 provides for mutual information and consultation, whereby Eurojust should be involved 'if appropriate'.[30] However, these instruments contain neither criteria for the choice of jurisdiction,[31] nor competence to take decisions at Union level[32] or to transfer proceedings to another State. On the latter, the European Convention on Transfer of Proceedings of 15 May 1972[33] applies to 13 EU Member States, but attempts to create a similar EU instrument did not produce results.[34] In contrast, once a decision has been taken in a Member State where it has the force of *res judicata*, criminal prosecutions anywhere else in the Union are excluded. The *ne bis in idem* principle contained in Article 54 of the Convention Implementing the Schengen Agreement (CISA) is incorporated in the Union *acquis* and valid in all Member States.[35] Based on the principle of mutual recognition and the right to free movement, the ECJ has developed it into a full-fledged fundamental right, which beyond court judgments applies to any decision that bars further prosecution under national law.[36] It remains to be seen whether certain restrictions and national reservations on Article 54, 55 CISA can be overcome via the parallel right in Article 50 CFR.[37]

However, *ne bis in idem* only provides a solution at the very end of proceedings, which may take years. Until then, it does not prevent parallel prosecution. In fact, it does not deal with the forum choice, but rather leads to a 'first come, first served' effect.[38] Wherever the first final decision occurs—and this may depend on random factors—it will exclude any other prosecution within the Union, no matter whether it took all the relevant interests, facts and circumstances into account, or not.

[29] Decision 2002/187/JHA establishing Eurojust, *OJ* 2002 L 63/1, amended by Decision 2009/426/JHA, *OJ* 2009 L 138/14; see especially Article 6(1)(a), 7(1)(a), (2).

[30] 2009/948/JHA, *OJ* 2009 L 328/42 (see especially Article 12(2)).

[31] Recital 9 of the Framework Decision refers to the 2003 Eurojust guidelines.

[32] *De lege ferenda,* the Union could confer on Eurojust the power to settle conflicts and/or to instruct to initiate an investigation (Article 85(1)(c) TFEU). Whether such instructions would be effective remains to be seen, as national authorities would stay in charge of the investigations.

[33] Council of Europe, ETS 73.

[34] See the draft framework decision in Council doc. 11119/09.

[35] *OJ* 2000 L 239/35 and Protocol No. 19 to the Treaty of Lisbon. For the application in the UK and Ireland see Council Decisions *OJ* 2000 L 131/43; 2002 L 64/20.

[36] ECJ 11 February 2003, Joined Cases C 187/01 & 385/01 *Gözütok and Brügge* [2003] ECR I-1345, para 38. On the development of the case law, see Wasmeier and Thwaites 2006; Vervaele 2013b.

[37] See Vervaele 2013b, pp. 225–227 (with case law references); however, on some aspects the text of Article 50 CFR is narrower than Article 54 CISA.

[38] Green Paper, Annex SEC(2005)1767, pt. 1; Klip 2012, p. 200; Asp et al. 2013, p. 441.

In turn, this 'Wild West solution'[39] can weaken mutual trust, which is an essential precondition for mutual recognition. Thus, the legal framework remains incomplete: *ne bis in idem* is only one side of the coin and makes the need to deal with conflicts among ongoing proceedings even more acute. The Commission has clearly identified this problem in its Green Paper on conflicts of jurisdiction and the principle of *ne bis in idem,*[40] although it has not yet presented a legislative proposal. This may be influenced by hesitation among the Member States.[41] However, the debate in academia has brought about several proposals.[42]

9.3 The Commission's Proposal for an EPPO

The choice of forum by EPPO should be seen against this background. In the *integrated model* proposed by the Commission, the European Public Prosecutor (EPP) as the Head of Office assigns cases to Delegated Prosecutors, who act in the national legal framework of their original authority.[43] Thus, the allocation of a case to a Delegated Prosecutor has at least a preliminary effect of determining jurisdiction and consequently the applicable national law. Where the EPP decides to conduct an investigation himself/herself, a jurisdictional choice can be made at another stage, at the latest, at the conclusion of the investigation.

9.3.1 Issues of Competence

At first, EPPO will have to verify its competence. Article 12 of the EPPO proposal defines the competence *ratione materiae* by reference to the offences in its proposal for a Directive on the fight against fraud to the Union's financial interests by means of criminal law (PIF Directive),[44] 'as implemented by national law'. The Commission has proposed rather detailed definitions of these offences, but a general

---

39 So pointedly Spencer 2013, p. 71.

40 Green Paper COM(2005)696 final and Annex SEC(2005)1767; see also COM(2000)495 final, pt. 13.2.

41 As demonstrated by the lack of support for an initiative presented by Greece, *OJ* 2003 C 100/24.

42 See Lagodny 2001, p. 99 et seq.; Van der Beken et al. 2002, p. 48 et seq.; 'Freiburg proposal', in: Biehler et al. 2003; Sinn (ed.) 2012, pp. 604–605 and 609–613 (draft models) and the references to the (former) Swiss law on intercantonal case allocation at Luchtman 2013, pp. 6/37 and Vervaele 2013a, pp. 180/181.

43 See Articles 6, 16, 18, 27 of the EPPO proposal.

44 See supra n. 3. These offences could be defined by means of a regulation, if one shares the Commission's view that Article 325(4) TFEU is an appropriate legal basis (it allows for 'measures', which includes regulations). However, several Member States contest this view, holding that the correct legal basis is Article 83(2) TFEU, which only provides for Directives.

approach reached by the Council in June 2013 establishes only minimum rules.[45] Under this approach, such a directive would not define all constituent elements of offences exhaustively and in a uniform manner; even the Commission proposal for such a directive may leave room for some variety in detail. In any case, at least in its incriminating aspects, such a directive will not be directly applicable (Article 288(3) TFEU).[46]

It remains to be seen whether this could even lead to situations, where the scope of EPPO's competence might not be exactly the same in all Member States, because of certain differences in the details of national definitions permitted by the directive. If this were the case, there would be the risk of a circular reasoning, even more so since EPPO's competence will be exclusive: if the limits of the competence depend on national law, the assignment of a case could have an influence on whether EPPO is competent or not.[47]

On the whole, it seems preferable to define the competence *ratione materiae* directly in a regulation with binding force and directly applicable in all Member States (Article 288(2) TFEU).[48] It is doubtful whether such a regulation could be based on Article 86, since its para (3) mainly refers to procedural rules. On the one hand, in the light of the principle of conferral in Articles 5(1) and 5(2) TEU, the words 'general rules applicable to the' EPPO may not be sufficiently specific;[49] on the other hand, such definitions could be needed in order to achieve the objectives of Article 86 TFEU.[50] A solution for this dilemma may be included in a regulation based on Article 325(4) TFEU.[51]

There are also other issues ensuing from the relationship between EPPO's competence and choice of jurisdiction. The first question concerns international jurisdiction: Article 14 of the EPPO proposal points to the principles of territoriality and active personality, the latter being extended to EU staff and members of EU institutions. Thus, where a Member State's international jurisdiction goes further (for instance, based on passive personality), EPPO would not be able to initiate an investigation on the basis of, e.g., the principle of passive personality; if in such situation the State does not act either, it could result in a 'negative conflict of jurisdiction'. A second question arises from the Office's ancillary competence for offences

---

[45] See Council doc. 10729/13. This difference is linked to the above mentioned controversy on the legal basis.

[46] Directives cannot create or aggravate criminal liability, see ECJ 8 October 1987, Case 80/86, *Kolpinghuis Nijmegen* [1987] ECR 3969; 3 May 2005, Cases C-387/02 et al. *Berlusconi* et al. [2005] ECR I-3565.

[47] See Article 11(4) of the EPPO proposal.

[48] See M. Pawlik, A. Klip in Chap. 11 in this book.

[49] Article 5 TEU requires a specific conferral, as it is clearly expressed in the German version of the Treaty (*Grundsatz der begrenzten Einzelermächtigung*), although this may be less clear in the English text.

[50] Cf. Delmas-Marty and Vervaele (eds.) 2000, p. 62 et seq, Articles 1–17 of the *Corpus Juris* (pp. 189–196).

[51] See supra n. 44.

inextricably linked with a predominant offence within its exclusive competence. According to Article 13(3) of the proposal, in case of disagreement, the competent national authority should be competent to decide. However, if there is an inextricable link to offences in several Member States, whose authority will then decide? Will EPPO then be able to choose from several jurisdictions? For instance, the facts of a fraud case may include a forgery of documents, a breach of trust or a tax fraud in several Member States. As the prosecution of such offences will not protect rights and interests of the Union directly, it does not seem appropriate to leave the choice to EPPO. Eurojust could play a useful role in resolving such dilemmas.[52]

9.3.2 Investigation

The act of initiating an investigation by EPPO and assigning it to a Delegated Prosecutor, *ipso facto* determines the applicable national law.[53] An initial suspicion may already be linked with the jurisdiction of several Member States. Taking the example of a manipulated procurement procedure, where goods and/or services are to be provided in various countries, the criminal behaviour may have occurred and/or damage may have been done in most or all of them. The *locus delicti* may extend over several countries, i.e. where the perpetrators acted (e.g. produced falsified documents, signed declarations, agreed to collude, etc.) or gained benefits, or where another significant economic impact occurred.[54] It could be argued that damage also occurs at the seat of the Commission as the institution responsible for executing the budget.

In addition, as mentioned above,[55] EU law often requires the Member States to establish extraterritorial jurisdiction, for instance by referring to the passive personality principle and/or where the offender is an official (civil servant) of the relevant State. In particular, this is true for the 1995 Convention on the protection of the Communities' financial interests (PIF Convention) and (regarding officials) the 1997 Corruption Convention.[56] Most likely, the expected future PIF Directive will include similar jurisdictional provisions.[57] Thus, it is to be expected that cases involving multiple jurisdiction will be frequent.

---

[52] See M. Coninsx, Chap. 3 and C. Deboyser, Chap. 6 in this book.

[53] See Article 16(2) of the EPPO proposal.

[54] Cf. Klip 2012, p. 191. Article 4(1) of the PFI Convention (see following note) requires its contracting parties to establish jurisdiction if the benefit was obtained in their territory.

[55] Supra n. 19.

[56] Convention of 26 July 1995 on the Protection of the European Communities' Financial Interests, O.J. 1995, C 316/49, Article 4; (First) Protocol of 27 September 1996 to the PFI Convention 1996, C 313/2, Article 6; Convention of 26 May 1997 on the fight against corruption involving officials of the European Communities or officials of Member States of the European Union, *OJ* 1997, C 195/2, Article 7.

[57] See Commission proposal for the PIF Directive, COM(2012)363 final, Article 11; cf. Council doc. 10729/13.

At the opening of an investigation, the assignment of the case to a Delegated Prosecutor may only have a preliminary effect, since it may be changed at any time.[58] Nonetheless, the initial assignment of an investigation may influence its further course, for instance with a view to investigative measures[59] and/or regarding a later dismissal.[60] As the Delegated Prosecutor in charge of the investigation will be guided by its own legal system, a switch to another jurisdiction and legal system may require a reorientation of the course of the investigation and/or of the steps taken. Thus, at least in factual terms the initial assignment may also 'set the agenda' towards a later choice of forum for an indictment. Therefore, Article 18(5) of the Proposal provides a list of substantive criteria. This list appears to be exhaustive, and seems to specify an overall determinant, which at this stage is the efficiency of the investigation.[61] In addition, according to Article 7(2), the internal rules of procedure 'shall include general rules on the allocation of cases'.

9.3.3 Conclusion of the Investigation

When a European Delegated Prosecutor considers an investigation completed, it submits to the EPP a summary of the case with a draft indictment, on the basis of which the latter decides on how to proceed further. The instructions contained in the EPP's decision should be based on a common prosecution policy.[62] The EPP has four options: to bring an indictment before a national court, to refer the case back for further investigations, to dismiss it, or to propose a transaction.

9.3.3.1 Indictment

The contents, purpose, admission and effect of an indictment depend on national law. Article 27(3) of EPPO proposal only requires that it lists the evidence to be adduced in trial. Anything more would presuppose a very far reaching approximation of criminal laws which is currently not foreseen. Regarding substantive criminal law, as mentioned above[63]; the Council has trimmed the Commission's proposal for a PIF directive, e.g. by removing minimum penalties for severe

---

[58] Article 16(2) of the EPPO proposal.

[59] In relation to investigative measures, the EPPO proposal reverses the usual *forum regit actum* principle, see Article 26(2), (4), (5), (7). Thus, the case allocation as such may have less impact. But even for investigative measures there may be a choice, e.g. where to arrest a person, or to seize assets.

[60] See infra, 9.3.3.2.

[61] Cf. Article 27(4) of the EPPO proposal (see infra 9.3.3.1).

[62] Article 27(2), Recital 30 of the EPPO proposal: If the Delegated Prosecutor proposes to dismiss a case, a draft indictment seems unnecessary; this could be clarified in the rules of procedure.

[63] Supra, Sect. 9.3.1.

cases.[64] Even if this was not the case, it is to be expected that some discretion for the national legislator will remain when implementing such a directive, e.g. as regards penalties (e.g. regarding aggravating and attenuating circumstances) and/or the very details of definitions of the relevant criminal offences.[65] Moreover, it is unlikely that the EU legislator would be able to define uniform fundamental concepts such as degrees and/or categories of criminality, involvement and culpability.[66] Furthermore, the procedural tenets differ fundamentally. Thus, the choice of forum at this stage is paramount. If the national court admits the indictment, this choice will be definitive and virtually irreversible and a resulting *res judicata* will ultimately bar any other prosecution within the EU.

Article 27(4) of the EPPO proposal defines criteria for the choice of forum as follows:

> The EPP shall choose, in close consultation with the European Delegated Prosecutor submitting the case and bearing in mind the proper administration of justice, the jurisdiction of trial and determine the competent national court taking into account the following criteria:
>
> (a) the place where the offence, or in case of several offences, the majority of the offences was committed;
> (b) the place where the accused person has his/her habitual residence;
> (c) the place where the evidence is located;
> (d) the place where the direct victims have their habitual residence.

This rather concise list takes into account the interests of the main 'stakeholders' (court, prosecution, defence and individuals) and allows, therefore, a balanced choice. The wording seems to suggest that the list is exhaustive, but this is not entirely clear. Other criteria may be of high relevance,[67] such as the nationality and/or civil servant status of concerned persons (in view of consistency with relevant EU instruments[68]), the seat of the EU and/or national institution or body managing the relevant budget and/or other places of important economic impact.[69] It should be clarified whether additional criteria can and should be taken into account and if

---

[64] See supra n. 45 and compare with COM(2012)363 final, Articles 7–8.

[65] For instance, fraud according to section 263 of the German Criminal Code requires a specific relation between the advantage sought by the offender and the damage caused (*Stoffgleichheit*); both need to be triggered by the same act the victim takes based on a deception. This specific relation may not be necessary in other national provisions (and is, by the way, not required for subsidy fraud according to section 264 of the German Criminal Code).

[66] Cf. Articles 9–13 *Corpus Juris* (General Criminal Law), supra n. 49.

[67] See e.g. the more extensive lists at Van der Beken et al. p. 51; section 1(3) of the 'Freiburg proposal' in: Biehler et al. 2003; Sinn, supra n. 42.

[68] Where EU law obliges States to establish jurisdiction based on certain criteria, see supra notes 19, 54, one may ask whether such criteria should not also play a role in the choice of jurisdiction (cf. also Article 14 of EPPO proposal).

[69] Cf. Article 6(1)(d) Protocol to the PFI Convention, supra n. 53; Model Rules EPPO 2013, no. 64(2) (where EPPO seems to stand for the Union interest); see Article 26(2)(c) *Corpus Juris* (on economic impact), supra n. 50.

so, which ones. Furthermore, since the Union is the main victim of offences against its financial interests[70] (and/or sometimes the Member States[71]), why should the residence of individual victims play a major role? At best this should be so in cases of ancillary competence ('mixed cases').

According to recital 30 of EPPO proposal, the EPP should choose the jurisdiction of trial 'on the basis of a set of transparent criteria'. While the abovementioned criteria are transparent and leave the necessary flexibility, the crucial questions here are: is there a limit to the discretion of the EPP, i.e. are there dispositions which exclude an arbitrary choice?[72] Given the enormous impact of the choice of forum at this stage, the question arises whether the list does guarantee that all legitimate interests are taken into account and balanced appropriately. One wonders whether such balancing can and should be achieved by a hierarchy of the different criteria. In a vein similar to the *Corpus Juris,* but unlike the Model Rules,[73] EPPO proposal does not, at least not expressly, rank the criteria. Admittedly, it may indeed be difficult to find an agreement on an order of sequence, as the previous attempts have shown.[74]

Because the proposal does not give an immediate answer to this problem, it has been criticised as not discouraging 'forum shopping'.[75] The response to such criticism depends on the interpretation of the proposed article. Firstly, as already mentioned, the proposal should be setting up an exclusive list of criteria. Understood in this way, Article 27(4) raises a certain barrier against extraneous, unreasonable considerations.[76] For instance, EPPO would not be able chose the forum on the basis of the availability of criminal sanctions or the length of proceedings. Secondly, the reference to the 'proper administration of justice' in Article 27(4) should be seen as a guiding principle, a *topos*, that pre-supposes a reasonable, non-arbitrary choice of forum and implies the duty to balance individual rights and interests with the interests of the prosecution.[77] Again, this would exclude a choice

---

[70] Cf. *Corpus Juris* and Model Rules EPPO 2013, which do not refer to individual victims.

[71] This could be considered for funds under shared management (see Articles 53, 53c EU Financial Regulation).

[72] See the references supra n. 23.

[73] See, on the one hand, Model Rules EPPO 2013, no. 64(1) of the ('in the following sequence'), on the other hand Article 26(2)(a) *Corpus Juris* ('principal criteria'). A certain ranking is foreseen in some EU framework decisions (see Green Paper, Annex SEC(2005)1767, pt. 3, however pointing to a lack of practical application).

[74] Cf. explanatory report to the European Transfer Convention (supra n. 33), paras 1–5, referring to failed attempts in the 1960s.

[75] See Council doc. 13863/13 (Council Presidency conference in Vilnius, September 2013), pp. 30, 34.

[76] Alternatively, it has been proposed to use a list of negative criteria, which might provide a stronger guarantee against extraneous considerations, see e.g. Article 9 in: Van der Beken et al. (2002), p. 51.

[77] However, it is not entirely clear whether the notion of 'proper administration of justice' comprises the defendants' interests, cf. Van der Beken et al. 2002, p. 20 et seq. (affirmative, as here); Asp et al. 2013, p. 441 (in the negative).

exclusively based on prosecutorial interests, such as sanction severity. This interpretation should include the respect of the legality principle and of the right to a fair trial as guaranteed by the CFR, which applies to any act by a Union body such as EPPO.[78] Some details could be set out in the rules of procedure according to Article 7 of EPPO proposal, as foreseen for the 'allocation of cases' in para 2.

However, with regard to the far-reaching legal impact of the forum choice, internal rules do not seem sufficient. It can be argued that the principle of legal certainty requires further clarification of the guiding principle, the criteria and their weight and the procedure (e.g. the duty to state reasons) in the text of the regulation. This also seems commendable with a view to stricter constitutional requirements on the clarity and certainty of law in some Member States.[79] While it remains to be seen what degree of legal certainty the courts will require in this new constellation, the relevant rules and principles should be as clear-cut and precise as possible, in order to guarantee the legitimacy and transparency of EPPO's acts. This is in the interest of EPPO, in order to prevent any reasonable suspicion of forum shopping, which would affect its credibility, acceptance and the necessary trust, especially from the national authorities.

9.3.3.2 Dismissal and Transaction

Most of the grounds for dismissal in the EPPO proposal[80] make reference to the national laws. Among the mandatory grounds in paragraph 1, this is especially true for lit. b (absence of a criminal offence), lit. c (amnesty and immunity[81]) and lit. d (expiry of the national statutory limitation). On *ne bis in idem* (lit. e), national law defines the details of 'finally acquitted or convicted' (as in Article 50 CFR), and there is room for diversity, especially if the word 'acquitted' will be interpreted in line with the case law on Article 54 CISA.[82] The optional grounds in para 2, too, depend on national law. On the core issue of whether there is sufficient evidence (b), this is obvious. On a dismissal *de minimis* (a), national law will at least determine the details, even if the Commission's proposal for an EU wide definition of 'minor offences' (a) were re-inserted into PIF Directive.[83]

The only option for which EPPO proposal provides autonomous rules is the 'transaction'.[84] EPPO may propose to the suspected person that he/she pays a 'lump-sum fine' to the EU, which when paid will entail a final dismissal. This

---

[78] See Article 51(1) CFR.

[79] Cf. Lagodny 2001, p. 114 on Article101 of the German *Grundgesetz* ('*gesetzlicher Richter*').

[80] Article 28 of EPPO proposal.

[81] For EU immunity see Protocol no. 7 to the Lisbon Treaty.

[82] For instance, out of court settlements can have the effect of *res judicata*, cf. ECJ *Gözütok and Brügge*, supra n. 36.

[83] The Council's current general approach, supra n. 45, does not contain it.

[84] Article 29.

instrument is subject to two conditions, which apparently do not depend on national law. Firstly, the damage caused must have been compensated, and secondly, the transaction should serve the proper administration of justice. In comparison with the relevant national rules, this provision is conspicuously simple.[85] National rules usually refer to a *de minimis* test, proportionality considerations, taking into account the seriousness of the offence, level of culpability, the harm caused and the impact on the community, as well as the public interest and/or the impact of the prosecution on the offender.[86] Sometimes, approval by a judge is required.[87]

In the interest of transparency and legal certainty, it would appear advisable to either add a complementary reference to national law or to elaborate more detailed conditions for transactions, at least in EPPO's internal rules of procedure,[88] but preferably in the regulation itself. Also, the role of the EPP and the European Delegated Prosecutor(s) should be clarified, as well as the nature of the 'fine', e.g. regarding a possible storage in national criminal records. National law tends to be much more explicit on these issues. Given the fact that Article 29 is conceived as an autonomous rule, it is doubtful whether and to what extent one could resort to national law in order to fill these 'gaps'. If national law were to play an important role regarding these aspects, then the case allocation within EPPO would determine the applicable law so that the above considerations on the choice of jurisdiction would have to be applied here as well.

9.3.4 Trial Phase and Judicial Review of Forum Choice

According to Article 36(1) of the proposal, for the purpose of judicial review, EPPO, 'when adopting procedural measures [...] shall be considered as a national authority'. Thus, an admission and/or review of indictments by EPPO will be processed in the same way as for other indictments. The national court will assess its competence and any other conditions for the opening of the trial. It depends on national law to what extent it may and will review the forum choice. One might ask whether this choice is to be considered a 'procedural measure' in the sense of Article 36(1). In the opinion of the author, given the importance of the legal impact of this choice and the principle of effective judicial protection, in terms of literal, grammatical and teleological interpretation, this question should be answered in the affirmative. In case of opposite answer, it would appear to be no judicial review at

[85] Cf. also Model Rules EPPO 2013, Annex to Rule 65.

[86] For example, see Code for Crown Prosecutors in England and Wales: http://www.cps.gov.uk/publications/docs/code2013english_v2.pdf. Accessed 5 November 2013; German Procedural Criminal Code, sections. 153–154c (11 sections), in English at: http://www.gesetze-im-internet.de/englisch_stpo/. Accessed 5 November 2013;

[87] Cf. German Procedural Criminal Code, sections. 153–153b, supra n. 86.

[88] Article 7 and recital 30 of the EPPO proposal ('common prosecution policy').

all, and that would mean that one of the most important decisions of EPPO would not be justiciable. That seems like a rather untenable conclusion.

One shall not forget, that national laws are drawn up from a national perspective; they define jurisdiction unilaterally, without taking into account the interests of other Member States.[89] In the absence of multilateral or European rules on jurisdiction, national courts lack both a mandate and parameters for identifying a suitable, or reasonable, forum.[90] Currently, the national law of most Member States is limited to the question whether or not jurisdiction has been established in a specific case. That means that the national courts will apply a test whether they *may* hear a case, but not whether, from a European perspective, a court in another Member State might be better placed for hearing a case. This is perfectly understandable: in order to undertake a fully informed decision from a European perspective, the national courts would first have to examine which Member States have established jurisdiction and/or which national criminal laws are applicable (taking into account the relevant national provisions of all Member States potentially concerned) and, secondly, identify and weigh the pros and cons of each jurisdiction.

In contrast, EPPO can and will have to make a choice from a European perspective. Unlike national judges and prosecutors, it can choose from any established jurisdiction. In other words, when determining jurisdiction, the EPPO will have to answer to an open question (i.e. which Member State?) as oppose to a closed question to which an answer can simply be 'yes' or 'no' (i.e. is there jurisdiction?). Its decision differs essentially from the existing 'horizontal' setting, where the national authorities either prosecute a case in their own system, or decide to let another country go ahead.[91] This is why many of the replies to the Commission's 2001 Green Paper on a European Prosecutor[92] expressed concerns about the possibility of 'forum shopping' and a preference for a solution on European level, especially a 'European Preliminary Chamber'.[93] While such an EU Court might neither be necessary nor could feasible, national courts only operate on an equal footing with EPPO and be able to effectively review its forum choice if they have an appropriate 'yardstick'. This can only be a legal framework on Union level; without it, national courts will hardly be in the position to review a multilateral choice of forum.

The core of such framework can be derived from an established fundamental rights canon, in particular the legality principle (*nullum crimen, nulla poena sine lege certa*)[94] and the right to a fair trial,[95] which includes the equality of arms

---

89 Cf. Vervaele 2013a, p. 171; Luchtman 2013, pp. 32, 37.

90 Cf. Luchtman 2013, pp. 34, 37.

91 Cf. Eurojust Decision, supra n. 29; European Transfer Convention, supra n. 33.

92 COM(2001)715 final.

93 The follow-up communication to the Green Paper, COM(2003)128 final, p. 17, mentions that eleven written contributions supported the idea of a European Preliminary Chamber; cf. Delmas-Marty and Vervaele (eds.) 2000, p. 50; Van der Beken (2002), p. 36.

94 Article 7 ECHR, Article 49 EUCFR.

95 Article 6 ECHR, Article 47 EUCFR.

between defence and prosecution[96] and to a certain extent the right to a lawful judge.[97] Given EPPO's 'competitive edge' and the legal impact of its forum choice, there might be a risk of eroding these rights if the defence could not challenge its limits. Thus, related concerns voiced in the context of horizontal cooperation[98] are even more acute here.

The case law of the ECtHR, which results rather from intra-state and/or mutual legal scenarios, makes clear that a choice of forum must be 'reasonable', i.e. non-arbitrary and free from extraneous considerations and that criminal liability must be accessible and foreseeable.[99] To a certain extent, this is holding true also for the possible range of penalties.[100] *A fortiori,* the test of reasonableness must apply where the choice of jurisdiction determines the applicable law and therefore has a higher impact, especially in a supranational context. Decisions by EPPO will be subject to control by the ECtHR once internal remedies have been exhausted. The 'legal fiction' contained in Article 36 of EPPO proposal may facilitate access to the ECtHR. When the Union accedes to the ECHR,[101] there may be a more direct route.[102] As an EU body EPPO will be subject to the CFR.[103] Articles 47-49 CFR are to be interpreted in a European perspective. It may be expected that any benchmark set by the ECJ will be at least as high as the one by the Strasbourg Court.[104] As far as judicial review of EPPO's choice of jurisdiction is concerned, it remains to be seen whether a forum choice by EPPO will be classified as an act of direct and individual concern to the accused person; its important legal impact could be an argument in favour. If so, the question arises whether it can be challenged directly before the ECJ under Article 263 TFEU, despite the 'legal fiction' in Article 36 of the EPPO proposal. Indeed, secondary law can only lay down 'specific conditions and arrangements'.[105] A counter argument may be, that a forum choice only becomes definitive when a national court has admitted an indictment.[106]

---

[96] Cf. Gless 2013a.

[97] Or 'natural judge', see Panzavolta 2013; Vervaele 2013a, p. 180.

[98] Supra, Sect. 9.2.1 and *notes*. 20, 23.

[99] ECtHR, cases *Coeme* v. *Belgium* and *Jorgic* v. *Germany*, supra n. 24.

[100] ECtHR, case *Camilleri* v. *Malta*, supra n. 24.

[101] Article 6(2) TEU.

[102] Probably following involvement of the EU Court of Justice via an exceptional preliminary ruling mechanism.

[103] See Article 51(1) CFR and Recital 17 of the EPPO proposal.

[104] It is important to note here that the ECJ has adhered to the ECtHR case law on 'foreseeability', e.g. in Case C-352/09 P *Thyssen Krupp Nirosta*, ECR [2011] I-2359 (cf. Klip 2012, p. 181; Gless 2011, p. 117; Luchtman 2013, p. 118).

[105] See Article 263(4), (5) TFEU. On the question, whether Article 86(3) authorises the Union to change the Treaty system on legal remedies, see also: J. Inghelram, Chap. 8 and A. Meij, Chap. 7 in this book.

[106] Cf. ECJ, 15 January 2003, Case C-377/00 et al. *Commission* v. *Philip Morris Int.* [2003] ECR II-1 para 79. See also Kuhl 2013, p. 98. However, it is difficult to draw conclusions from this judgment on the issues discussed here, as their factual and legal background is entirely different.

Similar questions arise for preliminary rulings regarding the validity of EPPO's acts according to Article 267 TFEU.[107]

In the light of these reflections, there is even more reason to further elaborate the relevant criteria and/or procedure.[108] They must be precise enough to enable the courts to verify whether a forum choice was reasonable. With regard to substantive criminal law, individuals must be able to foresee, by taking reasonable steps, whether their behaviour constitutes a criminal offence and what the possible penalty range may be.[109] Some authors plead for a *mens rea* test on this point.[110] In the absence of clear criteria for a forum choice, courts may be tempted to resort to such an approach, but this could hardly be seen as a comprehensive response to the problem. In any case, this does not mean that individuals must be able to foresee in which Member State a trial will finally take place.[111] It should be sufficient that they can foresee which choices would be reasonable and which ones not. For an efficient administration of justice, a considerable scope of discretion must remain for the prosecution. The present contribution does not recommend to introduce a comprehensive review, which would allow the courts to replace EPPO's choice, but only to avoid an unlimited discretion and to exclude arbitrary decisions.[112]

As concerns dismissals and transactions, *mutatis mutandis* the above remarks are also relevant. According to the EPPO proposal, dismissals are only subject to judicial review if the applicable national law so provides. One could take the view that the Union as the main victim should always be able to challenge dismissals,[113] but this may be countered by the argument that EPPO represents its interests in terms of criminal law.[114] With regard to the latter argument, a legal remedy for the Union may not seem indispensable. However, there is an issue of consistency, as the reference to national law would mean that the Union could challenge dismissals and/or transactions in some, but not in all cases.

For other victims, for instance in cases of ancillary competence, it may be difficult to accept that they cannot challenge a dismissal and/or launch a private prosecution, had they had such possibilities in another eligible jurisdiction.

[107] Recital 38 of the EPPO proposal.

[108] For possible approaches see infra at n. 121.

[109] See lately, ECtHR *Camilleri* v. *Malta*, supra n. 24.

[110] Cf. Luchtman 2013, p. 28, with further references; see also Gless 2011.

[111] Vervaele 2013a, p. 180. See, however, the arguments for a priority of the residence of the suspect derived from Article 3(2) TEU by Luchtman 2013, p. 18 et seq., 54 et seq.

[112] Cf. the instructive comparison of this approach with the abuse of process principle in common law and the '*Abwägungsfehlerlehre*' in Germany on the use of criminal evidence in: Van der Beken et al. 2002, p. 30.

[113] Cf. Model Rules EPPO 2013, no. 65(3).

[114] Otherwise, the EU's financial interests are represented by the Commission (Articles 317 TFEU) and/or the Budget Authority (Article 310 et seq. TFEU). Insofar, Articles 5(3), 52, 58(3) of the EPPO proposal provide for accountability.

Moreover, the national law 'chosen' by the EPP (by means of case allocation) will determine whether a dismissal triggers the *ne bis in idem* principle.[115] This shows that the assignment of a case can have the effect of a definitive choice of the applicable law. With regard to the legitimate interest of individual victims, it seems advisable to carefully examine whether or not there is a need for an EU-wide legal remedy, either on this choice, or on the dismissal itself. For transactions, which seem to be entirely under the regime of the Union law, Article 29(4) of EPPO proposal excludes any judicial review. Whether this is appropriate in view of the position of individual victims and/or of suspects[116] would go beyond the scope of this contribution and will, therefore, not be discussed further.

Finally, when it comes to the trial itself, Article 30(1) of the EPPO proposal is based on the mutual recognition of evidence. It declares evidence presented by EPPO admissible without any validation, even if the trial law provides for rules on the collection different from those in the Member State where the evidence was taken. However, the Member States' procedural systems still vary enormously.[117] This means that the forum will still be relevant.[118] 'Transplanting' a piece of evidence from one legal system into another bears risks of unforeseen consequences and a lack of transparency, which might compromise the fairness of the trial and particularly the equality of arms.[119] In this regard, prosecution by EPPO does not differ fundamentally from the general context of judicial cooperation.[120] Article 30 (1) of EPPO proposal attempts to mitigate these risks by permitting a fundamental rights test at the trial stage, with respect to procedural fairness and defence rights. It should be considered to extend such a 'European *ordre public*'[121] to all fundamental rights (e.g. also to Articles 7 and 8 CFR).

---

[115] On the relevant case law see supra n. 36. A dismissal because of lack of evidence will usually not bar further prosecution; this could be made a rule on Union level, as suggested in the Model Rules EPPO 2013, no. 65(2).

[116] Cf. Asp et al. 2013, p. 442.

[117] It may be sufficient here to recall the fundamental differences between adversarial and inquisitorial procedures, see supra n. 8.

[118] See, for instance, Vermeulen 2012, p. 129 et seq.

[119] Cf. Asp et al. 2013, p. 434 et seq. Gless 2013a; Spencer 2013, p. 65.

[120] Cf. the Framework Decision on a European Evidence Warrant, *OJ* 2008 L 350/72 (not applied in practice) and the negotiations on a European Investigation Order, Council doc 15196/13, available at: (http://www.statewatch.org/news/2013/oct/eu-council-eio-comprise-15196-13.pdf); cf. Vermeulen 2012, p. 129 et seq.

[121] This is to be distinguished from a national *ordre public,* which would allow (limited) grounds for refusal based on *national* (constitutional) law, as known in civil matters. It is much discussed whether this is needed and/or compatible with mutual recognition (cf. Asp et al. 2013, p. 436 et seq.; Mitsilegas 2013).

9.4 Final Remarks

The creation of EPPO entails several advantages compared to the *status quo*. It virtually excludes 'negative' conflicts of jurisdiction (which is a major reason for the proposal). As for the 'positive' conflicts, it will take responsibility for a choice of forum in a European perspective,[122] be able to take decisions swiftly and do away with parallel investigations and prosecutions. Of course, in case of enhanced cooperation, this is only true for the participating Member States.[123] The EPPO proposal procures a set of transparent and appropriate criteria for the choice of forum, particularly at the crucial stage of the indictment, while leaving flexibility in the interest of efficiency. Correctly interpreted, the overall concept of a 'proper administration of justice' includes the rights and legitimate interests of individuals and, thus, balances flexibility with certainty of the law and the need for procedural fairness. However, various questions regarding this balance remain unsettled. In particular, the limits of the EPP's executive discretion and the scope of judicial review of its choices are not yet sufficiently clear.

Since EPPO operates in a pluralistic legal environment, the allocation of cases among its Delegated Prosecutors is much more than just an organisational measure: it pre-determines the applicable law. On occasion, the allocation of a case by the EPP may be able to influence the legal regime which the Office has to subsequently respect; this could be regarded as a circularity. As a supranational authority operating in various, fundamentally different legal systems, EPPO will have a significantly wider range of possibilities than national prosecutors, who basically operate in a single legal system. When confronted with cross-jurisdictional cases, the latter can only *request* another state or entity to take over, or to close a procedure in view of a prosecution elsewhere, but is not able to choose from several jurisdictions. EPPO will be in the unique position to do so, and its power will be reinforced by its exclusive competence and a high degree of independence.[124] All this makes EPPO a *novum*, not only in comparison with other Union bodies, but also with those under international law.[125]

With power come responsibility and accountability. The present analysis shows that the approach taken in EPPO proposal on conflicts of jurisdiction needs to be further elaborated, preferably in the regulation itself rather than in internal rules of procedure. The limits of discretion on the choice of jurisdiction and the corresponding judicial review need to be shaped in a more transparent way. In the

[122] Cf. Luchtman 2013, p. 37: 'no one is really responsible'.

[123] For the cooperation of EPPO with other Member States, Eurojust could be an important player.

[124] See Articles 5, 8–10, 11(4) of the EPPO proposal. Several national prosecution services are not entirely independent.

[125] Cf. recital 36 of the EPPO proposal. As regards international law, the most prominent example is the International Criminal Court, which does not operate in a pluralistic, but in a single legal framework.

interest of effectiveness, trust by national authorities and the highest possible reputation and acceptance, EPPO should be above any possible reproach of 'forum shopping' or arbitrary decision making. It should meet the highest standards in terms of certainty of the law and due process (including 'equality of arms' regarding the defence).

In order to help ensure these objectives, the EU legislator can avail itself of a range of proposals which were developed in the general context of horizontal cooperation. They reach from reducing national jurisdiction to territoriality,[126] via a matrix of positive and/or negative criteria (with or without a priority and/or procedural sequence)[127] to a statutory system oriented at goals and legitimate interests.[128] A procedural starting point could be an obligation to state the reasons for a choice of forum (and/or allocation of a case to a Delegated Prosecutor). In substance, the case law of the ECtHR on the legality principle and the right to a fair trial, with its test of reasonableness and to a certain extent also of 'foreseeability' is pertinent. This test should at least be applied where the choice has definitive effects, particularly at the stage of the admission of an indictment by a national court. But it should be limited to the absence of extraneous aspects and/or an arbitrary choice, as there seems to be a wide consensus that a considerable scope of discretion is necessary.

If the legal parameters for such a test are defined on a Union level, then the judicial review can be left to national courts. Otherwise, this would be problematic. National criminal law is not designed in a European perspective. This can only be ensured at Union level. It is possible that future case law with regard to the CFR will promote a change towards such a multilateral perspective. Even so, with regard to legal certainty, the parameters in EPPO proposal itself would need to be further specified, also given the important impact of the forum choice. It is possible to set out certain details in EPPO's internal rules of procedure. But in the sensitive area of criminal law (from the point of view of fundamental rights), the essential decisions must be taken or at least approved by the EU legislator.[129] In the latter sense, it would be conceivable to set out more specific parameters for the forum choice in EPPO's rules of procedure subject to an approval by the Council and/or EP. Article 253(6) TFEU on the ECJ's Rules of Procedure could serve as an inspiration here.[130] Moreover, it follows from Article 263 TFEU that such rules would be subject to judicial review on Union level, in view of any significant impact on individual rights. On the whole, a rather small set of amendments and/or complementary

---

[126] Supra n. 16.

[127] Cf. Lagodny ('quality principle'), p. 104 et seq.; Van der Beken et al. 2002, p. 70 et seq. with further references, including to works in the Council of Europe, case law by the International Court of Justice and proposals by the American Law Institute; Eurojust Guidelines 2003; Biehler et al. 2003; Sinn 2012b, p. 603 et seq.

[128] Luchtman 2013, pp. 35–36, 57 (with references to the Swiss legal system).

[129] Cf. Article 52(1) EUCFR.

[130] Cf. also Article 10(2) of the Eurojust Decision, supra n. 29.

measures specifying the guiding principle of a reasonable choice[131] could enhance transparency and legal certainty and thereby also the public acceptance of an EPPO.

References

Asp P, Bitzilekis N, Bogdan S et al (2013) A manifesto on European criminal procedure law—European criminal policy initiative. Zeitschrift für Internationale Strafrechtsdogmatik (ZIS) 8:430–446

Biehler A, Kniebühler R, Lelieur-Fischer J, Stein S (eds) (2003) Freiburg proposal on concurrent jurisdictions and the prohibition of multiple prosecution in the European Union. Max-Planck Institute for Foreign and International Criminal Law, Freiburg

Böse M (2013) Choice of forum and jurisdiction. In: Luchtman M (ed.) Choice of the forum in cooperation against EU financial crime. Eleven International Publishing, The Hague, pp 73–88

Delmas-Marty M, Vervaele JAE (eds) (2000) The implementation of the *corpus juris* in the member states, vol I. Intersentia, Antwerp

Eurojust guidelines for deciding: which jurisdiction should prosecute? Annex to the annual report 2003 http://eurojust.europa.eu/doclibrary/corporate/eurojust%20Annual%20Reports/Annual%20Report%202003/Annual-Report-2003-EN.pdf. Accessed 7 November 2013

European Parliament, The future of Eurojust, Directorate-General for Internal Policies (2012), Study PE 462.451 http://www.europarl.europa.eu/committees/en/studies.html;jsessionid=68FC25F24BC6F82EC7E53AA086179048.node2#studies. Accessed 7 November 2013

Gless S (2011) A new test for *mens rea?* Safeguarding legal certainty in a European area of Freedom, Security and Justice, EuCLR 1:114–122

Gless S (2013a) Transnational cooperation in criminal matters and the guarantee of a fair trial: approaches to a general principle. Utrecht Law Rev 9:90–108

Gless S (2013b) Law should govern: aspiring general principles for transnational criminal justice (editorial). Utrecht Law Rev 9:1–10

Klip A (2012) European criminal law, 2nd edn. Intersentia, Cambridge

Kreß C (2009) International criminal law. In Wolfrum R (ed.), The Max Planck encyclopedia of public international law, pp 1–14. http://opil.ouplaw.com/home/EPIL. Accessed June 2014

Kuhl L (2013) Framework for coordination between judicial authorities and OLAF. In: Luchtman M (ed.) Choice of the forum in cooperation against EU financial crime. Eleven International Publishing, The Hague, pp 89–100

Lagodny O (2001) Empfiehlt es sich eine europäische Gerichtskompetenz für Strafgewaltskonflikte vorzusehen? Expert opinion for the German ministry of justice—*Bundesministerium der Justiz*, Berlin

Ligeti K, Simonato M (2013) The European public prosecutor's office: towards a truly European prosecution service. New J Eur Crim Law 4:7–21

Luchtman M (ed) (2013a) Choice of the Forum in cooperation against EU financial crime. Eleven International Publishing, The Hague

Luchtman M (2013b) Choice of forum and the prosecution of cross-border crime in the European Union—what role for the legality principle? In: Luchtman M (ed) Choice of the forum in cooperation against EU financial crime. Eleven International Publishing, The Hague, pp 3–60

Mitsilegas V (2013) Prosecution, national legal diversity and human rights after Lisbon (editorial). New J Eur Crim Law 4:3–6

[131] Cf. Van der Beken et al. 2002, p. 25 et seq.

Model Rules EPPO (2013) Model Rules for the procedure of the EPPO (project website, University of Luxembourg. http://www.eppo-project.eu/index.php/EU-model-rules/english). Accessed 7 Nov 2013

Panzavolta M (2013) Choice of forum and the lawful judge concept. In: Luchtman M (ed) Choice of the forum in cooperation against EU financial crime. Eleven International Publishing, The Hague, pp 142–165

Schmidt-Kessel M (2012) Das Internationale Privatrecht als Vorbild eines transnationalen Strafanwendungsrechts? In: Sinn A (ed) Jurisdiktionskonflikte bei grenzüberschreitender Kriminalität/Conflicts of jurisdiction in cross-border crime situations, V&R Unipress, Osnabrück, pp 65–83

Sinn A (2012a) Jurisdictional law as the key to resolving conflicts: comparative law observations. In: Sinn A (ed) Jurisdiktionskonflikte bei grenzüberschreitender Kriminalität/Conflicts of jurisdiction in cross-border crime situations, V&R Unipress, Osnabrück, pp 531–554

Sinn A (ed) (2012b) Jurisdiktionskonflikte bei grenzüberschreitender Kriminalität/Conflicts of jurisdiction in cross-border crime situations. V&R Unipress, Osnabrück

Spencer J (2002) Introduction. In: Spencer J, Delmas-Marty M (eds) European criminal procedures. Cambridge University Press, Cambridge, pp 1–80

Spencer J (2013) Mutual recognition and choice of forum. In: Luchtman M (ed.) Choice of the forum in cooperation against EU financial crime. Eleven International Publishing, The Hague, pp 61–72

Spronken T (2013) Effective defence. In: Vermeulen G (ed) 2012 Defence rights, Maklu, Antwerpen, Apeldoorn, pp 81–104

Van der Beken T, Vermeulen G, Steverlynck S, Thomaes S (2002) Finding the best place for prosecution. Maklu, Antwerpen/Apeldoorn

Vermeulen G (2012) Prisoners' rights in the EU & procedural rights in the context of EU cross-border gathering & use of evidence in criminal matters. In: Vermeulen G (ed.) Defence rights, Maklu, Antwerpen, Apeldoorn 2012, pp 105–137

Vervaele JAE (2013a) European territoriality and jurisdiction: the protection of the EU's financial interests in its horizontal and vertical (EPPO) dimension. In: Luchtman M (ed.) Choice of the forum in cooperation against EU financial crime. Eleven International Publishing, The Hague, pp 167–184

Vervaele JAE (2013b) *Ne bis in idem:* towards a transnational constitutional principle in the EU? Utrecht Law Rev 9:211–229

Wasmeier M (2006) Der europäische Haftbefehl vor dem Bundesverfassungsgericht. Zeitschrift für Europarechtliche Studien (ZEuS) 9:23–39

Wasmeier M, Thwaites N (2006) The development of *ne bis in idem* into a transnational fundamental right in EU law. E L Rev 13:565–578

Weyembergh A (2011) The development of Eurojust: potential and limitations of article 85 of the TFEU. New J Eur Crim Law 2:75–99

Part IV
Operational Foundations of the European Public Prosecutor's Office

Chapter 10
The European Public Prosecutor: Issues of Conferral, Subsidiarity and Proportionality

Kai M. Lohse

Abstract The legislative proposal of the European Commission on the establishment of the European Public Prosecutor's Office (EPPO) gives rise to questions concerning fundamental principles of European law as well as issues of practicability. Reflecting on the current situation of the criminal law systems and taking into consideration opportunities and risks of this project, this article considers some of the controversial issues from a practitioner's perspective. Pleading for a pragmatic approach, it emphasises the need for an independent office which should have positive effects on the position of the national prosecution offices. With regard to the options for the structure of this new European body a modification of the proposal is suggested. Collegial elements should be built into this Office, including the creation of chambers. Underlining the necessity of a close cooperation between European and national authorities, an exclusive competence of EPPO is rejected for reasons of practicability as well as subsidiarity and proportionality. In order to achieve a more suitable and flexible solution, the Office should be endowed with concurring competences having a right of evocation. Finally, some other issues are touched upon, such as the protection of individual rights, the determination of jurisdiction and the question of judicial review, suggesting that additional competences of the European Court of Justice are needed.

Keywords Criminal law system · Structure of the European Public Prosecutor's Office (EPPO) · Competence of EPPO · Subsidiarity · Individual rights · Proportionality · Article 86 TFEU

The author is a Senior Public Prosecutor at the Office of the Federal Public Prosecutor General in Karlsruhe, Germany. This article reflects his personal opinion and not that of his office.

K.M. Lohse (✉)
Der Generalbundesanwalt Beim Bundesgerichtshof, Brauerstraße 30,
76135 Karlsruhe, Germany
e-mail: poststelle@gba.bund.de

L.H. Erkelens et al. (eds.), *The European Public Prosecutor's Office*,
DOI 10.1007/978-94-6265-035-0_10

Contents

10.1 Introduction

The potential effects of establishing the European Public Prosecutor's Office could be looked upon in different ways: some may regard it as a threat to the current legal practice; others may welcome it as a new approach and an opportunity for a substantially positive impact, either immediately or in the long run. This contribution will take a moderate position, providing a plain and modest view from a practitioner's perspective, pointing at possible advantages, but at the same time taking note of potential risks and expressing some concerns with regard to the proposed regulation.

Before taking a closer look at the proposal of the European Commission[1] some general remarks must be made. First of all, it is necessary to identify clearly the problems which currently impede prosecution of complex cross-border cases and, furthermore, to gain clarity about the necessary preconditions of the functioning of EPPO. This project could only become a success, if it is based on a thorough analysis of the existing situation.

Thus, before evaluating the concept of the European Commission for the establishment of EPPO, we need to identify the relevant problems in the field of transnational criminal law. For one thing is the insufficient protection of the financial interests of the European Union, but as practical experience shows,

[1] Proposal for a Council Regulation on the establishment of the European Public Prosecutor's Office of July 17, 2013 COM (2013) 534 final. Hereafter EPPO proposal. See also the Appendix to this book.

another thing is the difficulties national prosecution offices in all Member States face, when dealing with complex cases with a cross-border dimension.

Undoubtedly, the establishment of EPPO will affect the national legal systems as a whole. This project is not designed only to improve the protection of the financial interests of the European Union, but also to significantly alter the basis of cooperation in criminal matters. In replacing mutual recognition by a new paradigm, a uniformed area of law, it may even be considered a key factor in opening a new era. In contrast to these ambitious goals, which could be directly or indirectly related to EPPO, the reasoning given by the Commission is much more modest. The European Commission justifies EPPO's establishment predominantly by referring to current deficiencies in the protection of the financial interests of the European Union by means of criminal law,[2] but shows to be reluctant in considering aims which go beyond this goal, especially with regard to the establishment of a new dimension in judicial cooperation in a single legal area.[3] The explanations provided in the proposal of the Commission widely leave out this important dimension of EPPO. From a political perspective, especially in the current financial crisis, the European Union's financial losses may be the most convincing way to justify an action by means of criminal law instruments. That is, perhaps, because it is easier to point to the shortcomings in the protection system, rather than to explain the need of substantial change in the cooperation between Member States and the Union when combating serious financial crimes.

Thus, it seems more adequate to analyse the causes of the difficulties which have occurred in the field of PIF crimes. The inefficiencies we face in this field uncover a much wider problem: an overall inability of national criminal legal systems to handle complex cases such as tax evasion, corruption or economic crimes, especially with a cross-border dimension. Clearly, such deficiencies do not only and exclusively relate to the prosecution of PIF crimes. If the Member States' authorities are not capable of investigating successfully those cases, neither can it be expected that they will be able to effectively protect the financial interests of the Union.

Therefore, in the current framework two major challenges can be noted. First of all, the weakness of national criminal law systems; and second of all, the considerable divergences between the Member States criminal law systems. The first issue could be resolved by, for example, granting the systems sufficient autonomy, including adequate human and financial resources. The second challenge has to be overcome regardless of setting up EPPO. The process of harmonisation by achieving comparable standards of law and practice remains more than ever a key for successful development of the capacities of the national criminal law systems in combatting cross-border crimes.

From this it follows, that for a successful establishment of EPPO several preconditions should be met. As a first precondition, EPPO must act on the basis of

---

2 See: Explanatory Memorandum to the EPPO proposal, p. 2.

3 See: Article 25(1) of the EPPO proposal.

mutual trust and in close cooperation with the national authorities. It should concentrate on those cases where its activity on a European level would provide real added value. As a consequence, a cautious approach is preferred as it seems neither necessary, nor desirable, to place too much burden on the new body, by granting it an exclusive competence, by obliging it to investigate all linked and minor cases, or by extending its competence to a wide range of crimes. Instead, at this phase, an effective EPPO should be limited to a function more complementary to that of national criminal law authorities. The new entity has to find its place among the different law authorities within the criminal law systems of the Member States. To a large extent, EPPO will have to rely on the support and acceptance of national authorities and prosecution offices. And there can be no doubt that it will take some time and some lessons to learn until its implementation will have achieved a satisfying degree of practical cooperation.

As a second precondition, EPPO should be able to exercise a considerable impact on the situation of the national law authorities, improving their standing in terms of independence, international cooperation and motivation. In such a situation, prosecutors in the Member States should welcome the establishment of this new authority and thus the project would be more likely to receive the acceptance it needs.

Finally, as the last precondition, the establishment of EPPO needs to be flanked by other measures on the European level: the European Public Prosecutor's Office is not a magic bullet, but just one element within a larger package of important instruments. Therefore, irrespective of the creation of EPPO, it remains essential to continue the harmonisation of procedural and substantive law, to facilitate the instruments of mutual legal assistance and to offer adequate judicial training regarding the application of EU criminal law. Many important actions are already conducted in order to promote these goals, although falling outside the scope of this contribution.

10.2 Issues of Conferral

Notwithstanding these general conditions for a successful functioning of EPPO, it is necessary to bear in mind that the competence to establish this EU body has been legally conferred upon the EU by the Member States. This well-established principle of conferral limits the Union competences,[4] which specifically means that 'the Union shall act only within the limits of the competences conferred upon it by the Member States in the Treaties to attain the objectives set out there in'.[5] The practical meaning thereof for a European prosecution system will be analysed from

---

[4] Article 5(1) TEU.

[5] Article 5(2) TEU.

the points of view of autonomy, accountability, structure and competences of the future Office.

10.2.1 Autonomy of EPPO

Autonomy is crucial and has been warranted because neither European, nor national institutions, can instruct or effectively influence the decisions of EPPO. This condition is not only important for the quality of the work of the Office, but also for the acceptance of this new institution. Therefore, it is essential that the, very welcomed statement in the proposal 'EPPO is independent'[6] will be enforced in practice. This includes providing EPPO with sufficient financial resources and personnel. It also means that any undue influence, whether from national authorities or other European institutions, has to be excluded. In particular, this principle has to be emphasised with respect to the appointment and dismissal of the members of EPPO.[7]

In order to secure EPPO's independence in the fulfilment of its daily tasks, additional procedural safeguards should be taken into consideration. To that end, a legal remedy to ensure the independent status of the European Prosecutors is suggested. In cases of various forms of undue influence, the European Public Prosecutor (EPP) should have the right to lodge a complaint to the European Court of Justice (ECJ), which could rule on an alleged violation of independence.[8] This should apply to any form of undue influence, whether resulting from the European institutions, or from the Member States. Such remedy could be implemented by an additional provision under Article 5(2) of the legislative proposal. It would correspond with the rights of the European Parliament, the European Council and the European Commission to may apply to the ECJ for a dismissal of the EPP.[9] Such an additional safeguard may be necessary particularly because a decision of the EPP to investigate may directly concern members of the mentioned European institutions,[10] as well as (high ranking) officials from the Member States.

---

[6] See: Article 5 of the EPPO proposal.

[7] See: Articles 8, 9 and 10 of the EPPO proposal.

[8] Recital 10 of the proposal calls for 'institutional safeguards to ensure its independence'.

[9] See: Article 8(4) of EPPO proposal.

[10] In this context, the issue of immunity as regulated in Article 19 of the EPPO proposal is of practical importance. Since the need to apply for a lifting of the immunity could hamper the speed and the success of the investigation, the establishment of a new European body with investigative powers like the EPPO should give rise to the question whether it is not time to abolish the existing immunity for EU servants.

10.2.2 Accountability

Independence and responsibility are two sides of the same coin.[11] An obligation of EPPO to regularly submit reports,[12] especially to the European Parliament, may be appropriate not only in order to establish a level of structural control, but also to ensure democratic legitimacy. As it has been mentioned in the introductory remarks, the lack of efficiency in the national criminal law systems is the main reason for the necessity to establish this new European body. Thus, an effective system of supervision and structural control as provided in Article 5, based on a system of regular reports as foreseen in Article 70 of the EPPO proposal, possibly with a right for the members of the European Parliament to inquire, will constitute an important tool enhancing the compliance of both EPPO and national prosecution authorities without affecting its autonomous status. As a consequence, such a system of scrutiny could not only increase the acceptance of EPPO, but also (indirectly) support the position of the national prosecutors in various ways. Irrespective of whether they act as European Delegated Prosecutors (EDPs) or whether they exercise (possibly as a result from the inter-institutional legislative negotiations) concurrent national jurisdiction in regard to PIF cases, the prosecutors would be put in a better position to reject any possible undue influence on the national level, because they could refer to their responsibility towards the European institutions. It may be expected that such a strengthening of the national prosecution offices will also have a positive long-term effect on the self-confidence and capability of these offices to investigate complex and delicate cases of corruption and tax evasion.

10.2.3 Structure

10.2.3.1 Centralised or Decentralised Model?

The European Commission has opted for a decentralised organisation of EPPO. It is a logical choice. A fully centralised body would not be feasible in view of the current state of the criminal law systems in the European Union and would have encountered severe, almost insurmountable difficulties given the vast powers of this new Office to instruct the national prosecution offices. Under the current conditions, EPPO would hardly have been able to take over the competences from the national authorities and fulfil its tasks effectively without having the possibility to resort to national legal authorities.

[11] Recital 11 of the EPPO proposal.

[12] See: Article 5(3) of the EPPO proposal.

10.2.3.2 Strict Hierarchy, College or Chamber? Advantages of a Hierarchical Structure

The decentralised model proposed by the Commission triggers a few questions with regard to the structure of the new body, also bearing in mind the EU framework of judicial cooperation and the legal challenges that lay ahead of it. Decentralised approach leaves at least three options open for structuring the European Public Prosecutor's Office: a model of strict hierarchy as proposed by the European Commission, a college-model and, on the basis of the latter, a model in which all Member States also may be represented through an integration of smaller units into EPPO, consisting of prosecutors from those Member States which are affected by the ongoing investigation.

In this respect, it should be underlined that in due course EPPO must be capable of reaching its goals through a clear division of responsibilities. National prosecutorial bodies reach their goals by means of a hierarchical structure. Similarly, the basis of EPPO needs to be hierarchically designed, enabling the entity to accomplish appropriately its daily casework.[13]

However, the European Prosecutors, irrespective of their level in the hierarchy, will hardly handle a case successfully without knowledge of the language, the legal culture and the mentality of the actors in the Member State affected. Although to a large extent, this challenge might be mastered by the establishment of EDPs, the central office of EPPO will bear the responsibility for supervising the case-handling by the EDPs and for taking important decisions like the initiation of investigations, the issuance of an indictment or the termination of the case as well as for the coordination of investigating measures in several Member States. Such decisions may include also difficult tactical issues. Therefore, it appears necessary to have national prosecutors from the concerned Member States to take part in the decision-making process at every level of the body. Only this would fulfil main requirements for an overall acceptance of EPPO and for the establishment of confidence and trust of the professionals and the public in the Member States.

The potential difficulties of the powers of an EPP to give instructions to EDPs or even to the police or other national authorities may be illustrated by the following, hypothetical scenario. The European Public Prosecutor struggling to instruct one hundred police or customs officers in a language he does not speak, trying to control their actions through procedural rules he does not understand, or being subject to motions of defence counsels he is not able to evaluate will hardly be very successful. Such worrying situations could possibly arise on the basis of the EPPO proposal, particularly where an EPP takes over the investigation from an EDP,[14] and are justifying an urgent need for EPPO to act through prosecutors who are familiar with the legal system of the Member State affected. For that reason also,

[13] This is also stressed in recital 8 of the EPPO proposal.

[14] See: Articles 18(2), 18(5) and 18(6) of the EPPO proposal.

every Member State should be represented at the highest level of the Office, in order to ensure the necessary expertise and acceptance.

This leads to the idea of looking for a combination of hierarchical and college elements, including the conditions of effective decision making and the participation of national prosecutors. With regard to the hierarchical structure of the Office, the legislative proposal certainly meets the basic requirements for reaching decisions rapidly and effectively. Therefore, amendments should be based on such a model, focusing on enabling the participation of prosecutors from the respective Member States on the different levels of hierarchy without hampering the capability of EPPO to act adequately and timely.

10.2.3.3 Strict Hierarchy, College or Chamber? Advantages of a College-Model

The legislative proposal attempts to take these facts into account by appointing EDPs, who will be responsible for executing the main parts of the procedure.[15] Under the 'double-hatted' model, they would belong to both EPPO and the national investigation authorities. However, from a perspective of a Member State, it seems insufficient to establish a national representation on the EDP level only, since it still appears to be possible, that the investigation would be conducted or supervised without the participation of competent prosecutors originating from the concerned legal system, though needed to ensure the availability of the necessary expertise. Besides, only a representative of Member States represented within EPPO would be able to provide views and experiences of the different national criminal law systems, in the process of establishing guidelines and common practice for the handling of the cases.[16]

A possible solution to that problem could be that every Member State appoints one national member. In addition to the EDPs, particularly in the course of their supervision, this person could play an important role in explaining national law to the other European Prosecutors and, on the other hand, in communicating the view of the European Office to the national prosecutors.

Furthermore, concerning the steering function,[17] which will have considerable impact on the development of coherent practice in combating fraud to the detriment of the European Union,[18] exclusive powers of a small panel consisting of the European Public Prosecutor and his four Deputies, do not seem to be indispensable; other models of the execution of internal competences in this field could be

[15] See: Article 6(4) and 6(5) of the EPPO proposal. See also: internal rules of procedure in Article 7.

[16] Article 7 of the EPPO proposal does not entirely fulfil this condition.

[17] Recital 12 of the EPPO proposal.

[18] EPPO will exert a strong influence on the practice of the national authorities in the handling of e.g. comparable national tax evasion cases or white-collar crimes.

considered.[19] General guidelines for prosecution, consensually adopted, or at least by a majority of the Member States, could be more influential.

10.2.3.4 Strict Hierarchy, College or Chamber? Advantages of the Integration of Chambers

A chamber model, as a further modification of EPPO's structure, is fulfilling both requirements of effective decision making as well as ensuring the participation of national prosecutorial experts. This means that through establishing a college, in which all Member States would be represented by national prosecutors, appropriate decisions on the highest level could be delegated to certain national members or—especially concerning important issues in the course of transnational proceedings—to chambers consisting of the national members of the affected Member State(s). Such a chamber should be able to react in a reasonable time. A comparison can be made with the practice of criminal courts, where panels of such size are not unusual. Having such a structure in place, it would be secured that a prosecutor from the Member State concerned would be able to take part in at least all decisions of major importance. It is worth mentioning that, although not completely comparable, such approach is successfully applied by the European Court of Human Rights. Through the ex-officio participation of a national judge from the State affected, it can be ensured that special knowledge of the respective legal system is taken into account in the decision-making process of the Court.[20]

This model would provide the additional advantage of ensuring a participation of prosecutors involved in cross-border cases ongoing in several Member States. Such a solution would in particular be a step forward towards reaching more effective, better coordinated, qualified and wider accepted prosecutorial decisions.

Finally, the establishing of such chambers within the structure of the European Public Prosecutor's Office would also allow for flexible responses in cases of unforeseen changes in the course of the investigation. This is particularly the case, if the need to collect evidence in other Member States occurs in the course of investigation. By providing a possibility to establish ad hoc chambers, EPPO could take recourse to a *forum* in which prosecutors may participate from all Member States affected.

The details regarding the competences of such chambers could be left to an autonomous decision of the European Public Prosecutors. This would allow for developing best practices in the most flexible way.

---

[19] E.g. the European Public Prosecutor and his deputies or a certain quantum of national members could have the right to initiate proposals, subject to subsequent confirmation by the College.

[20] Article 26(4) of the European Convention on Human Rights: 'There shall sit as an *ex-officio* member of the Chamber and the Grand Chamber the judge elected in respect of the High Contracting Party concerned. If there is none or if that judge is unable to sit, a person chosen by the President of the Court from a list submitted in advance by that Party shall sit in the capacity of judge'.

10.2.4 Delegated Prosecutors

It is without any doubt necessary to have European Delegated Prosecutors (EDPs) within the EPPO structure. However, especially for a Member State organised in a federal way like Germany, the implementation of Delegated Prosecutor into the national legal system will constitute a challenge.[21]

Criminal investigation processes often follow an unpredictable course. Therefore, in order to facilitate the investigative procedures, more flexible solutions could be considered. For instance: mechanisms allowing for quick reactions to unpredicted situations, such as an occurrence of a new suspect or criminal acts; or fast procedures enabling temporary appointments of additional Delegated Prosecutors.

10.2.5 Competences

A key issue regarding the establishment of EPPO in the light of the principle of conferral is the question of its competences. There are two aspects related to this subject-matter. First of all, the material scope of EPPO's competence and its precise delimitation in the relevant legislative document, and second of all, the choice between exclusive *versus* concurrent competence of the EPP to prosecute the crimes falling within that material scope of its competence.

10.2.5.1 Material Scope of Competence

The material scope of EPPO's competence is laid down in a proposal for a directive on the fight against fraud to the financial interests of the European Union.[22] This may lead to several problems with regard to the principle of sufficient certainty of criminal law. Offences, for which EPPO will have jurisdiction, should be exhaustively and conclusively enumerated in the regulation itself, and not by reference to the directive.[23] Furthermore, the competence of EPPO must be clearly defined. It should only result from the offence itself.

For the time being, it is difficult to foresee how many cases will be dealt with by EPPO and the consequences which may follow from the expected workload. It should nevertheless be of great importance that the material competence remains

---

[21] This issue cannot be elaborated here in more detail, because a number of questions are related to national administrative law.

[22] See Article 3 of the proposal for a Directive on the fight against fraud to the Union's financial interests by means of criminal law, COM (2012) 363 final of 11 July 2012.

[23] Marta Pawlik and Andre Klip scrutinise these issues precisely and in a rather convincing way in Chap. 11 in this book.

limited to PIF crimes, as laid down in the proposal.[24] The establishment of EPPO must not lead to a slippery slope, gradually shifting the competences regarding other offences, such as terrorism or organised crime, from national authorities to this European body, which is neither legally entitled nor prepared to take over such responsibilities. The experiences of Member States and their best practices in the field of offences to the detriment of the EU should be evaluated carefully before taking into consideration the possibility of proceeding towards a larger scope of competence. There is a high risk of hampering the functioning of existing structures.

The material scope of competence will also be delimited through EPPO's ancillary competence in mixed cases. These instances, where a PIF crime is linked to other offences under national criminal law, are not only of a complex nature, but also of high practical relevance, because of the fact that such dependency can frequently occur. The facts need to be inextricably linked, thus the question of double jeopardy is at stake. This sort of cases has to be distinguished from purely connected cases, which are only related in a certain way to the PIF crime, e.g. there being the same suspect or the same *modus operandi*.

A general competence of EPPO in mixed cases could be acceptably provided that the PIF crime is preponderant and the other criminal offences are based on identical facts.[25] However, some more precise criteria would be needed in order to determine the preponderance. In the event of ambiguity, a number of questions might arise: should only the amount of damage be of relevance, or should the circumstances of the case also be taken into account? More precise guidelines, though leaving some flexibility to the practitioners, would help to avoid such problems. This solution would be also beneficial for the procedure of determining the competence in case of divergent opinions between EPPO and national authorities. Another difficulty relates to the question how the power to determine the preponderance of a crime should be exercised. To what extent should the opinion of the EPP be taken into consideration? Or should it be up to a national office to decide? Undoubtedly, regardless concrete guidelines, again very close communication and the willingness on both sides to react, as soon as new facts occur in the course of an investigation, would be needed.

Unlike mixed cases, connected crimes do not fall within the scope of article 13. Since there is no legal basis for the assumption that EPPO will have competence for this category of cases, these will have to be dealt with by the national authorities after notifying EPPO. Again, close cooperation between the authorities is crucial. Such cooperation cannot be achieved by legal provisions only, but it has to develop through and to be based on mutual trust, personal contacts and positive experiences.

---

[24] See recital 21 of the EPPO proposal.

[25] See Article 13(1) of the EPPO proposal.

10.2.5.2 Exclusive Competence or Concurring Competence?

The proposal aims, at least indirectly, at the establishment of uniform standards of the prosecution of PIF crimes in the Member States. This aim might be better achieved by putting EPPO in a strong position towards the national prosecution offices. Nevertheless, from a practitioner's perspective for a number of reasons the introduction of concurring competences with a right of EPPO of evocation seems to be preferable. In general, this would mean that there is a competence both for EPPO and the authorities of the Member States, while it is up to EPPO to decide whether to execute its prevailing powers. Additionally, EPPO would be entitled to take over the case at every phase of the proceedings or, eventually, to return the case to the national authorities.

In the first place, in such a model, a more flexible and smooth handling could be achieved. On the basis of a steady flow of information, it would allow EPPO to decide on the execution of its competence depending on the particular circumstances and relevance of the case. EPPO would remain in control of the procedure and benefit from the expertise of national authorities in a better way. In urgent cases, the national authorities could act without prior dwelling on the issue of competence. Otherwise, at the expense of time and expediency, the file would have to be transferred to a different entity.[26] Furthermore, it has to be noted that easily a situation could occur in which, even after the dismissal of the case, new facts emerge on the national level.

Secondly, an additional advantage of such a split of competences would be the motivation for the national prosecutors to act responsibly, adding to a better execution of investigative measures. Therefore, national authorities should not generally be barred from action, particularly if they are well equipped to handle the case and they dealt already successfully with connected cases.

Thirdly, further reasons for not excluding national authorities could be found in the lack of seriousness of the concerned offence(s), lack of complexity of the investigation and lack of a cross-border dimension. EPPO would benefit from such a solution as well, since it allows for a more efficient division of resources to concentrate on more important criminal cases. With its right to take over the investigation at any given phase, EPPO would have sufficient strength in relation to the national prosecution offices. Finally, as a further major advantage, difficult problems in the cooperation with third states could be diminished.[27]

---

[26] According to Article 17 and recital 23 of the EPPO proposal, national authorities shall maintain a competence to take any urgent measures necessary to ensure effective investigation and prosecution.

[27] Should the EPPO be put in place in the framework of enhanced cooperation between some of the Member States, this aspect would gain even more importance.

10.3 Issues of Subsidiarity

The principle of subsidiarity as established in Article 5 TEU[28] is fundamental to the functioning of the European Union. Providing that the Union may only take action, where the same goal could not be otherwise achieved by Member States, the principle shall be applied by all of its institutions, and EPPO is certainly no exception in this regard. It is well understood, therefore, that a number of issues in the proposal seek to comply with the Article 5(3). This conclusion can be drawn not only from the decentralised model chosen for EPPO, but also from the proposed establishment of European Delegated Prosecutors who will remain national prosecutors within the national criminal law systems of the Member States. Further examples are the general competence of the courts of the Member States for the trial,[29] the applicability of the procedural law of the respective Member States without providing for an implementation of a comprehensive set of minimum rules[30] and the exercise of judicial review by the national courts.[31] While these are clear consequences of the application of the principle of subsidiarity, this contribution will concentrate on three more controversial issues related to this principle, namely the need for an additional prosecution office at a European level, the assumption of an exclusive competence and the right of EPPO to instruct national authorities.

10.3.1 Justification of the Establishment of a Prosecutor's Office on the European Level

The underlying question to be posed when analysing EPPO from the point of view of the subsidiarity principle, is whether there is an adequate justification for its establishment. Arguments brought forward in the proposed Council regulation relate, among others, to the clear-cut differences in the capabilities of the criminal

---

[28] Article 5.3. TEU provides:

'Under the principle of subsidiarity, in areas which do not fall within its exclusive competence, the Union shall act only if and in so far as the objectives of the proposed action cannot be sufficiently achieved by the Member States, either at central level or at regional and local level, but can rather, by reason of the scale or effects of the proposed action, be better achieved at Union level. The institutions of the Union shall apply the principle of subsidiarity as laid down in the Protocol on the application of the principles of subsidiarity and proportionality. National Parliaments ensure compliance with the principle of subsidiarity in accordance with the procedure set out in that Protocol'.

[29] Article 27 of the EPPO proposal.

[30] The procedural law is widely left to the Member States. Article 32 of the proposal refers to certain guarantees of the suspect, while all procedural rights under the respective national law remain applicable.

[31] Article 36 of the EPPO proposal.

law systems of the respective Member States to provide effective protection concerning cross-border crimes.[32] Considering the European Union as a whole, there is ground to believe that the creation of EPPO, implementing a supra-national level of prosecution, will enable a better protection of its financial interests by means of criminal law. And it seems to be almost impossible to prove that alternative concepts, such as for example support of the criminal law systems in some Member States, would be a more successful tool. This is particularly given the potential impact on the development of common standards within the European Union. Since EPPO's remit will not extend beyond the prosecution of PIF crimes, and even though it should help to achieve a stronger awareness of the European dimension as such, the fact is that—according to Article 86 TFEU—this matter falls under the prerogatives of the European Union. Therefore, the emphasis in the discussion on subsidiarity in EPPO's case should be focused on the question of its future shape and powers in relation to the criminal law authorities of the Member States.[33]

As a final remark regarding the compliance of the establishment of EPPO with the subsidiarity principle, it is necessary to stress that criminal law is only one of the instruments to prevent harm of the European Union's financial interests. Other useful measures, namely of a more administrative nature, should not be forgotten; this could include, for instance, stricter management of internal control in the field of subsidies of the European Union. The establishment of EPPO could be significantly strengthened and its credibility furthered through the simultaneous implementation of such additional steps.

10.3.2 Exclusive Competence

Related to the aforementioned aspect is the question, whether the establishment of EPPO's exclusive competence complies with the principle of subsidiarity. In relation to the Member States that have well-established, successful criminal law systems, especially those with a proven track record of dealing with complex, cross-border cases, one may wonder why transfer of the prosecutorial competence to the European level, even for crimes affecting EU finances, should be necessary. As far as the Member States are able to provide a sufficient protection, and if the case lacks a cross-border dimension, why should it not be handled on the national level? This is a further reason to maintain the option of concurring competences.

---

[32] See Introduction in Chap. 1 of this book.

[33] It should be noted, however, that the number of participating Member States will be of great importance for EPPO's capability to achieve real improvements in the protection of the EU's financial interests. If the number of participating Member States is insufficient, there may arise concerns with regard to the principle of subsidiarity.

10.3.3 The Right to Instruct National Prosecutors and Authorities

The decentralised model, including the European Delegated Prosecutors as provided for by the proposal, might be regarded as a less intrusive as the centralised one. Indeed, under most circumstances this model respects sufficiently the position of the Member States as secured also by the EDPs. Nevertheless, in some situations[34] EPPO might be able to investigate without relying on an EDP originating from a Member State. In such case, the competence of EPPO to instruct national authorities might be regarded as problematic in the light of the principle of subsidiarity.

Considerations on the problems of the choice of structure and on the consequences for the acceptance of such powers, as laid out afore, should be taken into account in this regard. Apart from legal and constitutional questions, it is for practical reasons that this competence should be exercised by prosecutors originating from the concerned Member State. Be it for the subsidiarity or simply to ensure a better functioning of EPPO.

10.4 Issues of Proportionality

Last but not least, the question whether the establishment of EPPO is sufficiently justified shall be analysed with regard to its compliance with the Treaty based principle of proportionality. According to this principle, 'the content and form of Union action shall not exceed what is necessary to achieve the objectives of the Treaties'.[35] With regard to the European Public Prosecutor, this principle shall be applied to its operations while ensuring that its impact on the legal orders and institutional structures of the Member States is the least intrusive possible.[36] This issue is important, especially from the point of view of a criminal suspect and his position in the course of an investigation.[37] From this perspective, a few proportionality aspects will be analysed in the following paragraphs.[38] The focus will be directed on the guarantees of individuals' rights, the question of the choice of jurisdiction and the question of judicial review.

---

[34] See Article 16(2) in conjunction with Articles 18(5), 18(6) and recital 9 of the EPPO proposal.

[35] Article 5(4) TEU.

[36] Recital 6 of the EPPO proposal alleges, that the impact on the legal order and the institutional structures of the Member States be 'the least intrusive possible'. This may be questioned considering the limited elements of a collegial system and the stipulation of an exclusive competence of EPPO.

[37] See Article 26(3) of the EPPO proposal in regard to the execution of investigative measures.

[38] This aspect is expressly stated in recitals 18 and 29 of the EPPO proposal.

10.4.1 Individual Rights and Coercive Measures

The proposal aims at the establishment of uniform standards for individual rights and coercive measures.[39] This approach to a stronger harmonisation is impaired by the narrow scope of applicability. PIF crimes (without connected crimes) only constitute a small piece of criminal law. This very circumstance may have an undue impact on what is strived for by this procedural harmonisation. Creating a special regime of procedural law for a relatively small piece of criminal law, may inevitably lead to vast problems in consistency between the criminal law systems of the Member States. The following example may illustrate that problem. According to Article 26(1)e of the EPPO proposal, a serious problem could rise if telephone-tapping would be allowed to investigate a PIF crime, whereas under German law such a measure would generally not be permitted in respect of a similar suspicion concerning tax fraud to the detriment of the Member State. Particularly in consideration of the general rule stipulated in Article 11(3) of the EPPO proposal, it remains ambiguous whether Germany will be obliged under European Law to allow such measures in PIF cases while refusing telephone-tapping in comparable cases under national criminal law. Taking into account the fact that PIF crimes will very often be accompanied by other crimes, this would lead to serious legal conflicts, which could hamper the development of a coherent application of law and could undermine the trust of citizens. We have to be aware that promoting harmonisation of procedural law on this small section may easily lead to severe frictions with the criminal law systems of the Member States. Therefore, as stated above, there is a need for general harmonisation of the law of the Member States which cannot be replaced by the establishment of EPPO.

What is more, it seems to be unclear to what extent higher standards of individual rights under the constitutional and procedural law of the Member States remain applicable.[40] A negative answer could hardly be acceptable, especially for reasons of proportionality. Individual rights granted under national law and even guaranteed by the constitution of the Member States should not be removed or watered down by the establishment of EPPO. Otherwise, the courts, at least the constitutional courts of some Member States and possibly the European Court of Human Rights, are likely to intervene sooner or later.

This problem becomes even more pressing due to the catalogue of coercive measures which should be implemented in the legal system of the Member States.[41] Specific standards, constitutional rights and safeguards for the protection of individual rights must be respected, also if they do not allow for particular measures at all. Otherwise, the well-balanced requirements of national law regarding the

---

[39] See Articles 26 and 32 of the EPPO proposal.

[40] Article 26(2) of the EPPO proposal is ambiguous. Nor it is clear whether Article 32(5) or recital 19 of the proposal could support a different opinion. Article 11(3) of the proposal does not seem to be sufficiently clear either.

[41] Article 26(1) of the EPPO proposal.

application of certain coercive measures, including guarantees for the protection of the individual, would be undermined. And PIF crimes are clearly not of such weight that, seen from a perspective of proportionality, every possible investigative measure should be made available.

Article 30 of the proposal, governing the admissibility of evidence, does not contribute to the clarification of this issue either. While referring to Articles 47 and 48 of the Charter of Fundamental Rights of the European Union, it remains silent on the much more precise and essential preconditions of procedural law of the Member States, which ought to safeguard the (constitutionally guaranteed) individual rights of the suspect.

10.4.2 Choice of Jurisdiction

Another much disputed issue is the choice of jurisdiction especially with a view to avoid forum shopping. The proposal of the European Commission obviously tries to exclude such a possibility.[42] However, more precise guidelines seem to be indispensable to achieve this objective. The criteria mentioned in Article 27(4) of the proposal grant a considerable amount of discretion, especially since they only have to be 'taken into account'. As an alternative, a clear hierarchy of these criteria should be introduced, starting with the place where the offence was committed.[43] Moreover, a choice of jurisdiction depending on the allocation of evidence[44] and the residence of the 'direct' victim[45] would contribute to further uncertainty, because these are rather vague criteria leaving an ample margin of appreciation.

Furthermore, to safeguard more effectively the objective of preventing arbitrariness in opting for a specific jurisdiction, it should be considered to create an additional competence of the ECJ. Thus, especially on a motion of the suspect, the ECJ could, under certain preconditions, decide whether the jurisdiction in charge has been determined without arbitrariness. There seems to be a need for this, particularly in the light of the likely future situation of having diverging approaches and decisions of national courts in the different Member States.

---

[42] Article 27 of the EPPO proposal.

[43] Article 27(4) a of the EPPO proposal.

[44] Article 27(4) c of the EPPO proposal.

[45] Article 27(4) d of the EPPO proposal. It should be noted that the concept of 'direct victim' is rather unclear. Since the EPPO will be established to protect the financial interests of the European Union, who should be regarded as a 'direct' victim. Consequently, who would be an 'indirect' victim?

10.4.3 Judicial Review

The issue of judicial review is of paramount importance, since the guarantees of individual rights have to be secured by effective legal remedies of the suspect and the accused. For reasons of practicability, although this is in breach of the well-established principles of European law, one could agree with the idea that judicial review should primarily be conducted by national courts.[46] That would, nevertheless, make the instrument of preliminary rulings by the ECJ all the more important in order to achieve sufficient common standards. However, to make sure that the relevant cases reach the ECJ, a modification of the proceedings for a preliminary ruling should be taken into consideration. Exceptionally, justified by the extraordinary competence of the national courts, it could be considered to give the defence a right to initiate a special procedure of preliminary ruling or even to lodge a complaint, enabling the ECJ to decide on cases which are of particular importance for the development of the European law or where the application by the national law is manifestly wrong.

Another problem relates to the fact that Article 13(4) of the proposal stipulates that the determination of ancillary competence shall not be subject to judicial review. Since the jurisdiction, the applicable law and choice of forum will depend on the execution of an ancillary competence, this provision might be in conflict with the constitutional right of the accused—as set out by some Member States—to have his case dealt with by a judge predetermined by law.

10.5 Conclusion

The legislative proposal of the Commission points into the right direction, especially if all or a vast majority of Member States participate in this project. However, adjustments seem necessary and should primarily affect the structure and the competences of EPPO in order to achieve a better cooperation with the national authorities. Furthermore, the concept of coercive measures should be reviewed in order to avoid frictions with the (constitutional) law of Member States. Other instruments to overcome divergences between the Member States, such as harmonisation of the law of the Member States, or better judicial training, must not be neglected. If EPPO fits in smoothly, one day it might become an important tool to combat crime. But one has to be aware of the consequences of a failure, including the possible loss of trust and decrease in acceptance of the European Union. And finally, there is a risk of facing not dragons, but a hydra of organised crime, if the ambitious goals set out in the proposal are not reached.

---

[46] Article 36 of the EPPO proposal.

Chapter 11
A Disappointing First Draft for a European Public Prosecutor's Office

Marta Pawlik and André Klip

Abstract The legislative proposal for the establishment of the European Public Prosecutor's Office resolves some doubts, but also raises further questions. This chapter attempts to analyse to what extent the legislative proposal as it stands now could serve as legal basis for the functioning of the new office. In particular, three main issues are tackled: first, the question of substantive law for EPPO's operations, second, accountability for human rights violations, and third, cooperation of the new body with Member States' authorities. An analysis of proposed provisions in the present paper leads to a conclusion that the document in the current form requires more work to be done on the part of the legislator in order to make the battle of EU's financial interests a won one.

Keywords European Public Prosecutor's Office · EPPO · European criminal law · EU's financial interests · Human rights · Accountability for human rights violations

Contents

At the time of writing this chapter, Marta Pawlik was research assistant at the T.M.C. Asser Institute in The Hague. She is a co-editor of the present EPPO volume. André Klip is professor of criminal law, criminal procedure and transnational criminal law at Maastricht University and Judge at the 's-Hertogenbosch Court of Appeal (criminal division).

M. Pawlik (✉)
Wroclaw, Poland
e-mail: martapawlik@gmail.com

A. Klip
Maastricht University, Maastricht, The Netherlands
e-mail: andre.klip@maastrichtuniversity.nl

L.H. Erkelens et al. (eds.), *The European Public Prosecutor's Office*,
DOI 10.1007/978-94-6265-035-0_11

11.1 Introduction

The legislative proposal on the establishment of the European Public Prosecutor's Office (EPPO) issued by the European Commission in July 2013 has been feared by many and hopefully expected by some. It answers some questions, but definitely raises a number of practical issues with regard to applicability of its provisions. An initial remark is one of disappointment. It was expected that the proposal would be based on three different constituent parts: first on substantive criminal law and jurisdiction, second on institutional matters and democratic accountability and lastly on criminal procedure and cooperation rules between Member States, non-EPPO participating Member States and third-party countries. The Commission proposal hardly deals with the first limb, does address some of the issues relating to the second and pays little attention to the third. The proposal establishes an EPPO in conjunction with an amendment of the rules applicable to Eurojust.

There is a number of issues arising from the initial analysis of provisions of the EPPO proposal. First of all, it is important to note that Article 86 TFEU provides that the Council, in order to combat crimes affecting the financial interests of the Union, may establish a EPPO from Eurojust. However, when analysing the provisions laid down for the establishment of EPPO, the question arises whether the formula 'from Eurojust' has not been taken too literally. The approach presented in the proposal appears to be significantly influenced by the partners in the drafting of the legislative proposal, the existing offices of Eurojust and OLAF, but, at the same time, by the conspicuous absence of EPPO.[1] That absence manifests itself in lack of appropriate protection for the interests of prosecutorial authorities and, consequently, a number of difficulties that the prosecution may face in various situations.

Second of all, another shortcoming that shows up in the legislative proposal is the highly ambiguous operational model chosen for EPPO. As it has been laid out in the EPPO proposal, the structure of the Office shall comprise a European Public Prosecutor, his Deputy and staff, as well as European Delegated Prosecutors located in the Member States.[2] It shall be the so-called 'double hatted' model, implying simultaneous dual capacities of prosecutors as representatives of both national, as well as European prosecutorial authorities. However, enabling the European

---

[1] Caianiello 2013, at p. 124: 'It looks more like a "reinforced Eurojust" than an European Public Prosecutor Office, that is, an organ empowered to give orders to the judicial authorities of the Member States rather than intervene directly in the field'.

[2] Article 6(1) of the proposal for a Council Regulation on the Establishment of the European Public Prosecutor's Office, COM(2013) 534 final, 17 June 2013 (hereafter: the 'EPPO proposal'). See also the Appendix to this book.

Delegated Prosecutors to perform their functions in parallel may, in fact, lead to lack of coherence, confusion and overall paralysis, when either of the roles is not entirely executed. An additional problem, which arises from this 'double hatted' model, is the division of tasks and competences. On the one hand, the Delegated Prosecutors shall be fully independent from the national prosecution bodies and have no obligations towards them when acting within their mandate under the Regulation.[3] On the other hand, they shall be able to exercise also their function as national prosecutors.[4] Such arrangements may not only lead to conflicts of competences, as operational capacities get intertwined with the rules on accountability, but may also be subject to a specific kind of national hierarchy.

Lastly, the proposal introduces a mandatory investigation principle,[5] apparently leaving no discretion to the European Prosecutor and obliging him to initiate an investigation, whenever certain offences are allegedly committed. The ambitions are sky high: 'every suspected offence will be systematically followed'.[6] What is conspicuous however, is the long list of grounds allowing for dismissal of a case.[7] This shows that the European legislator may have been overly ambitious to include the mandatory investigation provision judging by the amount of cases where such investigation may be impossible. One may draw a conclusion, that in the eyes of its architects, the EPPO is destined to perform considerably better than the prosecutions of the Member States, built upon centuries of experience and equipped with an ability to prosecute each case of fraud within the European Union. At the same time, two grounds for discretionary dismissal[8] raise doubts with regard to the supposedly obligatory nature of the EPPO's investigative powers.

Those questions are merely initial doubts one may have from the first analysis of the legislative proposal. The present paper will focus on three more specific aspects, which could potentially create difficulties for the future Office when it is applying the provisions in practice. Naturally assuming the regulation will be adopted in the form as put forward by the Commission. Those issues, as will be analysed in the following sections, relate to the substantive criminal law jurisdiction, the accountability for human rights violations and finally the mode of cooperation between the EPPO and the authorities of the Member States.

---

[3] Article 6(5) of the EPPO proposal.

[4] Article 6(6) of the EPPO proposal.

[5] As provided by Article 16(1): 'The European Public Prosecutor [...] shall initiate an investigation by written decision where there are reasonable grounds to believe that an offence within the competence of European Public Prosecutor's Office is being or has been committed'.

[6] Commission Document (2013) 533, Communication from the Commission to the European Parliament, the Council, the European Economic and Social Committee and the Committee of the Regions. Improving OLAF's governance and reinforcing procedural safeguards in investigations: A step-by-step approach to accompany the establishment of the European Public Prosecutor's Office, p. 6.

[7] Article 28(1) of the EPPO proposal.

[8] Article 28(2) of the EPPO proposal.

11.2 Substantive Criminal Law Jurisdiction

According to Article 12 of the proposal, the EPPO shall have competence with respect to criminal offences affecting the financial interests of the Union, as provided for by (what is currently still a proposal) a directive on the fight against fraud to the Union's financial interests by means of criminal law[9] and as subsequently implemented by national law. Thus, the substantive jurisdiction in the future is to be found in the Directive on Financial Interests and, by implementation, in national law. This legislative act, in addition to defining the Union's financial interests, also establishes necessary measures for the prevention of and fight against fraud and other illegal activities affecting them; therefore, it relates to the legal instruments that will, most probably, be adopted providing the substance necessary to complement the EPPO proposal.

Such fragmentation of substantive law, manifesting itself in this inclusion of provisions into various legislative acts, creates several conceptual problems. Firstly, it must be noted that the directive provides a common definition of the Union's financial interests, and consequently, a crime against that interest, that will, however, not be directly applicable in criminal proceedings. Thus, the relationship between the definitions implemented in the national legal systems on the basis of this directive raises some questions. First and foremost, a question of a greatest importance for the functioning of EPPO—which of the definitions shall initiate its operations.

There are at least three possible answers to the question. In one of them, the EPP would be able to apply the definition as provided by the Directive on Financial Interests, a common definition for the Member States. In the second option, the EPP could apply the definitions as implemented into the national criminal justice systems of the Member States. Nonetheless, there are as many as thirty such definitions of a criminal offence in the EU, which would constitute a wide variety of possibilities for the EPPO to choose from. Finally, the third solution provides a considerably different approach, not included in the present legislative proposal, but nonetheless offering possibly the best solution to the problem multiple definitions' problem. This option would be an inclusion of the definition directly into the regulation, instead of the directive, that requires implementation. It remains unknown why, even though Article 86(3) TFEU provides legal basis for inclusion of general and procedural rules directly in the regulation, previous attempts to establish criminal responsibility on the basis of a regulation have always been rejected. Such option would not only help avoiding questions with regard to the applicable definition, but also add to the certainty of law.

In addition to the problems stemming from the ambiguity of the definition of a crime affecting EU's interest, the functioning of EPPO might be handicapped due to the lack of clarity in defining 'suspect' and 'accused'. The subject is essential to

[9] Proposal for a Directive of the European Parliament and of the Council on the fight against fraud to the Union's financial interests by means of criminal law, COM(2012)363, 11 July 2012.

investigation and no prosecutorial office is able to start its operations without previous clarification of legal basis to the operational features. The questions of who shall be considered a suspect and, subsequently, an accused are fundamental for any authority obeying the rule of law. As these concepts do not have an autonomous notion under the EU law, different national definitions can be applied, leading to the question which Member State has jurisdiction over the crime.[10]

At this point, it must be noted that Article 13 of the proposal grants the EPPO additional jurisdiction over ancillary offences. Supplementary to the basic scope of EPPO's jurisdiction over criminal offences affecting financial interests of the Union, this provision gives the European Prosecutor the competence to conduct joint investigation and prosecution over offences inextricably linked to those mentioned in Article 12. In other words, this provision de facto broadens the EPPO's scope of jurisdiction, but only under a condition that the offences are preponderant and the other offences are based on identical facts. Such wording of Article 13 triggers further questions. The main concern with regard to ancillary competences, similarly as in case of the definitions, is how and by whom the term 'ancillary' will be interpreted. On the one hand, the determinant element could be the material facts, but on the other it could be defined by the legal characteristics of the crime. These two methodologies could bring different results; by applying the legal characteristic test, one would simply be referred to the Directive on Financial Interests, whereas the application of material facts as the decisive test, may result in connecting crimes of entirely different nature. This distinction poses practical difficulties with regard to the application of law. People who commit crimes do (generally) not obey the rules, they do not commit crimes as provided in specific article of a code, so as to make the legal classification easier.[11]

The proposed territorial and personal jurisdiction of the EPPO is no surprise. As derived from two classical jurisdictional models: territoriality and nationality principles, the EPPO will have competence over criminal offences committed wholly or partly on the territory of one or several Member States, as well as jurisdiction over Member States' nationals, Union staff members or members of the Institutions who commit one of the offences.[12] Thus, it should be recalled at this point, that the Member States have a wide variety of interpretation rules regarding the 'simple' principle of territorial jurisdiction. The question is therefore whether the terminology is to be interpreted on an autonomous basis or is it supposed to be given interpretation on the basis of national law. The Commission's proposal leaves the terminology issue unsolved, providing no interpretation guidelines, making it possible that both, national law or an autonomous Union law meaning could be applied.

[10] As some Member States have corporate criminal liability and others do not, and overlapping jurisdiction will often exist, the EPPO will have many choices to make.

[11] See: Caianiello 2013, p. 121.

[12] Article 14 of the EPPO proposal.

The last aspect of EPPO's jurisdiction is its temporal scope. This issue is only vaguely determined by the EPPO proposal, through a reference to statutory limitations. The proposal states that 'the European Public Prosecutor shall dismiss the case where prosecution has become impossible on account of [...] expiry of the national statutory limitation to prosecute'.[13] Without identifying which Member State's statute of limitations is relevant, this provision is prone to create a legal vacuum in the area of EU financial crimes. Bearing in mind the cross-border character and extraterritoriality, many Member States will most probably have jurisdiction over the crimes, resulting in several applicable limitations statutes. In theory, it might lead to a situation where EPPO could chose laws of a Member State with more lenient or stricter statutes of limitations. Taking these issues into account, a better solution, providing more certainty and equality, would be to include a statute of limitations in the EPPO regulation itself.

11.3 Accountability for Human Rights Violations

EPPO's operations are of a nature, which is likely to give rise to allegations of human rights violations. The characteristics of investigative proceedings, where the line between rights of an accused and obligations of the prosecutor is thin, will unavoidably lead to collision between those norms. International cooperation in criminal matters and judicial assistance between the Member States make it more difficult for victims of human rights violations committed jointly by Member States to allocate the responsibility. While the European Convention of Human Rights protective system takes exclusive accountability of individual states as a starting point, the practice of combating international crimes has evolved into shared responsibility.[14] This has made direct application of human rights norms more difficult.[15]

When it comes to protection of individual rights, the EPPO proposal makes solely reference to the rights enshrined in the Charter of Fundamental Rights of the European Union as the norms to be respected by the EPPO during its activities.[16] One remark must be made at this point with regard to this limited scope of protection, because seems rather short sighted to ignore the European Convention of Human Rights in the light of anticipated proximity of EU's accession to the ECHR. Such event has been prescribed in the Lisbon Treaty[17] and is facilitated by Article 59(2) of the Convention; thus, it surprises that the proposal does not include the ECHR in its provisions. Since the present analysis can only focus on the proposal as

---

13 Article 28(1)(d) of the EPPO proposal.

14 Similarly in the area of asylum policy, see ECtHR, 21 January 2011, Appl. 30696/09, *M.S.S* v. *Belgium and Greece*.

15 See: Klip 2012, p. 423.

16 Article 11(1) of the EPPO proposal.

17 Article 6(2) TEU.

it is written, the following sections will not deal with the benefits of having referral to the ECHR protection system included in the EPPO regulation.

The EPPO will be working within a national criminal justice system, but there must be a clear line of responsibility in case of human rights violations. The EPPO proposal indicates two options of accountability for human rights violations. First one, Article 4(3) provides that 'The European Public Prosecutor's Office shall exercise functions of a prosecutor in the competent courts of the Member States, which essentially means that the responsibility for the actions of the Prosecutor would lay on the relevant Member State. Should such violation occur and the Member State is subsequently held responsible before the European Court of Human Rights for the violations committed by the EPPO on its behalf, this Member State would most certainly in the future wish to influence the actions of the Prosecutor in order to prevent violations he can be held responsible for.

Second option with regard to the accountability for human rights violations is included in Article 6(7) which provides that 'acts performed by the European Public Prosecutor, European Delegated Prosecutors, any of the staff members of the European Public Prosecutor's Office [...] shall be attributed to the European Public Prosecutor's Office.[18] Such wording suggests that it would be the EPPO itself directly responsible, also under human rights obligations. As mentioned before, at a certain point complaints about human rights violations committed by the EPPO will occur and, with that in mind, it must be clear for the claimant against which entity or state he or she must bring the case. Whether that would be the Member State where the investigation was conducted or whether he or she shall directly apply against the EPPO as an EU body is a matter yet to be determined. This question is not sufficiently clarified in the legislative proposal.

Articles 32–35 provide the reader with some indication on the scope of the rights of the suspects. Through the reference to the Charter of Fundamental Rights of the European Union and, specifically, to the right to a fair trial and the rights of the defence, the provisions indicate a minimum of rights as they are provided in the Union's legislation and the national law of the Member State.[19] The subsequent paragraph provides a temporal framework for those rights—they shall be attributed to the suspect and accused from the moment a person is suspected of having committed an offence. At the same time, once the indictment has been acknowledged by the competent national court, their rights shall be based on the national regime applicable in the case. The obvious conclusion on the basis of these provisions is that the proposal assumes human rights protection only in the event that the EPPO brings the case to judicial proceedings.

One shall not forget, that not all investigations will ultimately lead to a charge and court proceedings. This is a point that the drafters of the legislative proposal seem to have forgotten. The responsibilities of EPPO and the judicial review provisions all relate to a situation where a case would eventually be brought to a

[18] Article 6(7) of the EPPO proposal.

[19] Article 32(1) of the EPPO proposal.

court. However, this is not the only possible scenario—the case might terminate earlier, but the rights and obligations of the individuals could still be injured. This demonstrates a potential need for a platform to resolve accusations of human rights abuses in the event a case does not get to the court.

The aforementioned Articles 32–35, regulating EPPO's procedural safeguards, set out the minimum standards to be applied by EPPO as those provided for by the EU legislation and the national law of the Member States. However and according to the principle of sincere cooperation[20] as elaborated by the Court of Justice,[21] the national systems must already include those rules, comply with them and should therefore be implemented. Thus, the question arises: why does the Commission see the need to emphasise the prevailing character of EU primary legislation?

A potential explanation might be that the European Public Prosecutor shall conduct some of the investigations himself. Even though, as a principle, the investigation initiated by the European Public Prosecutor shall subsequently be assigned to one of the European Delegated Prosecutors,[22] the contrary is also possible. In accordance with a set of criteria,[23] the Prosecutor can also conduct an investigation himself, which would explain the direct applicability of EU's legislation.

Another matter to be discussed here is the issue of the rights of an accused *vis-à-vis* the EPPO. A good example to illustrate this potential problem, is the right to access to essential materials. Especially in the preparatory phase where a judge is not yet involved, the defence counsel may be interested in viewing the files to better prepare their case. Would the accused or his attorney only be able to obtain such access through the national authorities? Or does the accused or his lawyer have a right *vis-à-vis* the EPPO to see the case related documents on allocation of the case on the basis of Directive 2012/13?[24]

The allocation of the case is in fact another interesting puzzle in the EPPO proposal. The draft regulation stipulates that the allocation of cases shall be governed by internal rules of procedure.[25] This provision should be read in conjunction with Article 16, which describes the procedure after the investigation is initiated—namely the assignment of the case to a European Delegated Prosecutor.[26] The Delegated Prosecutor shall subsequently conduct the investigation measures on

[20] Article 4(3) TEU.

[21] Case C-462/99, *Connect Austria Gesellschaft für Telekommunikation GmbH* v. *Telekom-Control-Kommission,* 22 May 2003, European Court Reports 2003 Page I-05197, para 38: '[…] the obligation arising from a directive for the Member States to achieve the result envisaged therein and their duty under Article 10 EC to take all appropriate measures, whether general or particular, to ensure compliance with that obligation is binding on all the authorities of Member States including, for matters within their jurisdiction, the courts'.

[22] Article 16(2) of the EPPO proposal.

[23] As set out in Article 18(5) of the EPPO proposal.

[24] Article 7 of the Directive 2012/13/EU on the right to information in criminal proceedings, 22 May 2012, *OJ* L 142/1, 1.6.2012.

[25] Article 7(2) of the EPPO proposal.

[26] Article 16(2) of the EPPO proposal.

his own or otherwise instruct the competent law enforcement authorities in the Member State where he is located.[27] In other words, the EPPO will have its own procedures to determine which Member State will eventually handle the case and consequently which legal system will be applied. This procedure is not yet established since it shall be adopted by a decision of the EPP, four Deputies and five Delegated Prosecutors. Due to the fact that the decision to allocate the case to a specific Member State determines the application of all substantive and procedural rules, the procedures to establish that should be laid down directly in the regulation.

11.4 Cooperation with Member States' Authorities

As the previous sections have shown, the functioning of EPPO will hinge on its ability to cooperate with Member States' authorities. In that regard, it is striking that the EPPO proposal lacks a distinction between EPPO participating and non-participating Member States. This absence may have potentially significant procedural implications when determining cooperation. The proposal uses by default the words 'Member States' without defining which states are covered by this definition. It could be an indication of an optimistic approach, or rather of wishful thinking, on the side of the Commission who simply assumes that all Member States will be participating in the EPPO structure. It may be one of the very issues relating to the EPPO that is not in dispute. If it is ever initiated—certainly not all Member States will be on board. From an institutional perspective, EPPO's cooperation struggle with non-participating Member States' authorities may be especially visible when responsibilities of those states need to be addressed. For example, Article 11(7) of the EPPO proposal, which stipulates that 'the competent authorities of the Member States shall actively assist and support the investigations and prosecutions of the EPPO at its request and shall refrain from any action, policy or procedure which may delay or hamper their progress'. This provision instigates curiosity with regard to the reasons for using such terminology, *in lieu* of terms such as 'mutual recognition' or 'international request'. Does this provision create an obligation on the part of Member States to comply with EPPO's requests? In a new draft of the proposal, the position of non-participating Member States would certainly have to be addressed.

11.5 Conclusions

The first draft of a proposal for a Council Regulation on the establishment of the EPPO has several deficiencies. First and the most evident, is the unregulated nature of the relationship between the EPPO and the Member States' authorities. The draft

[27] Article 18(1) of the EPPO proposal.

regulation makes it insufficiently clear, whether the terminology should be interpreted on an autonomous basis, i.e. in accordance with the Union manner or whether it should comply first and foremost with national law.

Secondly, some clarifications should be made regarding the procedural steps that need to be performed by the national criminal justice systems. The current legislative outline is to a large extent one-dimensional. The proposal provides that the EPPO shall rely on a relatively small set of EU wide rules, which might be insufficient for its proper functioning. Comparing it to the extensive procedural rules provided for the Prosecutor of the International Criminal Court, the proposed EPPO regulation appears significantly less elaborated, leaving out many, potentially very important for its functioning, issues unregulated. Furthermore, the proposal creates confusion with regard to applicability of the procedural rights and obligations. It is also inconsistent in determining whether the responsibilities are at the Union level or at the national level.

Finally, the exclusive competence of EPPO to investigate crimes against financial interests of the Union[28] might create an unintended consequence for the national authorities in leading their investigations, by discouraging them from taking any measures towards those crimes. A possible remedy for that could be to introduce complementary functions to the EPPO and leave the national competencies as they are. That might effect in stimulating the national authorities to continue to investigate the EU frauds.

When introducing the proposal to the public, the Commission repeatedly referred to its positive effects for tax payers' interests. If that remains the primary reason to establish the EPPO, it may become a major obstacle to convincing sceptical minds the EPPO's existence is justified. It still is, but on other grounds, and with a substantially amended proposal.

References

Caianiello M (2013) The proposal for a regulation on the European public prosecutor's office: everything changes or nothing changes? Eur J Crime, Crim Law Crim Justice 2:115–125

Klip A (2012) European criminal law. An integrative approach, 2nd edn. Intersentia Cambridge, Cambridge

[28] Article 11(4) of the EPPO proposal.

Part V
How Feasible is Enhanced Cooperation for the European Public Prosecutor's Office?

Chapter 12
Establishing Enhanced Cooperation Under Article 86 TFEU

Julian J.E. Schutte

Abstract Which are the legal implications of the procedure, set out in Article 86 para 1, 2nd and 3rd subparagraphs, of the Treaty on the Functioning of the European Union (TFEU) in the event that the Council does not unanimously support the proposal of the Commission for a regulation on the establishment and functioning of a European Public Prosecutor's Office (EPPO)? In this contribution, an analysis is made of this special procedure, involving the European Council, for allowing a limited number of at least nine Member States to resort to what the Treaties refer to as 'enhanced cooperation' among themselves. It seems unlikely that the proposed regulation will meet unanimity in the Council (even disregarding the special positions of DK, the UK and Ireland); a reference to the European Council is more probable (though far from certain). Consensus in the European Council in support of the draft regulation is not very realistic (where DK, the UK and Ireland have no special positions), although it is expected that the European Council discusses the principles involved. After that discussion, it remains to be seen whether a sufficiently large number of Member States wish to pursue the matter and proceed with enhanced cooperation between themselves. In that case, Article 86 TFEU imposes a strict time frame on them. If that time frame is not respected, the enhanced cooperation cannot be deemed to have been authorised. Participating in enhanced cooperation is not a game allowing those who 'opted in' to 'opt out' subsequently, even before the adoption of the regulation, or to be 'replaced' by another Member State. Extending the remit of the EPPO to other offences than those affecting the EU's financial interests requires a unanimous decision of all the members of the European Council under Article 86(4) TFEU, even if the EPPO regulation binds only a limited number of Member States. In its final part, the contribution discusses a number of implications of enhanced cooperation in relation to the proposed regulation. Can participating Member States

The author is a former Deputy Director General of the Legal Service of the General Secretariat of the Council of the European Union. He retired in 2012.

J.J.E. Schutte (✉)
Castelldefels, Spain
e-mail: julianschutte@yahoo.es

L.H. Erkelens et al. (eds.), *The European Public Prosecutor's Office*,
DOI 10.1007/978-94-6265-035-0_12

make use of bodies and agencies, other than the institutions? What is the role of the Council under its various provisions? To what extent can non-participating Member States be charged for the costs of the EPPO?

Keywords European Public Prosecutor · Enhanced cooperation · Article 86 TFEU · European Council · Crimes affecting the EU's financial interests · *Effet utile*

Contents

12.1 Introduction

Will there be nine? Will there be the minimum number of Member States required under Article 86(1) TFEU that will request that the draft Council Regulation on the establishment of the European Public Prosecutor's Office, proposed by the Commission in doc. COM(2013) 534 final of 17 July 2013, be referred to the European Council? And if no consensus is reached in the European Council, will there be at least nine Member States that wish to establish enhanced cooperation among themselves on the basis of the proposed draft regulation?

Will there be at least nine Member States recognising themselves in the rationale, the justification, given by the Commission for this regulation: do they share the assessment that their existing national-level efforts fail to address properly the problem of fraud against the Union's financial interests,[1] that the Union's financial interests remain insufficiently protected in those Member States[2] and that fraud, corruption and other offences affecting the Union's budget are largely non-prosecuted by them?[3] Do they agree that 'these offences are not always investigated and prosecuted by their national authorities, as law enforcement resources are limited',[4]

[1] Communication from the Commission to the European Parliament, the Council, the European Economic and Social Committee and the Committee of the Regions, 'Better protection of the Union's financial interests: Setting up the European Public Prosecutor's Office and reforming Eurojust', doc. COM(2013) 532 final of 17 July 2013, p. 3.

[2] Ibidem.

[3] Ibidem.

[4] Explanatory memorandum to the Commission's proposal in doc. COM(2013) 534 final, p. 2.

that 'gaps in the judicial action to fight fraud occur daily at different levels and between different authorities' in their countries and that these constitute 'a major impediment to the effective investigation and prosecution of offences affecting the Union's financial interests' at the national level?[5] Do they subscribe to the statement that 'the judicial action undertaken by them against fraud may not be considered as effective, equivalent and deterrent as required under the Treaty'[6] and that 'the present situation, in which the prosecution of offences against the Union's financial interests is exclusively in the hands of the authorities of the Member States is not satisfactory and does not sufficiently achieve the objective of fighting effectively against offences affecting the Union budget'?[7]

In other words, Member States which would support this draft regulation would implicitly recognise that at least with regard to EU fraud offences their public prosecution services are incompetent, incapable of coping with these types of offences or are allowed to disregard their investigation and that their governments are not able or willing to invest in remedying or improving the situation. They would acknowledge that they need a European Public Prosecutor, an outside body, acting autonomously and beyond the political control and responsibility of the national government and national Parliament, distinct from the existing national structures of judicial organisation and authority over police and other specialised law enforcement services.

And in exposing themselves as Member States whose public prosecution services apparently fail to adequately address fraud, corruption and similar offences affecting the financial interests of the Union, they at least raise questions as to the capacity of those services to cope with fraud, corruption, indeed white collar crime and organised crime in general, types of crime which would present a level of complexity as to their investigation, prosecution and further legal processing, similar to those for which the European Prosecutor's Office would be exclusively[8] competent.

Doubts as to the level of performance of the prosecuting services of Member States in these areas might eventually have a bearing on the development of the objectives of the Union in the field of justice and home affairs. A well-functioning and adequately equipped criminal justice system in each Member State is a precondition for the realisation of these objectives. Member States which acceded to the Union since 2004 have demonstrated to the satisfaction of the Union's institutions their willingness and the capacity of their national judicial system to comply with the EU's standards on such matters as the fight against corruption, fraud and organised crime, by having succeeded in complying with the requirements set out in

---

[5] Ibidem.

[6] Ibidem.

[7] Ibidem, p. 4.

[8] See recital (5) and Articles 11(4) and 14 of the draft regulation. Recital (23) states that the competence of the EPPO 'should take priority over national claims of jurisdiction' and that 'with regard to these offences the authorities of Member States should only act at the request of the EPPO', which, it seems, contradicts the notion of 'exclusive competence'.

the programmes for accession negotiations, and in particular in their requirements on Justice, Freedom and Security.

Would any of those Member States, by supporting the Commission's proposal and by accepting the interference of the European Public Prosecutor's Office into their judicial organisation, implicitly admit that, although having successfully completed the Union's clearing process, the action and capacity of their public prosecution services in the fight against offences affecting the Union's financial interests is, in fact, inadequate, insufficient and unsatisfactory?

Maybe the counter argument will run about as follows: the proposal presented by the Commission contradicts in essence its justification. According to the proposal, the functioning of the European Public Prosecutor's Office depends largely on what are called 'European Delegated Prosecutors' and their national staff. European Delegated Prosecutors are, in fact, members of the national public prosecution services who continue to exercise their national competences. They are considered to be at the same time members of the EPPO, but in practice they will act—indeed continue acting—as national prosecutors, within their national judicial organisation, in accordance with their national law and procedures. It is true that the proposed regulation contains some provisions in relation to the European Delegated Prosecutors which make their position in relation to the national judicial organisation somewhat ambiguous, but those ambiguities are likely to be ironed out of the text in the course of the legislative procedure. So in the end, not much will change in practice, compared to the actual situation: specialised national prosecutors who, under procedures still to be determined, will be entitled to add the title 'European Delegated Prosecutor' to their cv will do the work, while the EPP and his or her four Deputies in their luxurious offices in Luxembourg will be kept informed so as to allow them to write their annual report of activities in all languages of the institutions to the EP, national parliaments, the Council and the Commission. In practice, of course, the EPP and his or her Deputies would never investigate or prosecute themselves an offence before a court of a Member State.

So, the impact of the proposed regulation on the functioning of the national criminal justice systems is likely to be kept minimal: its importance will be mainly symbolic—at the estimated eventual costs of 35 million euros per annum.[9]

This counter argument may be valid but begs the obvious question 'why getting on with this exercise?'[10]

---

[9] Explanatory memorandum to the proposed regulation, p. 8.

[10] A more fundamental objection against the proposal would not be based on considerations of subsidiarity but on the very federalisation of a functional part of the criminal justice system. If there is indeed a problem in the functioning of the criminal justice systems of the Member States and in the cooperation and coordination between those systems with respect to offences affecting the financial interests of the Union, federalisation of the prosecution of these offences while disempowering the Member States is the wrong response. It runs counter to system of the Treaties, embodied in Article 4(3), second subparagraph TEU, which states that '(t)he Member States shall take any appropriate measure, general or particular, to ensure fulfillment of the obligations arising out of the Treaties or resulting from the acts of the institutions'. Member States, acting through their national institutions and services, are principally responsible for the full and correct

12.2 The Procedure of Article 86(1) TFEU and Its Implications

Let us suppose, however, that there will be sufficient support within the Council for the proposed regulation to initiate the procedure contemplated in Article 86(1) TFEU. What would this procedure exactly entail?

First, the Council would have to assess whether it is possible to adopt the proposed regulation with the unanimity of its members, as required by the second sentence of para 1 of Article 86 TFEU. Some members of the Council may make their support dependent on the willingness of others to accept certain amendments, which would require a certain period of discussions within the Council in order to find out which amendments would obtain unanimous support. These discussions would only be necessary, if there would be no delegations which would not be able to accept, under no circumstances whatsoever, the establishment of a European Public Prosecutor's Office. The Treaty respects the latter position: it does not require such establishment but states that the Council 'may' decide to do so. It may also decide not to.

Unanimity among the members of the Council does not include the votes of the representative of the Government of Denmark.[11] Nor does it include the votes of the representatives of the Governments of the United Kingdom and Ireland.[12] 'Unanimity' within the Council allows delegations entitled to vote to abstain from voting.

Let us further suppose that at a meeting of the Council specifically dedicated to the question whether there is, or there is not, unanimity to continue deliberations on the proposed regulation, it is concluded that no such unanimity can be reached. According to the second subparagraph of Article 86(1) TFEU, a group of at least nine Member States may then request that the draft regulation be referred to the European Council. Such a request would have to be addressed to the President of the European Council, who is responsible for convening and proposing the agenda

(Footnote 10 continued)
implementation of Union law in its broadest and exclusively responsible for applying criminal law measures to this end, and this should, in my view, remain the case. Existing shortcomings in the functioning of the judiciary in individual Member States or of judicial cooperation in criminal matters between Member States, if any, should be remedied by improving and enhancing their performances and responsibilities. In this respect, the Union legislator can play a useful role, as history has abundantly demonstrated over the last 20 years.

[11] See Article 1 of Protocol (N°22) on the position of Denmark, annexed to the TEU and the TFEU.

[12] See Article 1 of Protocol (N°21) on the position of the United Kingdom and Ireland in respect of the Area of Freedom, Security and Justice. If the UK and/or Ireland would have used their right, under Article 3 of the Protocol, to opt into the proposed regulation before it is adopted by the Council, their representatives would take part in the vote in Council. However, if the regulation could subsequently not be adopted because the UK and/or Ireland would not support it, the Council may adopt it without the participation of the UK and/or Ireland, as set out in Article 3(2) of the Protocol.

of European Council meetings. It is only in that case that the legislative procedure shall be suspended. As long as no group of at least nine Member States[13] has seized the European Council, the deliberations may continue within the Council, as well as the discussions with the European Parliament aiming at obtaining its consent, up to voting by both institutions.

If, however, the European Council has been seized by a sufficiently large group of Member States, the file is no longer at the desk of the Council and deliberations have to stop.

One can infer from the wording of Article 86, that the Member States concerned have to act as a group, i.e. that the request to the President of the European Council has to be made by the members of that group simultaneously and that no such member can withdraw from the group and that no other Member States can join the group later on as long as the European Council has not defined its position.

The group will have to submit a text of the draft regulation to the European Council on the basis of which it wishes the European Council to discuss and possibly reach a consensus. That text may be an amended version of the Commission's proposal. The European Council will have to discuss the matter in order to assess whether it is possible to reach a consensus. The Treaty does not specify whether there is a difference between 'consensus' to be reached in the European Council and 'unanimity' required in the Council. Within the context of Article 86 TFEU, there is one important difference: whereas at the level of the Council the representatives of Denmark, the UK and Ireland do not take part in the decision taking, at the level of the European Council the heads of government of these three Member States do. The exclusion of these three Member States from participation in the adoption of acts and measures in the area of justice and home affairs, applies, pursuant to Protocol N°22 on the position of Denmark and Protocol N°21 on the position of the United Kingdom and Ireland in respect of the area of Freedom, Security and Justice, only to the actions of the Council, not to those of the European Council. Consensus in the European Council implies, therefore, that also Denmark, the UK and Ireland join in the consensus. That has to be the case for all members of the European Council, including the President of the European Commission[14] and the President of the European Council himself.

The formal difference between 'unanimity' and 'consensus' is that unanimity is, or is supposed to be, the result of a vote. Consensus is not a voting rule,[15] but the confirmation by the President that all participants agree and that no one disagrees.

The European Council has to take a position within 4 months after it has been seized by the group of Member States, i.e. to express either consensus or

---

[13] Nothing has been stated as to the composition of the group. Theoretically Denmark, the UK and Ireland could be part of it.

[14] If the Commission would find that the text which the group of Member States referred to the European Council deviated too far from the proposal it submitted to the Council, its President would be in a position to prevent that this draft be referred back to the Council for adoption.

[15] See the reply by the Council of 11 March 2004 to a written question by a member of the European Parliament (P-3526/2003).

disagreement over the draft presented to it. Consensus as to the draft does not mean that it has to be adopted by the Council (and consented to by the European Parliament) without any further amendments. The European Council is not a legislative institution; its involvement in the procedure serves basically the purpose of ascertaining whether the European Council agrees that a European Public Prosecutor's Office should be established or not, given the fact that Article 86 TFEU only contemplates the possibility and does not require so.

In the event that the European Council does not reach consensus within the 4 months period Article 86 TFEU envisages two possibilities: either there are at least nine Member States, notifying their wish 'within the same timeframe' to the European Parliament, the Council, and the Commission to establish enhanced cooperation 'on the basis of the draft regulation concerned', or there are not. In the latter case, the procedure in the Council on the Commission's original draft remains suspended *sine die*, unless the Commission decided to withdraw it. What happens if the number of at least nine Member States is reached only beyond the time limit of 4 months? It seems that considering that in such a case the authorisation to proceed with enhanced cooperation would still be deemed to have been granted would constitute a violation of the rules set out in Article 86 TFEU and would therefore be illegal.[16]

Member States notifying their wish to establish enhanced cooperation do not necessarily have to act as a group; once the authorisation to proceed with enhanced cooperation has been deemed to have been granted (legally), the provisions on enhanced cooperation of the TFEU apply, including Article 331(1) which envisages the possibility for any Member State to participate in enhanced cooperation in progress, i.e. from the moment it has been authorised. Another question is whether Member States would be able to withdraw from enhanced cooperation, in particular before the draft regulation is adopted by the Council. It seems to me that this not the case. Clearly, a withdrawal which would leave the number of participating Member States below the threshold of nine would make the enhanced cooperation illegal and void. It would have to be stopped right away. But one cannot discriminate between Member States by letting the withdrawal of some without legal consequences for the enhanced cooperation (as long as the remaining number remains nine or more), whereas the same action by others would bring it to a halt. If one or more participating Member States would not be satisfied with the result of the negotiations within the Council or with the European Parliament, they would still have the option of voting against the adoption of the act.[17]

[16] Eventually to be confirmed by the Court of Justice.

[17] The only exception in this context would be the (unlikely) case in which the UK and/or Ireland would have been among the Member States wishing to establish the enhanced cooperation and would not join the unanimity required to adopt the act; Article 3(2) of Protocol n°21 allows the Council to adopt the act in such case without the participation of the UK and/or Ireland, it being understood that the remaining number of participating Member States remains nine or more.

This leads to the question whether it would be possible to re-establish an authorised enhanced cooperation which had to be stopped or otherwise failed, either because one or more Member States withdrew their participation or because the draft act embodying the enhanced cooperation was not adopted by the Council. The first case, in my view, would imply the commission of an illicit act by the withdrawing Member State that cannot be remedied by having one or more other Member States filling the gap. The second case is in essence not significantly different from the first: one cannot simply start a new enhanced cooperation (without the Member States whose delegations in the Council voted against) without violating the requirement of respecting a timeframe of 4 months set out in the third subparagraph of Article 86(1) TFEU. That would mean that one would have to start the procedure before the European Council for a second time and this, it seems, is not what the Treaty envisages. The procedure of Article 86(1) contemplates the involvement of the European Council only once in respect of the establishment of the Public Prosecutor's Office. If that procedure does not lead to the adoption by the Council of the regulation pursuing that objective, the game is over.

Needless to say that the procedure of Article 86(1) constitutes a *lex specialis* in relation to Articles 20(2) TEU and 329(1) TFEU, and that it is not possible to rely on the procedures set out in the latter provisions in order to establish enhanced cooperation for the establishment of a EPPO, in case where compliance with the procedure 86(1) led to a failure.

Before having a closer look at some of the implications of enhanced cooperation in the establishment and functioning of the European Public Prosecutor's Office, I wish to point out that the procedure, envisaged in Article 86(4), involving the European Council in a possible future extension of the remit of the EPPO to other crimes than those affecting the financial interests of the Union, requires the adoption of a decision of the European Council ('unanimously' this time, and not by 'consensus', since it is acting in a legislative capacity). Also in that case, all its members, including the heads of government of Denmark, the UK and Ireland, including the President of the Commission, as well as the President of the European Council, have the right to take part in the vote, even if the regulation establishing the EPPO has been adopted in enhanced cooperation and is applicable in a limited number of Member States only. As distinct from the procedure under para 1 of Article 86, the procedure under para 4 can be applied several times, even in order to provide the EPPO with extended powers which were initially refused to it. However, the existence of Article 86(4) TFEU excludes the possibility for Member States to follow the procedure of Article 329(1) TFEU in order to have the powers of the EPPO extended.

12.3 Some Implications of Enhanced Cooperation Under Article 86 TFEU

If the regulation proposed by the Commission were to be adopted by way of an authorised enhanced cooperation and therefore be binding on only a limited number of Member States, some of its provisions or concepts would raise questions as to their impact on other Union bodies and other Member States. For example, Article 20(1) TEU states that 'Member States which wish to establish enhanced cooperation between themselves within the framework of the Union's non-exclusive competences may make use of its institutions'. Thus, reliance on the European Court of Auditors, as foreseen in Articles 52 and 66 of the draft regulation, and reliance on the Court of Justice of the European Union under Articles 65 and 69, is compatible with Article 20(1) TEU. But that article refers only to 'the institutions' of the Union and not to other bodies. What would this mean for tasks attributed by the regulation to such bodies as OLAF,[18] the Ombudsman,[19] Eurojust[20] and the European Data Protection Supervisor,[21] which are not 'institutions' of the Union? Whereas OLAF can be considered as part of the institution 'European Commission', it would be more difficult to consider the Ombudsman as an extension of the institution 'European Parliament', and certainly both Eurojust and the EDPS are full-fledged Union bodies in their own right established by legislative acts involving the Council acting with all its members and being at the service (and charge!) of all Member States. It does not seem obvious to me that through an act adopted in enhanced cooperation, these bodies can be put at the service of the European Public Prosecutor's Office. In my view, this would require one or two separate legislative acts to be adopted by the same procedures as would require an amendment of the constitutive acts of Eurojust and the EDPS. If not, one would end up with different versions of these constitutive acts for different Member States, which is likely to lead to a legal labyrinth if those acts would have to be amended later on again.[22]

According to Article 330(1) TFEU 'all members of the Council may participate in its deliberations, but only members of the Council representing the Member States participating in enhanced cooperation shall take part in the vote'. This rule does not only apply to the regulation establishing the European Public Prosecutor's Office itself, but also, it seems, to acts to be adopted by the Council pursuant to that

[18] Article 66.

[19] Article 65.

[20] Article 57.

[21] EDPS, Articles 38, 39, 41, 42, 43, 45, 46 and 61.

[22] It may also run counter to the requirement of Article 288(2) TFEU that regulations shall be binding in their entirety and applicable in all Member States. Clearly, this provision does not mean that the institutions cannot adopt regulations which are binding and applicable only in Member States participating in an enhanced cooperation. But, at least in my view, it does prevent that regulations which are already binding on all Member States become amended in a way that does no longer make them binding in their entirety on all Member States.

regulation. For instance, this voting rule would apply to the appointment by the Council of the European Public Prosecutor[23] and his or her Deputies.[24] However, in some provisions,[25] reference is made to the Council in its capacity as part of the budgetary authority or when acting in the framework of the Union's budgetary procedures. In these cases, it acts with the participation of all its members, even if the basic act generating the budgetary expenditure has been adopted in enhanced cooperation.

Another case is the one foreseen in Articles 59(3) and 61(1), where the Council is acting pursuant to Article 218 TFEU (adopting negotiating directives for, and signature and conclusion of, agreements with third countries, for the purpose of establishing cooperative relations between the EPPO and the competent prosecutorial authorities of these countries). The case is special, because the Council would be acting not pursuant to the regulation, but by virtue of provisions of primary EU law. Both Article 218 TFEU and the provisions on enhanced cooperation of the TEU and the TFEU are silent on the exercise of the Union's external powers in matters that are internally the object of enhanced cooperation. However, there are precedents, in particular in the context of the Protocol (N°19) on the Schengen *acquis* integrated into the framework of the European Union. This Protocol, having recognised that it is necessary to make use of the provisions of the Treaties concerning closer cooperation[26] between some Member States (i.e. all, except the United Kingdom and Ireland), authorises in its Article 1 those Member States 'to establish closer cooperation among themselves in areas covered by provisions defined by the Council which constitute the Schengen *acquis*' (which) 'shall be conducted within the institutional and legal framework of the European Union and with respect for the relevant provisions of the Treaties'. And there are various examples of cases in which the Union has exercised its external competence with respect to matters belonging to the Schengen *acquis* (agreements on visa facilitation or exemption, for instance). In these cases, the Council acted under Article 218 TFEU (or its predecessor of the TEC) without the participation of the Member States not taking part in this enhanced cooperation. The same would therefore apply, *mutatis mutandis*, for the action of the Council as foreseen in Articles 59(3) and 61(1) of the proposed EPPO regulation.

Surprisingly,[27] the proposed regulation does not address the need of establishing cooperative relations between the EPPO and the competent prosecutorial authorities of Member States which as a result of enhanced cooperation would not become

---

[23] Article 8.

[24] Article 9 The requirement in Article 9(3) of the draft regulation that the shortlist of Deputies must reflect 'the demographic balance and geographical range of the Member States' sounds slightly peculiar if the Council would have to appoint four Deputy EPP's for only nine participating Member States.

[25] Articles 50(9), 52(11).

[26] The term 'closer cooperation' must be understood as being identical to 'enhanced cooperation' in this context.

[27] Since it is foreseeable that Denmark will not, and the UK and Ireland will probably not, take part in the adoption of the proposed regulation.

bound by it. If there is a need to establish such relations with third countries, there must be *a fortiori* a need to do so with regard to non-participating Member States. However, it is unclear how such relations could be established in a similar binding way, both from a legal and political point of view. The Treaties do not contemplate the possibility for the Union, acting with a view to bind the Member States participating in an enhanced cooperation, to conclude international agreements with non-participating Member States.[28] Article 327 TFEU limits itself to the obligation of non-participating Member States not to impede the implementation of an enhanced cooperation by the participating Member States. But that does not require them to enter into cooperative agreements or arrangements with the EPPO. Clearly, Article 327 TFEU allows them to insist on the continuation of existing forms of judicial cooperation between their judicial authorities and their counterparts in the other Member States, where it is stating that any enhanced cooperation shall respect the competences, rights and obligations of those Member States which do not participate in it. Politically, it is hard to see why Member States rejecting the concept of a European Public Prosecutor's Office by refusing to take part in its establishment, would be ready to cooperate with it and to allow it to exert its powers on their territory by requiring their authorities to take compulsory measures in pursuance of requests for judicial assistance. This raises of course the question when, under these circumstances, the establishment of a European Public Prosecutor's Office would have sufficient *effet utile*. This is highly doubtful if the number of participating Member States would only be nine. And even if that number would be between 15 and 20 only, there are probably good reasons to relinquish the project (depending also on who is in or out). This seems to be typically the sort of question the European Council should discuss whenever the draft regulation is referred to it by a group of Member States. It should try to give an indication on a minimum number of Member States to participate from the beginning in order to make the resort to enhanced cooperation in the establishment of the EPPO practically worthwhile.

Finally, according to Article 332 TFEU 'expenditure resulting from implementation of enhanced cooperation, other than administrative costs entailed for the institutions, shall be borne by the participating Member States, unless all members of the Council, acting unanimously after consulting the European Parliament, decide otherwise'.[29] What is the impact of this provision on the financing of the

---

[28] I am aware of two examples of such a situation: the Union concluded agreements with Denmark, at the latter's request,—one in the area of asylum law, and the other in the field of private international law—in order to fill lacunae resulting from Denmark's special position in relation to the Union's powers in the fields of Justice and Home Affairs. Community acts, which did not bind Denmark, replaced agreements between the EU Member States by which Denmark was bound. The Commission argued at the time that only this special situation justified the concept of an agreement between the Union and a Member State, but that this could not constitute a precedent for similar agreements between the EU and Denmark on any other subject in the area of Justice and Home Affairs.

[29] Similar provisions are contained in Protocol n°21 on the position of the United Kingdom and Ireland in respect of the area of freedom, security and justice (Article 5) and Protocol n°22 on the position of Denmark (Article 3).

as administrative expenditure for the Commission,[36] then all Member States would be charged, including those who refuse to participate in the enhanced cooperation, for the 'bonuses' on the salaries of the European Delegated Prosecutors in the Member States which do participate in that cooperation.

That would be exorbitant. If the legislative process is not brought to a halt at an early stage, the Council and the European Parliament should agree to review carefully the status and position of Delegated Public Prosecutors and in any event get rid of the first sentence of para 5 of Article 54 of the proposed regulation.[37]

12.4 Conclusion

It is too early to say what the prospects of the proposed regulation are. It is clear that it has raised serious misgivings in a number of national Parliaments, which has led to a sufficient number of reasoned opinions pursuant to Article 7(2) of Protocol (N°2) on the Application of the Principles of Subsidiarity and Proportionality on non-compliance with the principle of subsidiarity, to oblige the Commission to review its proposed draft. As a result, the Commission may decide to maintain, amend or withdraw its proposal. At the same time, initial discussions within the Council have revealed that several delegations, although accepting the establishment of a European Public Prosecutor's Office in principle, would wish to see the Commission's proposal amended in various respects, in order to allow their Member State to take part in any initiative triggering the procedure of enhanced cooperation set out in Article 86 TFEU. One may therefore expect a period of reflection and informal contacts between the Commission and a number of Member States, before the formal legislative procedure is pursued. If pursued, it will probably be by way of enhanced cooperation through a procedure in which the European Council will have to ponder the pros and cons of such cooperation in relation to the aim and purpose of the proposal and in the light of its perceived *effet utile*.

---

[36] Article 54(5) of the proposed regulation does not specify by whom European Delegated Prosecutors shall be engaged as Special Advisors. Paragraph 2 of Article 54 limits the power of the EPP to conclude contracts of employment to 'staff' of the EPPO and it remains to be seen whether Delegated Prosecutors can qualify as its 'staff'. If not—and I believe they should not—the power to conclude contracts of engagement of Delegated Prosecutors as Special Advisors would have to be exercised by the Commission itself which could then consider the costs involved as its own administrative expenditure.

[37] One does not have to be afraid that European Delegated Prosecutors remain penniless and understaffed: on the one hand Article 54(5), last sentence, of the draft regulation obliges the competent national authorities to provide the European Delegated Prosecutors with the resources and equipment necessary to exercise their functions under the regulation, and on the other hand Article 6(8) entitles the European Public Prosecutor to temporarily allocate resources and staff to European Delegated Prosecutors, where necessary for the purpose of an investigation or prosecution. Two bags of food indeed!

Chapter 13
Implications of Enhanced Cooperation for the EPPO Model and Its Functioning

Szymon Pawelec

Abstract Enhanced cooperation may be seen as a compromise, meant to save the EPPO project and allow it to enter into force in perspective of its wider recognition in the Union in the future. However, such a framework risks to undermine its functioning, conceiving it as territorially limited prosecutorial agency in the European Union. Basing the EPPO on enhanced cooperation is not suitable to establish a prosecutorial authority able to successfully act within the whole Union, replacing the horizontal cooperation of the national prosecutorial authorities in the restricted area of its competences. Outside the circle of the participating Member States, the prosecutorial cooperation will have to be put in practice in a similar horizontal setting as is presently prevailing in the Union. The proposal for the new EPPO regulation does not provide specifics on the relation between participating and non-participating Member States. Different scenarios of perception of the EPPO by the non-participating Member States may be analysed under the general framework of Article 327 TFEU, in particular where cooperation with EPPO in such Member States may not be conceived as collaboration between matching partners, but as a factual appropriation of existing competences of their national authorities by an entity which they decided not to support. Issues regarding conflicts of competences, multiplication of cases and coercive measures, 'forum shopping' and the risk of breaching the *ne bis in idem* principle do raise concerns not only about the effectiveness of the new authority, but in particular about the protection of the procedural position of suspects.

Keywords European public prosecutor's office · Enhanced cooperation · Participating member states · Non-participating member states · Conflict of competences · Procedural safeguards · Two-hat position · European delegated prosecutor

The author is assistant professor at the Institute of Criminal Law, Department of International Criminal Procedure of the University of Warsaw and barrister at the bar chamber in Warsaw.

S. Pawelec (✉)
University of Warsaw, Warsaw, Poland
e-mail: szymon.pawelec@wpia.uw.edu.pl

L.H. Erkelens et al. (eds.), *The European Public Prosecutor's Office*,
DOI 10.1007/978-94-6265-035-0_13

increase of number of EU Member States, more time and effort is needed to reach consensus that will ensure territorially coherent compliance with EU's fundamental aims—including prevention and combat of crime.[12] Under such conditions, attempts to find a way to promote new initiatives through cooperation among at least a part of the Member States seem understandable from the point of view of countries intending to proceed in a certain policy area. However, if misused, such actions raise doubts with regard to their compliance with Article 326 TFEU (which forbids undermining through enhanced cooperation the social and territorial cohesion between the participating and non-participating Member States) as well as their influence on Union's integrity and its ability to promote common values and harmonise legal systems outside the borders of the sub-unions created among the members of enhanced cooperation.[13]

It should be stressed that enhanced cooperation was designed not as an alternative cooperation procedure, but as an instrument of last resort—allowing to overcome the deadlock, where a proposal is blocked by one or a group of Member States unwilling to be part of the new initiative. In such situations, the Member States interested in the initiative and willing to make a step forward may start the new project, but limited only to their circle. That situation is an example of the concept of 'multi-speed' or 'two-speed' Europe. It is based on the assumption, as provided by pre enhanced-cooperation examples of the Schengen Area and the Eurozone that different parts of the Union may integrate on different levels and in different pace, according to the individual situation and political will of particular Member States.

Currently, enhanced cooperation mechanisms have been established in the field of intellectual property (European Union patent),[14] divorce law[15] and they might become the framework for the proposed financial transaction tax.[16] Comparative analysis of those arrangements may help determining the potential difficulties that a

---

[12] Article 3(2) TEU.

[13] As for the possibility of creating 'sub-unions' within European Union compare: Bordignon and Brusco 2006, pp. 2063–2090.

[14] As for the three major documents in this field see: Regulation (EU) No 1257/2012 of the European Parliament and of the Council of 17 December 2012 implementing enhanced cooperation in the area of the creation of unitary patent protection, *OJ* L 361/1; Council Regulation (EU) No 1260/2012 of 17 December 2012 implementing enhanced cooperation in the area of the creation of unitary patent protection with regard to the applicable translation arrangements, *OJ* L 361/89; Agreement on a Unified Patent Court (2013/C 175/01), 20 June 2013, *OJ* C 175/1.

[15] See Council Regulation (EU) No 1259/2010 of 20 December 2010 implementing enhanced cooperation in the area of the law applicable to divorce and legal separation, *OJ* L 343/10.

[16] See Proposal for a Council directive implementing enhanced cooperation in the area of financial transaction tax, COM(2013)71 final, 14 February 2013.

new EU body, functioning on a territorially limited area, might face. Such analysis may be especially valuable in finding solutions for EU internal cooperation in a mixed legal environment, where some Member States use the new uniform measures and some stick to the old, partially internal law, regulations. In such cases the obvious necessity is to find a connection between new and old solutions, in order to avoid duplication of legal regimes and chaos of the sources of law, applicable in cases with trans-border elements. However, the specific nature of the EPPO should always be kept in mind in such a comparative analysis. Due to the direct and far reaching competences of the proposed new supranational prosecutorial office (including deciding or initiating decisions concerning coercive measures and choice of jurisdiction), it is the procedural security of the suspect and not the effectiveness of prosecution in PIF cases which should prevail in the choice of applicable law and procedural safeguards. While respecting the basic pro-EPPO argument that the protection of financial interests of the European Union should be improved, it ought to be underlined that a suspect in criminal proceedings is in a weaker position than a public prosecutor. It may sound like a truism, but it is nevertheless worth repeating, that criminal responsibility of any entity may only be raised *in foro* if the applicable legal regime is easily identifiable.[17] At the same time, the suspect's defence may be effective only if it is clear which procedural rules define his position in penal proceedings. The possibility of negative impact on the suspect's position through a random or unclear choice of jurisdiction, as a result of vague correlation between the new, supranational powers of the EPPO and the old national rules of the non-participating Member States, should be minimized. Concerns with regard to a suspect's legal certainty, arising from the possibility of 'forum shopping' by the EPPO within the borders of the participating Member States, have already been put forward.[18] Increasing that risk through additional unclear rules governing the choice of jurisdiction between the EPPO and any of the non-participating Member States should be especially avoided.

[17] In some situations lack of knowledge of unlawfulness of certain conduct excludes the possibility of committing an offence or creates a basis for mitigation of penalty. Compare Article 30 of the Polish Penal Code of 6 June 1997: 'Whoever commits a prohibited act while being justifiably unaware of its unlawfulness, shall not commit an offence; if the mistake of the perpetrator is not justifiable, the court may apply an extraordinary mitigation of the penalty'. As for obtaining some clarity in the field of material penal law through harmonization of national legal regimes see the Proposal for a Directive of the European Parliament and of the Council on the fight against fraud to the Union's financial interests by means of criminal law, COM(2012)363 final, 11 July 2012.

[18] Steinborn 2012, p. 1277.

13.2 Enhanced Cooperation *Versus* the Federal Idea of the EPPO

EPPO is often described as an instrument federal by nature.[19] Its federal stature is considered to ensue from the federal character of the EU budget and the need for protecting it by a prosecutorial authority functioning on a supranational level.[20] In this regard, the Commission emphasises that due to the complex, trans-border character of many offences against the financial interests of the EU (PIF offences), they are not, and in fact cannot be, adequately dealt with by a fragmentary, slow and inefficient system of national criminal investigations and penal protection.[21] Moreover, though the Member States are bound by the 1995 Convention on the protection of the European Communities' financial interests[22] (and its additional protocols), obliging them to penalize financial abuse of the EU budget, they are still far from reaching a unified standard of protection of those interests. Such interests sometimes tend to be regarded as being of secondary importance in comparison with the direct financial interests of the Member States.[23] It is worth emphasising that tolerating such double-standard approach in prosecution of frauds against the interests of the Member States and against the Union itself would constitute a breach of the obligations put on the Member States in Article 325(2) TFEU. Through this provision Member States are required to take the same measures to counter fraud affecting the financial interests of the Union as they do to counter fraud affecting their own financial interests.

Thinking of EPPO as a clear example of European Union's federalist tendencies would be an exaggeration. The fact that according to Article 27(1) of the EPPO proposal[24] both the European Public Prosecutor (EPP) and his/her delegates (the European Delegated Prosecutor, EDP) will act in the criminal proceedings directly —having the same powers as national public prosecutors in respect of prosecution and bringing a case to judgement—is certainly unprecedented. Nevertheless, there are three particular solutions that the legislative proposal introduces. First of all, it underlines the decentralized structure of the EPPO, as linked with the two-hatted EDP.[25] Second of all, it does not propose a common federal penal procedure, but

[19] See Reding 2013, p. 1; Franssen 2013.

[20] See Reding 2013, p. 2.

[21] See: European Commission 2013, pp. 3–4, also in the Appendix to this book. See also relevant tables of PIF cases passed on to the Member States in 2011 available at: Representation of the European Commission in Poland 2013.

[22] See Council act of 26 July 1995 drawing up the Convention on the protection of the European Communities' financial interests (95/C 316/03), *OJ* C 316/48.

[23] Nürnberger 2009, p. 495.

[24] The term 'proposed regulation' means the Proposal from 17 July 2013 for a Council Regulation on the establishment of the European Public Prosecutor's Office, COM(2013)534 final, 2013/0255 (APP).

[25] Article 6(1) of the EPPO proposal.

relies on national regulations, supported by automatic mutual recognition and a catalogue of harmonizing principles.[26] Lastly, it does not attempt to introduce a system of federal criminal courts for PIF cases but remains limited[27] to an EU office competent only for investigating, prosecuting and bringing to judgement the suspects of PIF fraud.

However, the federal aspect of the EPPO lies in the fundamental assumption that breaching certain interests of the Union as a whole should be treated as a problem of the whole community and not as a sum of individual problems of the Member States. Hence violations affecting the Union should be investigated throughout the whole Union by one specialized agency, possessing possibly uniform investigation powers, taking direct actions against the suspects, and organised in hierarchical command structure of one decision taking entity. Such an approach appears justified especially if one looks at the structure of the PIF offences, which become significantly more transnational,[28] based on networks not limited to the territory of one Member State, benefiting broadly from the EU's four freedoms. Applying a national prosecutorial approach to such criminal activities may result in losing the overall picture of a crime.[29] Instead of searching for the roots of criminal activity, fighting it swiftly under supranational command and according to common European interest, it may just focus on investigating the national manifestations of the criminal conduct, leaving the very core aside. The risk of such an approach may be compared to a surveillance of a place conducted by local police, with stolen goods delivered by foreign people, and terminated with pressing charges against the owner of the establishment, but without continuing to investigate where those items came from and who was involved in stealing them.

Bearing in mind the abovementioned federal outline of the EPPO, the shortest characteristic of the implications for the model and functioning of the EPPO resulting from using the institution of enhanced cooperation for its introduction could be presented as follows: on the one hand, enhanced cooperation is a compromise, meant to save the EPPO project and allow it to enter into force—although in a diminished scope—with the hope for a wider recognition in the Union in the future. On the other hand, however, it undermines the whole idea of the model of the EPPO and corrupts its functioning, making it just another territorially limited prosecutorial agency (like the existing national ones) in the European Union.

A Union divided into participating and non-participating Member States means, that the idea of a single body able to pool investigative and prosecutorial powers of the Member States in order to ensure efficient and complex decision making, would be implemented only partially. Judicial cooperation with the non-participating

[26] Articles 30 and 32–35 of the EPPO proposal.

[27] Fully in accordance with Article 86 TFEU on establishing EPPO.

[28] For more details see: The OLAF Report 2012—Thirteenth report of the European Anti-Fraud Office, 1 January to 31 December 2012. For a more general overview of the problem of transborder crimes in Europe see: Sieber 1998, pp. 1–42; Velkova and Georgievski 2005, pp. 64–77; Den Boer 2001, pp. 259–272.

[29] Analogically: Ligeti and Simonato 2013, p. 9.

Member States would not change fundamentally and would be pursued through the existing legal cooperation mechanisms, although with one difference. Instead of cooperation between two or more national prosecutorial authorities from different Member States, a new kind of cooperation, between the EPPO and national authorities of the non-participating Member States would have to be arranged.

The enhanced cooperation scenario requires a new set of rules with regard to interaction and cooperation of EPPO within the European Union, but outside the EPPO's structures and competences. It does not matter that much whether it is just one non-participating Member State or two, four, or six of them. The unity of the structure will be affected even if one Member State remains outside the EPPO framework.

13.3 Functioning of the EPPO in Relation to Non-Participating Member States

Inevitably the EPPO has to be set up on the basis of an enhanced cooperation framework.[30] This framework raises the question of how the competences and functioning of the EPPO will be perceived by the non-participating Member States. It is difficult to predict what it will mean that not all Member States do support the proposed regulation and that some of them don't want to take part in establishing the EPPO. How will the non-participating Member States react to the new entity and its way of operating in the policy Area of Freedom, Security and Justice (AFSJ)? Will they be inclined to cooperate or coordinate their actions with those of the EPPO? In the following subsection, two alternative scenarios offering two different answers to these questions are discussed. Subsequently, some more specific issues are addressed.

13.3.1 Solidarity or Refusal: Non-Participating Member States and the EPPO

When considering possible reactions of the non-participating Member States to the EPPO, two different scenarios can be distinguished. One—the optimistically realistic—is that although certain Member States do not want to take part in the EPPO project, they will, nevertheless, demonstrate their attachment to the principles of sincere cooperation[31] and solidarity[32] and will thus recognize the status of the

[30] The UK and Denmark both have already made clear that they will not participate to a future EPPO.

[31] Article 4(3) TEU.

[32] Article 3(3) TEU.

EPPO as a European body authorized to cooperate with their national criminal justice authorities in order to fulfil the general objectives set out in, *inter alia*, Article 325 TFEU, obliging both the EU and the Member States to counter fraud and any other illegal activities affecting the financial interests of the Union.[33] As a consequence of such approach, they will, naturally, have to carry the burdens stemming from the requests presented by that authority in the course of its prosecutorial and investigative activity—not only of purely factual or legal character, but also generating calculable financial costs.

The second—and more pessimistic—scenario regarding a possible attitude of the non-participating Member States to the EPPO involves their refusal to recognize the EPPO's competences (as it limits the competences and rights of their national criminal judicial authorities), arguing that if they wanted to cooperate with the EPPO, they would have joined the enhanced cooperation agreement. In this way they could avoid the inevitable burden for their criminal law systems resulting from the cooperation with EPPO, as well as exclude the possibility of the overlap of competences between the EPPO and their national authorities.

In support of the optimistically realistic scenario one could argue that in spite of the unwillingness of some Member States, the established enhanced cooperation has to be respected. It can be argued that those Member States cannot refuse to recognize acts adopted through the enhanced cooperation procedure. Article 20(4) TEU directly provides that acts adopted in the framework of enhanced cooperation shall bind only the participating Member States. These acts should therefore not have any external effect on the non-participating Member States. Besides, the first sentence of Article 327 TFEU confirms, that any enhanced cooperation shall respect the competences, rights, and obligations of the non-participating Member States. That means that enhanced cooperation results in a specific construction within the legal framework of the Union, separating the competences, rights, and obligations of both categories of Member States. Nevertheless, the non-participating Member States are and remain fully fledged members of the Union and, in accordance with the second sentence of Article 327 TFEU, they are obliged not to impede the implementation of the foreseen enhanced cooperation by the participating Member States.[34] Member States have to recognise the existence and way of functioning of the enhanced cooperation as a *sui generis* construction meant to further goals and objectives of the Union, in particular in relation to the protection of the interests of the Union and the strengthening of its integration.[35] With regard to the EPPO this could imply that the non-participating Member States also have to recognise rights and competences of the EPPO as a perfectly competent public prosecutor within the

[33] About the connection between Article 86 TFEU and Article 325 TFEU, see: Steinborn 2012, p. 1265. Steinborn characterizes the creation of the EPPO under Article 86 TFEU as an activity aimed at fulfilling the general obligation from Article 325(1) TFEU to combat PIF offences.

[34] Article 327 TFEU: Any enhanced cooperation shall respect the competences, rights and obligations of those Member States which do not participate in it. Those Member States shall not impede its implementation by the participating Member States.

[35] In conformity with Article 20(1) TEU, second para.

legal order of the Union, entitled to apply EU criminal law instruments of the Union available to it, also outside the *sui generis* construction of the enhanced cooperation framework. If non-participating Member States would not be ready to recognise the EPPO, nor would they be prepared to provide a follow-up to EPPO requests for legal cooperation (e.g. as regards an issued European Arrest Warrant), they would impede the implementation of the concerned enhanced cooperation, including its results and thus infringing Article 327 TFEU. That way, non-complying and non-participating Member States would also hinder the protection of the interests of the Union as stipulated in Article 20(1) TEU. And more specifically, according to Article 325 TFEU, one of those interests pertains to EU finances; and both, Member States and Union, have an obligation to counter fraud and any other illegal activities affecting these interests.

The obligation of the non-participating Members States to respect the position and powers of the EPPO stems also from the Article 86 TFEU itself. Leaving aside the issue of the opt-out clauses, the entering into force of the Lisbon Treaty has been preceded by its ratification—including the present Article 86 TFEU—by all Member States. This in turn means, that the Member States have already given their initial approval for the existence and activity of such an authority, and thus they cannot disregard it, even if they stay outside the enhanced cooperation circle.

Comparing the abovementioned two contradicting scenarios, it appears impossible for the non-participating Member States to ignore the existence of the EPPO and to refuse to cooperate with it in trans-border PIF cases. Nevertheless, there is room to raise the question to what extent in practice the non-participating Member States will feel obliged to carry the burdens stemming from such cooperation. Especially if, compared to previously existing horizontal contacts between the national prosecutorial agencies, such cooperation would result in additional financial costs, or, if it starts to be regarded not as collaboration between equal partners, but as a factual appropriation of existing competences of their national authorities, they decide not to join in the first place.

Assuming that the non-participating Member States recognize the status of the EPPO, a practical problem concerning the functioning of the EPPO under enhanced cooperation procedure would still need to be solved. This is the question of how in that situation an EDP will seek the cooperation of national justice authorities in the non-participating Member States. Despite the fact that it is difficult to imagine the EPPO functioning without such cooperation, there is no clear legal basis for such cooperation stemming from the proposed regulation.[36] It may be only guessed why the non-participating Member States were not taken into account in the proposed regulation—perhaps because it might look like an act of giving up on full participation and agreeing to a territorially limited EPPO, even before the discussion has started. Nonetheless, even if the non-participating Member States were mentioned in the proposal, it follows from the very nature of enhanced cooperation that they

[36] Cf.: Hamran and Szabova 2013, p. 49.

could not be bound by the obligations imposed on them by a regulation which they have not accepted.

Otherwise, a legal reasoning supporting the above mentioned optimistically realistic scenario can be formulated, based on the Treaty, opening up a gateway for providing mutual legal assistance between the EPPO and the criminal law authorities of non-participating Member States. An alternative route to establishing such a cooperation could possibly be found through formulating an analogy with the cooperation with third countries as presented in Articles 25(2), 56(1) and 59(1) of the EPPO proposal. Accordingly, this would result in establishing working arrangements and/or formal agreements between the EPPO and the non-participating Member States. However, taking that route would be extremely laborious and time-consuming. It would also leave some uncertainty as to whether the EPPO is going to be regarded by the non-participating Member States as the successor of all rights and obligations of the national prosecutorial agencies of the participating Member States in PIF cases, or as some kind of new entity, whose new status makes the development of new rules of trans-border cooperation necessary.

A practical solution in such a situation, bypassing the problem of creating new ways of cooperation with a new legal entity, is to make use of the double hatted position of the European Delegated Prosecutors. The double hatted construction (also known as the 'hybrid function') evolves out of the *Corpus Juris* idea of the integrated model of the EPPO, where there is a steering, central 'head' (EPP and his deputies) and Delegated Prosecutors located in the Members States.[37] According to the legislative proposal the EDP's are making part of the national criminal justice system, while at the same time holding the position of national prosecutor.[38,39] Therefore, making use of such double position would mean that, in order to cooperate with the non-participating Member States, the Delegated Prosecutors could switch back to their national prosecutorial positions and make use of the existing EU and international instruments applicable in the relations between their home Member States and the non-participating Member States.

Such practice could be regarded as acceptable by the non-participating Member States. Through the double hatted construction they could in fact cooperate with a new European prosecutorial agency by using the same legal instruments (for instance the European Arrest Warrant) and possibly even liaising with the same persons as in other bilateral contacts between the authorities. Nevertheless, the use of such a double hatted position could also lead to defence's allegations of abuse of the national prosecutor's position. It should be kept in mind that in a PIF case an

[37] Cf. Article 18(3) of the *Corpus Juris 2000* (known as the 'Florence' version) and its concepts of the European Director of Public Prosecutions (with office in Brussels) and European Delegated Public Prosecutors (with offices in the Member States).

[38] See Article 6(4) of the EPPO proposal. Cf.: Ligeti and Simonato 2013, pp. 15–17.

[39] Integration of the European Delegated Prosecutors within their national system is described not only in Article 6(6) of the EPPO proposal, stating that the EDP's may also exercise their function as national prosecutors, but also in Article 10(2) of the proposal, stating that Member States shall appoint the EDP as a prosecutor under national law, if he/she did not have this status already.

EDP acts, according to Article 6(5) of the proposed regulation, under the exclusive authority of the EPP and under his instructions. For example, an EDP requesting legal help from a non-participating Member State in order to obtain evidence, freeze possible proceeds of a committed crime or requesting other investigative measures is exclusively entitled to do so in his capacity as 'an integral part' of the EPPO, acting under the exclusive authority of the EPP. It means that, although the EDP uses his national position to contact a non-participating Member State, he in fact fully represents the entity which this Member State has rejected by not joining the enhanced cooperation. The argument of the abuse of position may be used especially in situations where procedural consequences for a suspect originating from a non-participating Member State would be much more severe than under regular bilateral horizontal cooperation, with no EPPO involved. That involves *inter alia* the anxieties concerning the applicable law, risk of 'forum shopping' or even 'simple' problems with the access to case files, resulting from much wider competences of the EPP with regard to the choice of jurisdiction or the determination of a national court, than those available to any national prosecutor.[40]

13.3.2 Criminal Procedure Issues in the Relationship Between the EPPO and Non-Participating Member States

In a Union divided into participating and non-participating Member States, problems related to lack of uniformity on the one hand and the exclusive position of the EPPO on the other, could manifest themselves also through the classic complications of the plurality of decision centres. Consequently, the issues of conflict of competences,[41] parallel investigations, multiplication of cases and coercive measures, and a risk of breaching the *ne bis in idem* principle should be taken into account. It should be mentioned, that throughout the years a lot has been done in the EU, in order to minimize the extent of the conflict of jurisdictions and to promote the *ne bis in idem* principle,[42] especially in the field of preventing parallel

---

[40] See: the criteria of choosing the jurisdiction of trial and determination of the competent national court set out in Article 27(4) of the proposed regulation.

[41] Cf.: Rogacka-Rzewnicka 2009, p. 69, signalizing generally that the risk of conflict of competences stems from insufficient determination of EPPO competences in relation to other authorities involved in national penal proceedings, especially in the light of unclear perspectives of extending the EPPO competences under the clause from Article 86(4) TFEU.

[42] As for the legal regime governing the observance of the *ne bis in idem* principle on the territory of European Union compare—Sakowicz 2012, pp. 555–582. See also: Van Bockel 2010; Sakowicz 2011, pp. 293–463.

investigations through exchange of information between the Member States.[43] Nevertheless, as the 'Green Paper on conflicts of jurisdiction and the *ne bis in idem* principle in criminal proceedings'[44] shows, even the diagnosis of the problem turns out to be very complicated, and thus the creation of a coherent system solving judicial conflicts between the Member States is regarded by some authors as impossible to achieve in the near future.[45]

One of the specific issues ensuing from such a divided Union relates to PIF but sometimes also to other, inextricably linked offences committed wholly or partly on the territory of a non-participating Member State. According to Article 14 of the legislative proposal, the EPPO shall exercise its exclusive competences to investigate and prosecute PIF offences and offences inextricably linked therewith,[46] when wholly or partly committed on the territory of one or several Member States, or by one of their nationals, or by Union staff members, or a member of the Institutions. However, such exclusivity regards only the participating Member States whilst the non-participating Member States will rely on their own authorities and the rules of their own criminal law systems, whether they are ready to investigate and prosecute a specific offence committed (partly) on their territory—or not. Hence, a lot will be left to daily judicial practice and case by case analysis whether under such circumstances the EPPO and relevant authorities of non-participating Member States will agree to prosecute or to cooperate in prosecuting such cross-border cases. However, it must be stressed that Articles 28 and 29 of the legislative proposal do not provide for a possibility of dismissing a case by the EPPO due to prior criminal proceedings (in case of the same act, committed by the same person) still pending in a non-participating Member State. The lack of such a *lis pendens* clause may mean that in trans-border cases involving one or more non-participating Member States, the EPPO should have to try to force its jurisdiction regardless of the proceedings already taking place in such countries.

Besides *lites pendentes*, attention should be paid also to cross-border cases consisting of two or more offences, one being a PIF offence committed wholly or partly on the territory of a participating Member State and another one, inextricably linked to this PIF offence, committed wholly or partly on the territory of a non-participating Member State. In many such cases the authorities would like to agree on having one national authority prosecuting jointly those inextricably linked crimes (in the sense of the EPPO proposal). Even if a non-participating Member State agrees to have the prosecution concerning a PIF offence carried out by the EPPO (rather than by their own national authorities), there may be no consent with regard to the establishment of EPPO's ancillary competence, as laid down in Article

---

[43] Cf. Articles 5–9 of the Council Framework Decision 2009/948/JHA of 30 November 2009 on prevention and settlement of conflicts of exercise of jurisdiction in criminal proceedings, *OJ* L 328/42.

[44] Green Paper On Conflicts of Jurisdiction and the Principle of *ne bis in idem* in Criminal Proceedings, COM(2005)696 final, 23 December 2005.

[45] See: Hofmański 2006, p. 5.

[46] Articles 12 and 13 of the EPPO proposal.

13 of the proposed regulation.[47] The procedure only applies to the participating Member States, but no similar procedure has been suggested in the proposal with regard to non-participating Member States. In such cases, without recognising EPPO's ancillary competence regarding the other crime inextricably linked to the PIF offence, the prosecution will be split up between the EPPO and the authorities of a non-participating Member State. Such a situation will engender all sorts of procedural problems, like lack of concentration of evidence, procedural economy and a speedy trial. Under certain conditions, one could argue that in such cases the EPPO could consider applying the principle of 'the interest of a good administration of justice', as set in Article 13(1) of the legislative proposal, however not in order to execute the EPPO ancillary competences, but in order to allow the non-participating Member State to carry out the whole prosecution. The main condition would be that if the national element of the case is preponderant, as compared with the part dealing strictly with the PIF issue, and the non-participating Member State conducts its own prosecution, not willing to hand it over, the EPPO could allow such Member State's prosecutorial authorities to deal with the entire case—just 'in the interest of good administration of justice'—in order to finish the proceedings in a reasonable time, and to be able to make use of the full set of evidence collected and analyzed directly in a concentrated way.[48]

13.4 The Model of the EPPO Under Enhanced Cooperation

Concerning the implications of enhanced cooperation for the proposed decentralised model of the EPPO, it should be assumed that the 'arms' of this model (i.e. the EDP's) will embrace only the participating Member States. Since the appointment of an EDP starts with presenting at least three candidates by each concerned Member State,[49] the final list of Delegated Prosecutors will be limited to the officials proposed by the participating Member States residing therein. As has been already mentioned, the EDPs will either be selected from the ranks of already active national prosecutors or he or she will obtain such status upon appointment for an EDP.[50]

The absence of an EDP in the non-participating Member States would not only limit the prosecutorial powers of the EPPO, but also impede the flow of

[47] Cases of disagreements between the EPPO and the national prosecution authorities over the ancillary competence of the EPPO will be subject to decision of the national juridical authorities—see Article 13(3) of the proposed regulation.

[48] Although reasonable and probably effective, such scenario may raise opposition of the ardent supporters of the EPPO project, since it takes us back to the start of discussion on the need of creating an EPPO and its effectiveness under the limited jurisdiction set by the borders of enhanced cooperation.

[49] Article 10(1) of the EPPO proposal.

[50] Cf.: Articles 6(6) and 10(2) of the EPPO proposal.

information. In such situation, it should be expected, that Eurojust will sustain and develop its statutory role of stimulating investigative and prosecutorial co-ordination among the Member States. Eurojust should therefore facilitate effective judicial cooperation and coordination between the EPPO and the judicial authorities of the non-participating Member States.[51]

An interesting, albeit complicated question is whether the 'Head' of the EPPO and/or any of the four deputies, could originate from a non-participating Member State. Contrary to the appointment rules concerning the EDPs, the choice of the EPP relies on an open call for candidates, which fulfil the requirements to be appointed for a high level judicial office and possess relevant prosecutorial experience. This procedure would be concluded by an appointment by the Council, upon approval of the European Parliament, supported by an opinion of a panel of experts.[52] Although one might suppose, that a candidate from a non-participating Member State could become an EPP, this would, arguably, require a strong confidence in a non-discrimination principle over any other arguments. Whether one of the deputies of the European Prosecutor could be a national of a non-participating Member State is a different question and could appear to be more justified. After all, having a qualified professional of a non-participating Member State in the proximity of the EPP could help stimulate contacts of the EPPO with those States thereby create a solid basis for further synergy in the area of criminal procedure or future enlargement of the enhanced cooperation circle. The bottom line is, whatever the choice of the deputies will be, it seems indispensable for the EPP's effective decision making process, that his/her delegates include prosecutors trained and experienced in the legal systems of non-participating Member States. That point of view appears especially justified if one looks at the differences between major European legal traditions and the characteristics of criminal procedure rooted in common law, adversarial legal tradition.[53]

13.5 Conclusions

Aspiring for a coherent integration of all 28 Member States—at the same time, at the same level and in all policy areas—is an idealistic and difficult goal in the ever enlarging European organism. Nevertheless, the history of the European (Economic) Communities and the European Union offers many examples of differences in the levels of integration—to mention the beginning of the Schengen area and the Eurozone, or the most recent examples of enhanced cooperation in the fields of patent and divorce law. The risks linked with such a multi-speed approach are well known, especially in view of fears for preserving the institutional framework of the

[51] See M. Coninsx, Chap. 6 in this book.

[52] Article 8(1)–(3) of the EPPO proposal.

[53] Cf.: Cape et al. 2007, pp. 5–8, 59–78; Kruszyński and Pawelec 2010, pp. 18–26.

Union and the risk of misusing the enhanced cooperation as an instrument of permanent separation of the leading Member States from the less integrated ones.

Bearing that in mind, an important question is whether the currently delicate and relatively weakly harmonised criminal law area is a proper place for introducing a full-fledged prosecutorial authority. The EPPO will not only act on the basis of a legal system fundamentally differing between participating and non-participating Member States (i.e. in respect of setting aside the national prosecutorial authorities or cooperating with them under the two-hat procedure), but also strongly combining various criminal law systems of participating Member States in one supranational criminal procedure to prosecute trans-border PIF offences. Additionally, Member States' prosecutorial authorities will be obliged to apply legal regimes of other Member States before their national courts. Due to significant differences, especially seen in some fields of criminal procedure (*inter alia*: differences in rules of admissibility of evidence, differences in the interpretation of defendant's passivity in the light of the principle of presumption of innocence, different approaches towards aims and functions of the investigative stage of criminal process), the risk of 'forum shopping' and deterioration of the defendant's procedural security should be taken into account. The issue of the timeframe is also important. The effects of the proposed harmonisation of the fight against fraud to the Union's financial interests by means of criminal law[54] are still unknown. The options of developing the existing measures of combating PIF crimes through mutual cooperation between national prosecutorial agencies, national authorities, and the current EU bodies, do not seem be exhausted yet. Since the proposed EPPO regulation does not in itself harmonise the substantive criminal law differences between the Member States and presents only a minimum catalogue of harmonizing principles in the area of criminal procedure, the most problematic issue consists of choosing the right moment to introduce a new, supranational body that will be able to swap between the national criminal law systems without a risk of falling and breaking its (or the suspects') neck due to insufficient level of integration in those areas.[55] Such concerns make some argue that the creation of the EPPO should be preceded by further standardization, at least in the field of instruments concerning individual rights in criminal proceedings and the establishment of common rules concerning gathering and admissibility of evidence.[56]

An even more important question is whether introducing such a new, supranational authority in one part of the European Union would not result, at least initially, in effects opposite to those expected—fuelling conflicts of competence and enabling perpetrators of (PIF) crimes to hide behind the unclearness of a border

[54] Proposal for a Directive of the European Parliament and of the Council on the fight against fraud to the Union's financial interests by means of criminal law, COM(2012)363 final, 11 July 2012.

[55] Consider e.g. only the problem of securing adequate time and facilities for the preparation of the defence. Compare Article 6(3)(b) of the Convention for the Protection of Human Rights and Fundamental Freedoms.

[56] Cf.: Hofmański 2009, p. 24; Council of Bar and Law Societies of Europe 2013, p. 5.

between the legal regimes functioning inside and outside the enhanced cooperation circle.

Basing the EPPO on an enhanced cooperation framework is very much unlike establishing an EU-wide prosecutorial authority which could successfully act within the whole Union substituting the current horizontal cooperation between the national prosecutorial authorities by a more vertical or centralised approach. Firstly, the cooperation between EPPO and the non-participating Member States will have to be organised along the lines of the current horizontal dimension. To that end, a legal reasoning based upon the Treaty is presented (see Sect. 13.3.1). Perhaps this solution should be implemented through an 'honest' cooperation between two or more national prosecutors, one of which is an EDP representing EPPO in a concerned case, but at the same time acting in his capacity of a national prosecutor together with the public prosecutor of the non-participating Member State. All in all, the big unknown in this area and at the same time a big gap remaining after the presentation of the EPPO legislative proposal, is the character of the relationship between the participating and non-participating Member States in the enhanced cooperation. Potential conflicts of competences raise concerns with regard to the effectiveness of the new authority and the protection of procedural position of the suspects. In such a situation, only general predictions can be made. But the design of this relationship will clearly rely on the practical approach of the Member States and the Union itself. Secondly, most significant are the implications of the general primary law provisions concerning the nature of enhanced cooperation and—thirdly—the common duty of all Member States and the Union alike in realising the principles regarding the countering of fraud and other illegal activities affecting the EU's financial interests as laid down in Article 325(1) TFEU.

Since we are talking about an entity taking or initiating procedural decisions concerning people's liberty and their assets, the stake seems too high for giving a green light to extensive experiments where regulatory gaps are left, just under the banner of looking for better ways of protecting the financial interests of the Union. However, leaving such fears aside and having a strong belief in the wise self-control of the EPPO and even wiser judicial control over it, the territorially limited EPPO may prove to be a positive catalyst for further synergy between national criminal law regimes, especially in the field of criminal law procedures.

References

Bordignon M, Brusco S (2006) On enhanced cooperation. J Public Econ 90:2063–2090

Cape E et al (2007) Suspects in Europe. Procedural rights at the investigative stage of the criminal process in the European Union. Intersentia, Antwerpen-Cambridge

Cremona M (2009) Enhanced cooperation and the common foreign and security and defence policies of the EU. EUI Working Papers—Law 21:1–17

Commissariat Général du Plan (1980) L'Europe les vingt prochaines années. La Documentation Française

Council of Bar and Law Societies of Europe (2013) A European public prosecutor's office—report, 7 Feb 2013. www.ccbe.eu/fileadmin/user_upload/NTCdocument/EN_07022013_EPPOpdf1_1360678235.pdf. Accessed 18 Aug 2013

Dahrendorf R (1979) A third Europe? European University Institute, Florence

Den Boer M (2001) The fight against organised crime in Europe: a comparative perspective. Eur J Crim Policy Res 9:259–272

Europa (2013) Enhanced cooperation. www.europa.eu/legislation_summaries/institutional_affairs/treaties/lisbon_treaty/ai0018_en.htm. Accessed March 2014

European Commission (2013) Communication from the commission to the European Parliament, the council, the European economic and social committee and the committee of the regions, 17 July 2013, COM(2013)532 final

Franssen V (2013) Proposed regulation on the European public prosecutor—thinking federal? http://europeanlawblog.eu/?p=1887#sthash.3xCB0LQO.dpuf. Accessed 18 Aug 2013

Grabitz E (ed) (1984) Abgestufte Integration. Engel, Kehl am Rein

Hamran L, Szabova E (2013) European public prosecutor's office—*cui bono*? New J Eur Crim Law 4:40–58

Hofmański P (2006) Przyszłość ścigania karnego w Europie. Europejski Przegląd Sądowy 12:4–11

Hofmański P (2009) Ochrona interesów finansowych Unii Europejskiej w kontekście idei utworzenia urzędu Prokuratury Europejskiej. In: Nowak C (ed) Ochrona interesów finansowych a przemiany instytucjonalne Unii Europejskiej. Wydawnictwa Akademickie i Profesjonalne, Warsaw

Kruszyński P, Pawelec S (2010) Uwagi nad szansami dla europejskiej kodyfikacji karnoprocesowej. In: Kruszyński P et al. (2010) Europejski kodeks postępowania karnego. Stowarzyszenie Absolwentów Wydziału Prawa i Administracji UW, Warsaw, pp 15–26

Lamers K, Schäuble W (1994) Reflection on European policy, document by the CDU/CSU group in the German *Bundestag*, Europe Doc. 1895/96, 1 Sept 1994

Ligeti K, Simonato M (2013) The European public prosecutor's office: towards a truly European prosecution service? New J Eur Crim Law 4:7–21

Nürnberger S (2009) Die zukünftige Europäische Staatsanwaltschaft—Eine Einführung. Zeitschrift für das Juristische Studium 5:494–505

Papagianni G (2001) Flexibility in justice and home affairs: an old phenomenon taking new forms. In: de Witte B, Hanf D, Vos E (eds) The many faces of differentiation in EU law. Intersentia, Antwerpen, pp 101–128

Reding V (2013) Establishing a European public prosecutor's office—a federal budget needs federal protection. Materials from a press conference, speech/13/644. http://europa.eu/rapid/press-release_SPEECH-13-644_en.htm. Accessed 18 Sept 2013

Representation of the European Commission in Poland (2013) Powstanie Prokuratura Europejska. http://ec.europa.eu/polska/news/130717_prokuratura_europejska_pl.htm. Accessed 18 Sept 2013

Rogacka-Rzewnicka M (2009) Przemiany procesu karnego po utworzeniu urzędu Prokuratury Europejskiej. In: Nowak C (ed) Ochrona interesów finansowych a przemiany instytucjonalne Unii Europejskiej. Wydawnictwa Akademickie i Profesjonalne, Warsaw, pp 59–70

Sakowicz A (2009) Wzmocniona współpraca a powołanie Prokuratury Europejskiej. Niebezpieczeństwo wielobiegunowej współpracy w ochronie interesów finansowych Unii Europejskiej. In: Nowak C (ed) Ochrona interesów finansowych a przemiany instytucjonalne Unii Europejskiej. Wydawnictwa Akademickie i Profesjonalne, Warsaw

Sakowicz A (2011) Zasada *ne bis in idem* w prawie karnym w ujęciu paneuropejskim. Temida 2, Białystok

Sakowicz A (2012) In: Grzelak A et al. Europejskie prawo karne. Wydawnictwo C. H. Beck, Warsaw

Sieber U (1998) Euro-fraud: organised fraud against the financial interests of the European Union. Law Soc Change 30:1–42

Steinborn S (2012) In: Wróbel A (ed.) Traktat o funkcjonowaniu Unii Europejskiej. Komentarz Lex, vol I. Wolters Kluwer Polska, Warsaw

Szwarc M (2005) Zróżnicowania integracja i wzmocniona współpraca w prawie Unii Europejskiej. Wydawnictwo Prawo i Praktyka Gospodarcza, Warsaw

Tekin F, Wessels W (2008) Flexibility within the Lisbon treaty: trademark or empty promise? Eipascope 1:25–31

Tindemans L (1976) European Union. Bullet Eur Comm. Suppl 1(76):5–35

Van Bockel B (2010) The *ne bis in idem* principle in EU law. Alphen aan den Rijn

Velkova E, Georgievski S (2005) Fighting trans-border organized crime in southeast Europe through fighting corruption in customs agencies. In: Athanassopoulou E (ed) Fighting organised crime in southeast Europe. Routledge, New York, pp 64–77

Appendix
European Commission Proposal

EUROPEAN
COMMISSION

Brussels, 17.7.2013
COM(2013) 534 final
2013/0255 (APP)

Proposal for a

Council Regulation

On the Establishment of the European Public Prosecutor's Office

{SWD(2013) 274 final}
{SWD(2013) 275 final}

EXPLANATORY MEMORANDUM

1. CONTEXT OF THE PROPOSAL

Prosecuting offences against the EU budget is currently within the exclusive competence of Member States and no Union authority exists in this area. While their potential damage is very significant, these offences are not always investigated and prosecuted by the relevant national authorities, as law enforcement resources are limited. As a result, national law enforcement efforts remain often fragmented in this area and the cross-border dimension of these offences usually escapes the attention of the authorities.

Whereas tackling cross-border fraud cases would require closely coordinated and effective investigations and prosecutions at European level, the current levels of information exchange and coordination are not sufficient to achieve this, despite the intensified efforts of Union bodies, such as Eurojust, Europol and the European Anti-Fraud Office (OLAF). Coordination, cooperation and information exchange face numerous problems and limitations owing to a split of responsibilities between authorities belonging to diverse territorial and functional jurisdictions. Gaps in the judicial action to fight fraud occur daily at different levels and between different authorities and are a major impediment to the effective investigation and prosecution of offences affecting the Union's financial interests.

L.H. Erkelens et al. (eds.), *The European Public Prosecutor's Office*,
DOI 10.1007/978-94-6265-035-0

Eurojust and Europol have a general mandate to facilitate exchange of information and coordinate national criminal investigations and prosecutions, but lack the power to carry out acts of investigation or prosecution themselves. The European Anti-Fraud Office (OLAF) has a mandate to investigate fraud and illegal activities affecting the EU, but its powers are limited to administrative investigations. Action by national judicial authorities remains often slow, prosecution rates on the average low and results obtained in the different Member States over the Union as a whole unequal. Based on this track record the judicial action undertaken by Member States against fraud may currently not be considered as effective, equivalent and deterrent as required under the Treaty.

As Member States' criminal investigation and prosecution authorities are currently unable to achieve an equivalent level of protection and enforcement, the Union not only has the competence but also the obligation to act. Article 325 of the Treaty so requires from a legal perspective, but taking into account the specific Union rules which apply in this field the Union is also best placed to protect its own financial interests, including via the prosecution of offences against these interests. Article 86 of the Treaty provides the necessary legal basis for such a new Union-level prosecution system, the purpose of which is to correct the deficiencies of the current enforcement regime exclusively based on national efforts and add consistency and coordination to these efforts.

The current proposal seeks to set up the European Public Prosecutor's Office and define its competences and procedures. It complements an earlier legislative proposal[1] which defines the criminal offences as well as the applicable sanctions.

This proposal is part of a legislative package as it will be accompanied by a proposal concerning the reform of Eurojust.

2. RESULTS OF CONSULTATIONS WITH THE INTERESTED PARTIES AND IMPACT ASSESSMENTS

In order to prepare this Regulation, the Commission has consulted widely with stakeholders, on a number of occasions, also building on earlier discussions related to the European Public Prosecutor's Office, which have been going on for more than a decade.[2] Preparatory consultations in view of the present proposal have covered the main issues addressed in this Regulation, including various options with regard to the institutional, legal, organisational and operational set-up of a European system for the investigation and prosecution of the relevant offences.

---

[1] Proposal for a Directive of the European Parliament and of the Council on the fight against fraud to the Union's financial interests by means of criminal law, 11 July 2012 COM (2012) 363 final

[2] See Green Paper on criminal law protection of the financial interests of the Community and the establishment of a European Public Prosecutor, 11 December 2001 COM (2001)715 final and its follow up report, 19 March 2003 COM (2003)128 final

Early in 2012, two questionnaires were published and distributed on-line, one to justice professionals and another to the general public, respectively. In general, the replies were positive towards taking new actions to strengthen the material and procedural framework to counter offences affecting the EU's financial interests, and most also expressed support for the idea to set up a European Public Prosecutor's Office. A number of more detailed suggestions, concerns and questions were also voiced, in particular on the relationship between such the European Public Prosecutor's Office and national prosecution authorities, the competence of the European Public Prosecutor's Office to direct and coordinate investigations at national level, or the possible difficulties with any harmonised European rules of procedure in the European Public Prosecutor's Office's proceedings. In parallel, field research has been conducted in a number of Member States, as part of the external study in support of this report. In addition, throughout 2012 and at the beginning of 2013, a number of discussions or meetings took place at European level:

- The network of Public Prosecutors or equivalent institutions at the Supreme Judicial Courts of the Member States, Budapest, 25–26 May 2012.
- Conference: A Blueprint for the European Public Prosecutor's Office? Luxembourg, 13–15 June 2012. The conference gathered experts and high level representatives from academia, EU institutions and Member States.
- Vice-President Reding's consultation meeting with Prosecutors General and Directors of Public Prosecution from Member States, Brussels, 26 June 2012. The meeting permitted an open discussion on specific issues regarding the protection of the Union's financial interests.
- On 18 October 2012, the Commission organised a consultation meeting on issues relating to a possible reform of Eurojust, in which questions related to the setting up of a European Public Prosecutor's Office were also discussed with representatives of Member States. The meeting generally supported establishing a close link between Eurojust and the European Public Prosecutor's Office.
- The 10th OLAF Conference of Fraud Prosecutors, Berlin, 8-9 November 2012, was an opportunity to explore the ways in which national prosecutors would interact with the European Public Prosecutor's Office, if set up.
- The informal consultation held on 26 November 2012 with defence lawyers (CCBE and ECBA) looked at procedural safeguards for suspects and made useful recommendations in that regard.
- ERA seminar "Towards the European Public Prosecutor's Office (EPPO)", 17 and 18 January 2013.
- Meeting of the Commission Expert Group on European Criminal Policy, Brussels, 23 January 2013.
- Further consultation meeting with ECBA and CCBE, Brussels, 9 April 2013.

Also, numerous bilateral consultation meetings with Member States' authorities have taken place over the second half of 2012 and the beginning of 2013.

The Commission conducted an Impact Assessment of policy alternatives taking account *inter alia* an external study (Specific contract No. JUST/2011/JPEN/FW/0030.A4) which has considered various options involving the establishment of a

European Public Prosecutor's Office. According to the analysis of the Impact Assessment, setting up the European Public Prosecutor's Office as a decentralised integrated office of the Union, which relies on national judicial systems, offers the most benefits and generates the lowest costs.

3. LEGAL ELEMENTS OF THE PROPOSAL

3.1 The Legal Basis

The legal basis of the proposal is Article 86 of the Treaty. According to the first paragraph of that provision, "[i]n order to combat crimes affecting the financial interests of the Union, the Council, by means of regulations adopted in accordance with a special legislative procedure, may establish a European Public Prosecutor's Office from Eurojust. The Council shall act unanimously after obtaining the consent of the European Parliament". The second paragraph of that provision defines the responsibility of the European Public Prosecutor's Office as follows: "[t]he European Public Prosecutor's Office shall be responsible for investigating, prosecuting and bringing to judgment, where appropriate in liaison with Europol, the perpetrators of, and accomplices in, offences against the Union's financial interests, as determined by the regulation provided for in paragraph 1. It shall exercise the functions of prosecutor in the competent courts of the Member States in relation to such offences". Finally, the third paragraph of Article 86 of the Treaty defines the substantive scope of the regulations to be adopted pursuant to it: "[t]he regulations referred to in paragraph 1 shall determine the general rules applicable to the European Public Prosecutor's Office, the conditions governing the performance of its functions, the rules of procedure applicable to its activities, as well as those governing the admissibility of evidence, and the rules applicable to the judicial review of procedural measures taken by it in the performance of its functions".

3.2 Subsidiarity and Proportionality

There is a need for the Union to act because the foreseen action has an intrinsic Union dimension. It implies Union-level steering and coordination of investigations and prosecutions of criminal offences affecting its own financial interests, the protection of which is required both from the Union and the Member States by Articles 310 (6) and 325 TFEU. In accordance with the subsidiarity principle, this objective can only be achieved at Union level by reason of its scale and effects. As stated above, the present situation, in which the prosecution of offences against the Union's financial interests is exclusively in the hands of the authorities of the Member States is not satisfactory and does not sufficiently achieve the objective of fighting effectively against offences affecting the Union budget.

In accordance with the principle of proportionality, this Regulation does not go beyond what is necessary to achieve this objective. Throughout the proposed text, the options chosen are those that are least intrusive for the legal orders and the institutional structures of the Member States. Key features of the proposal, such as the choice of the law that applies to investigative measures, the figure of Delegated Prosecutors, the decentralised character of the European Public Prosecutor's Office and the system of judicial review, were designed in order not to go beyond what was necessary to achieve the main objectives of the proposal.

The Union's competence to counter fraud and other offences affecting its financial interests is unambiguously stipulated by Articles 86 and 325 of the Treaty. As this Union competence is not accessory to that of Member States and exercising it has become necessary to achieve a more effective protection of the Union's financial interests, the proposed package complies with the requirement of subsidiarity.

3.3 Explanation of the Proposal by Chapters

The main objectives of the proposal are:

- To contribute to the strengthening of the protection of the Union's financial interests and further development of an area of justice, and to enhance the trust of EU businesses and citizens in the Union's institutions, while respecting all fundamental rights enshrined in the Charter of Fundamental Rights of the European Union.
- To establish a coherent European system for the investigation and prosecution of offences affecting the Union's financial interests.
- To ensure a more efficient and effective investigation and prosecution of offences affecting the EU's financial interests.
- To increase the number of prosecutions, leading to more convictions and recovery of fraudulently obtained Union funds.
- To ensure close cooperation and effective information exchange between the European and national competent authorities.
- To enhance deterrence of committing offences affecting the Union's financial interests.

3.3.1 Chapter I Subject Matter and Definitions

This Chapter sets out the subject matter of the Regulation, which is the setting up of the European Public Prosecutor's Office. In addition, it defines a certain number of terms used in the text, such as the "financial interests of the Union".

3.3.2 Chapter II: General Rules

This Chapter regulates the fundamental features of the European Public Prosecutor's Office, its status and structure as a new Union office with investigation and prosecution functions. In doing so, it provides specific rules on the appointment and dismissal of the European Public Prosecutor and his/her delegates. It also sets out the basic principles of its functioning.

Section 1 (Status, organisation and structure of the European Public Prosecutor's Office) clarifies how the European Public Prosecutor's Office is set up and what functions will be entrusted to it. The text provides for its establishment as a new Union body with legal personality and sets out its relationship with Eurojust. Among the key features of the European Public Prosecutor's Office, the text refers to independence and accountability, which should guarantee that it is able to exercise its functions and use its powers in a way that makes it immune from any improper influence. The main characteristics of the structure of the European Public Prosecutor's Office are also described in the text.

Section 2 (Appointment and dismissal of the members of the European Public Prosecutor's Office) provides the rules applicable to the appointment and dismissal procedure of the European Public Prosecutor, his/her Deputies and staff. The appointment procedure for the European Public Prosecutor is designed in a way that guarantees his independence and accountability towards Union institutions, whereas his/her dismissal procedure rests with the Court of Justice of the European Union. For the European Delegated Prosecutors, who will be appointed and dismissed by the European Public Prosecutor, the procedure ensures their integration into national prosecution systems.

Section 3 (Basic principles) describes the main legal principles that will govern the activities of the European Public Prosecutor's Office, including conformity with the Charter of Fundamental Rights of the European Union, proportionality, national law being applicable to implement the Regulation, procedural neutrality, legality and celerity of investigations, Member States' duty to assist the investigations and prosecutions of the European Public Prosecutor's Office.

Section 4 (Competence of the European Public Prosecutor's Office) clarifies the criminal offences which fall within the material competence of the European Public Prosecutor's Office. These offences are to be defined by reference to national law implementing Union law (Directive 2013/xx/EU). The text distinguishes between two categories of offences, the first of which falls automatically within the competence of the European Public Prosecutor's Office (Article 12) and the second (Article 13) which requires to establish its competence where there are certain connecting links with offences of the first category. The Section also describes how the European Public Prosecutor's Office will exercise its competence over these offences.

3.3.3 Chapter III: Rules of Procedure on Investigations, Prosecutions and Trial Proceedings

This Chapter covers the essential features of the investigations and prosecutions of the European Public Prosecutor's Office, including provisions on how they should be controlled by national courts, what decisions the European Public Prosecutor's

Office could take once the investigation is completed, how it would exercise its prosecution functions and how the evidence collected would be used in trial courts.

Section 1 (Conduct of the investigation) provides the general rules that apply to the investigations of the European Public Prosecutor's Office, including the sources of information used, how investigations are initiated and conducted and how the European Public Prosecutor's Office may obtain further information from databases or data collected at its request.

Section 2 (Processing of information) explains the functioning of the Case Management System.

Section 3 (Investigation measures) sets out the types and conditions of the individual investigation measures which the European Public Prosecutor's Office will be able to use. The text does not regulate in detail each of these measures but requires the application of national law.

Section 4 (Termination of the investigation and powers of prosecution) stipulates the different types of decisions which the European Public Prosecutor's Office may take at the end of the investigation, including indictments and dismissals.

Section 5 (Admissibility of evidence) regulates the admissibility of evidence collected and presented by the European Public Prosecutor's Office in trial courts.

Section 6 (Confiscation) regulates the disposition of the assets confiscated by national courts as a result of the prosecution conducted by the European Public Prosecutor's Office.

3.3.4 Chapter IV: Procedural Safeguards

The rules of this Chapter provide safeguards for suspects and other persons involved in the proceedings of the European Public Prosecutor's Office, which will need to comply with the relevant standards, in particular the Charter of Fundamental Rights of the European Union. The rules refer to Union legislation (Directives on various procedural rights in criminal proceedings) with regard to certain rights but also define autonomously other rights which have not yet been regulated in Union legislation. As such, these rules provide an additional layer of protection compared to national law so that suspects and other persons may benefit directly from a Union-level protection.

3.3.5 Chapter V: Judicial Review

Article 86(3) of the Treaty prescribes the Union legislator to determine the rules applicable to the judicial review of procedural measures taken by the European Public Prosecutor's Office in the performance of its functions. This possibility reflects the specific nature of the European Public Prosecutor's Office, which is different from that of all other Union bodies and agencies and requires special rules regarding judicial review.

Article 86(2) of the Treaty requires that the European Public Prosecutor's Office exercise its functions of prosecutor in the competent courts of the Member States.

The acts of investigation of the European Public Prosecutor's Office are also closely related to an eventual prosecution and will mainly deploy their effects in the legal orders of the Member States. In most cases they will also be carried out by national law enforcement authorities acting under the instructions of the European Public Prosecutor's Office, and sometimes also after having obtained the authorisation of a national court. The European Public Prosecutor's Office is therefore a Union body whose action will mainly be relevant in the national legal orders. It is therefore appropriate to consider the European Public Prosecutor's Office as a national authority for the purpose of the judicial review of its acts of investigation and prosecution. As a result, national courts should be entrusted with the judicial review of all the challengeable acts of investigation and prosecution of the European Public Prosecutor's Office, and the Union courts should not be directly competent with regard to those acts pursuant to Articles 263, 265 and 268 of the Treaty, since such acts should not be considered as acts of an office of the Union for the purpose of judicial review.

In accordance with Article 267 of the Treaty, national courts are able or, in certain circumstances, bound to refer to the Court of Justice questions for preliminary rulings on the interpretation or the validity of provisions of Union law which are relevant for the judicial review of acts of investigation and prosecution of the European Public Prosecutor's Office. This may include questions on the interpretation of this Regulation. Since the European Public Prosecutor's Office will be considered a national authority for the purpose of judicial review, national courts will only be able to refer questions on interpretation to the Court of Justice regarding its acts. The preliminary rulings procedure will thus ensure that this Regulation is applied uniformly throughout the Union, whereas the validity of the acts of the European Public Prosecutor's Office may be challenged before national courts in accordance with national law.

3.3.6 Chapter VI: Data Protection

This Chapter provides for rules governing the data protection regime which in the specific context of the European Public Prosecutor's Office particularise and complement the Union legislation applicable to processing of personal data by EU bodies (in particular Regulation (EC) No 45/2001 of the European Parliament and of the Council of 18 December 2000 on the protection of individuals with regard to the processing of personal data by the Community institutions and bodies and on the free movement of such data). The supervision of all personal data processing in the context of the activities of the European Public Prosecutor's Office has been entrusted to the European Data Protection Supervisor (EDPS).

3.3.7 Chapter VII: Financial and Staff Provisions

The rules of this Chapter regulate how the European Public Prosecutor's Office shall handle its budget and staff. They are based on the applicable Union legislation, i.e. for budget matters on Regulation (EU, Euratom) No 966/2012 of the European Parliament and of the Council of 25 October 2012 on the financial rules applicable to the general budget of the Union and repealing Council Regulation (EC, Euratom) No 1605/2002, and for staff matters on Regulation 31 (EEC), as amended.

3.3.8 Chapter VIII: Provisions on the Relations of the European Public Prosecutor's Office

This Chapter regulates the relationship of the European Public Prosecutor's Office with Union institutions or other bodies as well as actors outside the Union. Special rules apply to the relationship of the European Public Prosecutor's Office with Eurojust, given the special links that tie them together in the area of operational activities, administration and management.

3.3.9 Chapter IX: General Provisions

These provisions address institutional matters which arise with the setting up of any new Union office or agency. They are largely inspired by the "Common Approach on decentralised agencies" but take into account the specific (judicial) nature of the European Public Prosecutor's Office. The provisions covers matters such as legal status and operating conditions, language arrangements, transparency requirements, rules on the prevention of fraud, handling classified information, administrative enquiries and liability rules.

3.3.10 Chapter X: Final Provisions

These provisions deal with the implementation of the Regulation and provide for the adoption of implementing provisions, transitional provisions, administrative rules and entry into force.

4. BUDGETARY IMPLICATION

The proposal seeks to be cost-efficient for the EU budget: part of OLAF's current resources will be used for setting up the central headquarters of the European Public Prosecutor's Office, which in turn will rely on the administrative support of Eurojust.

Limited additional costs will arise in relation to the position of the European Delegated Prosecutors who will be located in the Member States and will be an integral part of the European Public Prosecutor's Office. Given their dual status as both Union and national prosecutors, they will receive remuneration from the EU budget and will be covered by the Staff Regulations.

As the set-up phase of the European Public Prosecutor's Office will probably take several years, staff members will be gradually transferred from OLAF to the European Public Prosecutor's Office. The equivalent number of the staff transferred and the corresponding credits to finance this staff will be reduced in the establishment plan and budget of OLAF. The European Public Prosecutor's Office will reach cruising speed once the full staff levels are achieved. The full staff level will be achieved in 2023 with 235 staff, of which 180 establishment plan posts and 55 external staff. The estimated cost for 2023 with this staff level is approximately 35 million EUR.

2013/0255 (APP)

Proposal for a

COUNCIL REGULATION

on the establishment of the European Public Prosecutor's Office

THE COUNCIL OF THE EUROPEAN UNION,
Having regard to the Treaty on the Functioning of the European Union, and in particular Article 86 thereof,
Having regard to the proposal from the European Commission,
After transmission of the draft legislative act to the national Parliaments, Having regard to the consent of the European Parliament,
After consulting the European Data Protection Supervisor, Acting in accordance with a special legislative procedure,
Whereas:

(1) Both the Union and the Member States have an obligation to protect the Union's financial interests against criminal offences, which generate significant financial damages every year. Yet, these offences are currently not sufficiently investigated and prosecuted by the relevant national authorities.
(2) The setting up of the European Public Prosecutor's Office is foreseen by the Treaty on the Functioning of the European Union (TFEU) in the context of the area of freedom, security and justice.
(3) The Treaty expressly requires that the European Public Prosecutor's Office be established from Eurojust, which implies that this Regulation should establish links between them.
(4) The Treaty provides that the mandate of the European Public Prosecutor's Office is to combat crime affecting the Union's financial interests.
(5) In accordance with the principle of subsidiarity, combatting crimes affecting the financial interests of the Union can be better achieved at Union level by reason of its scale and effects. The present situation, in which the prosecution of offences against the Union's financial interests is exclusively in the hands

of the authorities of the Member States does not sufficiently achieve that objective. Since the objectives of this Regulation, namely the setting up of the European Public Prosecutor's Office, cannot be achieved by the Member States given the fragmentation of national prosecutions in the area of offences committed against the Union's financial interests and can therefore, by reason of the fact that the European Public Prosecutor's Office is to have exclusive competence to prosecute such offences, be better achieved at Union level, the Union may adopt measures, in accordance with the principle of subsidiarity as set out in Article 5 of the Treaty on European Union.

(6) In accordance with the principle of proportionality, as set out in Article 5 of the Treaty on European Union, this Regulation does not go beyond what is necessary in order to achieve these objectives and ensures that its impact on the legal orders and the institutional structures of the Member States is the least intrusive possible.

(7) The mandate of the European Public Prosecutor's Office should be to investigate, prosecute and bring to judgment the perpetrators of offences against the Union's financial interests. This requires autonomous powers of investigation and prosecution, including the ability to carry out investigations in cross-border or complex cases.

(8) The organisational structure of the European Public Prosecutor's Office should also allow quick and efficient decision-making in the conduct of criminal investigations and prosecutions, whether they involve one or several Member States.

(9) As a rule, the investigations of the European Public Prosecutor's Office should be carried out by European Delegated Prosecutors in the Member States. In cases involving several Member States or cases which are of particular complexity, the efficient investigation and prosecution may require that the European Public Prosecutor also exercise his powers by instructing national law enforcement authorities.

(10) Since the European Public Prosecutor's Office is to be granted powers of investigation and prosecution, institutional safeguards should be put in place to ensure its independence as well as its accountability towards the Union institutions.

(11) Strict accountability is a complement to the independence and the powers granted to it under this Regulation. The European Public Prosecutor is fully accountable for the performance of his/her duties as the head of the European Public Prosecutor's Office and as such he/she carries an overall institutional accountability for its general activities before the Union institutions. As a result, any of the Union institutions can apply to the Court of Justice of the European Union with a view to his/her removal under certain circumstances, including in cases of serious misconduct. This accountability should be combined with a strict regime of judicial control whereby the European Public Prosecutor's Office can only use coercive investigation powers subject to prior judicial authorisation and the evidence presented to the trial court should be subject to verification by that court as to its compliance with the Charter of Fundamental Rights of the European Union.

(12) To ensure consistency in its action and thus an equivalent protection of the Union's financial interests, the organisational structure of the European Public Prosecutor's Office should enable central coordination and steering of all investigations and prosecutions within its competence. The European Public Prosecutor's Office should therefore have a central structure where decisions are taken by the European Public Prosecutor.

(13) To maximise efficiency and mimimise costs, the European Public Prosecutor's Office should respect the principle of decentralisation whereby it should in principle have recourse to European Delegated Prosecutors located in the Member States to carry out investigations and prosecutions. The European Public Prosecutor's Office should rely on national authorities, including police authorities, in particular for the execution of coercive measures. Under the principle of loyal cooperation, all national authorities and the relevant Union bodies, including Europol, Eurojust and OLAF, are obliged to actively support the investigations and prosecutions of the European Public Prosecutor's Office as well as to cooperate with it to the fullest extent possible.

(14) The operational activities of the European Public Prosecutor's Office should be carried out under the instruction and on behalf of the European Public Prosecutor by the designated European Delegated Prosecutors or their national staff in the Member States. The European Public Prosecutor and the Deputies should have the staff necessary to carry out their functions under this Regulation. The European Public Prosecutor's Office should be considered indivisible.

(15) The procedure for the appointment of the European Public Prosecutor should ensure his/her independence and his/her legitimacy should be drawn from Union institutions. The Deputies of the European Public Prosecutor should be appointed by the same procedure.

(16) The procedure for the appointment of the European Delegated Prosecutors should ensure that they are an integral part of the European Public Prosecutor's Office, and that they are integrated at both an operational and functional level into the national legal systems and prosecution structures.

(17) The Charter of Fundamental Rights of the European Union constitutes the common basis for the protection of rights of suspected persons in criminal proceedings during the pre-trial and trial phase. The activities of the European Public Prosecutor's Office should in all instances be carried out in full respect of those rights.

(18) The investigations and prosecutions of the European Public Prosecutor's Office should be guided by the principles of proportionality, impartiality and fairness towards the suspect. This includes the obligation to seek all types of evidence, inculpatory as well as exculpatory.

(19) It is necessary to determine the rules of procedure applicable to the activities of the European Public Prosecutor's Office. As it would be disproportionate to provide detailed provisions on the conduct of its investigations and prosecutions, this Regulation should only list the measures of investigation

that the European Public Prosecutor's Office may need to use and leave the other matters, in particular rules related to their execution, to national law.

(20) In order to ensure legal certainty and zero tolerance towards offences affecting the Union's financial interests, the investigation and prosecution activities of the European Public Prosecutor's Office should be based on the principle of mandatory prosecution, whereby it should initiate investigations and, subject to further conditions, prosecute every offence within its competence.

(21) The material scope of competence of the European Public Prosecutor's Office should be limited to criminal offences affecting the financial interests of the Union. Any extension of this competence to include serious crimes having a cross-border dimension would require a unanimous decision of the European Council.

(22) Offences against the Union's financial interests are often closely connected to other offences. In the interest of procedural efficiency and to avoid a possible breach of the principle *ne bis in idem*, the competence of European Public Prosecutor's Office should also cover offences which are not technically defined under national law as offences affecting the Union's financial interests where their constituent facts are identical and inextricably linked with those of the offences affecting the financial interests of the Union. In such mixed cases, where the offence affecting the Union's financial interests is preponderant, the competence of the European Public Prosecutor's Office should be exercised after consultation with the competent authorities of the Member State concerned. Preponderance should be established on the basis of criteria such as the offences' financial impact for the Union, for national budgets, the number of victims or other circumstances related to the offences' gravity, or the applicable penalties.

(23) The competence of the European Public Prosecutor's Office regarding offences affecting the financial interests of the Union should take priority over national claims of jurisdiction so that it can ensure consistency and provide steering of investigations and prosecutions at Union level. With regard to these offences the authorities of Member States should only act at the request of the European Public Prosecutor's Office, unless urgent measures are required.

(24) As the European Public Prosecutor's Office should bring prosecutions before national courts, its competence should be defined by reference to the criminal law of the Member States, which criminalises acts or omissions affecting the Union's financial interests and determines the applicable penalties by implementing the relevant Union legislation, in particular [*Directive 2013/xx/ EU*[3]], in national legal systems.

---

[3] Proposal for a Directive of the European Parliament and of the Council on the fight against fraud to the Union's financial interests by means of criminal law, 11 July 2012 COM (2012) 363 final.

(25) The European Public Prosecutor's Office should exercise its competence as broadly as possible so that its investigations and prosecutions may extend to offences committed outside the territory of the Member States. The exercise of its competence should therefore be aligned with the rules pursuant to [*Directive 2013/xx/EU*].

(26) Since the European Public Prosecutor's Office has exclusive competence to deal with offences affecting the Union's financial interests, the investigations it conducts on the territory of Member States should be facilitated by the competent national authorities and the relevant Union bodies, including Eurojust, Europol and OLAF, from the moment a suspected offence is reported to the European Public Prosecutor's Office until it determines whether to prosecute or otherwise dispose of the case.

(27) In order to comply fully with their obligation to inform the European Public Prosecutor's Office where a suspicion of an offence within its competence is identified, the national authorities of the Member States as well as all institutions, bodies, offices and agencies of the Union should follow the existing reporting procedures and have in place efficient mechanisms for a preliminary evaluation of allegations reported to them. The institutions, bodies, offices and agencies of the Union may make use of OLAF to that effect.

(28) It is essential for the effective investigation and prosecution of offences affecting the Union's financial interests that the European Public Prosecutor's Office can gather evidence throughout the Union by using a comprehensive set of investigative measures, while bearing in the mind the principle of proportionality and the need to obtain judicial authorisation for certain investigative measures. These measures should be available with regard to the offences within the mandate of the European Public Prosecutor's Office for the purpose of its investigations and prosecutions. Once ordered by the European Public Prosecutor's Office or by the competent judicial authority at its request, they should be carried out in accordance with national law. In addition, the European Public Prosecutor's Office should have access to all relevant data sources, including public and private registers.

(29) The use of the investigative measures provided for by this Regulation should comply with the conditions set out in it, including the need to obtain judicial authorisation for certain coercive investigative measures. Other investigative measures may be subject to judicial authorisation if this is required by the national law of the Member State where the investigation measure is to be carried out. The general requirements of proportionality and necessity should apply to the ordering of the measures by the European Public Prosecutor's Office and to their authorisation by the competent national judicial authority pursuant to this Regulation.

(30) Article 86 of the Treaty requires the European Public Prosecutor's Office to exercise the functions of the prosecutor, which includes taking decisions on a suspect's indictment and the choice of jurisdiction. The decision whether to indict the suspect should be made by the European Public Prosecutor so that

there is a common prosecution policy. The jurisdiction of trial should be chosen by the European Public Prosecutor on the basis of a set of transparent criteria.

(31) Taking into account the principle of mandatory prosecution, the investigations of the European Public Prosecutor's Office should normally lead to prosecution in the competent national courts in cases where there is solid evidence and no legal ground bars prosecution. In the absence of such evidence and where there is no high prospect that the required evidence could be produced in trial the case can be dismissed. Additionally the European Public Prosecutor's Office should have the possibility to dismiss the case where the offence is a minor one. Where the case is not dismissed on such grounds but prosecution is not justified either, the European Public Prosecutor's Office should have the possibility of proposing a transaction to the suspect, if this would be in the interest of the proper administration of justice. The rules applicable to transactions, and those which apply to the calculation of the fines to be imposed, should be clarified in the administrative rules of the European Public Prosecutor's Office. The closure of a case through a transaction in accordance with this Regulation should not affect the application of administrative measures by the competent authorities, as far as those measures do not refer to penalties that could be equated to criminal penalties.

(32) The evidence presented by the European Public Prosecutor's Office to the trial court should be recognised as admissible evidence, and thus presumed to meet any relevant evidentiary requirements under the national law of the Member State where the trial court is located, provided that court considers it to respect the fairness of the procedure and the suspect's rights of defence under the Charter of Fundamental Rights of the European Union. The trial court cannot exclude the evidence presented by the European Public Prosecutor's Office as inadmissible on the ground that the conditions and rules for gathering that type of evidence are different under the national law applicable to it.

(33) This Regulation respects fundamental rights and observes the principles recognised by the Charter of Fundamental Rights of the European Union. It requires the European Public Prosecutor's Office to respect, in particular, the right to a fair trial, the rights of the defence and the presumption of innocence, as enshrined in Articles 47 and 48 of the Charter. Article 50 of the Charter, which protects the right not to be tried or punished twice in criminal proceedings for the same offence (*ne bis in idem*), ensures that there will be no double jeopardy as a result of the prosecutions brought by European Public Prosecutor's Office. The activities of the European Public Prosecutor's Office shall thus be exercised in full compliance with these rights and the Regulation shall be applied and interpreted accordingly.

(34) Article 82(2) of the Treaty allows the Union to establish minimum rules on rights of individuals in criminal proceedings, in order to ensure that the rights of defence and the fairness of the proceedings are respected. Although the

Union has already established a significant acquis, some of these rights have not yet been harmonised under Union law. In respect of those rights, this Regulation should lay down rules which would apply exclusively for the purposes of this Regulation.

(35) The rights of defence already provided for in the relevant Union legislation, such as Directive 2010/64/EU of the European Parliament and of the Council of 20 October 2010 on the right to interpretation and translation in criminal proceedings[4], Directive 2012/13/EU of the European Parliament and of the Council of 22 May 2012 on the right to information in criminal proceedings[5], and *[Directive 2013/xx/EU of the European Parliament and of the Council of xx xxxx 2013 on the right of access to a lawyer in criminal proceedings and on the right to communicate upon arrest]*, as implemented by national law, should apply to the activities of the European Public Prosecutor's Office. Any suspected person in respect of whom the European Public Prosecutor's Office initiates an investigation should benefit from them.

(36) Article 86(3) of the Treaty allows the Union legislator to determine the rules applicable to the judicial review of procedural measures taken by the European Public Prosecutor's Office in the performance of its functions. This competence granted to the legislator reflects the specific nature of the European Public Prosecutor's Office, which is different from that of all other Union bodies and agencies and requires special rules regarding judicial review.

(37) Article 86(2) of the Treaty requires that the European Public Prosecutor's Office exercise its functions of prosecutor in the competent courts of the Member States. Acts undertaken by the European Public Prosecutor's Office in the course of its investigations are closely related to the prosecution which may result therefrom and have effects in the legal order of the Member States. In most cases they will be carried out by national law enforcement authorities acting under the instructions of European Public Prosecutor's Office, sometimes after having obtained the authorisation of a national court. It is therefore appropriate to consider the European Public Prosecutor's Office as a national authority for the purpose of the judicial review of its acts of investigation and prosecution. As a result, national courts should be entrusted with the judicial review of all acts of investigation and prosecution of the European Public Prosecutor's Office which may be challenged, and the Court of Justice of the European Union should not be directly competent with regard to those acts pursuant to Articles 263, 265 and 268 of the Treaty, since such acts should not be considered as acts of a body of the Union for the purpose of judicial review.

(38) In accordance with Article 267 of the Treaty, national courts are able or, in certain circumstances, bound to refer to the Court of Justice questions for

---

[4] OJ L 280, 26.10.2010, p. 1.

[5] OJ L 142, 1.6.2012, p. 1.

preliminary rulings on the interpretation or the validity of provisions of Union law, including this Regulation, which are relevant for the judicial review of the acts of investigation and prosecution of the European Public Prosecutor's Office. National courts should not be able to refer questions on the validity of the acts of the European Public Prosecutor's Office to the Court of Justice, since those acts should not be considered acts of a body of the Union for the purpose of judicial review.

(39) It should also be clarified that issues concerning the interpretation of provisions of national law which are rendered applicable by this Regulation should be dealt with by national courts alone. In consequence, those courts may not refer questions to the Court of Justice relating to the interpretation of national law to which this Regulation refers.

(40) As the Treaty prescribes that the European Public Prosecutor's Office is to be set up from Eurojust, they should organically, operationally and administratively co-exist, co-operate and complement each other.

(41) The European Public Prosecutor's Office should also work closely with other Union institutions and agencies in order to facilitate the exercise of its functions under this Regulation and establish, where necessary, formal arrangements on detailed rules relating to exchange of information and cooperation. Cooperation with Europol and OLAF should be of particular importance to avoid duplication and enable the European Public Prosecutor's Office to obtain the relevant information at their disposal as well as to draw on their analyis in specific investigations.

(42) Regulation (EC) 45/2001 of the European Parliament and of the Council of 18 December 2000 on the protection of individuals with regard to the processing of personal data by the Community institutions and bodies and on the free movement of such data[6] applies to the processing of personal data performed by the European Public Prosecutor's Office. This concerns the processing of personal data in the framework of the objectives and tasks of the European Public Prosecutor's Office, personal data related to staff members as well as administrative personal data held by it. The European Data Protection Supervisor should monitor the processing of personal data by the European Public Prosecutor's Office. The principles set out in (EC) No Regulation 45/2001 should be particularised and complemented as regards the processing of operational personal data by the European Public Prosecutor's Office when necessary. When the European Public Prosecutor's Office transfers operational personal data to an authority of a third country or to an international organisation or Interpol by virtue of an international agreement concluded pursuant to Article 218 of the Treaty, the adequate safeguards adduced with respect to the protection of privacy and fundamental

6 OJ L 8, 12.1.2001, p. 1.

rights and freedoms of individuals should ensure that the data protection provisions of this Regulation are complied with.

(43) [Directive 2013/xx/EU on the protection of individuals with regard to the processing of personal data and on the free movement of such data] applies to the processing of personal data by Member States competent authorities for the purposes of the prevention, investigation, detection or prosecution of criminal offences or the execution of criminal penalties.

(44) The data processing system of the European Public Prosecutor's Office should build on the Case Management System of Eurojust, but its temporary work files should be considered case- files from the time an investigation is initiated.

(45) The financial, budgetary and staff regime of the European Public Prosecutor's Office should follow the relevant Union standards applicable to bodies referred to in Article 208 of Regulation (EU, EURATOM) No 966/2012 of the European Parliament and of the Council[7], with due regard, however, to the fact that the competence of the European Public Prosecutor's Office to carry out investigations and prosecutions at Union-level is unique. The European Public Prosecutor's Office should be subject to an annual reporting obligation.

(46) The general rules of transparency applicable to Union agencies should also apply to the European Public Prosecutor's Office but only with regard to its administrative tasks so as not to jeopardise in any manner the requirement of confidentiality in its operational work. In the same manner, administrative inquiries conducted by the European Ombudsman should respect the requirement of confidentiality of the European Public Prosecutor's Office.

(47) In accordance with Article 3 of Protocol (No 21) on the position of the United Kingdom and Ireland in respect of the Area of Freedom, Security and Justice, annexed to the Treaty on European Union and to the Treaty on the Functioning of the European Union, those Member States have notified their wish [not] [to take part] in the adoption and application of this Regulation.

(48) In accordance with Articles 1 and 2 of Protocol (No 22) on the position of Denmark, annexed to the Treaty on European Union and to the Treaty on the Functioning of the European Union, Denmark is not taking part in the adoption of this Regulation and is not bound by it or subject to its application,

(49) The Representatives of the Member States, meeting at Head of State or Government level in Brussels on 13 December 2003 have determined the seat of the European Public Prosecutor's Office,

---

[7] Regulation (EU, EURATOM) No 966/2012 of the European Parliament and of the Council of 25 October 2012 on the financial rules applicable to the general budget of the Union and repealing Council Regulation (EC, Euratom) No 1605/2002, OJ L 298, 26.10.2012, p. 1

HAS ADOPTED THIS REGULATION:

CHAPTER I
SUBJECT MATTER AND DEFINITIONS

Article 1

Subject matter

This Regulation establishes the European Public Prosecutor's Office and sets out rules concerning its functioning.

Article 2

Definitions

For the purposes of this Regulation, the following definitions apply:

a) 'person' means any natural or legal person;
b) 'criminal offences affecting the financial interests of the Union' means the offences provided for by Directive 2013/xx/EU, as implemented by national law;
c) 'financial interests of the Union' means all revenues, expenditures and assets covered by, acquired through, or due to the Union budget and the budgets of institutions, bodies, offices and agencies established under the Treaties and budgets managed and monitored by them;
d) 'administrative personal data' means all personal data processed by the European Public Prosecutor's Office except for operational personal data;
e) 'operational personal data' means all personal data processed by the European Public Prosecutor's Office to meet the purposes laid down in Article 37.

CHAPTER II
GENERAL RULES

Section 1
Status, organisation and structure of the European Public Prosecutor's Office

Article 3

Establishment

1. The European Public Prosecutor's Office is established as a body of the Union with a decentralised structure.
2. The European Public Prosecutor's Office shall have legal personality.
3. The European Public Prosecutor's Office shall cooperate with Eurojust and rely on its administrative support in accordance with Article 57.

Article 4
Tasks

1. The task of the European Public Prosecutor's Office shall be to combat criminal offences affecting the financial interests of the Union.
2. The European Public Prosecutor's Office shall be responsible for investigating, prosecuting and bringing to judgment the perpetrators of, and accomplices in the criminal offences referred to in paragraph 1. In that respect the European Public Prosecutor's Office shall direct and supervise investigations, and carry out acts of prosecution, including the dismissal of the case.
3. The European Public Prosecutor's Office shall exercise the functions of prosecutor in the competent courts of the Member States in respect of the offences referred to in paragraph 1, including lodging the indictment and any appeals until the case has been finally disposed of.

Article 5
Independence and accountability

1. The European Public Prosecutor's Office shall be independent.
2. The European Public Prosecutor's Office, including the European Public Prosecutor, his/her Deputies and the staff, the European Delegated Prosecutors and their national staff, shall neither seek nor take instructions from any person, any Member State or any institution, body, office or agency of the Union in the performance of their duties. The Union institutions, bodies, offices or agencies and the Member States shall respect the independence of the European Public Prosecutor's Office and shall not seek to influence it in the exercise of its tasks.
3. The European Public Prosecutor shall be accountable to the European Parliament, the Council and the European Commission for the general activities of the European Public Prosecutor's Office, in particular by giving an annual report in accordance with Article 70.

Article 6
Structure and organisation of the European Public Prosecutor's Office

1. The structure of the European Public Prosecutor's Office shall comprise a European Public Prosecutor, his/her Deputies, the staff supporting them in the execution of their tasks under this Regulation, as well as European Delegated Prosecutors located in the Member States.
2. The European Public Prosecutor's Office shall be headed by the European Public Prosecutor, who shall direct its activities and organise its work. The European Public Prosecutor shall be assisted by four Deputies.
3. The Deputies shall assist the European Public Prosecutor in all his/her duties and act as a replacement, in accordance with the rules adopted pursuant to Article 72 (d), when he/she is absent or prevented from attending to them. One of the Deputies shall be responsible for the implementation of the budget.
4. The investigations and prosecutions of the European Public Prosecutor's Office shall be carried out by the European Delegated Prosecutors under the direction

and supervision of the European Public Prosecutor. Where it is deemed necessary in the interest of the investigation or prosecution, the European Public Prosecutor may also exercise his/her authority directly in accordance with Article 18(5).

5. There shall be at least one European Delegated Prosecutor in each Member State, who shall be an integral part of the European Public Prosecutor's Office. The European Delegated Prosecutors shall act under the exclusive authority of the European Public Prosecutor and follow only his/her instructions, guidelines and decisions when they carry out investigations and prosecutions assigned to them. When they act within their mandate under this Regulation, they shall be fully independent from the national prosecution bodies and have no obligations with regard to them.
6. The European Delegated Prosecutors may also exercise their function as national prosecutors. In the event of conflicting assignments, the European Delegated Prosecutors shall notify the European Public Prosecutor, who may, after consultation with the competent national prosecution authorities, instruct them in the interest of the investigations and prosecutions of the European Public Prosecutor's Office to give priority to their functions deriving from this Regulation. In such cases, the European Public Prosecutor shall immediately inform the competent national prosecution authorities thereof.
7. Acts performed by the European Public Prosecutor, European Delegated Prosecutors, any of the staff members of the European Public Prosecutor's Office or any other person acting on behalf of it in the performance of their duties shall be attributed to the European Public Prosecutor's Office. The European Public Prosecutor shall represent the European Public Prosecutor's Office towards the Union Institutions, the Member States and third parties.
8. Where necessary for the purpose of an investigation or prosecution, the European Public Prosecutor may temporarily allocate resources and staff to European Delegated Prosecutors.

Article 7

Internal rules of procedure of the European Public Prosecutor's Office

1. The internal rules of procedure of the European Public Prosecutor's Office shall be adopted by a decision of the European Public Prosecutor, his/her four Deputies and five European Delegated Prosecutors, who shall be chosen by the European Public Prosecutor on the basis of a system of strictly equal rotation, reflecting the demographic and geographical range of all the Member States. The decision shall be taken by simple majority, all members having
2. The internal rules of procedure shall govern the organisation of the work of the European Public Prosecutor's Office and shall include general rules on the allocation of cases.

Section 2
Appointment and dismissal of the members of the European Public Prosecutor's Office

Article 8
Appointment and dismissal of the European Public Prosecutor

1. The European Public Prosecutor shall be appointed by the Council with the consent of the European Parliament for a term of eight years, which shall not be renewable. The Council shall act by simple majority.
2. The European Public Prosecutor shall be chosen from persons whose independence is beyond doubt and who possess the qualifications required for appointment to high judicial office and relevant prosecutorial experience.
3. The selection shall be based on an open call for candidates, to be published in the Official Journal of the European Union, following which the Commission shall draw up and submit a shortlist to the European Parliament and the Council. Before the shortlist is submitted, the Commission shall seek the opinion of a panel set up by it and composed of seven persons chosen from among former members of the Court of Justice, members of national supreme courts, national public prosecution services and/or lawyers of recognised competence, one of whom shall be proposed by the European Parliament, as well as the President of Eurojust as an observer.
4. If the European Public Prosecutor no longer fulfils the conditions required for the performance of his/her duties or if he/she has been guilty of serious misconduct, the Court of Justice of the European Union may, on application by the European Parliament, the Council, or the Commission dismiss him/her.

Article 9
Appointment and dismissal of the Deputies of the European Public Prosecutor

1. The Deputies of the European Public Prosecutor shall be appointed in accordance with the rules set out in Article 8(1).
2. The Deputies of the European Public Prosecutor shall be chosen from persons whose independence is beyond doubt and who possess the qualifications required for appointment to high judicial office and relevant prosecutorial experience.
3. The selection shall be based on an open call for candidates, to be published in the Official Journal, following which the European Commission shall draw up and submit, in agreement with the European Public Prosecutor, a shortlist to the European Parliament and the Council, reflecting the demographic balance and geographical range of the Member States.
4. The Deputies may be dismissed in accordance with the rules set out in Article 8(4), on the initiative of the European Public Prosecutor.

Article 10

Appointment and dismissal of the European Delegated Prosecutors

1. The European Delegated Prosecutors shall be appointed by the European Public Prosecutor from a list of at least three candidates, who comply with the requirements set out in paragraph 2, submitted by the Member State(s) concerned. They shall be appointed for a term of five years, which shall be renewable.
2. The European Delegated Prosecutors shall possess the qualifications required for appointment to high judicial office and have relevant prosecutorial experience. Their independence should be beyond doubt. Member States shall appoint the European Delegated Prosecutor as a prosecutor under national law, if at the time of his/her appointment as a European Delegated Prosecutor, he/she did not have this status already.
3. European Delegated Prosecutors may be dismissed by the European Public Prosecutor if they no longer fulfil the requirements set out in paragraph 2, or the criteria applicable to the performance of their duties, or if they have been found guilty of serious misconduct. European Delegated Prosecutors shall not be dismissed as national prosecutors by the competent national authorities without the consent of the European Public Prosecutor during the exercise of their functions on behalf of the European Public Prosecutor's Office.

Section 3
Basic Principles

Article 11

Basic principles of the activities of the European Public Prosecutor's Office

1. The European Public Prosecutor's Office shall ensure that its activities respect the rights enshrined in the Charter of Fundamental Rights of the European Union.
2. The actions of the European Public Prosecutor's Office shall be guided by the principle of proportionality as referred to in Article 26(3).
3. The investigations and prosecutions of the European Public Prosecutor's Office shall be governed by this Regulation. National law shall apply to the extent that a matter is not regulated by this Regulation. The applicable national law shall be the law of the Member State where the investigation or prosecution is conducted. Where a matter is governed by national law and this Regulation, the latter shall prevail.
4. The European Public Prosecutor's Office shall have exclusive competence to investigate and prosecute criminal offences against the Union's financial interests.

5. The European Public Prosecutor's Office shall conduct its investigations in an impartial manner and seek all relevant evidence, whether inculpatory or exculpatory.
6. The European Public Prosecutor's Office shall initiate investigations without undue delay and ensure that investigations and prosecutions are conducted speedily.
7. The competent authorities of the Member States shall actively assist and support the investigations and prosecutions of the European Public Prosecutor's Office at its request and shall refrain from any action, policy or procedure which may delay or hamper their progress.

Section 4
Competence of the European Public Prosecutor's Office

Article 12
Criminal offences within the competence of the European Public Prosecutor's Office

The European Public Prosecutor's Office shall have competence in respect of the criminal offences affecting the financial interests of the Union, as provided for by Directive 2013/xx/EU and implemented by national law.

Article 13
Ancillary competence

1. Where the offences referred to in Article 12 are inextricably linked with criminal offences other than those referred to in Article 12 and their joint investigation and prosecution are in the interest of a good administration of justice the European Public Prosecutor's Office shall also be competent for those other criminal offences, under the conditions that the offences referred to in Article 12 are preponderant and the other criminal offences are based on identical facts. If those conditions are not met, the Member State that is competent for the other offences shall also be competent for the offences referred to in Article 12.
2. The European Public Prosecutor's Office and the national prosecution authorities shall consult each other in order to determine which authority has competence pursuant to paragraph 1. Where appropriate to facilitate the determination of such competence Eurojust may be associated in accordance with Article 57.
3. In case of disagreement between the European Public Prosecutor's Office and the national prosecution authorities over competence pursuant to in paragraph 1, the national judicial authority competent to decide on the attribution of

competences concerning prosecution at national level shall decide on ancillary competence.

4. The determination of competence pursuant to this Article shall not be subject to review.

Article 14

Exercise of the competence of the European Public Prosecutor's Office

The European Public Prosecutor's Office shall exercise its exclusive competence to investigate and prosecute any criminal offence referred to in Articles 12 and 13, where such offence was wholly or partly committed

a) on the territory of one or several Member States, or
b) by one of their nationals, or by Union staff members or members of the Institutions.

CHAPTER III
RULES OF PROCEDURE ON INVESTIGATIONS, PROSECUTIONS AND TRIAL PROCEEDINGS

SECTION 1
CONDUCT OF INVESTIGATIONS

Article 15

Sources of investigation

1. All national authorities of the Member States and all institutions, bodies, offices and agencies of the Union shall immediately inform the European Public Prosecutor's Office of any conduct which might constitute an offence within its competence.
2. Where European Delegated Prosecutors become aware of any conduct which might constitute an offence within the competence of the European Public Prosecutor's Office, they shall immediately inform the European Public Prosecutor.
3. The European Public Prosecutor's Office may collect or receive information from any person on conduct which might constitute an offence within its competence.
4. Any information brought to the attention of the European Public Prosecutor's Office shall be registered and verified by the European Public Prosecutor or the European Delegated Prosecutors. Where they decide, upon verification, not to initiate an investigation, they shall close the case and note the reasons in the Case Management System. They shall inform the national authority, the Union institution, body, office or agency, which provided the information, thereof, and at their request, where appropriate, the persons who provided the information.

Article 16
Initiation of investigations

1. The European Public Prosecutor or, on his/her behalf, the European Delegated Prosecutors shall initiate an investigation by written decision where there are reasonable grounds to believe that an offence within the competence of the European Public Prosecutor's Office is being or has been committed.
2. Where the investigation is initiated by the European Public Prosecutor, he/she shall assign the case to a European Delegated Prosecutor unless he/she wishes to conduct the investigation himself/herself in accordance with the criteria set out in Article 18(5). Where the investigation is initiated by a European Delegated Prosecutor, he/she shall inform the European Public Prosecutor immediately. Upon receipt of such notification, the European Public Prosecutor shall verify that an investigation has not already been initiated by him/her or another European Delegated Prosecutor. In the interest of the efficiency of the investigation the European Public Prosecutor may allocate the case to another European Delegated Prosecutor or decide to take over the case himself/herself in accordance with the criteria set out in Article 18(5).

Article 17
Urgent measures and referrals

1. Where immediate action with regard to an offence within the competence of the European Public Prosecutor's Office is required, the national authorities shall take any urgent measures necessary to ensure effective investigation and prosecution. The national authorities shall subsequently refer the case without delay to the European Public Prosecutor's Office. In that case, the European Public Prosecutor's Office shall confirm, if possible within 48 hours from the initiation of its investigation, the measures taken by the national authorities, even if such measures have been undertaken and executed under rules other than those of this Regulation.
2. At any stage of the investigation, where the case gives rise to doubts as to its competence, the European Public Prosecutor's Office may consult the national prosecution authorities to determine which authority is competent. Pending a decision on competence, the European Public Prosecutor's Office shall take any urgent measures necessary to ensure effective investigation and prosecution of the case. Where the competence of the national authority is established, the national authority shall confirm within 48 hours from the initiation of the national investigation the urgent measures taken by the European Public Prosecutor's Office.
3. Where an investigation initiated by the European Public Prosecutor's Office reveals that the conduct subject to investigation constitutes a criminal offence, which is not within its competence, the European Public Prosecutor's Office shall refer the case without delay to the competent national law enforcement and judicial authorities.

4. Where an investigation initiated by national authorities subsequently reveals that the conduct constitutes an offence within the competence of the European Public Prosecutor's Office, the national authorities shall refer the case without delay to the European Public Prosecutor's Office. In that case, the European Public Prosecutor's Office shall confirm, if possible within 48 hours from the initiation of its investigation, the measures taken by the national authorities, even if such measures have been undertaken and executed under rules other than those of this Regulation.

Article 18
Conducting the investigation

1. The designated European Delegated Prosecutor shall lead the investigation on behalf of and under the instructions of the European Public Prosecutor. The designated European Delegated Prosecutor may either undertake the investigation measures on his/her own or instruct the competent law enforcement authorities in the Member State where he/she is located. These authorities shall comply with the instructions of the European Delegated Prosecutor and execute the investigation measures assigned to them.
2. In cross-border cases, where investigation measures need to be executed in a Member State other than the one where the investigation was initiated, the European Delegated Prosecutor who initiated it, or to whom the case was assigned by the European Public Prosecutor, shall act in close consultation with the European Delegated Prosecutor where the investigation measure needs to be carried out. That European Delegated Prosecutor shall either undertake the investigation measures himself/herself or instruct the competent national authorities to execute them.
3. In cross-border cases the European Public Prosecutor may associate several European Delegated Prosecutors with the investigation and set up joint teams. He/she may instruct any European Delegated Prosecutor to collect relevant information or undertake specific investigation measures on his/her behalf.
4. The European Public Prosecutor shall monitor the investigations conducted by the European Delegated Prosecutors and ensure their coordination. He/she shall instruct them where necessary.
5. The European Public Prosecutor may reallocate the case to another European Delegated Prosecutor or himself/herself lead the investigation if this appears necessary in the interest of the efficiency of the investigation or prosecution on the grounds of one or more of the following criteria:

   a) the seriousness of the offence;
   b) specific circumstances related to the status of the alleged offender;
   c) specific circumstances related to the cross-border dimension of the investigation;
   d) the unavailability of national investigation authorities; or
   e) a request of the competent authorities of the relevant Member State.

6. Where the investigation is undertaken by the European Public Prosecutor directly, he/she shall inform the European Delegated Prosecutor in the Member State where the investigation measures need to be carried out. Any investigation measure conducted by the European Public Prosecutor shall be carried out in liaison with the authorities of the Member State whose territory is concerned. Coercive measures shall be carried out by the competent national authorities.
7. Investigations carried out under the authority of the European Public Prosecutor's Office shall be protected by the rules concerning professional secrecy under the applicable Union legislation. Authorities participating in the investigations of the European Public Prosecutor's Office are also bound to respect professional secrecy as provided under the applicable national law.

Article 19
Lifting privileges or immunities

1. Where the investigations of the European Public Prosecutor's Office involve persons protected by privileges or immunities under national law, and such privilege or immunity presents an obstacle to a specific investigation being conducted, the European Public Prosecutor's Office shall make a reasoned written request for its lifting in accordance with the procedures laid down by that national law.
2. Where the investigations of the European Public Prosecutor's Office involve persons protected by privileges or immunities under Union law, in particular the Protocol on the privileges and immunities of the European Union, and such privilege or immunity presents an obstacle to a specific investigation being conducted, the European Public Prosecutor's Office shall make a reasoned written request for its lifting in accordance with the procedures laid down by Union law.

Section 2
Processing of information

Article 20
Access to information by the European Public Prosecutor's Office

From the moment it registers a case, the European Public Prosecutor's Office shall be able to obtain any relevant information stored in national criminal investigation and law enforcement databases, as well as other relevant registers of public authorities, or have access to such information through European Delegated Prosecutors.

Article 21
Collection of information

1. Where necessary for the purpose of its investigations, the European Public Prosecutor's Office shall obtain, at its request, from Eurojust and Europol, any relevant information concerning an offence within its competence, and may also ask Europol to provide analytical support to a specific investigation conducted by the European Public Prosecutor's Office.
2. The institutions, bodies, offices and agencies of the Union and Member States' authorities shall provide the necessary assistance and information to the European Public Prosecutor's Office upon its request.

Article 22
Case Management System, index and temporary work files

1. The European Public Prosecutor's Office shall establish a Case Management System composed of temporary work files and of an index which contain personal data as referred to in the Annex and non-personal data.
2. The purpose of the Case Management System shall be to:
   a) support the management of investigations and prosecutions conducted by the European Public Prosecutor's Office, in particular by the cross-referencing of information;
   b) facilitate access to information on on-going investigations and prosecutions;
   c) facilitate the monitoring of lawfulness and compliance with the provisions of this Regulation concerning the processing of personal data.
3. The Case Management System may be linked to the secure telecommunications connection referred to in Article 9 of Decision 2008/976/JHA[8].
4. The index shall contain references to temporary work files processed within the framework of the work of the European Public Prosecutor's Office and may contain no personal data other than those referred to in points (a) to (i), (k) and (m) of point (1) and in point 2 of the Annex.
5. In the performance of its duties under this Regulation, the European Public Prosecutor's Office may process data on the individual cases on which it is working in a temporary work file. The European Public Prosecutor's Office shall allow the Data Protection Officer provided for in Article 41 to have access to the temporary work file. The European Public Prosecutor's Office shall inform the Data Protection Officer each time a new temporary work file containing personal data is opened.
6. For the processing of case related personal data, the European Public Prosecutor's Office may not establish any automated data file other than the Case Management System or a temporary work file.

---

[8] OJ L 348, 24.12.2008, p. 130.

Article 23
Functioning of temporary work files and the index

1. A temporary work file shall be opened by the European Public Prosecutor's Office for every case with respect to which information is transmitted to it in so far as this transmission is in accordance with this Regulation or other applicable legal instruments. The European Public Prosecutor's Office shall be responsible for the management of the temporary work files which it has opened.
2. The European Public Prosecutor's Office shall decide, on a case-by-case basis, whether to keep the temporary work file restricted or to give access to it or to parts of it to members of its staff, where necessary to enable such staff to carry out its tasks.
3. The European Public Prosecutor's Office shall decide which information related to a temporary work file shall be introduced in the index. Unless otherwise decided by the European Public Prosecutor, information registered and subject to verification in accordance with Article 15(4) shall not be introduced in the index.

Article 24
Access to the Case Management System

European Delegated Prosecutors and their staff, in so far as they are connected to the Case Management System, may only have access to:

a) the index, unless such access has been expressly denied;
b) temporary work files opened by the European Public Prosecutor's Office related to investigations or prosecutions taking place in their Member State;
c) temporary work files opened by the European Public Prosecutor's Office related to investigations or prosecutions taking place in another Member State in as far as they relate to investigations or prosecutions taking place in their Member State.

SECTION 3
INVESTIGATION MEASURES

Article 25
The European Public Prosecutor's Office's authority to investigate

1. For the purpose of investigations and prosecutions conducted by the European Public Prosecutor's Office, the territory of the Union's Member States shall be considered a single legal area in which the European Public Prosecutor's Office may exercise its competence.
2. Where the European Public Prosecutor's Office decides to exercise its competence over an offence which was partly or wholly committed outside the territory of the Member States by one of their nationals, by Union staff

members or by members of the Institutions, it shall seek assistance to obtain the cooperation of the third country concerned pursuant to the instruments and procedures referred to in Article 59.

Article 26
Investigation measures

1. The European Public Prosecutor's Office shall have the power to request or to order the following investigative measures when exercising its competence:
   a) search any premises, land, means of transport, private home, clothes and any other personal property or computer system;
   b) obtain the production of any relevant object or document, or of stored computer data, including traffic data and banking account data, encrypted or decrypted, either in original or in some other specified form;
   c) seal premises and means of transport and freezing of data, in order to preserve their integrity, to avoid the loss or contamination of evidence or to secure the possibility of confiscation;
   d) freeze instrumentalities or proceeds of crime, including freezing of assets, if they are expected to be subject to confiscation by the trial court and there is reason to believe that the owner, possessor or controller will seek to frustrate the judgement ordering confiscation;
   e) intercept telecommunications, including e-mails, to and from the suspected person, on any telecommunication connection that the suspected person is using;
   f) undertake real-time surveillance of telecommunications by ordering instant transmission of telecommunications traffic data to locate the suspected person and to identify the persons who have been in contact with him at a specific moment in time;
   g) monitor financial transactions, by ordering any financial or credit institution to inform the European Public Prosecutor's Office in real time of any financial transaction carried out through any specific account held or controlled by the suspected person or any other accounts which are reasonably believed to be used in connection with the offence;
   h) freeze future financial transactions, by ordering any financial or credit institution to refrain from carrying out any financial transaction involving any specified account or accounts held or controlled by the suspected person;
   i) undertake surveillance measures in non-public places, by ordering the covert video and audio surveillance of non-public places, excluded video surveillance of private homes, and the recording of its results;
   j) undertake covert investigations, by ordering an officer to act covertly or under a false identity;

k) summon suspected persons and witnesses, where there are reasonable grounds to believe that they might provide information useful to the investigation;
l) undertake identification measures, by ordering the taking of photos, visual recording of persons and the recording of a person's biometric features;
m) seize objects which are needed as evidence;
n) access premises and take samples of goods;
o) inspect means of transport, where reasonable grounds exist to believe that goods related to the investigation are being transported;
p) undertake measures to track and control persons, in order to establish the whereabouts of a person;
q) track and trace any object by technical means, including controlled deliveries of goods and controlled financial transactions;
r) undertake targeted surveillance in public places of the suspected and third persons;
s) obtain access to national or European public registers and registers kept by private entities in a public interest;
t) question the suspected person and witnesses;
u) appoint experts, ex officio or at the request of the suspected person, where specialised knowledge is required.

2. Member States shall ensure that the measures referred to in paragraph 1 may be used in the investigations and prosecutions conducted by the European Public Prosecutor's Office. Such measures shall be subject to the conditions provided for in this Article and those set out in national law. Investigation measures other than those referred to in paragraph 1 may only be ordered or requested by the European Public Prosecutor's Office if available under the law of the Member State where the measure is to be carried out.
3. The individual investigative measures referred to in paragraph 1 shall not be ordered without reasonable grounds and if less intrusive means can achieve the same objective.
4. Member States shall ensure that the investigative measures referred to in points (a)–(j) of paragraph 1 are subject to authorisation by the competent judicial authority of the Member State where they are to be carried out.
5. The investigative measures referred to in points (k) – (u) of paragraph 1 shall be subject to judicial authorisation if required by the national law of the Member State where the investigation measure is to be carried out.
6. If the conditions set out in this Article as well as those applicable under national law for authorising the measure subject to the request are met, the authorisation shall be given within 48 hours in the form of a written and reasoned decision by the competent judicial authority.
7. The European Public Prosecutor's Office may request from the competent judicial authority the arrest or pre-trial detention of the suspected person in accordance with national law.

Section 4
Termination of the investigation and powers of prosecution

Article 27
Prosecution before national courts

1. The European Public Prosecutor and the European Delegated Prosecutors shall have the same powers as national public prosecutors in respect of prosecution and bringing a case to judgement, in particular the power to present trial pleas, participate in evidence taking and exercise the available remedies.
2. When the competent European Delegated Prosecutor considers the investigation to be completed, he/she shall submit a summary of the case with a draft indictment and the list of evidence to the European Public Prosecutor for review. Where he/she does not instruct to dismiss the case pursuant to Article 28, the European Public Prosecutor shall instruct the European Delegated Prosecutor to bring the case before the competent national court with an indictment, or refer it back for further investigations. The European Public Prosecutor may also bring the case to the competent national court himself/herself.
3. The indictment submitted to the competent national court shall list the evidence to be adduced in trial.
4. The European Public Prosecutor shall choose, in close consultation with the European Delegated Prosecutor submitting the case and bearing in mind the proper administration of justice, the jurisdiction of trial and determine the competent national court taking into account the following criteria:
   a) the place where the offence, or in case of several offences, the majority of the offences was committed;
   b) the place where the accused person has his/her habitual residence;
   c) the place where the evidence is located;
   d) the place where the direct victims have their habitual residence.
5. Where necessary for the purposes of recovery, administrative follow-up or monitoring, the European Public Prosecutor shall notify the competent national authorities, the interested persons and the relevant Union institutions, bodies, agencies of the indictment.

Article 28
Dismissal of the case

1. The European Public Prosecutor shall dismiss the case where prosecution has become impossible on account of any of the following grounds:
   a) death of the suspected person;
   b) the conduct subject to investigation does not amount to a criminal offence;

c) amnesty or immunity granted to the suspect;
d) expiry of the national statutory limitation to prosecute;
e) the suspected person has already been finally acquitted or convicted of the same facts within the Union or the case has been dealt with in accordance with Article 29.

2. The European Public Prosecutor may dismiss the case on any of the following grounds:
   a) the offence is a minor offence according to national law implementing *Directive 2013/XX/EU on the fight against fraud to the Union's financial interests by means of criminal law*;
   b) lack of relevant evidence.
3. The European Public Prosecutor's Office may refer cases dismissed by it to OLAF or to the competent national administrative or judicial authorities for recovery, other administrative follow-up or monitoring.
4. Where the investigation was initiated on the basis of information provided by the injured party, the European Public Prosecutor's Office shall inform that party thereof.

Article 29
Transaction

1. Where the case is not dismissed and it would serve the purpose of proper administration of justice, the European Public Prosecutor's Office may, after the damage has been compensated, propose to the suspected person to pay a lump-sum fine which, once paid, entails the final dismissal of the case (transaction). If the suspected person agrees, he/she shall pay the lump sum fine to the Union.
2. The European Public Prosecutor's Office shall supervise the collection of the financial payment involved in the transaction.
3. Where the transaction is accepted and paid by the suspected person, the European Public Prosecutor shall finally dismiss the case and officially notify the competent national law enforcement and judicial authorities and shall inform the relevant Union institutions, bodies, agencies thereof.
4. The dismissal referred to in paragraph 3 shall not be subject to judicial review.

SECTION 5
ADMISSIBILITY OF EVIDENCE

Article 30
Admissibility of evidence

1. Evidence presented by the European Public Prosecutor's Office to the trial court, where the court considers that its admission would not adversely affect the fairness of the procedure or the rights of defence as enshrined in Articles 47 and

48 of the Charter of Fundamental Rights of the European Union, shall be admitted in the trial without any validation or similar legal process even if the national law of the Member State where the court is located provides for different rules on the collection or presentation of such evidence.
2. Once the evidence is admitted, the competence of national courts to assess freely the evidence presented by the European Public Prosecutor's Office at trial shall not be affected.

SECTION 6
CONFISCATION

Article 31

Disposition of the confiscated assets

Where at the request of the European Public Prosecutor's Office the competent national court has decided by a final ruling to confiscate any property related to, or proceeds derived from, an offence within the competence of the European Public Prosecutor's Office, the monetary value of such property or proceeds shall be transferred to the Union's budget, to the extent necessary to compensate the prejudice caused to the Union.

CHAPTER IV
PROCEDURAL SAFEGUARDS

Article 32

Scope of the rights of the suspects and accused persons as well as other persons involved

1. The activities of the European Public Prosecutor's Office shall be carried out in full compliance with the rights of suspected persons enshrined in the Charter of Fundamental Rights of the European Union, including the right to a fair trial and the rights of defence.
2. Any suspect and accused person involved in the proceedings of the European Public Prosecutor's Office shall, as a minimum, have the following procedural rights as they are provided for in Union legislation and the national law of the Member State:
   (a) the right to interpretation and translation, as provided for in Directive 2010/64/EU of the European Parliament and of the Council,
   (b) the right to information and access to the case materials, as provided for in Directive 2012/13/EU of the European Parliament and of the Council,
   (c) the right of access to a lawyer and the right to communicate with and have third persons informed in case of detention, as provided for in [*Directive 2013/xx/EU of the European Parliament and of the Council of xx xxxx*

2013 on the right of access to a lawyer in criminal proceedings and on the right to communicate upon arrest],

(d) the right to remain silent and the right to be presumed innocent,

(e) the right to legal aid,

(f) the right to present evidence, appoint experts and hear witnesses.

3. Suspects and accused persons shall have the rights listed in paragraph 2 from the time that they are suspected of having committed an offence. Once the indictment has been acknowledged by the competent national court, the suspect and accused person's procedural rights shall be based on the national regime applicable in the relevant case.
4. The rights listed in paragraph 2 shall also apply to any person other than a suspect or accused person who is heard by the European Public Prosecutor's Office if, in the course of questioning, interrogation or hearing, he/she becomes suspected of having committed a criminal offence.
5. Without prejudice to the rights provided in this Chapter, suspects and accused persons as well as other persons involved in the proceedings of the European Public Prosecutor's Office shall have all the procedural rights available to them under the applicable national law.

Article 33

Right to remain silent and to be presumed innocent

1. The suspect and accused person involved in the proceedings of the European Public Prosecutor's Office shall have, in accordance with national law, the right to remain silent when questioned, in relation to the facts that he/she is suspected of having committed, and shall be informed that he/she is not obliged to incriminate himself/herself.
2. The suspect and accused person shall be presumed innocent until proven guilty according to national law.

Article 34

Right to legal aid

Any person suspected or accused of an offence within the scope of the competence of the European Public Prosecutor's Office shall have, in accordance with national law, the right to be given legal assistance free or partially free of charge by national authorities if he/she has insufficient means to pay for it.

Article 35

Rights concerning evidence

1. The suspect and accused person shall have, in accordance with national law, the right to present evidence to the consideration of the European Public Prosecutor's Office.

2. The suspect and accused person shall have, in accordance with national law, the right to request the European Public Prosecutor's Office to gather any evidence relevant to the investigation, including appointing experts and hearing witnesses.

CHAPTER V
JUDICIAL REVIEW

Article 36
Judicial review

1. When adopting procedural measures in the performance of its functions, the European Public Prosecutor's Office shall be considered as a national authority for the purpose of judicial review.
2. Where provisions of national law are rendered applicable by this Regulation, such provisions shall not be considered as provisions of Union law for the purpose of Article 267 of the Treaty.

CHAPTER VI
DATA PROTECTION

Article 37
Processing of personal data

1. The European Public Prosecutor's Office may process by automated means or in structured manual files in accordance with this Regulation only the personal data listed in point 1 of the Annex, on persons who, under the national legislation of the Member States concerned are suspected of having committed or having taken part in an offence in respect of which the European Public Prosecutor's Office is competent, or who have been convicted of such an offence, for the following purposes:
   - criminal investigations and prosecutions undertaken in accordance with the present Regulation;
   - information exchange with the competent authorities of Member States and other Union bodies in accordance with the present Regulation;
   - co-operation with third countries in accordance with the present Regulation.
2. The European Public Prosecutor's Office may process only the personal data listed in point 2 of the Annex, on persons who, under the national legislation of the Member States concerned, are regarded as witnesses or victims in a criminal investigation or prosecution regarding one or more of the types of offence for which the European Public Prosecutor's Office is competent, or persons under

the age of 18. The processing of such personal data may only take place if it is strictly necessary for the purposes specified in paragraph 1.

3. In exceptional cases, the European Public Prosecutor's Office may also, for a limited period of time which shall not exceed the time needed for the conclusion of the case related to which the data are processed, process personal data other than those referred to in paragraphs 1 and 2 relating to the circumstances of an offence where they are immediately relevant to and included in on-going investigations which the European Public Prosecutor's Office is pursuing and when their processing is strictly necessary for the purposes specified in paragraph 1, provided that the processing of such specific data takes place in accordance with this Regulation. The Data Protection Officer referred to in Article 41 shall be informed immediately of recourse to this paragraph.
4. Personal data, processed by automated or other means, revealing racial or ethnic origin, political opinions, religious or philosophical beliefs, trade union membership, and data concerning health or sex life may be processed by the European Public Prosecutor's Office only when such data are strictly necessary for his investigations and if they supplement other personal data already processed. The Data Protection Officer shall be informed immediately of recourse to this paragraph. Such data may not be processed in the Index referred to in Article 22(4). Where such other data refer to witnesses or victims within the meaning of paragraph 2, the decision to process them shall be taken by the European Public Prosecutor.
5. Regulation (EC) No 45/2001 shall apply to the processing of personal data by the EPPO in the context of its activities. This Regulation particularises and complements Regulation (EC) No 45/2001 in as far as operational personal data are concerned.

Article 38
Time limits for the storage of personal data

1. Personal data processed by the European Public Prosecutor's Office may not be stored beyond the first applicable among the following dates:
   a) the date on which prosecution is barred under the statute of limitations of all the Member States concerned by the investigation and prosecutions;
   b) the date on which the person has been acquitted and the judicial decision became final;
   c) three years after the date on which the judicial decision of the last of the Member States concerned by the investigation or prosecutions became final;
   d) the date on which the European Public Prosecutor's Office established that it was no longer necessary for it to continue the investigation or prosecution.

2. Observance of the storage deadlines referred to in paragraph 1 shall be reviewed constantly by appropriate automated processing. Nevertheless, a review of the need to store the data shall be carried out every three years after they were entered. If data concerning persons referred to in the Annex are stored for a period exceeding five years, the European Data Protection Supervisor shall be informed accordingly.
3. When one of the storage deadlines referred to in paragraph 1 has expired, the European Public Prosecutor's Office shall review the need to store the data longer in order to enable it to perform its tasks and it may decide by way of derogation to store those data until the following review. The reasons for the continued storage shall be justified and recorded. If no decision is taken on the continued storage of personal data, those data shall be deleted automatically after three years.
4. Where, in accordance with paragraph 3, data has been stored beyond the dates referred to in paragraph 1, a review of the need to store those data shall take place every three years by the European Data Protection Supervisor.
5. Where a file exists containing non-automated and unstructured data, once the deadline for storage of the last item of automated data from the file has elapsed all documents in the file and any copies shall be destroyed.

Article 39

Logging and documentation

1. For the purposes of verification of the lawfulness of the data processing, self-monitoring and ensuring proper data integrity and security, the European Public Prosecutor's Office shall keep records of any collection, alteration, access, disclosure, combination or erasure of personal data used for operational purposes. Such logs or documentation shall be deleted after 18 months, unless the data are further required for on-going control.
2. Logs or documentation prepared under paragraph 1 shall be communicated on request to the European Data Protection Supervisor. The European Data Protection Supervisor shall use this information only for the purpose of data protection supervision, ensuring proper data processing, and data integrity and security.

Article 40

Authorised access to personal data

Only the European Public Prosecutor, the European Delegated Prosecutors and authorised members of their staff may, for the purpose of achieving their tasks and within the limits provided for in this
Regulation, have access to personal data processed by the European Public Prosecutor's Office for its operational tasks.

Article 41

Data protection officer

1. The European Public Prosecutor shall appoint a Data Protection Officer in accordance with Article 24 of Regulation (EC) No 45/2001.
2. When complying with the obligations set out in Article 24 of Regulation (EC) No 45/2001, the Data Protection Officer shall:
   a) ensure that a written record of the transfer of personal data is kept;
   b) cooperate with the staff of the European Public Prosecutor's Office responsible for procedures, training and advice on data processing;
   c) prepare an annual report and communicate that report to the European Public Prosecutor and to the European Data Protection Supervisor.
3. In the performance of his tasks, the Data Protection Officer shall have access to all the data processed by the European Public Prosecutor's Office and to all of the Office's premises.
4. The staff members of the European Public Prosecutor's Office assisting the Data Protection Officer in the performance of his/her duties shall have access to the personal data processed by it and to its premises to the extent necessary for the performance of their tasks.
5. If the Data Protection Officer considers that the provisions of Regulation (EC) No 45/2001 or this Regulation related to the processing of personal data have not been complied with, he/she shall inform the European Public Prosecutor, requiring him/her to resolve the non- compliance within a specified time. If the European Public Prosecutor does not resolve the non-compliance of the processing within the specified time, the Data Protection Officer shall refer the matter to the European Data Protection Supervisor.
6. The European Public Prosecutor shall adopt the implementing rules referred to in Article 24(8) of Regulation (EC) No 45/2001.

Article 42

Modalities regarding the exercise of the right of access

1. Any data subject may exercise the right of access to personal data in accordance with Regulation (EC) No 45/2001 and in particular Article 13 thereof.
2. When the right of access is restricted in accordance with Article 20 paragraph 1 of Regulation (EC) No 45/2001, the European Public Prosecutor's Office shall inform the data subject in accordance with Article 20(3) in writing. The information about the principal reasons on which the application of the restriction is based may be omitted where the provision of such information would deprive the restriction of its effect. The data subject shall at least be informed that all necessary verifications by the European Data Protection Supervisor have taken place.

3. The European Public Prosecutor's Office shall document the grounds for omitting the communication of the principal reasons on which the restriction referred to in paragraph 2 is based.
4. When in application of Articles 46 and 47 of Regulation (EC) No 45/2001, the European Data Protection Supervisor checks the lawfulness of the processing performed by the European Public Prosecutor's Office, he/she shall inform the data subject at least that all necessary verifications by the European Data Protection Supervisor have taken place.

Article 43

Right to rectification, erasure and restrictions on processing

1. If personal data processed by the European Public Prosecutor's Office have to be rectified, erased or whose processing has to be restricted in accordance with Articles 14, 15 or 16 of Regulation (EC) No 45/2001 the European Public Prosecutor's Office shall rectify, erase or restrict the processing of such data.
2. In the cases referred to in Articles 14, 15 or 16 of Regulation (EC) No 45/2001, all addressees of such data shall be notified forthwith in accordance with Article 17 of Regulation (EC) No 45/2001. In accordance with rules applicable to them, the addressees shall then rectify, erase or restrict the processing of those data in their systems.
3. The European Public Prosecutor's Office shall inform the data subject in writing without undue delay and in any case within three months of the receipt of the request that data concerning him or her have been rectified, erased or their processing restricted.
4. The European Public Prosecutor's Office shall inform the data subject in writing on any refusal of rectification, of erasure or of restrictions to the processing, and the possibility of lodging a complaint with the European Data Protection Supervisor and seeking a judicial remedy.

Article 44

Responsibility in data protection matters

1. The European Public Prosecutor's Office shall process personal data in such a way that that it can be established which authority provided the data or where the personal data has been retrieved from.
2. The responsibility for compliance with Regulation (EC) No 45/2001 and this Regulation shall lie with the European Public Prosecutor. The responsibility for the legality of transfer of personal data provided to the European Public Prosecutor's Office shall lie with the provider of the personal data, and with the European Public Prosecutor's Office for the personal data provided to Member States, Union bodies and third countries or organisations.
3. Subject to other provisions in this Regulation, the European Public Prosecutor's Office shall be responsible for all data processed by it.

Article 45

Cooperation between the European Data Protection Supervisor and national data protection authorities

1. The European Data Protection Supervisor shall act in close cooperation with national authorities competent for data protection supervision with respect to specific issues requiring national involvement, in particular if the European Data Protection Supervisor or a national authority competent for data protection supervision finds major discrepancies between practices of the Member States or potentially unlawful transfers using the communication channels of the European Public Prosecutor's Office, or in the context of questions raised by one or more national supervisory authorities on the implementation and interpretation of this Regulation.
2. In cases referred to under paragraph 1 the European Data Protection Supervisor and the national authorities competent for data protection supervision may, each acting within the scope of their respective competences, exchange relevant information, assist each other in carrying out audits and inspections, examine difficulties of interpretation or application of this Regulation, study problems related to the exercise of independent supervision or to the exercise of the rights of data subjects, draw up harmonised proposals for joint solutions to any problems and promote awareness of data protection rights, as necessary.
3. The National Supervisory Authorities and the European Data Protection Supervisor shall meet for the purposes outlined in this Article, as needed. The costs and servicing of these meetings shall be for the account of the European Data Protection Supervisor. Rules of procedure shall be adopted at the first meeting. Further working methods shall be developed jointly as necessary.

Article 46

Right to lodge a complaint with the European Data Protection Supervisor

1. Where a complaint introduced by a data subject pursuant to Article 32(2) of Regulation (EC) No 45/2001 relates to a decision as referred to in Article 43, the European Data Protection Supervisor shall consult the national supervisory bodies or the competent judicial body in the Member State which was the source of the data or the Member State directly concerned. The decision of the European Data Protection Supervisor, which may extend to a refusal to communicate any information, shall be taken in close cooperation with the national supervisory body or competent judicial body.
2. Where a complaint relates to the processing of data provided to the European Public Prosecutor's Office by Union bodies, third countries or organisations or private parties, the European Data Protection Supervisor shall ensure that the necessary checks have been carried out by the European Public Prosecutor's Office.

Article 47
Liability for unauthorised or incorrect processing of data

1. The European Public Prosecutor's Office shall be liable, in accordance with Article 340 of the Treaty, for any damage caused to an individual which results from unauthorised or incorrect processing of data carried out by it.
2. Complaints against the European Public Prosecutor's Office pursuant to the liability referred to in paragraph 1 shall be heard by the Court of Justice in accordance with Article 268 of the Treaty.

CHAPTER VII
FINANCIAL AND STAFF PROVISIONS

SECTION 1
FINANCIAL PROVISIONS

Article 48
Financial actors

1. The European Public Prosecutor shall be responsible for taking decisions on financial and budgetary matters.
2. The Deputy designated by the European Public Prosecutor in accordance with Article 6(3) shall be responsible for the implementation of the budget of the European Public Prosecutor's Office as authorising officer.

Article 49
Budget

1. Estimates of all the revenue and expenditure of the European Public Prosecutor's Office shall be prepared for each financial year, corresponding to the calendar year, and shall be shown in its budget.
2. The budget of the European Public Prosecutor's Office shall be balanced in terms of revenue and of expenditure.
3. Without prejudice to other resources, the revenue of the European Public Prosecutor's Office shall comprise:
   a) a contribution from the Union entered in the general budget of the Union;
   b) charges for publications and any service provided by the European Public Prosecutor's Office.
4. The expenditure of the European Public Prosecutor's Office shall include staff remuneration, administrative and infrastructure expenses, and operating costs.
5. Where European Delegated Prosecutors act within the framework of the tasks of the European Public Prosecutor's Office, the relevant expenditure related to these activities shall be regarded as operational expenditure.

Article 50
Establishment of the budget

1. Each year the Deputy of the European Public Prosecutor referred to in Article 48 shall draw up a provisional draft estimate of the revenue and expenditure of the European Public Prosecutor's Office for the following financial year. The European Public Prosecutor shall, on the basis of that draft, produce a provisional draft estimate of the revenue and expenditure of the European Public Prosecutor's Office for the following financial year.
2. The provisional draft estimate of the revenue and expenditure of the European Public Prosecutor's Office shall be sent to the Commission no later than 31 January each year. The European Public Prosecutor shall send a final draft estimate, which shall include a draft establishment plan, to the Commission by 31 March.
3. The Commission shall send the statement of estimates to the European Parliament and the Council (the budgetary authority) together with the draft general budget of the Union.
4. On the basis of the statement of estimates, the Commission shall enter in the draft general budget of the Union the estimates it considers necessary for the establishment plan and the amount of the contribution to be charged to the general budget, which it shall submit to the budgetary authority in accordance with Articles 313 and 314 of the Treaty.
5. The budgetary authority shall authorise the appropriations for the contribution of the European Public Prosecutor's Office.
6. The budgetary authority shall adopt the establishment plan of the European Public Prosecutor's Office.
7. The European Public Prosecutor shall adopt the budget of the European Public Prosecutor's Office. It shall become final following final adoption of the general budget of the Union. Where necessary, it shall be adjusted accordingly.
8. For any building project likely to have significant implications for the budget the European Public Prosecutor's Office shall inform the European Parliament and the Council as early as possible in accordance with the provisions of Article 203 of Regulation (EU, Euratom) No 966/2012.
9. Except in cases of force majeure referred to in Article 203 of Regulation (EU, Euratom) No 966/2012 shall deliberate upon the building project within four weeks of its receipt by both institutions. The building project shall be deemed approved at the expiry of this four-week period, unless the European Parliament or the Council take a decision contrary to the proposal within that period of time. If the European Parliament or the Council raise duly justified concerns within that four-week period, that period shall be extended once by two weeks. If the European Parliament or the Council take a decision contrary to the building project, the European Public Prosecutor's Office shall withdraw its proposal and may submit a new one.

10. The European Public Prosecutor's Office may finance a budget acquisition project through a loan subject to prior approval of the budgetary authority in accordance with Article 203(8) of Regulation (EU, Euratom) No 966/2012.

Article 51

Implementation of the budget

1. The Deputy of the European Public Prosecutor referred to in Article 48, acting as the authorising officer of the European Public Prosecutor's Office, shall implement its budget under his or her own responsibility and within the limits authorised in budget.
2. Each year the Deputy of the European Public Prosecutor referred to in Article 48 shall send to the budgetary authority all information relevant to the findings of the evaluation procedures.

Article 52

Presentation of accounts and discharge

1. The accounting officer of Eurojust shall act as the accounting officer of the European Public Prosecutor's Office in the implementation of its budget. The necessary arrangements so as to avoid any conflict of interest shall be made.
2. By 1 March following each financial year, the accounting officer of the European Public Prosecutor's Office shall send the provisional accounts to the Commission's Accounting Officer and the Court of Auditors.
3. The European Public Prosecutor's Office shall send the report on the budgetary and financial management to the European Parliament, the Council and the Court of Auditors, by 31 March of the following financial year.
4. By 31 March following each financial year, the Commission's accounting officer shall send the provisional accounts of the European Public Prosecutor's Office consolidated with the Commission's accounts to the Court of Auditors.
5. In accordance with Article 148(1) of Regulation (EU, Euratom) No 966/2012, the Court of Auditors shall, by 1 June of the following year at the latest, make its observations on the provisional accounts of the European Public Prosecutor's Office.
6. On receipt of the Court of Auditors' observations on the provisional accounts of the European Public Prosecutor's Office pursuant to Article 148 of Regulation (EU, Euratom) No 966/2012, the accounting officer of the European Public Prosecutor's Office shall draw up its final accounts under his/her own responsibility.
7. The accounting officer of the European Public Prosecutor's Office shall, by 1 July following each financial year, send the final accounts to the European Parliament, the Council, the Commission and the Court of Auditors.

8. The final accounts of the European Public Prosecutor's Office shall be published in the Official Journal of the European Union by 15 November of the following year.
9. The deputy of the European Public Prosecutor referred to in Article 48 shall send the Court of Auditors a reply to its observations by 30 September of the following year at the latest. The replies of the European Public Prosecutor's Office shall be sent to the Commission at the same time.
10. The Deputy of the European Public Prosecutor referred to in Article 48 shall submit to the European Parliament, at the latter's request, any information required for the smooth application of the discharge procedure for the financial year in question in accordance with Article 165(3) of Regulation (EU, Euratom) No 966/2012.
11. On a recommendation from the Council acting by a qualified majority, the European Parliament, shall, before 15 May of year N + 2, give a discharge to the deputy of the European Public Prosecutor referred to in Article 48 in respect of the implementation of the budget for year N.

Article 53
Financial rules

The financial rules applicable to the European Public Prosecutor's Office shall be adopted by the European Public Prosecutor in accordance with [Regulation 2343/2002 of 23 December 2002 on the framework Financial Regulation for the bodies referred to in Article 185 of Council Regulation (EC, Euratom) No 1605/2002 on the Financial Regulation applicable to the general budget of the European Communities] and after consultation with the Commission. They shall not depart from [*Regulation 2343/2002*] unless such departure is specifically required for the operation of the European Public Prosecutor's Office and the Commission has given its prior consent.

SECTION 2
STAFF PROVISIONS

Article 54
General provisions

1. The Staff Regulations of the European Union[9] and the Conditions of Employment of Other Servants of the European Union and the rules adopted by agreement between the institutions of the European Union for giving effect to those Staff Regulations and those Conditions of Employment of Other Servants

[9] Council Regulation No 31 (EEC), 11 (EAEC) of 18 December 1961 laying down the Staff Regulations for Officials and the Conditions of Employment of Other Servants of the European Economic Community and the European Atomic Energy Community, OJ P 045, 14.6.1962, p. 1385, as amended, in particular, by Council Regulation 259/68, of 29 February 1968 (OJ L 56, 4.3.1968, p. 1), as itself subsequently amended.

shall apply to the European Public Prosecutor, the Deputies and the staff of the European Public Prosecutor's Office, unless otherwise stipulated in this Section.
2. The powers conferred on the appointing authority by the Staff Regulations and by the Conditions of Employment of Other Servants to conclude Contracts of Employment shall be exercised by the European Public Prosecutor with respect to the staff of the European Public Prosecutor's Office.
3. The European Public Prosecutor shall adopt appropriate implementing rules to the Staff Regulations and the Conditions of Employment of Other Servants in accordance with Article 110 of the Staff Regulations. The European Public Prosecutor shall also adopt staff resource programming as part of the programming document.
4. The Protocol on the Privileges and Immunities of the European Union shall apply to the European Public Prosecutor's Office and its staff.
5. European Delegated Prosecutors shall be engaged as Special Advisors in accordance with Articles 5, 123 and 124 of the Conditions of Employment of Other Servants of the European Union. The competent national authorities shall facilitate the exercise of the functions of European Delegated Prosecutors under this Regulation and refrain from any action or policy which may adversely affect their career and status in the national prosecution system. In particular, the competent national authorities shall provide the European Delegated Prosecutors with the resources and equipment necessary to exercise their functions under this Regulation, and ensure that they are fully integrated into their national prosecution services.

Article 55

Seconded national experts and other staff

1. The European Public Prosecutor's Office may make use of Seconded national experts or other persons not employed by it. The Seconded national experts shall be subject to the authority of the European Public Prosecutor in the exercise of tasks related to the functions of the European Public Prosecutor's Office.
2. The European Public Prosecutor shall adopt a decision laying down rules on the secondment of national experts to the European Public Prosecutor's Office and further implementing provisions as may be necessary.

CHAPTER VIII
PROVISIONS ON THE RELATIONS OF THE EUROPEAN PUBLIC PROSECUTOR'S OFFICE WITH ITS PARTNERS

Section 1
COMMON PROVISIONS

Article 56
Common provisions

1. In so far as necessary for the performance of its tasks, the European Public Prosecutor's Office may establish and maintain cooperative relations with Union bodies or agencies in accordance with the objectives of those bodies or agencies, the competent authorities of third countries, international organisations and the International Criminal Police Organisation (Interpol).
2. In so far as relevant to the performance of its tasks, the European Public Prosecutor's Office may, in accordance with Article 61, directly exchange all information, with the exception of personal data, with the entities referred to in paragraph 1.
3. The European Public Prosecutor's Office may receive, in accordance with Article 4 of Regulation (EC) No 45/2001, and process personal data received from the entities referred to in paragraph 1 in so far as necessary for the performance of its tasks and subject to the provisions of Section 3.
4. Personal data shall only be transferred by the European Public Prosecutor's Office to third countries, international organisations, and Interpol if this is necessary for preventing and combating offences that fall under the competence of the European Public Prosecutor's Office and in accordance with this Regulation.
5. Onward transfers to third parties of personal data received from the European Public Prosecutor's Office by Member States, Union bodies or agencies, third countries and international organisations or Interpol shall be prohibited unless the European Public Prosecutor's Office has given its explicit consent after considering the circumstances of the case at hand, for a specific purpose that is not incompatible with the purpose for which the data was transmitted.

SECTION 2
RELATIONS WITH PARTNERS

Article 57
Relations with Eurojust

1. The European Public Prosecutor's Office shall establish and maintain a special relationship with Eurojust based on close cooperation and the development of operational, administrative and management links between them as defined below.

2. In operational matters, the European Public Prosecutor's Office may associate Eurojust with its activities concerning cross-border or complex cases by:
   a) sharing information, including personal data, on its investigations, in particular where they reveal elements which may fall outside the material or territorial competence of the European Public Prosecutor's Office;
   b) requesting Eurojust or its competent national member(s) to participate in the coordination of specific acts of investigation regarding specific aspects which may fall outside the material or territorial competence of the European Public Prosecutor's Office;
   c) facilitating the agreement between the European Public Prosecutor's Office and the Member State(s) concerned on ancillary competence in accordance with Article 13 without prejudice to a possible settlement by the judicial authority of the Member State concerned and competent to decide on the matter;
   d) requesting Eurojust or its competent national member(s) to use the powers attributed to them by Union legislation or national law regarding specific acts of investigation which may fall outside the material or territorial competence of the European Public Prosecutor's Office;
   e) sharing information with Eurojust or its competent national member(s) on prosecution decisions referred to at Articles 27, 28 and 29 before their submission to the European Public Prosecutor where Eurojust competences may be affected and this is appropriate in the light of Eurojust's previous involvement in the case;
   f) requesting Eurojust or its competent national member(s) to provide support in the transmission of its decisions or requests for mutual legal assistance to, and execution in, States members of Eurojust but not taking part in the establishment of the European Public Prosecutor's Office or third countries.
3. The European Public Prosecutor's Office shall have access to a mechanism for automatic cross-checking of data in Eurojust's Case Management System. Whenever a match is found between data entered into the Case Management System by the European Public Prosecutor's Office and data entered by Eurojust, the fact that there is a match will be communicated to both Eurojust and the European Public Prosecutor's Office, as well as the Member State which provided the data to Eurojust. In cases where the data was provided by a third country, Eurojust will only inform that third country of the match found with the consent of the European Public Prosecutor's Office.
4. The cooperation established in accordance with paragraph 1 shall entail the exchange of information, including personal data. Any data thus exchanged shall only be used for the purposes for which it was provided. Any other usage of the data shall only be allowed in as far as such usage falls within the mandate of the body receiving the data, and subject to the prior authorisation of the body which provided the data.

5. The European Public Prosecutor shall designate the staff members authorised to have access to the results of the cross-checking mechanism and inform Eurojust thereof.
6. The European Public Prosecutor's Office shall rely on the support and resources of the administration of Eurojust. The details of this arrangement shall be regulated by an Agreement. Eurojust shall provide the following services to the European Public Prosecutor's Office:
   a) technical support in the preparation of the annual budget, the programming document containing the annual and multi-annual programming, and the management plan;
   b) technical support in staff recruitment and career-management;
   c) security services;
   d) Information Technology services;
   e) financial management, accounting and audit services;
   f) any other services of common interest.

Article 58

Relations with Union institutions, agencies and other bodies

1. The European Public Prosecutor's Office shall develop a special relationship with Europol.
2. The cooperation established in accordance with paragraph 1 shall entail the exchange of information, including personal data. Any data thus exchanged shall only be used for the purposes for which it was provided. Any other usage of the data shall only be allowed in as far as such usage falls within the mandate of the body receiving the data, and subject to the prior authorisation of the body which provided the data.
3. The European Public Prosecutor's Office shall cooperate with the Commission, including OLAF, for the purpose of implementing the obligations under Article 325(3) of the Treaty. To this end, they shall conclude an agreement setting out the modalities of their cooperation.
4. The European Public Prosecutor's Office shall establish and maintain cooperative relations with other Union institutions, bodies, offices and agencies.

Article 59

Relations with third countries and international organisations

1. The European Public Prosecutor's Office may establish working arrangements with the entities referred to in Article 56(1). Such working arrangements may, in particular, concern the exchange of strategic information and the secondment of liaison officers to the European Public Prosecutor's Office.
2. The European Public Prosecutor's Office may designate, in agreement with the competent authorities, contact points in third countries in order to facilitate cooperation.

3. In accordance with Article 218 of the Treaty, the European Commission may submit to the Council proposals for the negotiation of agreements with one or more third countries regarding the cooperation between the European Public Prosecutor's Office and the competent authorities of these third countries with regard to legal assistance in criminal matters and extradition in cases falling under the competence of the European Public Prosecutor's Office.
4. Concerning the criminal offences within its material competence, the Member States shall either recognise the European Public Prosecutor's Office as a competent authority for the purpose of the implementation of their international agreements on legal assistance in criminal matters and extradition, or, where necessary, alter those international agreements to ensure that the European Public Prosecutor's Office can exercise its functions on the basis of such agreements when it assumes its tasks in accordance with Article 75(2).

SECTION 3
TRANSFER OF PERSONAL DATA

Article 60
Transfer of personal data to Union bodies or agencies

Subject to any restrictions pursuant to this Regulation, the European Public Prosecutor's Office may directly transfer personal data to Union bodies or agencies in so far as it is necessary for the performance of its tasks or those of the recipient Union body or agency.

Article 61
Transfer of personal data to third countries and international organisations

1. The European Public Prosecutor's Office may transfer personal data to an authority of a third country or to an international organisation or Interpol, in so far as this is necessary for it to perform its tasks, only on the basis of:
   a) a decision of the Commission adopted in accordance with [Articles 25 and 31 of Directive 95/46/EC] that that country or international organisation, or a processing sector within that third country or international organisation ensures an adequate level of protection (adequacy decision); or
   b) an international agreement concluded between the Union and that third country or international organisation pursuant to Article 218 of the Treaty adducing adequate safeguards with respect to the protection of privacy and fundamental rights and freedoms of individuals.

Such transfer does not require further authorisation.

The European Public Prosecutor's Office may conclude working arrangements to implement such agreements or adequacy decisions.

2. By way of derogation from paragraph 1, the European Public Prosecutor may authorise the transfer of personal data to third countries or international organisations or Interpol on a case- by-case basis if:
   a) the transfer of data is absolutely necessary to safeguard the essential interests of the Union, including its financial interests, within the scope of the objectives of the European Public Prosecutor's Office;
   b) the transfer of the data is absolutely necessary in the interests of preventing imminent danger associated with crime or terrorist offences;
   c) the transfer is otherwise necessary or legally required on important public interest grounds of the Union or its Member States, as recognised by Union law or by national law, or for the establishment, exercise or defence of legal claims; or
   d) the transfer is necessary to protect the vital interests of the data subject or another person.
3. Moreover the European Public Prosecutor may, in agreement with the European Data Protection Supervisor, authorise a set of transfers in conformity with points a) to d) above, taking into account the existence of safeguards with respect to the protection of privacy and fundamental rights and freedoms of individuals, for a period not exceeding one year, renewable.
4. The European Data Protection Supervisor shall be informed of cases where paragraph 3 was applied.
5. The European Public Prosecutor's Office may transfer administrative personal data in accordance with Article 9 of Regulation (EC) No 45/2001.

CHAPTER IX
GENERAL PROVISIONS

Article 62
Legal status and operating conditions

1. In each of the Member States the European Public Prosecutor's Office shall enjoy the most extensive legal capacity accorded to legal persons under their laws. It may, in particular, acquire and dispose of movable and immovable property and be party to legal proceedings.
2. The necessary arrangements concerning the accommodation provided for the European Public Prosecutor's Office and the facilities made available by the host Member State together with the specific rules applicable in that Member State to the European Public Prosecutor, his/her Deputies and their staff, and members of their families, shall be laid down in a Headquarters Agreement concluded between the European Public Prosecutor's Office and the host Member State no later than [2 years after the entry into force of this regulation].

3. The host Member State of the European Public Prosecutor's Office shall provide the best possible conditions to ensure the functioning of the European Public Prosecutor's Office, including multilingual, European-oriented schooling and appropriate transport connections.

Article 63

Language arrangements

1. Regulation No 1[10] shall apply to the acts provided in Articles 7 and 72.
2. The translation services required for the functioning of the European Public Prosecutor's Office shall be provided by the Translation Centre of the bodies of the European Union.

Article 64

Confidentiality

1. The European Public Prosecutor, the Deputies and the staff, European Delegated Prosecutors and their national staff shall be bound by an obligation of confidentiality with respect to any information which has come to their knowledge in the course of the performance of their tasks.
2. The obligation of confidentiality shall apply to all persons and to all bodies called upon to work with the European Public Prosecutor's Office.
3. The obligation of confidentiality shall also apply after leaving office or employment or after the termination of the activities of the persons referred to in paragraphs 1 and 2.
4. The obligation of confidentiality shall apply to all information received by the European Public Prosecutor's Office, unless that information has already been made public or is accessible to the public.
5. Members and the staff of the European Data Protection Supervisor shall be subject to the obligation of confidentiality with respect to any information which has come to their knowledge in the course of the performance of their tasks.

Article 65

Transparency

1. Regulation (EC) No 1049/2001 shall apply to documents which relate to the administrative tasks of the European Public Prosecutor's Office.
2. The European Public Prosecutor shall, within six months of the date of its establishment adopt the detailed rules for applying Regulation (EC) No 1049/2001.
3. Decisions taken by the European Public Prosecutor's Office under Article 8 of Regulation (EC) No 1049/2001 may form the subject of a complaint to the Ombudsman or of an action before the Court of Justice of the European Union, under the conditions laid down in Articles 228 and 263 of the Treaty respectively.

[10] OJ L 17, 6.10.1958, p. 385.

Article 66

OLAF and the European Court of Auditors

1. In order to facilitate combating fraud, corruption and other unlawful activities under Regulation (EC) No 1073/1999 of the European Parliament and of the Council[11], within six months from the day the European Public Prosecutor's Office becomes operational, it shall accede to the Interinstitutional Agreement of 25 May 1999 concerning internal investigations by OLAF and adopt the appropriate provisions applicable to all the employees of the European Public Prosecutor's Office using the template set out in the Annex to that Agreement.
2. The European Court of Auditors shall have the power of audit, on the basis of documents and on the spot, over all grant beneficiaries, contractors and subcontractors who have received Union funds from the European Public Prosecutor's Office.
3. OLAF may carry out investigations, including on-the-spot checks and inspections, in accordance with the provisions and procedures laid down in Regulation (EC) No 1073/1999 and Council Regulation (Euratom, EC) No 2185/96[12] with a view to establishing whether there have been any irregularities affecting the financial interests of the Union in connection with expenditure funded by the European Public Prosecutor's Office.
4. Without prejudice to paragraphs 1, 2 and 3, working arrangements with third countries and international organisations or Interpol, contracts, grant agreements and grant decisions of the European Public Prosecutor's Office shall contain provisions expressly empowering the European Court of Auditors and OLAF to conduct such audits and investigations, according to their respective competences.

Article 67

Security rules on the protection of classified information

The European Public Prosecutor's Office shall apply the security principles contained in the Commission's security rules for protecting European Union Classified Information (EUCI) and sensitive non-classified information, as set out in the annex to Commission Decision 2001/844/EC, ECSC, Euratom[13]. This shall cover, inter alia, provisions for the exchange, processing and storage of such information.

---

[11] OJ L 136, 31.5.1999, p. 1.

[12] OJ L 292, 15.11.1996, p. 2.

[13] OJ L 317, 3.12.2011, p. 1.

Article 68
Administrative inquiries

The administrative activities of the European Public Prosecutor's Office shall be subject to the inquiries of the European Ombudsman in accordance with Article 228 of the Treaty.

Article 69
General regime of liability

1. The contractual liability of the European Public Prosecutor's Office shall be governed by the law applicable to the contract in question.
2. The Court of Justice of the European Union shall have jurisdiction to give judgment pursuant to any arbitration clause contained in a contract concluded by the European Public Prosecutor's Office.
3. In the case of non-contractual liability, the European Public Prosecutor's Office shall, in accordance with the general principles common to the laws of the Member States and independently of any liability under Article 47, make good any damage caused by the European Public Prosecutor's Office or its staff in the performance of their duties in so far as it may be imputed to them.
4. Paragraph 3 shall also apply to damage caused through the fault of a European Delegated Prosecutor in the performance of his duties.
5. The Court of Justice of the European Union shall have jurisdiction in disputes over compensation for damages referred to in paragraph 3.
6. The national courts of the Member States competent to deal with disputes involving the liability of the European Public Prosecutor's Office as referred to in this Article shall be determined by reference to Council Regulation (EC) No 44/2001[14]
7. The personal liability of its staff towards the European Public Prosecutor's Office shall be governed by the provisions laid down in the Staff Regulations or Conditions of Employment applicable to them.

Article 70
Reporting

1. The European Public Prosecutor's Office shall issue an Annual Report on its general activities. It shall transmit this report to the European Parliament and to national Parliaments, as well as to the Council and the Commission.
2. The European Public Prosecutor shall appear once a year before the European Parliament and the Council to give account of the general activities of the European Public Prosecutor's Office, taking into account the obligation of discretion and confidentiality. Upon request, he/she shall also appear before the Commission.

---

[14] OJ L 12, 16.1.2001, p. 1. Regulation (EC) 44/2001 is replaced by Regulation (EU) No 1215/2012 as from 10.01.2015.

3. National Parliaments may invite the European Public Prosecutor or European Delegated Prosecutors to participate in an exchange of views in relation to the general activities of the European Public Prosecutor's Office.

CHAPTER X
FINAL PROVISIONS

Article 71
Transitional provisions

1. Before exercising its tasks the European Public Prosecutor shall take any measures necessary for the setting up of the European Public Prosecutor's Office.
2. Without prejudice to Article 9, the first appointment of two of the Deputies to the European Public Prosecutor, to be chosen by lot, shall be made for a period of 6 years.
3. Member States shall remain competent until the date on which the European Public Prosecutor's Office has been set up and assumed its tasks in accordance with Article 75(2). The European Public Prosecutor's Office shall exercise its competence with regard to any offence within its competence committed after that date. The European Public Prosecutor's Office may also exercise its competence with regard to any offence within its competence committed before that date if no competent national authority is already investigating or prosecuting it.

Article 72
Administrative rules and programme documents

The European Public Prosecutor shall:
a) adopt each year the programming document containing annual and multi-annual programming of the European Public Prosecutor's Office;
b) adopt an anti-fraud strategy, which is proportionate to the fraud risks having regard to the cost-benefit of the measures to be implemented;
c) adopt rules for the prevention and management of conflicts of interest in respect of the European Delegated Prosecutors;
d) adopt rules on the status, performance criteria, rights and obligations of the Deputies and the European Delegated Prosecutors, as well as the rotation of European Delegated Prosecutors for the purpose of implementing Article 7;
e) adopt rules on the handling of transactions made in accordance with Article 29 and the modalities to calculate the amounts of the fine to be paid;
f) adopt rules on the modalities of giving feedback to persons or entities which have provided information to the European Public Prosecutor's Office;

g) adopt detailed rules concerning the application of Regulation (EC) No 1049/2001 in its activities;
h) implementing rules referred to in Article 24(8) of Regulation (EC) No 45/2001.

Article 73
Notifications

Each Member State shall designate the authorities which are competent for the purposes of Articles 6(6), 13(3), 17(2) and 26(4). Information on the designated authorities, as well as on any subsequent change, shall be notified simultaneously to the European Public Prosecutor, the Council and the Commission.

Article 74
Review clause

1. By [*five years after the start of application of this Regulation*] at the latest the Commission shall present its evaluation report to the European Parliament and the Council on the implementation of this Regulation, which may be accompanied by any legislative proposals. The report shall contain its findings on the feasibility and advisability of extending the competence of the European Public Prosecutor's Office to other criminal offences in accordance with Article 86(4) of the Treaty.
2. The Commission shall submit legislative proposals to the European Parliament and the Council if it concludes that more detailed rules on the setting up of the European Public Prosecutor's Office, its functions or the procedure applicable to its activities are necessary. It may recommend to the European Council the extension of the competence of the European Public Prosecutor's Office in accordance with Article 86(4) of the Treaty.

Article 75
Entry into force

1. This Regulation shall enter into force on the twentieth day following that of its publication in the *Official Journal of the European Union.*
2. The European Public Prosecutor's Office shall assume the investigative and prosecutorial tasks conferred on it by this Regulation on a date to be determined by a decision of the Commission on a proposal of the European Public Prosecutor once the European Public Prosecutor's Office is set up. The decision of the Commission shall be published in the Official Journal of the European Union.

This Regulation shall be binding in its entirety and directly applicable in the Member States in accordance with the Treaties.
Done at Brussels,

For the Council
The President

The manufacturer's authorised representative in the EU is Springer Nature Customer Service Centre GmbH, Europaplatz 3, 69115 Heidelberg, Germany. If you have any concerns regarding our products, please contact ProductSafety@springernature.com

Printed and bound by CPI Group (UK) Ltd, Croydon, CR0 4YY
30/09/2026
02225446-0007